UNCTAD/DITE/4(Vol. XIII)

United Nations Conference on Trade and Development
Division on Investment, Technology and Enterprise Development

International Investment Instruments: A Compendium

Volume XIII

United Nations
New York and Geneva, 2005

Note

UNCTAD serves as the focal point within the United Nations Secretariat for all matters related to foreign direct investment and transnational corporations. In the past, the Programme on Transnational Corporations was carried out by the United Nations Centre on Transnational Corporations (1975-1992) and the Transnational Corporations and Management Division of the United Nations Department of Economic and Social Development (1992-1993). In 1993, the Programme was transferred to the United Nations Conference on Trade and Development. UNCTAD seeks to further the understanding of the nature of transnational corporations and their contribution to development and to create an enabling environment for international investment and enterprise development. UNCTAD's work is carried out through intergovernmental deliberations, technical assistance activities, seminars, workshops and conferences.

The term "country", as used in the boxes added by the UNCTAD secretariat at the beginning of the instruments reproduced in this volume, also refers, as appropriate, to territories or areas; the designations employed and the presentation of the material do not imply the expression of any opinion whatsoever on the part of the Secretariat of the United Nations concerning the legal status of any country, territory, city or area or of its authorities, or concerning the delimitation of its frontiers or boundaries. Moreover, the country or geographical terminology used in the boxes may occasionally depart from standard United Nations practice when this is made necessary by the nomenclature used at the time of negotiation, signature, ratification or accession of a given international instrument.

To preserve the integrity of the texts of the instruments reproduced in this volume, references to the sources of the instruments that are not contained in their original text are identified as "note added by the editor".

The texts of the instruments included in this volume are reproduced as they were written in one of their original languages or as an official translation thereof. When an obvious linguistic mistake has been found, the word "sic" has been added in brackets.

The materials contained in this volume have been reprinted with special permission of the relevant institutions. For those materials under copyright protection, all rights are reserved by the copyright holders.

It should be further noted that this collection of instruments has been prepared for documentation purposes only, and its contents do not engage the responsibility of UNCTAD.

UNCTAD/DITE/4 Vol. XIII

UNITED NATIONS PUBLICATION

Sales No. E.05.II.D.7

ISBN 92-1-112664-9

MAY 1 3 2005

PREFACE

International Investment Instruments: A Compendium contains a collection of international instruments relating to foreign direct investment (FDI) and transnational corporations (TNCs). The collection is presented in fourteen volumes. The first three volumes were published in 1996. *Volumes IV* and *V* were published in 2000 followed by *Volume VI* in 2001. *Volumes VII, VIII, IX* and X were published in 2002. *Volumes XI* and *XII* were published in 2003 bringing the collection up to date. The present publication comprises *volumes XIII* and *XIV*.

The collection has been prepared to make the texts of international investment instruments conveniently available to interested policy-makers, scholars and business executives. The need for such a collection has increased in recent years as bilateral, regional, interregional and multilateral instruments dealing with various aspects of FDI have proliferated, and as new investment instruments are being negotiated or discussed at all levels.

While by necessity selective, the *Compendium* seeks to provide a faithful record of the evolution and present status of intergovernmental cooperation concerning FDI and TNCs. Although the emphasis of the collection is on relatively recent documents, it was deemed useful to include important older instruments as well, with a view to providing some indications of the historical development of international concerns about FDI in the decades since the end of the Second World War.

The core of this collection consists of legally binding international instruments, mainly multilateral conventions, regional agreements, and bilateral treaties that have entered into force. In addition, a number of "soft law" documents, such as guidelines, declarations and resolutions adopted by intergovernmental bodies, have been included since these instruments also play a role in the evolution of international agreements concerning FDI. In an effort to enhance the understanding of this evolution, certain draft instruments that never entered into force, or texts of instruments on which the negotiations were not concluded, are also included; prototypes of bilateral investment treaties are reproduced as well. Included also are a number of influential documents prepared by business, consumer and labour organizations, as well as by other non-governmental organizations. It is clear from the foregoing that no conclusions concerning the legal status or the legal effect of an instrument can be drawn from its inclusion in this collection.

In view of the great diversity of the instruments in this *Compendium* -- in terms of subject matter, approach, legal form and extent of participation of States -- the simplest possible method of presentation was deemed the most appropriate. With regard to previous volumes, the structure and content are indicated in the table of content which is included below (see pp. ix-xl). As far as volumes XIII and XIV are concerned relevant instruments are distributed as follows:

Volume XIII is divided into the following three parts:

- Part One contains additional regional instruments, including agreements and other texts from regional organizations with an inclusive geographical context.

- Part Two reproduces investment-related provisions in a number of additional free trade, economic partnership arrangements and framework agreements not covered in previous volumes.

- Part Three contains the texts of a number of additional prototype BITs not covered in previous volumes.

Volume XIV is divided into the following two parts:

- Part One reproduces investment-related provisions in three free trade agreements and a framework agreement not covered in previous volumes.

- Part Two contains the text of a number of an additional prototype BIT not covered in previous volumes.

Within each of these subdivisions and in previous volumes, instruments are reproduced in chronological order, except for the sections dedicated to prototype instruments.

The multilateral and regional instruments covered are widely differing in scope and coverage. Some are designed to provide an overall, general framework for FDI and cover many, although rarely all, aspects of investment operations. Most instruments deal with particular aspects and issues concerning FDI. A significant number address core FDI issues, such as the promotion and protection of investment, investment liberalization, dispute settlement and insurance and guarantees. Others cover specific issues, of direct but not exclusive relevance to FDI and TNCs, such as transfer of technology, intellectual property, avoidance of double taxation, competition and the protection of consumers and the environment. A relatively small number of instruments of this last category has been reproduced, since each of these specific issues often constitutes an entire system of legal regulation of its own, whose proper coverage would require an extended exposition of many kinds of instruments and arrangements.[a]

The *Compendium* is meant to be a collection of instruments, not an anthology of relevant provisions. Indeed, to understand a particular instrument, it is normally necessary to take its entire text into consideration. An effort has been made, therefore, to reproduce complete instruments, even though, in a number of cases, reasons of space and relevance have dictated the inclusion of excerpts. Owing to their size, annexes containing the list of reservations and exceptions are excluded in many cases. The excerpts are meant to reflect all provisions directly relevant to investment in an international agreement. There are other provisions that have an indirect bearing on investment but are not covered in the *Compendium*. The mark "[...]" has been inserted to indicate missing text.

The UNCTAD secretariat has deliberately refrained from adding its own commentary to the texts reproduced in the *Compendium*. The only exception to this rule is the boxes added to each instrument. They provide some basic facts, such as its date of adoption and date of entry into force and, where appropriate, signatory countries. Also, a list of agreements containing investment-related provisions signed by the EFTA countries and by the EC countries with third

---

[a]   For a collection of instruments (or excerpts therefrom) dealing with transfer of technology, see UNCTAD, *Compendium of International Arrangements on Transfer of Technology: Selected Instruments* (Geneva: United Nations), United Nations publication, Sales No. E.01.II.D.28.

countries or regional groups are reproduced in the *Compendium*. Moreover, to facilitate the identification of each instrument in the table of contents, additional information has been added, in brackets, next to each title, on the year of its signature and the name of the relevant institution involved.

Carlos Fortin
Officer-in-Charge of UNCTAD

Geneva, February 2005

ACKNOWLEDGEMENTS

Volume XIII of the *Compendium* was prepared by Abraham Negash under the supervision of Torbjörn Fredriksson and the overall guidance of Anne Miroux and Karl P. Sauvant. Comments and inputs were received from James Zhan, Amare Bekele, Hamid El-Khadi, Gabriele Koehler, Moritz Meier-Ewert and Elisabeth Tuerk. The cooperation of the relevant countries and organizations from which the instruments originate is acknowledged with gratitude.

VOLUME XIII

PART ONE
REGIONAL AND INTERREGIONAL INSTRUMENTS

PART TWO
BILATERAL INSTRUMENTS

PART THREE
PROTOTYPE INSTRUMENTS

CONTENTS OF OTHER VOLUMES

VOLUME I

MULTILATERAL INSTRUMENTS

VOLUME II

REGIONAL INSTRUMENTS

REGIONAL INSTRUMENTS

VOLUME III

REGIONAL INTEGRATION, BILATERAL AND NON-GOVERNMENTAL INSTRUMENTS

ANNEX C. NON-GOVERNMENTAL INSTRUMENTS

VOLUME IV

MULTILATERAL AND REGIONAL INSTRUMENTS

PART ONE

MULTILATERAL INSTRUMENTS

PART TWO

REGIONAL INSTRUMENTS

VOLUME V

REGIONAL INTEGRATION, BILATERAL AND NON-GOVERNMENTAL INSTRUMENTS

PART ONE

INVESTMENT-RELATED PROVISIONS IN FREE TRADE AND ECONOMIC INTEGRATION AGREEMENTS

PART TWO

INVESTMENT-RELATED PROVISIONS IN ASSOCIATION AGREEMENTS, BILATERAL AND INTERREGIONAL COOPERATION AGREEMENTS

ANNEX A. INVESTMENT-RELATED PROVISIONS IN FREE TRADE AGREEMENTS SIGNED BETWEEN THE COUNTRIES MEMBERS OF THE EUROPEAN FREE TRADE ASSOCIATION AND THIRD COUNTRIES AND LIST OF AGREEMENTS SIGNED (END-1999)

ANNEX B. INVESTMENT-RELATED PROVISIONS IN ASSOCIATION, PARTNERSHIP AND COOPERATION AGREEMENTS SIGNED BETWEEN THE COUNTRIES MEMBERS OF THE EUROPEAN COMMUNITY AND THIRD COUNTRIESAND LIST OF AGREEMENTS SIGNED (END-1999)

ANNEX C. OTHER BILATERAL INVESTMENT-RELATED AGREEMENTS

PART THREE

PROTOTYPE BILATERAL INVESTMENT TREATIES AND LIST OF BILATERAL INVESTMENT TREATIES (MID-1995 — END-1998)

PART FOUR

NON-GOVERNMENTAL INSTRUMENTS

VOLUME VI

PART ONE

MULTILATERAL INSTRUMENTS

PART TWO

INTERREGIONAL AND REGIONAL INSTRUMENTS

PART THREE

INVESTMENT-RELATED PROVISIONS IN FREE TRADE AND ECONOMIC INTEGRATION AGREEMENTS

PART FOUR

INVESTMENT-RELATED PROVISIONS IN ASSOCIATION AGREEMENTS, BILATERAL AND INTERREGIONAL COOPERATION AGREEMENTS

PART FIVE

PROTOTYPE BILATERAL INVESTMENT TREATIES

PART THREE

PROTOTYPE INSTRUMENTS

VOLUME VIII

PART ONE

INTERREGIONAL AND REGIONAL INSTRUMENTS

PART TWO

BILATERAL INSTRUMENTS

PART THREE

PROTOTYPE INSTRUMENTS

VOLUME IX

PART ONE

INTERREGIONAL AND REGIONAL INSTRUMENTS

PART TWO

BILATERAL INSTRUMENTS

PART THREE

PROTOTYPE INSTRUMENTS

VOLUME X

PART ONE

BILATERAL INSTRUMENTS

PART TWO

PROTOTYPE INSTRUMENTS

VOLUME XI

PART ONE

MULTILATERAL INSTRUMENTS

PART TWO

REGIONAL AND INTERREGIONAL INSTRUMENTS

PART THREE

BILATERAL INSTRUMENTS

VOLUME XII

Selected UNCTAD publications on transnational corporations and

VOLUME XIV

PART ONE
BILATERAL INSTRUMENTS

PART TWO
PROTOTYPE INSTRUMENTS

PART ONE

REGIONAL AND INTERREGIONAL INSTRUMENTS

ECOWAS ENERGY PROTOCOL[*]
[excerpts]

(ECONOMIC COMMUNITY OF WEST AFRICAN STATES)

The ECOWAS Energy Protocol was signed on 31 January 2003. Pursuant to Article 40, the Protocol is provisionally implemented pending its entry into force. ECOWAS comprises Benin, Burkina Faso, Cape Verde, Côte d'Ivoire, Gambia, Ghana, Guinea, Guinea-Bissau, Liberia, Mali, Niger, Nigeria, Senegal, Sierra Leone and Togo.

PREAMBLE

THE HIGH CONTRACTING PARTIES
[...]

CONSIDERING that the principles articulated and adopted by 51 nations of Europe and Asia, and memorialised in the document known as the Energy Charter Treaty which was signed in December, 1994, and which went into effect in April, 1998, represent the leading internationally accepted basis for the promotion, cooperation, integration and development of energy investment projects and energy trade among sovereign nations;
[...]

CONVINCED that adherence to the terms and principles of the Energy Charter Treaty by Member States of the Community will demonstrate to international investors and capital markets that the ECOWAS Region is a very attractive region for investing in energy projects and infrastructure;

WISHING to implement the basic concept of the Energy Charter initiative, which is to catalyse economic growth in the ECOWAS region by means of measures to liberalize energy investment and trade in energy;

AFFIRMING that the Member States of ECOWAS attach the highest importance to implementing the most favoured nation treatment and that such commitments will make it possible to realize investments in accordance with this Protocol;
[...]

DETERMINED to progressively remove technical, administrative and other barriers to trade in electricity, gas and other Energy Materials and Energy-Related Equipment, technologies and services;
[...]

---

[*] *Source*: The Economic Community of West African States (2003). "ECOWAS Energy Protocol", ECOWAS (A/P4/1/03); available on the Internet (http://www.sec.ecowas.int/sitecedeao/ English /protocoles/ WA_ EC_ Protocol _English-_DEFINITIF.pdf). [Note added by the editor.]

RECOGNIZING the vital role of the private sector in promoting and implementing energy investments, and intent on ensuring a favourable institutional framework for economically viable investment in energy infrastructure;

CONVINCED of the urgency of the need to promote energy sector investment and energy trade in West Africa; and

RECOGNIZING that adoption of the highest international trade standards is the most efficient course to pursue to attract energy sector investors to the ECOWAS Region

HAVE AGREED AS FOLLOWS:

CHAPTER I
DEFINITIONS AND PURPOSE

ARTICLE 1
DEFINITIONS

As used in this Protocol:
[...]

(12)   "Intellectual Property" includes copyrights and related rights, trademarks, geographical indications, industrial designs, patents, layout designs of integrated circuits and the protection of undisclosed information.

(13)   "Investment" means every kind of asset, owned or controlled directly or indirectly by an Investor and includes:

(a)   tangible and intangible, and movable and immovable, property, and any property rights such as leases, mortgages, liens, and pledges;

(b)   a company or business enterprise, or shares, stock, or other forms of equity participation in a company or business enterprise, and bonds and other debt of a company or business enterprise;

(c)   claims to money and claims to performance pursuant to contract having an economic value and associated with an Investment;

(d)   Intellectual Property;

(e)   Returns;

(f)   any right conferred by law or contract or by virtue of any licences and permits granted pursuant to law to undertake any Economic Activity in the Energy Sector.

A change in the form in which assets are invested does not affect their character as investments and the term "Investment" includes all investments, whether existing at or made after the later of the date of entry into force of this Protocol for the Contracting Party of the Investor making the investment and that for the Contracting Party in the Area of which the investment is made (hereinafter referred to as the "Effective Date") provided that this Protocol shall only apply to matters affecting such investments after the Effective Date.

"Investment" refers to any investment associated with an Economic Activity in the Energy Sector and to investments or classes of investments designated by a Contracting Party in its Area as "efficiency projects" and so notified to the Executive Secretariat of ECOWAS.

(14)   "Investor" means:

(a)   a natural person having the citizenship or nationality of, or who resides or establishes an office in the Area of, a Contracting Party in accordance with its applicable laws; or,

(b)   a company or other organization organized, or registered, in accordance with the law applicable in that Contracting Party.

(15)   "Make Investments" or "Making of Investments" means establishing new Investments, acquiring all or part of existing Investments or moving into different fields of Investment activity.
[…]

(18)   "Returns" means the amounts derived from or associated with an Investment, irrespective of the form in which they are paid, including profits, dividends, interest, capital gains, royalty payments, management, technical assistance or other fees and payments in kind.
[…]

ARTICLE 2
PURPOSE OF THE PROTOCOL

This Protocol establishes a legal framework in order to promote long-term co-operation in the energy field, based on complementarities and mutual benefits, with a view to achieving increased investment in the energy sector, and increased energy trade in the West Africa region.
[…]

CHATPER II
COMMERCE

ARTICLE 5
TRADE-RELATED INVESTMENT MEASURES

(1)   A Contracting Party shall not apply any trade-related investment measure that is inconsistent with the provisions of article III or XI of the GATT 1994; this shall be without prejudice to the Contracting Party's rights and obligations under the WTO Agreement and Article 29 of this Protocol.

(2)   Such measures include any investment measure which is mandatory or enforceable under domestic law or under any administrative ruling, or compliance with which is necessary to obtain an advantage, and which requires:

(a) the purchase or use by an enterprise of products of domestic origin or from any domestic source, whether specified in terms of particular products, in terms of volume or value of products, or in terms of a proportion of volume or value of its local production; or

(b) that an enterprise's purchase or use of imported products be limited to an amount related to the volume or value of local products that it exports;

or which restricts:

(c) the importation by an enterprise of products used in or related to its local production, generally or to an amount related to the volume or value of local production that it exports;

(d) the importation by an enterprise of products used in or related to its local production by restricting its access to foreign exchange to an amount related to the foreign exchange inflows attributable to the enterprise; or

(e) the exportation or sale for export by an enterprise of products, whether specified in terms of particular products, in terms of volume or value of products, or in terms of a proportion of volume or value of its local production.

(3) Nothing in paragraph (1) shall be construed to prevent a Contracting Party from applying the trade-related investment measures described in subparagraphs (2)(a) and (c) as a condition of eligibility for export promotion, foreign aid, government procurement or preferential tariff or quota programmes.

(4) Notwithstanding paragraph (1), a Contracting Party may temporarily continue to maintain trade-related investment measures which were in effect more than 180 days before its signature of this Protocol, subject to the notification and phase-out provisions set out in Annex C.

ARTICLE 8
TRANSFER OF TECHNOLOGY

(1) The Contracting Parties agree to promote access to and transfer of energy technology on a commercial and non-discriminatory basis to assist effective trade in Energy Materials and Products and Investment and to implement the objectives of this Protocol subject to their laws and regulations, and to the protection of Intellectual Property rights.

(2) Accordingly, to the extent necessary to give effect to paragraph (1) the Contracting Parties shall eliminate existing obstacles and create no new ones to the transfer of technology in the field of Energy Materials and Products and related equipment and services, subject to non-proliferation and other international obligations.

ARTICLE 9
ACCESS TO CAPITAL

(1) The Contracting Parties acknowledge the importance of open capital markets in encouraging the flow of capital to finance trade in Energy Materials and Products and for the making of and assisting with regard to Investments in Economic Activity in the Energy Sector in

the Areas of other Contracting Parties. Each Contracting Party shall accordingly endeavour to promote conditions for access to its capital market by companies and nationals of other Contracting Parties, or, any other third state, for the purpose of financing trade in Energy Materials and Products and for the purpose of Investment in Economic Activity in the Energy Sector in the Areas of those other Contracting Parties, on a basis no less favourable than that which it accords in like circumstances to its own companies and nationals or companies and nationals of any other Contracting Party or any third state, whichever is the most favourable.

(2)   A Contracting Party may adopt and maintain programmes providing for access to their Investors to public loans, grants, guarantees or insurance for facilitating trade or Investment within the Area of other Contracting Parties. It shall make such facilities available, consistent with the objectives, constraints and criteria of such programmes (including any objectives, constraints or criteria relating to the place of business of an applicant for any such facility or the place of delivery of goods or services supplied with the support of any such facility) for Investments in the Economic Activity in the Energy Sector of other Contracting Parties or for financing trade in Energy Materials and Products with other Contracting Parties.

(3)   Contracting Parties shall, in implementing programmes in Economic Activity in the Energy Sector to improve the economic stability and investment climates of the Contracting Parties, seek as appropriate to encourage the operations and take advantage of the expertise of relevant international financial institutions.

(4)   Nothing in this Article shall prevent:

   (a)   financial institutions from applying their own lending or underwriting practices based on market principles and prudential considerations; or

   (b)   a Contracting Party from taking prudent measures, including:

      (i)   steps to protect its investors, consumers, depositors, insured or persons to whom a fiduciary duty is owed by a financial service supplier; or

      (ii)   steps to ensure the integrity and stability of its financial system and capital markets.

CHAPTER III
INVESTMENT PROMOTION AND PROTECTION

ARTICLE 10
PROMOTION, PROTECTION AND TREATMENT OF INVESTMENTS

(1)   Each Contracting Party shall, in accordance with the provisions of this Protocol, encourage and create stable, equitable, favourable and transparent conditions for Investors to make Investments in its Area. Such conditions shall include a commitment to accord at all times to Investments of Investors fair and equitable treatment. Such Investments shall also enjoy the most constant protection and security and no Contracting Party shall in any way impair by unreasonable or discriminatory measures their management, maintenance, use, enjoyment or disposal.

In no case shall such Investments be accorded treatment less favourable than that required by international law, including treaty obligations. Each Contracting Party shall observe any obligations it has entered into with an Investor or with respect to an Investment.

(2)   Each Contracting Party shall endeavour to accord to Investors, as regards the Making of Investments in its Area, the Treatment described in paragraph (3).

(3)   For the purposes of this Article, "Treatment" means treatment accorded by a Contracting Party which is no less favourable than that which it accords to its own Investors or to Investors of any other Contracting Party or, indeed, of any third state, whichever is the most favourable.

(4)   Each Contracting Party shall, as regards the Making of Investments in its Area, endeavour to:

      (a)   limit to the minimum the exceptions to the Treatment described in paragraph (3);

      (b)   progressively remove existing restrictions affecting Investors.

(5)   (a)   A Contracting Party may, as regards the Making of Investments in its Area, at any time declare voluntarily to the Meeting of Energy Ministers, through the Executive Secretariat of ECOWAS, its intention not to introduce new exceptions to the Treatment described in paragraph (3).

      (b)   A Contracting Party may, furthermore, at any time make a voluntary commitment to accord to Investors, as regards the Making of Investments in some or all Economic Activities in the Energy Sector in its Area, the Treatment described in paragraph (3). Such commitments shall be notified to the Executive Secretariat of ECOWAS and shall be binding under this Protocol.

(6)   Each Contracting Party shall, in its Area, accord to Investments of Investors and their related activities including management, maintenance, use, enjoyment or disposal, treatment no less favourable than that which it accords to its own Investors or of the Investors of any third state and their related activities including management, maintenance, use, enjoyment or disposal, whichever is the most favourable.

(7)   The modalities of application of paragraph (6) may exclude programmes under which a Contracting Party provides to its own national investors grants or other financial assistance, or enters into contracts, for energy technology research and development. Each Contracting Party shall through the Executive Secretariat of ECOWAS keep the Meeting of Energy Ministers informed of the modalities it applies to the programmes described in this paragraph.

(8)   Each state or Regional Economic Integration Organization which signs or accedes to this Protocol shall, on the date it signs the Protocol or deposits its instrument of accession, submit to the Executive Secretariat of ECOWAS a report summarizing all laws, regulations or other measures relevant to:

      (a)   exceptions to paragraph (2); or

      (b)   the programs referred to in paragraph (7).

A Contracting Party shall keep its report up to date by promptly submitting amendments to the Executive Secretariat of ECOWAS. The Meeting of Energy Ministers shall review these reports periodically.

In respect of subparagraph (a) the report may designate parts of the energy sector in which a Contracting Party accords to Investors the Treatment described in paragraph (3).

In respect of subparagraph (b) the review by the Meeting of Energy Ministers may consider the effects of such programmes on competition and Investments.

(9)   Notwithstanding any other provision of this Article, the treatment described in paragraphs (3) and (6) shall not apply to the protection of Intellectual Property; instead, the treatment shall be as specified in the corresponding provisions of the applicable international agreements for the protection of Intellectual Property rights to which the respective Contracting Parties are parties.

(10)   For the purposes of Article 26, the application by a Contracting Party of a traderelated investment measure as described in Article 5(1) and (2) to an Investment of an Investor existing at the time of such application shall, subject to Article 5(3) and (4), be considered a breach of an obligation of the former Contracting Party under this Part.

(11)   Each Contracting Party shall ensure that its domestic law provides effective means for the assertion of claims and the enforcement of rights with respect to Investments, investment agreements, and investment authorizations.

ARTICLE 11
KEY PERSONNEL

(1)   A Contracting Party shall, subject to its laws and regulations relating to the entry, stay and work of natural persons, examine in good faith requests by Investors and key personnel who are employed by such Investors or by Investments of such Investors, to enter and remain temporarily in its Area to engage in activities connected with the making or the development, management, maintenance, use, enjoyment or disposal of relevant Investments, including the provision of advice or key technical services.

(2)   A Contracting Party shall permit Investors which have Investments in its Area, and Investments of such Investors, to employ any key person of the Investor's or the Investment's choice regardless of nationality and citizenship provided that such key person has been permitted to enter, stay and work in the Area of the Contracting Party and that the employment concerned conforms to the terms, conditions and time limits of the permission granted to such key person.

ARTICLE 12
COMPENSATION FOR LOSSES

(1)   Except where Article 13 applies, an Investor which suffers a loss with respect to any Investment in the Area of a Contracting Party owing to war or other armed conflict, state of national emergency, civil disturbance, or other similar event in that Area, shall be accorded by the latter Contracting Party, as regards restitution, indemnification, compensation or other settlement, treatment which is the most favourable of that which that Contracting Party accords

to any other Investor, whether its own Investor, the Investor of any other Contracting Party, or the Investor of any third state.

(2)   Without prejudice to paragraph (1), an Investor which, in any of the situations referred to in that paragraph, suffers a loss in the Area of a Contracting Party resulting from

(a)   requisitioning of its Investment or part thereof by the latter's forces or authorities;or

(b)   destruction of its Investment or part thereof by the latter's forces or authorities, which was not required by the necessity of the situation, shall be accorded restitution or compensation which in either case shall be prompt, adequate and effective.

ARTICLE 13
EXPROPRIATION

(1)   Investments of Investors in the Area of any Contracting Party shall not be nationalized, expropriated or subjected to a measure or measures having effect equivalent to nationalization or expropriation (hereinafter referred to as "Expropriation") except where such Expropriation is:

(a)   for a purpose which is in the public interest;
(b)   not discriminatory;
(c)   carried out under due process of law; and
(d)   accompanied by the payment of prompt, adequate and effective compensation.

Such compensation shall amount to the fair market value of the Investment expropriated at the time immediately before the Expropriation or impending Expropriation became known in such a way as to affect the value of the Investment (hereinafter referred to as the "Valuation Date").

Such fair market value shall at the request of the Investor be expressed in a Freely Convertible Currency on the basis of the market rate of exchange existing for that currency on the Valuation Date. Compensation shall also include interest at a commercial rate established on a market basis from the date of Expropriation until the date of payment.

(2)   The Investor affected shall have a right to prompt review, under the law of the Contracting Party making the Expropriation, by a judicial or other competent and independent authority of that Contracting Party, of its case, of the valuation of its Investment, and of the payment of compensation, in accordance with the principles set out in paragraph (1).

(3)   For the avoidance of doubt, Expropriation shall include situations where a Contracting Party expropriates the assets of a company or enterprise in which an Investor has an Investment, including through the ownership of shares.

ARTICLE 14
TRANSFERS RELATED TO INVESTMENTS

(1)   Each Contracting Party shall with respect to Investments made in its Area by Investors guarantee the freedom of transfer into and out of its Area, including the transfer of:

(a)   the initial capital plus any additional capital for the maintenance and development of an Investment;

(b)   Returns;

(c)   payments under a contract, including amortization of principal and accrued interest payments pursuant to a loan agreement;

(d)   unspent earnings and other remuneration of personnel engaged from abroad in connection with that Investment;

(e)   proceeds from the sale or liquidation of all or any part of an Investment;

(f)   payments arising out of the settlement of a dispute;

(g)   payments of compensation pursuant to Articles 12 and 13.

(2)   Transfers under paragraph (1) shall be effected without delay and (except in case of a Return in kind) in a Freely Convertible Currency.

(3)   Transfers shall be made at the market rate of exchange existing on the date of transfer with respect to spot transactions in the currency to be transferred. In the absence of a market for foreign exchange, the rate to be used will be the most recent rate applied to inward investments or the most recent exchange rate for conversion of currencies into Special Drawing Rights, whichever is more favourable to the Investor.

(4)   Notwithstanding paragraphs (1) to (3), a Contracting Party may protect the rights of creditors, or ensure compliance with laws on the issuing, trading and dealing in securities and the satisfaction of judgements in civil, administrative and criminal adjudicatory proceedings, through the equitable, non-discriminatory, and good faith application of its laws and regulations.

(5)   Notwithstanding subparagraph (1)(b), a Contracting Party may restrict the transfer of a Return in kind in circumstances where the Contracting Party is permitted under Article 29(2) or the WTO Agreement to restrict or prohibit the exportation or the sale for export of the product constituting the Return in kind; provided that a Contracting Party shall permit transfers of Returns in kind to be effected as authorized or specified in an investment agreement, investment authorization, or other written agreement between the Contracting Party and either an Investor or its Investment.

ARTICLE 15
SUBROGATION

(1)   If a Contracting Party or its designated agency (hereinafter referred to as the "Indemnifying Party") makes a payment under an indemnity or guarantee given in respect of an Investment of an Investor (hereinafter referred to as the "Party Indemnified") in the Area of another Contracting Party (hereinafter referred to as the "Host Party"), the Host Party shall recognize:

(a)   the assignment to the Indemnifying Party of all the rights and claims in respect of such Investment; and

(b)   the right of the Indemnifying Party to exercise all such rights and enforce such claims by virtue of subrogation.

(2)   The Indemnifying Party shall be entitled in all circumstances to:

(a)   the same treatment in respect of the rights and claims acquired by it by virtue of the assignment referred to in paragraph (1); and

(b)   the same payments due pursuant to those rights and claims, as the Party Indemnified was entitled to receive by virtue of this Protocol in respect of the Investment concerned.

(3)   In any proceeding under Article 26, a Contracting Party shall not assert as a defence, counterclaim, right of set-off or for any other reason, that indemnification or other compensation for all or part of the alleged damages has been received or will be received pursuant to an insurance or guarantee contract.

ARTICLE 16
RELATION TO OTHER AGREEMENTS

Where two or more Contracting Parties have entered into a prior international agreement, or enter into a subsequent international agreement, whose terms in either case concern the subject matter of Chapter III or V of this Protocol,

(1)   nothing in Chapter III or V of this Protocol shall be construed to derogate from any provision of such terms of the other agreement or from any right to dispute resolution with respect thereto under that agreement; and

(2)   nothing in such terms of the other agreement shall be construed to derogate from any provision of Chapter III or V of this Protocol or from any right to dispute resolution with respect thereto under this Protocol, where any such provision is more favourable to the Investor or Investment.

ARTICLE 17
NON-APPLICATION OF CHAPTER III IN CERTAIN CIRCUMSTANCES

Each Contracting Party reserves the right to deny the advantages of the provisions of Chapter III to:

(1)   a legal entity if citizens or nationals of a third state own or control such entity and if that entity has no substantial business activities in the Area of the Contracting Party in which it is organized; or

(2)   an Investment, if the denying Contracting Party establishes that such Investment is an Investment of an Investor of a third state with or as to which the denying Contracting Party:

(a)   does not maintain a diplomatic relationship; or

(b)   adopts or maintains measures that:

(i)   prohibit transactions with Investors of that state; or

(ii)   would be violated or circumvented if the benefits of this Chapter were accorded to Investors of that state or to their Investments.

CHAPTER IV
MISCELLANEOUS PROVISIONS

ARTICLE 18
SOVEREIGNTY OVER ENERGY RESOURCES

(1)   The Contracting Parties recognize state sovereignty and sovereign rights over energy resources. They reaffirm that these must be exercised in accordance with and subject to the rules of international law.

(2)   Without affecting the objectives of promoting access to energy resources, and exploration and development thereof on a commercial basis, this Protocol shall in no way prejudice the rules in Contracting Parties governing the system of property ownership of energy resources.

(3)   Each state continues to hold in particular the rights to decide the geographical areas within its Area to be made available for exploration and development of its energy resources, the optimization of their recovery and the rate at which they may be depleted or otherwise exploited, to specify and enjoy any taxes, royalties or other financial payments payable by virtue of such exploration and exploitation, and to regulate the environmental and safety aspects of such exploration, development and reclamation within its Area, and to participate in such exploration and exploitation, inter alia, through direct participation by the government or through state enterprises.

(4)   The Contracting Parties undertake to facilitate access to energy resources, inter alia, by allocating in a non-discriminatory manner on the basis of published criteria authorizations, licences, concessions and contracts to prospect and explore for or to exploit or extract energy resources.

[...]

ARTICLE 21
TAXATION

(1)   Except as otherwise provided in this Article, nothing in this Protocol shall create rights or impose obligations on Investors with respect to Taxation Measures of the Contracting Parties. In the event of any inconsistency between this Article and any other provision of this Protocol, this Article shall prevail to the extent of the inconsistency.

(2)   Article 7(3) shall apply to Taxation Measures other than those on income or on capital, except that such provision shall not apply to:

(a)   an advantage accorded by a Contracting Party pursuant to the tax provisions of any convention, agreement or arrangement described in subparagraph (7)(a)(ii); or (b)　　any Taxation Measure aimed at ensuring the effective collection of taxes, except where the measure of a Contracting Party arbitrarily discriminates against Energy Materials and Products originating in, or destined for the Area of another Contracting Party or arbitrarily restricts benefits accorded under Article 7(3).

(3)　　Article 10(2) and (6) shall apply to Taxation Measures of the Contracting Parties other than those on income or on capital, except that such provisions shall not apply to:

(a)　　impose most favoured nation obligations with respect to advantages accorded by a Contracting Party pursuant to the tax provisions of any convention, agreement or arrangement described in subparagraph (7)(a)(ii) or resulting from membership of any Regional Economic Integration Organization; or

(b)　　any Taxation Measure aimed at ensuring the effective collection of taxes, except where the measure arbitrarily discriminates against an Investor or arbitrarily restricts benefits accorded under the Investment provisions of this Protocol.

(4)　　Article 29(2) to (8) shall apply to Taxation Measures other than those on income or on capital.

(5)　　(a)　　Article 13 shall apply to taxes.

(b)　　Whenever an issue arises under Article 13, to the extent it pertains to whether a tax constitutes an expropriation or whether a tax alleged to constitute an expropriation is discriminatory, the following provisions shall apply:

(i)　　The Investor or the Contracting Party alleging expropriation shall refer the issue of whether the tax is an expropriation or whether the tax is discriminatory to the relevant Competent Tax Authority. Failing such referral by the Investor or the Contracting Party, bodies called upon to settle disputes pursuant to Article 26(2)(c) or 27(2) shall make a referral to the relevant Competent Tax Authorities;

(ii)　　The Competent Tax Authorities shall, within a period of six months of such referral, strive to resolve the issues so referred. Where non-discrimination issues are concerned, the Competent Tax Authorities shall apply the nondiscrimination provisions of the relevant tax convention or, if there is no non-discrimination provision in the relevant tax convention applicable to the tax or no such tax convention is in force between the Contracting Parties concerned, they shall apply the non-discrimination principles under the Model Tax Convention on Income and Capital of the Organisation for Economic Co-operation and Development or any other model agreed upon by the Contracting Parties;

(iii)　　Bodies called upon to settle disputes pursuant to Article 26(2)(c) or 27(2) may take into account any conclusions arrived at by the Competent Tax Authorities regarding whether the tax is an expropriation. Such bodies shall take into account any conclusions arrived at within the six-month period prescribed in subparagraph (b)(ii) by the Competent Tax Authorities regarding whether the tax is discriminatory. Such bodies may also take into account any conclusions arrived at by the Competent Tax Authorities after the expiry of the six-month period;

    (iv)   Under no circumstances shall involvement of the Competent Tax Authorities, beyond the end of the six-month period referred to in subparagraph (b)(ii), lead to a delay of proceedings under Articles 26 and 27.

(6)   For the avoidance of doubt, Article 14 shall not limit the right of a Contracting Party to impose or collect a tax by withholding or other means.

(7)   For the purposes of this Article:

    (a)   The term "Taxation Measure" includes:

        (i)   any provision relating to taxes of the domestic law of the Contracting Party or of a political subdivision thereof or a local authority therein; and

        (ii)   any provision relating to taxes of any convention for the avoidance of double taxation or of any other international agreement or arrangement by which the Contracting Party is bound.

    (b)   There shall be regarded as taxes on income or on capital all taxes imposed on total income, on total capital or on elements of income or of capital, including taxes on gains from the alienation of property, taxes on estates, inheritances and

    (c)   A "Competent Tax Authority" means the competent authority pursuant to a double taxation agreement in force between the Contracting Parties or, when no such agreement is in force, the minister or ministry responsible for taxes or their authorized representatives.

    (d)   For the avoidance of doubt, the terms "tax provisions" and "taxes" do not include customs duties.

    [...]

CHAPTER V
DISPUTE SETTLEMENT

ARTICLE 26
SETTLEMENT OF DISPUTES BETWEEN AN INVESTOR AND A CONTRACTING PARTY

(1)   Disputes between a Contracting Party and an Investor relating to an Investment of the latter in the Area of the former, which concern an alleged breach of an obligation of the former under Chapter III shall, if possible, be settled amicably.

(2)   If such disputes can not be settled according to the provisions of paragraph (1) within a period of three months from the date on which either party to the dispute requested amicable settlement, the Investor party to the dispute may choose to submit it for resolution:

(a)   to the courts or administrative tribunals of the Contracting Party to the dispute;

(b)   in accordance with any applicable, previously agreed dispute settlement procedure; or

(c)   in accordance with the following paragraphs of this Article.

(3)   Each Contracting Party hereby gives its unconditional consent to the submission of a dispute to international arbitration or conciliation in accordance with the provisions of this Article.

(4)   In the event that an Investor chooses to submit the dispute for resolution under subparagraph (2)(c), the Investor shall further provide its consent in writing for the dispute to be submitted to:

(a)   (i)   The International Centre for Settlement of Investment Disputes, established pursuant to the Convention on the Settlement of Investment Disputes between States and Nationals of other States opened for signature at Washington, 18 March 1965 (hereinafter referred to as the "ICSID Convention"), if the country of origin of the Investor and the Contracting Party to the dispute are both parties to the ICSID Convention; or

        (ii)   The International Centre for Settlement of Investment Disputes, established pursuant to the Convention referred to in subparagraph (a)(i), under the rules governing the Additional Facility for the Administration of Proceedings by the Secretariat of the Centre (hereinafter referred to as the "Additional Facility Rules"), if the country of origin of the Investor or the Contracting Party to the dispute, but not both, is a party to the ICSID Convention; or

(b)   a sole arbitrator or ad hoc arbitration tribunal established under the Arbitration Rules of the United Nations Commission on International Trade Law (hereinafter referred to as "UNCITRAL"); or

(c)   an arbitral proceeding under the Arbitration Institute of the Stockholm Chamber of Commerce; or

(d)   an arbitral proceeding under the organization for the Harmonization of Trade Laws in Africa (OHADA).

(5)   (a)   The consent given in paragraph (3) together with the written consent of the Investor given pursuant to paragraph (4) shall be considered to satisfy the requirement for:

        (i)   written consent of the parties to a dispute for purposes of Chapter II of the ICSID Convention and for purposes of the Additional Facility Rules;

        (ii)   an "agreement in writing" for purposes of article II of the United Nations Convention on the Recognition and Enforcement of Foreign Arbitral

Awards, done at New York, 10 June 1958 (hereinafter referred to as the "New York Convention"); and

    (iii)   "the parties to a contract [to] have agreed in writing" for the purposes of article 1 of the UNCITRAL Arbitration Rules.

    (b)   Any arbitration under this Article shall at the request of any party to the dispute be held in a state that is a party to the New York Convention. Claims submitted to arbitration hereunder shall be considered to arise out of a commercial relationship or transaction for the purposes of article I of that Convention.

(6)   A tribunal established under paragraph (4) shall decide the issues in dispute in accordance with this Protocol and applicable rules and principles of international law.

(7)   An Investor other than a natural person which has the nationality of a Contracting Party to the dispute on the date of the consent in writing referred to in paragraph (4) and which, before a dispute between it and that Contracting Party arises, is controlled by Investors of another Contracting Party, shall for the purpose of article 25(2)(b) of the ICSID Convention be treated as a "national of another Contracting Party" and shall for the purpose of article 1(6) of the Additional Facility Rules be treated as a "national of another State".

(8)   The awards of arbitration, which may include an award of interest, shall be final and binding upon the parties to the dispute. An award of arbitration concerning a measure of a sub-national government or authority of the disputing Contracting Party shall provide that the Contracting Party may pay monetary damages in lieu of any other remedy granted. Each Contracting Party shall carry out without delay any such award and shall make provision for the prompt and effective enforcement in its Area of such awards.

[...]

*

DECISIÓN 578 RÉGIMEN PARA EVITAR LA DOBLE TRIBUTACIÓN Y PREVENIR LA EVASIÓN FISCAL*

(ANDEAN COMMUNITY)

Decision 578 of the Andean Community on the Regime for the Avoidance of Double Taxation and Prevention of Tax Evasion was signed on 14 May 2004.

LA COMISION DE LA COMUNIDAD ANDINA,

VISTOS: Los artículos 3, 22 literales a) y b), 30 literal c), 51 y 54 del Acuerdo de Cartagena, la Decisión 40 de la Comisión y el artículo 19 de la Decisión 292 de la Comisión;

CONSIDERANDO: Que es necesario eliminar la doble imposición a las actividades de las personas naturales y jurídicas, domiciliadas en los Países Miembros de la Comunidad Andina, que actúan a nivel comunitario y establecer un esquema y reglas para la colaboración entre las administraciones tributarias con tal fin;

Que, asimismo, es indispensable actualizar las normas referentes a evitar la doble tributación entre los Países Miembros, con el fin de fomentar los intercambios entre los Países Miembros, atraer la inversión extranjera y prevenir la evasión fiscal;

DECIDE:

Establecer el presente:

RÉGIMEN PARA EVITAR LA DOBLE TRIBUTACIÓN Y PREVENIR LA EVASIÓN FISCAL

CAPITULO I
AMBITO DE APLICACIÓN Y DEFINICIONES GENERALES

Artículo 1.- Ámbito de Aplicación

La presente Decisión es aplicable a las personas domiciliadas en cualquiera de los Países Miembros de la Comunidad Andina, respecto de los impuestos sobre la renta y sobre el patrimonio. Se aplica principalmente a los siguientes:

En Bolivia, Impuesto a la renta.

En Colombia, Impuesto a la renta.

En el Ecuador, Impuesto a la renta.

---

* *Source*: The Andean Community (2004). "Decisión 578 Régimen para evitar la Doble Tributación y Prevenir la Evasión Fiscal", available on the Internet (http://www.comunidadandina.org/ingles/treaties.htm). [Note added by the editor.]

En el Perú, Impuesto a la renta.

En Venezuela, Impuesto sobre la renta e Impuesto a los activos empresariales.

Las normas previstas en esta Decisión tienen por objeto evitar la doble tributación de unas mismas rentas o patrimonios a nivel comunitario.

La presente Decisión se aplicará también a las modificaciones que se introdujeran a los referidos impuestos y a cualquier otro impuesto que, en razón de su base gravable o materia imponible, fuera esencial y económicamente análogo a los anteriormente citados y que fuere establecido por cualquiera de los Países Miembros con posterioridad a la publicación de esta Decisión.

Artículo 2.- Definiciones Generales

Para los efectos de la presente Decisión y a menos que en el texto se indique otra cosa:

a) Los términos "Países Miembros" servirán para designar indistintamente a Bolivia, Colombia, Ecuador, Perú y Venezuela.

b) La expresión "territorio de uno de los Países Miembros" significará indistintamente los territorios de Bolivia, Colombia, Ecuador, Perú y Venezuela.

c) El término "persona" servirá para designar a:

1. Una persona física o natural

2. Una persona moral o jurídica

3. Cualquier otra entidad o grupo de personas, asociadas o no, sujetas a responsabilidad tributaria.

d) El término "empresa" significará una organización constituida por una o más personas que realiza una actividad lucrativa.

e) Una persona física o natural será considerada domiciliada en el País Miembro en que tenga su residencia habitual.

Se entiende que una empresa está domiciliada en el País que señala su instrumento de constitución. Si no existe instrumento de constitución o éste no señala domicilio, la empresa se considerará domiciliada en el lugar donde se encuentre su administración efectiva.

Cuando, no obstante estas normas, no sea posible determinar el domicilio, las autoridades competentes de los Países Miembros interesados resolverán el caso de común acuerdo.

f) La expresión "fuente productora" se refiere a la actividad, derecho o bien que genere o pueda generar una renta.

g) La expresión "actividades empresariales" se refiere a actividades desarrolladas por empresas.

h) Los términos "empresa de un País Miembro" y "empresa de otro País Miembro" significan una empresa domiciliada en uno u otro País Miembro.

i) El término "regalía" se refiere a cualquier beneficio, valor o suma de dinero pagado por el uso o el derecho de uso de bienes intangibles, tales como marcas, patentes, licencias, conocimientos técnicos no patentados u otros conocimientos de similar naturaleza en el territorio de uno de los Países Miembros, incluyendo en particular los derechos del obtentor de nuevas variedades vegetales previstos en la Decisión 345 y los derechos de autor y derechos conexos comprendidos en la Decisión 351.

j) La expresión "ganancias de capital" se refiere al beneficio obtenido por una persona en la enajenación de bienes que no adquiere, produce o enajena habitualmente dentro del giro ordinario de sus actividades.

k) El término "pensión" significa un pago periódico hecho en consideración a servicios prestados o por daños padecidos, y el término "anualidad" significa una suma determinada de dinero pagadera periódicamente durante un lapso determinado a título gratuito o en compensación de una contraprestación realizada o apreciable en dinero.

l) El término "intereses" significa los rendimientos de cualquier naturaleza, incluidos los rendimientos financieros de créditos, depósitos y captaciones realizados por entidades financieras privadas, con o sin garantía hipotecaria, o cláusula de participación en los beneficios del deudor, y especialmente, las rentas provenientes de fondos públicos (títulos emitidos por entidades del Estado) y bonos u obligaciones, incluidas las primas y premios relacionados con esos títulos. Las penalizaciones por mora en el pago atrasado no se considerarán intereses a efecto del presente articulado.

m) La expresión "autoridad competente" significa en el caso de:

Bolivia, el Ministro de Hacienda o su delegado.

Colombia, el Ministro de Hacienda y Crédito Público o su delegado.

Ecuador, el Ministro de Economía y Finanzas o su delegado.

Perú, el Ministro de Economía y Finanzas o su delegado.

República Bolivariana de Venezuela, el Superintendente Nacional Aduanero y Tributario del Servicio Nacional Integrado de Administración Aduanera y Tributaria (SENIAT) o su delegado.

CAPITULO II
IMPUESTO A LA RENTA

Artículo 3.- Jurisdicción Tributaria

Independientemente de la nacionalidad o domicilio de las personas, las rentas de cualquier naturaleza que éstas obtuvieren, sólo serán gravables en el País Miembro en el que tales rentas tengan su fuente productora, salvo los casos de excepción previstos en esta Decisión.

Por tanto, los demás Países Miembros que, de conformidad con su legislación interna, se atribuyan potestad de gravar las referidas rentas, deberán considerarlas como exoneradas, para los efectos de la correspondiente determinación del impuesto a la renta o sobre el patrimonio.

Artículo 4.- Rentas provenientes de bienes inmuebles

Las rentas de cualquier naturaleza provenientes de bienes inmuebles sólo serán gravables por el País Miembro en el cual estén situados dichos bienes.

Artículo 5.- Rentas provenientes del derecho a explotar recursos naturales

Cualquier beneficio percibido por el arrendamiento o subarrendamiento o por la cesión o concesión del derecho a explotar o a utilizar en cualquier forma los recursos naturales de uno de los Países Miembros, sólo será gravable por ese País Miembro.

Artículo 6.- Beneficios de las empresas

Los beneficios resultantes de las actividades empresariales sólo serán gravables por el País Miembro donde éstas se hubieren efectuado.

Se considerará, entre otros casos, que una empresa realiza actividades en el territorio de un País Miembro cuando tiene en éste:

a)   Una oficina o lugar de administración o dirección de negocios;

b)   Una fábrica, planta o taller industrial o de montaje;

c)   Una obra de construcción;

d)   Un lugar o instalación donde se extraen o explotan recursos naturales, tales como una mina, pozo, cantera, plantación o barco pesquero;

e)   Una agencia o local de ventas;

f)   Una agencia o local de compras;

g)   Un depósito, almacén, bodega o establecimiento similar destinado a la recepción, almacenamiento o entrega de productos;

h)   Cualquier otro local, oficina o instalación cuyo objeto sea preparatorio o auxiliar de las actividades de la empresa;

i)   Un agente o representante.

Cuando una empresa efectúe actividades en dos o más Países Miembros, cada uno de ellos podrá gravar las rentas que se generen en su territorio, aplicando para ello cada País sus disposiciones internas en cuanto a la determinación de la base gravable como si se tratara de una empresa distinta, independiente y separada, pero evitando la causación de doble tributación de acuerdo con las reglas de esta Decisión. Si las actividades se realizaran por medio de representantes o utilizando instalaciones como las indicadas en el párrafo anterior, se atribuirán a dichas personas o instalaciones los beneficios que hubieren obtenido si fueren totalmente independientes de la empresa.

Artículo 7.- Empresas Asociadas o Relacionadas

1.   Cuando

a)   una empresa de un País Miembro participe directa o indirectamente en la dirección, el control o el capital de una empresa de otro País Miembro, o

b)   unas mismas personas participen directa o indirectamente en la dirección, el control o el capital de una empresa de un País Miembro y de una empresa de otro País Miembro,

y en uno y otro caso las dos empresas estén, en sus relaciones comerciales o financieras, unidas por condiciones aceptadas o impuestas que difieren de las que serían acordadas por empresas independientes, las rentas que habrían sido obtenidas por una de las empresas de no existir dichas condiciones, y que de hecho no se han realizado a causa de las mismas, podrán incluirse en la renta de esa empresa y sometidas en consecuencia a imposición.

2.   Cuando un País Miembro incluya en la renta de una empresa de ese País, y someta, en consecuencia, a imposición, la renta sobre la cual la empresa del otro País Miembro ha sido sometida a imposición en ese otro País Miembro, y la renta así incluida es renta que habría sido realizada por la empresa del País Miembro mencionado en primer lugar si las condiciones convenidas entre las dos empresas hubieran sido las que se hubiesen convenido entre las empresas independientes, ese otro País practicará el ajuste correspondiente de la cuantía del impuesto que ha percibido sobre esa renta. Para determinar dicho ajuste se tendrán en cuenta las demás disposiciones de la presente Decisión y las autoridades competentes de los Países Miembros se consultarán en caso necesario.

Artículo 8.- Beneficios de empresas de transporte

Los beneficios que obtuvieren las empresas de transporte aéreo, terrestre, marítimo, lacustre y fluvial, sólo estarán sujetos a obligación tributaria en el País Miembro en que dichas empresas estuvieren domiciliadas.

Artículo 9.- Regalías

Las regalías sobre un bien intangible sólo serán gravables en el País Miembro donde se use o se tenga el derecho de uso del bien intangible.

Artículo 10.- Intereses

Los intereses y demás rendimientos financieros sólo serán gravables en el País Miembro en cuyo territorio se impute y registre su pago.

Artículo 11.- Dividendos y participaciones

Los dividendos y participaciones sólo serán gravables por el País Miembro donde estuviere domiciliada la empresa que los distribuye.

El País Miembro en donde está domiciliada la empresa o persona receptora o beneficiaria de los dividendos o participaciones, no podrá gravarlos en cabeza de la sociedad receptora o inversionista, ni tampoco en cabeza de quienes a su vez sean accionistas o socios de la empresa receptora o inversionista.

Artículo 12.- Ganancias de capital

Las ganancias de capital sólo podrán gravarse por el País Miembro en cuyo territorio estuvieren situados los bienes al momento de su venta, con excepción de las obtenidas por la enajenación de:

a)   Naves, aeronaves, autobuses y otros vehículos de transporte, que sólo serán gravables por el País Miembro donde estuviere domiciliado el propietario, y

b)   Títulos, acciones y otros valores, que sólo serán gravables por el País Miembro en cuyo territorio se hubieren emitido.

Artículo 13.- Rentas provenientes de prestación de servicios personales

Las remuneraciones, honorarios, sueldos, salarios, beneficios y compensaciones similares, percibidos como retribuciones de servicios prestados por empleados, profesionales, técnicos o por servicios personales en general, incluidos los de consultoría, sólo serán gravables en el territorio en el cual tales servicios fueren prestados, con excepción de sueldos, salarios, remuneraciones y compensaciones similares percibidos por:

a)   Las personas que presten servicios a un País Miembro, en ejercicio de funciones oficiales debidamente acreditadas; estas rentas sólo serán gravables por ese País, aunque los servicios se presten dentro del territorio de otro País Miembro.

b)   Las tripulaciones de naves, aeronaves, autobuses y otros vehículos de transporte que realizaren tráfico internacional; estas rentas sólo serán gravables por el País Miembro en cuyo territorio estuviere domiciliado el empleador.

Artículo 14.- Beneficios empresariales por la prestación de servicios, servicios técnicos, asistencia técnica y consultoría

Las rentas obtenidas por empresas de servicios profesionales, técnicos, de asistencia técnica y consultoría, serán gravables sólo en el País Miembro en cuyo territorio se produzca el beneficio de tales servicios. Salvo prueba en contrario, se presume que el lugar donde se produce el beneficio es aquél en el que se imputa y registra el correspondiente gasto.

Artículo 15.- Pensiones y Anualidades

Las pensiones, anualidades y otras rentas periódicas semejantes sólo serán gravables por el País Miembro en cuyo territorio se halle situada su fuente productora.

Se considerará que la fuente está situada en el territorio del País donde se hubiere firmado el contrato que da origen a la renta periódica y cuando no existiere contrato, en el País desde el cual se efectuare el pago de tales rentas.

Artículo 16.- Rentas provenientes de actividades de entretenimiento público

Los ingresos derivados del ejercicio de actividades artísticas y de entretenimiento público, serán gravables solamente en el País Miembro en cuyo territorio se hubieren efectuado las actividades, cualquiera que fuere el tiempo que las personas que ejercen dichas actividades permanecieren en el referido territorio.

CAPITULO III
IMPUESTOS SOBRE EL PATRIMONIO

Artículo 17.- Impuestos sobre el Patrimonio

El patrimonio situado en el territorio de un País Miembro, será gravable únicamente por éste.

CAPITULO IV
DISPOSICIONES GENERALES

Artículo 18.- Tratamiento tributario aplicable a las personas domiciliadas en los otros Países Miembros

Ningún País Miembro aplicará a las personas domiciliadas en los otros Países Miembros, un tratamiento menos favorable que el que aplica a las personas domiciliadas en su territorio, respecto de los impuestos que son materia de la presente Decisión.

Artículo 19.- Consultas e información

Las autoridades competentes de los Países Miembros celebrarán consultas entre sí e intercambiarán la información necesaria para resolver de mutuo acuerdo cualquier dificultad o duda que se pueda originar en la aplicación de la presente Decisión y para establecer los controles administrativos necesarios para evitar el fraude y la evasión fiscal.

La información que se intercambie en cumplimiento de lo establecido en el párrafo anterior será considerada secreta y no podrá transmitirse a ninguna persona distinta de las autoridades encargadas de la administración de los impuestos que son materia de la presente Decisión.

Para los efectos de este artículo, las autoridades competentes de los Países Miembros podrán comunicarse directamente entre sí, realizar auditorías simultáneas y utilizar la información obtenida para fines de control tributario.

En ningún caso las disposiciones del primer párrafo del presente artículo podrán interpretarse en el sentido de obligar a un País Miembro a:

a)   adoptar medidas administrativas contrarias a su legislación o práctica administrativa, o a las del otro País Miembro;

b)   suministrar información que no se pueda obtener sobre la base de su propia legislación o en el ejercicio de su práctica administrativa normal, o de las del otro País Miembro;

c)   suministrar información que revele secretos comerciales, industriales o profesionales, procedimientos comerciales o informaciones cuya comunicación sea contraria al orden público.

Artículo 20.- Interpretación y Aplicación

La interpretación y aplicación de lo dispuesto en esta Decisión se hará siempre de tal manera que se tenga en cuenta que su propósito fundamental es el de evitar doble tributación de unas mismas rentas o patrimonios a nivel comunitario.

No serán válidas aquellas interpretaciones o aplicaciones que permitan como resultado la evasión fiscal correspondiente a rentas o patrimonios sujetos a impuestos de acuerdo con la legislación de los Países Miembros.

Nada de lo dispuesto en esta Decisión impedirá la aplicación de las legislaciones de los Países Miembros para evitar el fraude y la evasión fiscal.

Artículo 21.- Asistencia en los procesos de recaudación

Los Países Miembros se prestarán asistencia en la recaudación de impuestos adeudados por un contribuyente determinado mediante actos firmes o ejecutoriados, según la legislación del País solicitante.

El requerimiento de asistencia para ayuda solamente podrá realizarse si los bienes de propiedad del deudor tributario ubicado en el País Miembro acreedor, no fueren suficientes para cubrir el monto de la obligación tributaria adeudada.

A menos que sea convenido de otra manera por las autoridades competentes de los Países Miembros, se entenderá que:

a)   Los costos ordinarios incurridos por un País Miembro que se compromete a proporcionar su ayuda serán asumidos por ese País.

b)   Los costos extraordinarios incurridos por el País Miembro que se compromete a proporcionar su ayuda serán asumidos por el País Miembro solicitante y serán pagaderos sin consideración al monto a ser recuperado en su favor.

Este artículo será interpretado de conformidad con la legislación interna de los Países Miembros.

Artículo 22.- Vigencia

La presente Decisión entrará en vigencia respecto al impuesto sobre la renta y al impuesto sobre el patrimonio que se obtengan y a las cantidades que se paguen, acrediten, o se contabilicen como gasto, a partir del primer día del ejercicio fiscal siguiente a la publicación de esta Decisión en la Gaceta Oficial del Acuerdo de Cartagena.

Dada en la ciudad de Lima, Perú, a los cuatro días del mes de mayo del año dos mil cuatro.

*

PART TWO

BILATERAL INSTRUMENTS

MAINLAND AND HONG KONG
CLOSER ECONOMIC PARTNERSHIP ARRANGEMENT[*]
[excerpts]

The Mainland and Hong Kong Closer Economic Partnership Arrangement was signed on 29 June 2003. It entered into force on 1 January 2004.

Preamble

To promote the joint economic prosperity and development of the Mainland[1] and the Hong Kong Special Administrative Region (hereinafter referred to as the "two sides"), to facilitate the further development of economic links between the two sides and other countries and regions, the two sides decided to sign the Mainland and Hong Kong Closer Economic Partnership Arrangement (hereinafter referred to as the "CEPA").

CHAPTER 1

GENERAL PRINCIPLES

Article 1
Objectives

To strengthen trade and investment cooperation between the Mainland and the Hong Kong Special Administrative Region (hereinafter referred to as "Hong Kong") and promote joint development of the two sides, through the implementation of the following measures:

1.   progressively reducing or eliminating tariff and non-tariff barriers on substantially all the trade in goods between the two sides;

2.   progressively achieving liberalization of trade in services through reduction or elimination of substantially all discriminatory measures;

3.   promoting trade and investment facilitation.

[...]

---

[*] *Source*: The Government of the People's Republic of China (2004). "Mainland and Hong Kong Closer Economic Partnership Arrangement", available on the Internet (http://www.tid.gov.hk/english/cepa/files/main_e.doc). [Note added by the editor.]
[1] In the "CEPA", the "Mainland" refers to the entire customs territory of China.

CHAPTER 4
TRADE IN SERVICES

Article 11
Market Access

1.   Either side will progressively reduce or eliminate existing restrictive measures against services and service suppliers of the other side in accordance with the content and timetable set out in Annex 4.

2.   At the request of either side, the two sides may, through consultation, pursue further liberalization of trade in services between them.

3.   Any new measures on liberalization of trade in services implemented pursuant to paragraph 2 of this Article shall be added to Annex 4.

Article 12
Service Suppliers

1.   The definition and related provisions on "service suppliers" under the "CEPA" are set out in Annex 5.

2.   Service suppliers of other WTO Members that are juridical persons established under the laws of one side will be entitled to preferential treatments granted by the other side under the "CEPA", provided that they are engaged in substantive business operations as stipulated in Annex 5 in the area of the former side.

Article 13
Financial Cooperation

The two sides shall adopt the following measures to further strengthen cooperation in the areas of banking, securities and insurance:

1.   The Mainland supports wholly state-owned commercial banks and certain joint-equity commercial banks in re-locating their international treasury and foreign exchange trading centres to Hong Kong.

2.   The Mainland supports its banks in developing network and business activities in Hong Kong through acquisition.

3   The Mainland supports the full utilization of financial intermediaries in Hong Kong during the process of reform, restructuring and development of the financial sector in the Mainland.

4.   The two sides shall strengthen cooperation and information sharing between their financial regulators.

5.   The Mainland shall, in line with the principles of observing market rules and enhancing regulatory efficiency, support eligible Mainland insurance companies and other companies, including private enterprises, in listing in Hong Kong.

Article 14
Cooperation in Tourism

1.   In order to further promote the development of the tourism industry of Hong Kong, the Mainland will allow residents in Guangdong Province to visit Hong Kong individually. This measure will be implemented on a trial basis first in Dongguan, Zhongshan and Jiangmen and it will be extended to the entire Guangdong Province no later than 1 July 2004.

2.   The two sides shall strengthen cooperation in tourism promotion, including promotion of tourism between each other and development of external promotion programmes centered around the Pearl River Delta.

3.   The two sides shall cooperate to raise the service standards of their tourism industries and protect the legitimate rights and interests of tourists.

Article 15
Mutual Recognition of Professional Qualifications

1.   The two sides shall encourage mutual recognition of professional qualifications and promote the exchange of professional talents between each other.

2.   Competent authorities and professional bodies of both sides will, in consultation with each other, consider and design specific methodologies for mutual recognition of professional qualifications.

CHAPTER 5
TRADE AND INVESTMENT FACILITATION

Article 16
Measures

The two sides shall promote trade and investment facilitation through greater transparency, standard conformity and enhanced information exchange.

Article 17
Areas of Cooperation

1.   The two sides will promote cooperation in the following areas:

1.   trade and investment promotion;
2.   customs clearance facilitation;
3.   commodity inspection and quarantine, food safety and quality and standardization;
4.   electronic business;
5.   transparency in laws and regulations;
6.   cooperation of small and medium enterprises;
7.   cooperation in Chinese traditional medicine and medical products sector.

2.   Details on the areas of cooperation listed in paragraph 1 of this Article are set out in Annex 6.

3.   At the request of either side, the two sides may expand the scope and content of trade and investment facilitation through consultation.

4.   Any new scope or content concluded under paragraph 3 of this Article shall be added to Annex 6.

[…]

Annex 4

Specific Commitments on Liberalization of Trade in Services

1.   Pursuant to the Mainland and Hong Kong Closer Economic Partnership Arrangement (hereinafter referred to as the "CEPA"), the Mainland and Hong Kong Special Administrative Region have concluded this Annex on the specific commitments on liberalization of trade in services.

2.   As from 1 January 2004, the Mainland will apply to services and service suppliers of Hong Kong the specific commitments set out in Table 1 of this Annex. Table 1 forms an integral part of this Annex. The commitments on value-added telecommunications services will apply as from 1 October 2003.

3.   In respect of the service sectors, sub-sectors or relevant measures not covered by this Annex, the Mainland will apply Annex 9 of the "Schedule of Specific Commitments on Services List of Article II MFN Exemptions" of the "Protocol on the Accession of the People's Republic of China".

4.   In respect of the implementation of the specific commitments set out in Table 1 of this Annex, apart from applying the provisions of this Annex, the relevant laws and regulations, and administrative regulations of the Mainland should also be applicable.

5.   As from 1 January 2004, Hong Kong will not impose any new discriminatory measures on Mainland's services and service suppliers in the areas of services covered in Table 1 of this Annex.

6.   The two sides will, through consultations, formulate and implement further liberalization of Hong Kong's service sectors for the Mainland. The relevant specific commitments will be listed in Table 2. Table 2 forms an integral part of this Annex.

7.   The two sides will, through consultations, formulate and implement specific commitments of Hong Kong in relation to Mainland people obtaining professional qualifications of Hong Kong.

8.   In the event that the implementation of this Annex causes substantial impact on the trade and relevant sectors of either side, the two sides will conduct consultations on the relevant provisions of this Annex at the request of either side.

9.   This Annex will come into effect on the day of signature by the representatives of the two sides.

Signed in duplicate in Hong Kong, this 29th day of September 2003 in the Chinese language.

Table 1
The Mainland's Specific Commitments on Liberalization of Trade in Services for Hong Kong[1]

Sectors or sub-sectors	1. Business services
	A. Professional services
	a. Legal services (CPC861)
Specific commitments	1. To allow Hong Kong law firms (offices) that have set up representative offices in the Mainland to operate in association with Mainland law firms, except in the form of partnership. Hong Kong lawyers participating in such association may not handle matters of Mainland law. 2. To allow Mainland law firms to employ Hong Kong legal practitioners[2]. Such practitioners who are employed by Mainland law firms must not handle matters of Mainland law. 3. To allow the 15 Hong Kong lawyers who have already acquired Mainland lawyer qualifications to intern and practise on non-litigation legal work in the Mainland. 4. To allow Hong Kong permanent residents with Chinese citizenship to sit the legal qualifying examination in the Mainland and acquire Mainland legal professional qualification in accordance with the "State Judicial Examination Implementation Measures". 5. To allow those who have acquired Mainland legal professional qualification under item 4 above to engage in non-litigation legal work in Mainland law firms in accordance with the "Law of the People's Republic of China on Lawyers". 6.The minimum residency requirement is waived for all Hong Kong representatives stationed in the Mainland representative offices of Hong Kong law firms (offices) located in Shenzhen and Guangzhou. For the Hong Kong representatives stationed in the Mainland representative offices of Hong Kong law firms (offices) located in places other than Shenzhen and Guangzhou, their minimum residency requirement is 2 months each year.
Sectors or sub-sectors	1. Business services
	A. Professional services
	b. Accounting, auditing and bookkeeping services (CPC862)
Specific commitments	1. Hong Kong accountants who have already qualified as Chinese Certified Public Accountants (CPAs) and practised in the Mainland (including partnership) are treated on par with Chinese CPAs in respect of the requirement for annual residency in the Mainland.

---

[1] Sectoral classification is based on WTO's GATS Services Sectoral Classification List (GNS/W/120). For the contents of the sectors, reference is made to the relevant CPC, United Nations Provisional Central Product Classification.

[2] In this Annex, Hong Kong legal practitioners refer to solicitors and barristers of Hong Kong.

	2. The validity period of the "Temporary Auditing Business Permit" applied by Hong Kong accounting firms to conduct temporary auditing services in the Mainland is 1 year.
Sectors or sub-sectors	1. Business services
	A. Professional services
	d. Architectural services (CPC8671) e. Engineering services (CPC8672) f. Integrated engineering services (CPC8673) g. Urban planning and landscape architectural services (except general urban planning) (CPC8674)
Specific commitments	To allow Hong Kong service suppliers to provide, in the form of wholly-owned operations, architectural services, engineering services, integrated engineering services, urban planning and landscape architectural services in the Mainland.[1]
Sectors or sub-sectors	1. Business services
	A. Professional services
	h. Medical and dental services (CPC9312)
Specific commitments	1. The majority of medical personnel employed by Hong Kong-Mainland joint venture hospitals or clinics can be Hong Kong permanent residents. 2. The maximum duration of the licence to provide short-term medical, dental and Chinese medicine services in Mainland is 3 years for practitioners who are legally eligible to practise in the Hong Kong Special Administrative Region. On expiry, the licence for short term practice is renewable.
	3. To allow Hong Kong permanent residents, who have acquired a medical degree from the University of Hong Kong, or the Chinese University of Hong Kong, and who are legally eligible to practise in Hong Kong and have completed 1 year internship in Hong Kong, to sit the Mainland's qualification examination. A "medical practitioner's qualification certificate" of the Mainland will be issued to those who pass the examination. 4. To allow Hong Kong permanent residents who have acquired a dental degree from the University of Hong Kong and who are legally eligible to practise in Hong Kong and have practised for more than 1 year to sit the Mainland's qualification examination. A "medical (dental) practitioner's qualification certificate" of the Mainland will be issued to those who pass the examination. 5. To allow Hong Kong permanent residents in possession of a medicine higher degree from a full-time tertiary institution approved by the Education Administration Department of the Mainland State Council to sit the Mainland's qualification examination after they have passed the Hong Kong qualification examination, and after they have completed one year of internship and become legally eligible to practise in Hong Kong. A "medical practitioner's qualification certificate" of the Mainland will be issued to those who pass the examination. 6. To allow Hong Kong permanent residents in possession of a dental higher degree from a full-time tertiary institution approved by the Education Administration Department of the Mainland State Council to sit the Mainland's dental qualification examination after they have become legally eligible to practise through examination in Hong Kong and after they have been licensed to practise for over one year. A "medical (dental) practitioner's qualification

---

[1] Hong Kong service suppliers may set up wholly-owned engineering consultancy companies in the Mainland to provide the above services.

certificate" of the Mainland will be issued to those who pass the examination.

7. Hong Kong permanent residents in possession of a medicine or dental higher degree from a full-time tertiary institution approved by the Education Administration Department of the Mainland State Council may sit the Mainland's qualification examination in accordance with paragraphs 5 and 6 above. They may also sit the Mainland's qualification examination after they have completed one year's internship in the Mainland and passed an assessment in accordance with the relevant requirements. A "medical (or medical (dental)) practitioner's qualification certificate" of the Mainland will be issued to those who pass the examination.

8. To allow Hong Kong permanent residents who have acquired a Chinese medicine degree from the Chinese University of Hong Kong or the Hong Kong Baptist University and are legally eligible to practise in Hong Kong to sit the Mainland's qualification examination on the condition that they have completed 1 year's internship in a third-level traditional Chinese medicine hospital in the Mainland and have passed the performance test; or that they have been practising in Hong Kong for more than 1 year. A "medical (traditional Chinese medicine) practitioner's qualification certificate" of the Mainland will be issued to those who pass the examination.

9. To allow Hong Kong permanent residents who are in possession of a Chinese medicine higher degree from a full-time tertiary institution approved by the Education Administration Department of the Mainland State Council to sit the Mainland's medical qualification examination after they have become legally eligible to practise in Hong Kong for over one year through the Chinese medicine qualification examination for one year. They may also sit the Mainland's medical qualification examination after they have completed one year of internship in the Mainland and passed an assessment in accordance with the relevant requirements. A "medical (traditional Chinese medicine) practitioner's qualification certificate" of the Mainland will be issued to those who pass the examination.

10. The categories of medical qualification examinations that Hong Kong permanent residents may apply to sit are clinical medicine, traditional Chinese medicine and dental medicine.

Sectors or sub-sectors	1. Business services
	D. Real estate services
	Real estate services involving own or leased property (CPC821) Real estate services on a fee or contract basis (CPC822)
Specific commitments	1. To allow Hong Kong service suppliers to provide, in the form of wholly-owned operations, high standard real estate project services in the Mainland.[1] 2. To allow Hong Kong service suppliers to provide, in the form of wholly-owned operations, real estate services on a fee or contract basis in the Mainland.
Sectors or sub-sectors	1. Business services
	F. Other business services
	a. Advertising services (CPC871)
Specific commitments	To allow Hong Kong service suppliers[1] to set up wholly-owned advertising firms in the Mainland.

---

[1] High standard real estate projects refer to the real estate projects with construction costs per unit two times more than the average construction costs per unit in the same city.

Sectors or sub-sectors	1. Business services
	F. Other business services
	c. Management Consulting services (CPC86501, 86502, 86503, 86504, 86505, 86506, 86509)
Specific commitments	1. To allow Hong Kong service suppliers to provide, in the form of wholly-owned operations, management consulting services, including general management consulting services, financial management consulting services (except business tax), marketing management consulting services, human resource management consulting services, production management consulting services, public relations services and other management consulting services in the Mainland. 2. The minimum registered capital requirement for Hong Kong service suppliers providing management consulting services in the Mainland follows the requirements in the "Company Law of the People's Republic of China".
Sectors or sub-sectors	1. Business services
	F. Other business services
	Convention services and exhibition services (CPC87909)
Specific commitments	To allow Hong Kong service suppliers to provide, in the form of wholly-owned operations, convention services and exhibition services in the Mainland.[1]
Sectors or sub-sectors	2. Communications services
	C. Telecommunications services
	Valued-added services
Specific commitments	1. As from 1 October 2003, to allow Hong Kong service suppliers to set up joint venture enterprises in the Mainland to provide the following five types of value-added telecommunications services.[1] (1) internet data centre services; (2) store and forward services; (3) call centre services; (4) internet access services; (5) content services. 2. Hong Kong service suppliers' shareholding in the joint venture enterprises engaging in the value-added telecommunications services mentioned in item 1 above should not exceed 50%. 3. There will be no geographic restriction for the joint venture enterprises formed by Hong Kong service suppliers and the Mainland to provide value-added telecommunications services mentioned in item 1 above.
Sectors or sub-sectors	2. Communications services
	D. Audiovisual services
	Videos distribution services (CPC83202), Sound recording products distribution services Cinema theatre services Chinese language motion pictures and motion pictures jointly produced
Specific commitments	Videos, sound recording products distribution services 1. To allow Hong Kong service suppliers to provide, in the form of joint venture,

[1] In this sector, a Hong Kong service supplier must be an enterprise juridical person engaging in advertising services (but not necessarily as its principal business).
[1] Excluding exhibitions outside the Mainland.
[1] To implement in accordance with the Mainland's "Telecommunication business classification".

	videos and sound recording products (including motion picture products) distribution services in the Mainland.[1] 2. To allow majority shareholding, not exceeding 70%, for Hong Kong service suppliers.
	Cinema theatre services 1. To allow Hong Kong service suppliers to construct, renovate and operate cinema theatres on an equity joint venture or contractual joint venture basis. 2. To allow majority shareholding, not exceeding 75%, for Hong Kong service suppliers.
	Chinese language motion pictures and motion pictures jointly produced 1. Chinese language motion pictures produced in Hong Kong may be imported for distribution in the Mainland on a quota-free basis, after vetting and approval by the relevant Mainland authority. 2. Chinese language motion pictures produced in Hong Kong refer to those motion pictures made by production companies which are set up or established in accordance with the relevant laws of the Hong Kong Special Administrative Region, and which own more than 75% of the copyright of the motion pictures concerned. Hong Kong residents should comprise more than 50% of the total principal personnel[1] in the motion pictures concerned. 3. Motion pictures jointly produced by Hong Kong and the Mainland are treated as Mainland motion pictures for the purpose of distribution in the Mainland. Translated versions of the motion pictures in languages of other Chinese ethnic groups and Chinese dialects, which are based on the Putonghua version, are allowed to be distributed in the Mainland. 4. For motion pictures jointly produced by Hong Kong and the Mainland, there is no restriction on the percentage of principal creative personnel[2] from Hong Kong, but at least one-third of the leading artistes must be from the Mainland; there is no restriction on where the story takes place, but the plots or the leading characters must be related to the Mainland.
Sectors or sub-sectors	3. Construction and related engineering services
	CPC511, 512, 513[1], 514, 515, 516, 517, 518[2]
Specific commitments	1. For construction enterprises set up in the Mainland by Hong Kong service suppliers, the performance of both the enterprises in Hong Kong and in the Mainland is taken into account in assessing the qualification of the construction enterprises in the Mainland. However, the number of managerial and technical staff in the construction enterprises in the Mainland will be the actual number of staff working there.

---

[1] In undertaking distribution services in the Mainland in respect of videos and sound recording products, Hong Kong service suppliers should comply with the relevant laws, regulations and requirements of the review system in the Mainland.

[1] Principal personnel includes personnel performing the roles of director, screenwriter, leading actor, leading actress, supporting actor, supporting actress, producer, cinematographer, editor, art director, costume designer, action choreographer, and composer of the original film score.

[2] Major creative personnel refers to personnel performing the roles of director, screenwriter, cinematographer and leading artistes. Leading artistes refer to leading actor, leading actress, leading supporting actor and leading supporting actress.

[1] Including dredging services relating to infrastructure construction.

[2] Coverage is limited only to the rental and leasing services of construction and/or demolition machines (with operators) which are owned and used by foreign construction enterprises in the course of providing services.

	2. To allow Hong Kong service suppliers to wholly acquire construction enterprises in the Mainland.
	3. Construction enterprises in the Mainland set up and invested by Hong Kong service suppliers are exempted from foreign investment restrictions when undertaking Chinese-foreign joint construction projects.
	4. Construction enterprises in the Mainland invested by Hong Kong service suppliers will follow the relevant laws and regulations in the Mainland for application of construction qualification certificates. Those which have acquired such certification are permitted in accordance with laws to bid for construction projects in all parts of the Mainland.
Sectors or sub-sectors	4. Distribution services
	Commission agents' services (excluding salt and tobacco) Wholesale trade services (excluding salt and tobacco)
Specific commitments	1. To allow Hong Kong service suppliers to provide, in the form of wholly-owned operations, commission agents' services and wholesale trade services and to set up wholly-owned external trading companies in the Mainland.[1] 2. To apply for the setting up of wholesale commercial enterprises in the Mainland on a wholly-owned, equity joint venture, or contractual joint venture basis, Hong Kong service suppliers must fulfill the following conditions: The average annual sales value of a Hong Kong service supplier in the preceding 3 years is not less than US$30 million; the asset in the preceding year is not less than US$10 million; the minimum registered capital for setting up an enterprise in the Mainland is RMB 50 million. For setting up a wholesale commercial enterprise in the Central and Western Region[2], the average annual sales value of a Hong Kong service supplier in the preceding 3 years is not less than US$20 million; the minimum registered capital is RMB 30 million. 3. To apply for the setting up of external trading companies in the Mainland on a wholly-owned, equity joint venture or contractual joint venture basis, the Hong Kong service suppliers must fulfill the following conditions: The average annual trade value with the Mainland of a Hong Kong service supplier in the preceding 3 years is not less than US$10 million; for setting up an external trading company in the Central and Western Region, the average annual trade value with the Mainland of a Hong Kong service supplier in the preceding 3 years is not less than US$5 million; the minimum registered capital for setting up a company in the Mainland is RMB 20 million; for setting up an external trading company in the Central and Western Region, the minimum registered capital is RMB 10 million. 4. There are no geographic restrictions for Hong Kong service suppliers to provide, in the form of wholly-owned operations, commission agents' services and wholesale trade services in the Mainland.
Sectors or sub-sectors	4. Distribution services
	C. Retailing services (excluding tobacco)

---

[1] The wholesale trade services and commission agents' services provided by Hong Kong service suppliers in the Mainland in respect of books, newspapers, magazines, pharmaceutical products, pesticides, mulching film, chemical fertilizers, processed oil and crude oil remain subject to Mainland's commitments to members of the World Trade Organization.

[2] In this Annex, the Central and Western Region include Central Region and Western Region. Western Region refers to 12 provinces/autonomous regions/municipality including Chongqing, Sichuan, Guizhou, Yunnan, Tibet, Shaanxi, Gansu, Qinghai, Ningxia, Xinjiang, Inner Mongolia and Guangxi; and Xianxi Tugia-Miao Autonomous Prefecture of Hunan Province, Enshi Tugia-Miao Autonomous Prefecture of Hubei Province and Yanbian Korean Autonomous Prefecture of Jilin Province. Central Region refers to 8 provinces including Heilongjiang, Jilin, Shanxi, Henan, Hubei, Hunan, Anhui and Jiangxi.

Specific commitments	1. To allow Hong Kong service suppliers to set up wholly-owned retail commercial enterprises in the Mainland.[1] 2. To apply for the setting up of retail commercial enterprises in the Mainland on a wholly-owned, equity joint venture or contractual joint venture basis, Hong Kong service suppliers must fulfill the following conditions: 3. The average annual sales value of a Hong Kong service supplier in the preceding 3 years is not less than US$100 million; the minimum asset in the previous year is US$10 million; the minimum registered capital for setting up an enterprise in the Mainland is RMB 10 million. For setting up a retail commercial enterprise in the Central and Western Region, the minimum registered capital is RMB 6 million. 4. To allow Hong Kong service suppliers to set up wholly owned retailing enterprises in the Mainland for sale of motor vehicles.[2] 5. To allow Hong Kong permanent residents with Chinese citizenship to set up, in accordance with the relevant laws , regulations and administrative regulations, individually owned stores in Guangdong to provide retailing services excluding franchising operation, without being subject to the approval procedures applicable to foreign investments. The sales area of such stores should not exceed 300 square metres.
Sectors or sub-sectors	4. Distribution services
	D. Franchising
Specific commitments	To allow Hong Kong service suppliers to engage, in the form of wholly-owned operations, in franchising in the Mainland.[1]
Sectors or sub-sectors	7. Financial services
	A. All insurance and insurance-related services
	Life, health and pension/ annuities insurance Non-life insurance Reinsurance Services auxiliary to insurance
Specific commitments	1. To allow groups formed by Hong Kong insurance companies through re-grouping and strategic mergers to enter the Mainland insurance market subject to established market access conditions (total assets held by the group of over US$ 5 billion; more than 30 years of establishment experience attributable to one of the Hong Kong insurance companies in the group; and a representative office established in the Mainland for over 2 years by one of the Hong Kong insurance companies in the group). 2. The maximum limit of capital participation by a Hong Kong insurance company in a Mainland insurance company is 24.9%. 3. To allow Hong Kong residents with Chinese citizenship, after obtaining the Mainland's professional qualifications in actuarial science, to practise in the Mainland without prior approval. 4. To allow Hong Kong residents, after obtaining the Mainland's insurance

---

[1] The retailing services provided by Hong Kong service suppliers in the Mainland in respect of books, newspapers, magazines, pharmaceuticals, pesticides, mulching film, chemical fertilizers, staple food, vegetable oil, edible sugar, cotton and processed oil remain subject to Mainland's commitments to members of the World Trade Organization.

[2] Chain stores with more than 30 outlets remain subject to Mainland's commitments to members of the World Trade Organization.

[1] The relevant laws and regulations will be promulgated separately.

	qualifications and being employed or appointed by a Mainland insurance institution, to engage in the relevant insurance business.
Sectors or sub-sectors	7. Financial services
	B. Banking and other financial services (excluding insurance and securities)
	a. Acceptance of deposits and other repayable funds from the public;
	b. Lending of all types, including consumer credit, mortgage credit, factoring and financing of commercial transaction;
	c. Financial leasing;
	d. All payment and money transmission services, including credit, charge and debit cards, travellers cheques and bankers drafts (including import and export settlement);
	e. Guarantees and commitments;
	f. Trading for own account or for account of customers: foreign exchange.
Specific commitments	1. For Hong Kong banks to set up branches or body corporates in the Mainland, the total asset requirement at the end of the year preceding application is not less than US$ 6 billion; for finance companies to set up body corporates, the total asset requirement at the end of the year preceding application is not less than US$ 6 billion.
	2. There will be no requirement for setting up a representative office in the Mainland before a Hong Kong bank establishes a joint venture bank or joint venture finance company in the Mainland, or before a Hong Kong finance company establishes a joint venture finance company in the Mainland.
	3. For Mainland branches of Hong Kong banks to apply to conduct RMB business:
	(1) they should have been operating in the Mainland for more than 2 years;
	(2) in conducting profitability assessment, the relevant authorities will base their assessment on the overall profitability position of all branches of the bank in the Mainland instead of the profitability position of its individual branches.
Sectors or sub-sectors	7. Financial services
	B. Banking and other financial services
	Securities
Specific commitments	1. To allow the Hong Kong Exchanges and Clearing Limited to set up a representative office in Beijing.
	2. To simplify the relevant procedures for Hong Kong professionals[1] applying in the Mainland for securities and futures industry qualifications. Hong Kong professionals applying to obtain securities and futures industry qualifications of the Mainland need only to undertake training and pass examination on Mainland laws and regulations; and examination on professional knowledge is not required.
Sectors or sub-sectors	9. Tourism and travel related services

---

[1] In this sector, professionals refer to Hong Kong permanent residents who have been licensed by the Securities and Futures Commission of Hong Kong.

Specific commitments	A. Hotels (including apartment buildings) and restaurants (CPC641-643) B. Travel agency and tour operator (CPC7471) Others
	1. To allow Hong Kong service suppliers to construct, renovate and operate, on a wholly-owned basis, hotels, apartment buildings and restaurant establishments in the Mainland. 2. There will be no geographic restriction on Hong Kong travel agencies forming joint venture travel agencies in the Mainland where the Mainland agencies have majority shareholding. 3. To allow residents of Beijing, Shanghai, and Guangzhou, Shenzhen, Zhuhai, Dongguan, Zhongshan, Jiangmen, Foshan and Huizhou of the Guangdong Province to visit Hong Kong individually for tourism, and to allow the same in respect of the whole of Guangdong Province not later than 1 July 2004.
Sectors or sub-sectors	11. Transport services
	A. Maritime transport services H. Auxiliary services
	International transport (freight and passengers) (CPC7211, 7212, less cabotage transport services) Container station and depot services Others
Specific commitments	1. To allow Hong Kong service suppliers[1] to set up wholly-owned enterprises in the Mainland to operate international ship management services, storage and warehousing for international maritime freight, container station and depot services, and non-vessel operating common carrying services. 2. To allow Hong Kong service suppliers to set up wholly-owned shipping companies in the Mainland to provide regular business services for vessels that they own or operate, such as shipping undertaking, issuance of bills of lading, settlement of freight rates, signing of service contracts, etc.
	3. To allow Hong Kong service suppliers to use liner vessels serving main routes to move, without any restrictions, empty containers that they own or rent, as long as customs procedures are observed.
Sectors or sub-sectors	11. Transport services
	F. Road transport services
	Freight transportation by road in trucks or cars (CPC7123) Road passenger transportation (CPC7121, 7122)
Specific commitments	1. To allow Hong Kong service suppliers to set up wholly-owned enterprises in the Mainland to provide road freight transport services. 2. To allow Hong Kong service suppliers to provide direct non-stop road freight transport services between Hong Kong and individual provinces, cities and autonomous regions in the Mainland.[1] 3. To allow Hong Kong service suppliers to set up wholly-owned enterprises in the Western Region of the Mainland to provide road passenger transport services
Sectors or sub-sectors	11. Transport services

---

[1] In this sector, the Hong Kong service suppliers must be enterprise juridical persons.

[1] Non-stop services mean direct road transport services between Hong Kong and the Mainland. In this sector, Hong Kong service suppliers supplying non-stop services must be enterprise juridical persons.

	H. Services auxiliary to all modes of transport
	Storage and warehouse services (CPC742)
Specific commitments	1. To allow Hong Kong service suppliers to provide, in the form of wholly-owned operations, storage and warehousing services in the Mainland. 2. The minimum registered capital requirement for storage and warehousing enterprises in the Mainland set up and invested by Hong Kong service suppliers will be the same as that for Mainland enterprises.
Sectors or sub-sectors	11. Transport services
	H. Services auxiliary to all modes of transport
	Freight forwarding agency services (CPC748, 749, excluding freight inspection)
Specific commitments	1. To allow Hong Kong service suppliers[1] to provide, in the form of wholly-owned operations, freight forwarding agency services in the Mainland. 2. The minimum registered capital requirement for international freight forwarding agency enterprises in the Mainland set up and invested by Hong Kong service suppliers will be the same as that for Mainland enterprises.
Sectors or sub-sectors	Service sectors (sectors not set out in GNS/W/120)
	Logistics services
Specific commitments	To allow Hong Kong service suppliers to provide, in the form of wholly-owned operations, logistics services in the Mainland, which include road transport, storage and warehousing, loading and unloading, value adding processing, packaging, delivery and related information and consultancy services for ordinary road freight; freight transport agency services within the Mainland; and the management and operation of logistics services through computer network.

Table 2

Hong Kong's Specific Commitments on Liberalization of Trade in Services for the Mainland[1]

*

Annex 5

Definition of "Service Supplier" and Related Requirements

1.   Pursuant to the Mainland and Hong Kong Closer Economic Partnership Arrangement (hereinafter referred to as the "CEPA"), the Mainland and Hong Kong Special Administrative Region have concluded this Annex on the definition of "service supplier" and related requirements.

2.   Unless otherwise stipulated in the "CEPA" and its Annexes, "service supplier" as used in the "CEPA" and its Annexes refers to any person that supplies a service. In this context:

2.1.   "person" means either a natural person or a juridical person;

---

[1] In this sector, Hong Kong service suppliers must be enterprise juridical persons.
[1] The two sides will, through consultations, formulate and implement further liberalization of Hong Kong's service sectors for the Mainland. The relevant specific commitments will be listed in this table.

2.2. "natural person":

2.2.1. in the case of the Mainland, means a citizen of the People's Republic of China;

2.2.2. in the case of Hong Kong, means a permanent resident of the Hong Kong Special Administrative Region of the People's Republic of China;

2.3. "juridical person" means any legal entity duly constituted or otherwise organized under the applicable laws of the Mainland or the Hong Kong Special Administrative Region, whether for profit or otherwise, and whether privately-owned or governmentally-owned, including any corporation, trust, partnership, joint venture, sole proprietorship or association (business association).

3. The specific criteria for Hong Kong service suppliers who provide services in the form of juridical persons:

3.1. with the exception of the legal services sector, a Hong Kong service supplier, when applying to provide the relevant services under Annex 4 in the Mainland, should:

3.1.1. be incorporated or established pursuant to the Companies Ordinance or other relevant laws of the Hong Kong Special Administrative Region,[1] and have obtained a valid Business Registration Certificate. If required by law, it should also have obtained the licence or permit for providing such services; and

3.1.2. engage in substantive business operations in Hong Kong. The criteria for determination are:

(1) The nature and scope of business

The nature and scope of the services provided by a Hong Kong service supplier in Hong Kong should encompass the nature and scope of the services it intends to provide in the Mainland.

(2) Years of operation required

A Hong Kong service supplier should be incorporated or established in Hong Kong, and have engaged in substantive business operations for 3 years or more.[2]

---

[1] Any overseas company, representative office, liaison office, "mail box company" and company specifically established for providing certain services to its parent company, which is registered in Hong Kong, is not a Hong Kong service supplier under this Annex.

[2] From the day the "CEPA" comes into effect, where more than 50% of the equity interest of a Hong Kong service supplier has been owned for at least one year since a merger or acquisition by a service supplier other than one from either side, the service supplier which has been acquired or merged will be regarded as a Hong Kong service supplier.

A Hong Kong service supplier providing construction and related engineering services should be incorporated or established in Hong Kong, and have engaged in substantive business operations for 5 years or more; there is no limitation on the years of substantive business operations in Hong Kong for Hong Kong service suppliers providing real estate services;

A Hong Kong service supplier providing banking and other financial services (excluding insurance and securities), i.e. a Hong Kong bank or finance company should have engaged in substantive business operations for 5 years or more after it has been granted a relevant licence by the Monetary Authority pursuant to the Banking Ordinance;

A Hong Kong service supplier providing insurance and related services, i.e. a Hong Kong insurance company should be incorporated or established in Hong Kong and have engaged in substantive business operations for 5 years or more.

(3)   Profits tax

During the period of substantive business operations in Hong Kong, a Hong Kong service supplier should have paid profits tax in accordance with the law.

(4)   Business premises

A Hong Kong service supplier should own or rent premises in Hong Kong to engage in substantive business operations. The scale of its business premises should be commensurate with the scope and the scale of its business.

For a Hong Kong service supplier providing maritime transport services, 50% or more of the ships owned by it, calculated in terms of tonnage, should be registered in Hong Kong.

(5)   Employment of staff more than 50% of the staff employed in Hong Kong by the Hong Kong service supplier should be residents staying in Hong Kong without limit of stay, and people from the Mainland staying in Hong Kong on One Way Permit.

3.2.   A Hong Kong law firm (office) of the legal services sector, when applying to provide the relevant services under Annex 4 in the Mainland, should:

3.2.1. be registered and established as a Hong Kong law firm (office) and have obtained a valid Business Registration Certificate pursuant to the relevant legislation of the Hong Kong Special Administrative Region.

3.2.2. The sole proprietor and all the partners of the law firm (office) should be registered Hong Kong practising lawyers.

3.2.3. The principal scope of business of the law firm (office) should be to provide Hong Kong legal services in Hong Kong.

3.2.4. The law firm (office) or its sole proprietor or partners should pay profits tax in accordance with the law.

3.2.5. The law firm (office) should have engaged in substantive business operations in Hong Kong for 3 years or more.

3.2.6. The law firm (office) should own or rent premises in Hong Kong to engage in substantive business operations.

4. Unless otherwise stipulated in the "CEPA" and its Annexes, Hong Kong service suppliers providing services in the form of natural persons should be permanent residents of the Hong Kong Special Administrative Region of the People's Republic of China.

5. Service suppliers of the Mainland should fulfil the definition of Article 2 of this Annex. Specific criteria will be determined by the two sides through consultation.

6. To obtain the treatment under the "CEPA", a Hong Kong service supplier should provide:

6.1. In the event that the Hong Kong service supplier is a juridical person, the Hong Kong service supplier should submit the following documents and information, and statutory declaration, which have been verified by relevant institutions (persons) of Hong Kong, as well as the certificate issued by the Government of the Hong Kong Special Administrative Region:

6.1.1. Documents and information (if applicable)

(1) Copy of the Certificate of Incorporation issued by the Companies Registry of the Hong Kong Special Administrative Region;

(2) Copies of the Business Registration Certificate of the Hong Kong Special Administrative Region and an Extract of Information in the Register of Businesses;

(3) Annual reports or audited financial statements of the Hong Kong service supplier for the past 3 years (or 5 years);

(4) Original or copy of document(s) substantiating that the Hong Kong service supplier owns or rents business premises in Hong Kong;[3]

(5) Copy of the Profits Tax Returns, Notice of Assessment and Demand for Tax in respect of the Hong Kong service supplier for the past 3 years (or 5 years); in the event of loss, the Hong Kong service supplier should provide supporting document(s) from the

---

[3] A Hong Kong service supplier applying to provide maritime transport services in the Mainland should separately submit document(s) or its copy (verified) to attest that 50% or more of the ships owned by it, calculated in terms of tonnage, is registered in Hong Kong.

relevant department of the Hong Kong Special Administrative Region attesting to the loss;

(6)   Copy of the Employer's Return of Remuneration and Pensions of the Hong Kong service supplier in respect of the remuneration and pension of its employees in Hong Kong, and the original or a copy of other relevant document(s) substantiating that the company fulfils the requirement of Article 3.1.2.(5) of this Annex on the percentage threshold;

(7)   Original or copy of other relevant document(s) that can substantiate the nature and scope of the business in Hong Kong of the Hong Kong service supplier.

6.1.2.   Statutory declaration

For any Hong Kong service supplier applying to obtain treatment under the "CEPA", its authorized representative should make a statutory declaration pursuant to the procedures and requirements of the Oaths and Declarations Ordinance of the Hong Kong Special Administrative Region.[4] The form of the declaration will be determined by the relevant authorities of the Mainland and the Hong Kong Special Administrative Region through consultation.

6.1.3.   Certificate

A Hong Kong service supplier should submit the documents and information, and the statutory declaration as required under Article 6.1.1 and 6.1.2 of this Annex to the Trade and Industry Department of the Hong Kong Special Administrative Region (hereinafter referred to as the "TID") for examination. The "TID" may, in the circumstances it considers necessary, entrust other government departments of the Hong Kong Special Administrative Region, statutory bodies, or independent professional institutions (personnel) to conduct verification.[5] The "TID" will issue a certificate to the applicants that it considers to have fulfilled the criteria of Hong Kong service suppliers as required under this Annex. The contents and form of the certificate will be determined by the relevant authorities of the Mainland and the Hong Kong Special Administrative Region through consultation.

6.2.   In the event that a Hong Kong service supplier is a natural person, the Hong Kong service supplier should provide identification of his or her Hong Kong permanent resident status. For Chinese citizens among such service suppliers, their Home

---

[4] A person is subject to criminal liability of Hong Kong if he wilfully makes a false or untrue declaration pursuant to the Oaths and Declarations Ordinance.

[5] In the telecommunications sector, the "TID" will entrust the authority of the Government of the Hong Kong Special Administrative Region that regulates telecommunications to conduct verification with a view to substantiating the nature and scope of business of the Hong Kong service suppliers providing internet data centre services, call centre services, and content services.

Visit Permit for Hong Kong and Macau Residents or Hong Kong Special Administrative Region passport should also be provided.

    6.3.   Copies of the statutory declarations and the identification documents of natural persons, as well as the documents and information that the "TID" considers should be attested by a lawyer, as required under Article 6.1.1 and 6.1.2 and 6.2 of this Annex, should be attested by attesting officers recognized by the Mainland.

7.   When applying to the Mainland's examining authorities to obtain treatment under the "CEPA", a Hong Kong service supplier should follow the following procedures:

    7.1.   When it applies to provide the services under Annex 4 in the Mainland, a Hong Kong service supplier should submit to the Mainland's examining authorities the documents and information, statutory declaration and certificate as required under Article 6 of this Annex.

    7.2.   Pursuant to the powers conferred under Mainland laws and regulations, the Mainland examining authorities, in examining the application for supplying Hong Kong services, should at the same time verify the qualifications of the Hong Kong service supplier.

    7.3.   When holding a different view in respect of the qualification of the Hong Kong service supplier, the Mainland examining authority should inform the Hong Kong service supplier within a stipulated period, and notify the Ministry of Commerce. The Ministry of Commerce will in turn inform the "TID", giving the reasons for the divergent views. The Hong Kong service supplier may, through the "TID" and with written justification, request the Ministry of Commerce for reconsideration. The Ministry of Commerce should give a written reply to the "TID" within a stipulated period.

8.   Hong Kong service suppliers who have already been providing services in the Mainland should apply for obtaining treatment under the "CEPA" in accordance with the requirements of Articles 6 and 7 of this Annex.

9.   This Annex will come into effect on the day of signature by the representatives of the two sides.

Annex 6
Trade and Investment Facilitation

1.   Pursuant to the Mainland and Hong Kong Closer Economic Partnership Arrangement (hereinafter referred to as the "CEPA"), the Mainland and the Hong Kong Special Administrative Region have concluded this Annex on cooperation in trade and investment facilitation.

2.   The two sides agree to cooperate in trade and investment facilitation in seven areas, namely, trade and investment promotion; customs clearance facilitation; commodity inspection and quarantine, food safety, quality and standardization; electronic business; transparency in

laws and regulations; cooperation of small and medium enterprises, and cooperation in Chinese traditional medicine and medical products sector. Cooperation in these areas will follow the guidance and coordination of the Joint Steering Committee set up in accordance with Article 19 of the "CEPA".

3.   Trade and Investment Promotion

The two sides recognize the importance of mutual trade and investment to their economic and social development. Taking into account the actual development of trade and investment as well as the need for growth, the two sides agree to strengthen cooperation in trade and investment promotion.

3.1.   Cooperation Mechanism

Relevant working groups under the Joint Steering Committee will be made full use of in guiding and coordinating cooperation in trade and investment promotion between the two sides.

3.2.   Content of Cooperation

Based on past cooperation experience, as well as the development of economic and trade exchanges between both sides, the two sides will strengthen cooperation in the following areas:

3.2.1. Notify and publicize their respective policies and regulations on external trade and foreign investment promotion, with a view to achieving information sharing.

3.2.2. Exchange views and conduct consultations to solve common problems relating to trade and investment of both sides.

3.2.3. Strengthen communication and cooperation in mutual investment and joint promotion of overseas investment.

3.2.4. Strengthen cooperation in organizing exhibitions and arranging delegations to participate in overseas exhibitions.

3.2.5. Conduct exchanges on other issues of mutual concern relating to trade and investment promotion.

3.3.   Participation of Other Entities

The two sides note that the participation of semi-official and non-official organizations in the area of trade and investment promotion has positive effect and significance. The two sides agree to support and assist these organizations in various ways to launch trade and investment promotion activities.

4.   Customs Clearance Facilitation

Recognizing the importance of close and long-term cooperation between the two Customs Administrations and of the implementation of customs clearance facilitation to their economic and social development, the two sides agree to strengthen cooperation in customs clearance facilitation.

4.1. Cooperation Mechanism

The two sides will steer and coordinate cooperation in customs clearance facilitation through the Annual Review Meeting between the senior leaders of the General Administration of Customs and the Customs and Excise Department of Hong Kong, and will promote the launch of cooperation in customs clearance facilitation through expert groups of the Customs Administrations and relevant departments of the two sides.

4.2. Content of Cooperation

Taking into account the need for different customs clearance systems and monitoring modes as well as experience in cooperation, the two sides agree to strengthen cooperation in the following areas:

4.2.1. Establish a reciprocal notification system to report their respective policies and regulations on customs clearance and management of clearance facilitation.

4.2.2. Conduct studies and exchanges on the differences between their respective customs clearance systems and on existing problems, with a view to enriching the specific content of cooperation in customs clearance facilitation.

4.2.3. Explore the expansion of the scope for further cooperation in strengthening control and enhancing efficiency in respect of customs clearance in areas such as sea and land transportation, intermodal operation and logistics.

4.2.4. Strengthen cooperation in establishing a crisis management mechanism at control points and adopt effective measures to maintain as far as possible smooth clearance on the two sides.

4.2.5. Establish a regular liaison mechanism, to make full use of the Guangdong and Hong Kong Customs Working Group on Operational Efficiency of Control Points set up under the Guangdong Branch of the General Administration of Customs and the Customs and Excise Department of Hong Kong.

4.2.6. Strengthen the work of the Expert Group on Cargo Data Sharing and Road Cargo Clearance set up under the two Customs Administrations, study the feasibility of data interchange and development of electronic customs clearance system at control points, strengthen the risk management of customs clearance and enhance its efficiency with technical solutions.

5.   Commodity Inspection and Quarantine, Food Safety and Quality and Standardization

Recognizing the importance of protecting the health and safety of Mainland and Hong Kong people in the course of trade in goods and movement of persons, the two sides agree to strengthen cooperation in the areas of commodity inspection and quarantine, food safety, health and quarantine of people, and certification, accreditation and standardization.

5.1.   Cooperation Mechanism

The two sides will make use of the existing cooperation channels of relevant departments to promote the launch of cooperation in the relevant areas through reciprocal visits, discussions and other modes of communication.

5.2.   Content of Cooperation

The two sides agree to strengthen cooperation in the following areas:

5.2.1. Inspection and supervision of electrical and mechanical products

To ensure the safety of consumers of both sides, the two sides will enhance information flow and exchanges through established communication channels, in particular the exchange of information and intelligence on the safety of electrical and mechanical products, so as to jointly prevent safety problems associated with these products. The two sides will also promote cooperation in the training of inspection and supervisory officers.

The two sides are committed to implementing the "Cooperation Arrangement on Electrical and Mechanical Products Safety" signed between the State General Administration for Quality Supervision and Inspection and Quarantine, and the Electrical and Mechanical Services Department of Hong Kong on 12 February 2003.

5.2.2. Inspection and quarantine of animals and plants, and food safety

The two sides will make use of the existing coordination mechanism to step up cooperation in inspection and quarantine of animals and plants as well as in food safety, so as to enable both sides to enforce their respective regulations more effectively.

5.2.3. Monitoring of health and quarantine issues

The two sides will make use of the existing channels to regularly notify each other of the information on epidemic outbreaks and to step up academic exchange and joint research on health and quarantine issues; discuss health monitoring issues in respect of small vessels plying between the control points of Guangdong and Shenzhen; enhance cooperation in areas such as investigation and prevention of tropical infectious diseases and live vectors, surveillance and control of special articles and radioactive articles, transportation of biological disease factors and the related inspection, treatment and control measures.

5.2.4. Certification, accreditation and standardization management

The two sides will urge their respective organizations to strengthen cooperation with a view to promoting conformity assessment (including testing, certification and inspection), accreditation and standardization management.

6. Electronic Business

The two sides recognize that the application and promotion of electronic business will create more trade and investment opportunities for both sides. They agree to step up exchange and cooperation in the area of electronic business.

6.1. Cooperation Mechanism

Under the guidance and coordination of the Joint Steering Committee, the two sides will set up a working group to act as a communication channel as well as a consultation and coordination mechanism for cooperation in electronic business, with a view to promoting cooperation and joint development in the area of electronic business.

6.2. Content of Cooperation

The two sides agree to cooperate in the following areas:

6.2.1. Cooperate in specialized projects in respect of the study and formulation of rules, standards and regulations of electronic business, with a view to creating a favourable environment for promoting and ensuring the healthy development of electronic business.

6.2.2. Strengthen exchange and cooperation in areas such as corporate application, promotion and training. Make full use of the relevant government departments of the two sides in promotion and coordination, step up promotion for electronic business, foster interaction between the enterprises of the two sides, and facilitate the launching of electronic business among the enterprises through demonstration projects.

6.2.3. Strengthen cooperation in implementing e-government, intensify exchange and cooperation in the development of e-government at various levels.

6.2.4. Cooperate in economic and trade information exchange, and expand the scope and extent of cooperation.

7. Transparency in Laws and Regulations

The two sides recognize that enhanced transparency in laws and regulations is an important foundation for promoting economic and trade flow between both sides. In the spirit of serving the commercial and industrial enterprises in the two places, the two sides agree to strengthen cooperation in the area of enhanced transparency of laws and regulations.

7.1. Cooperation Mechanism

The two sides will cooperate through relevant working groups under the Joint Steering Committee as well as their respective representative agencies.

7.2. Content of Cooperation

The two sides agree to strengthen cooperation in the following areas:

7.2.1. Exchange information on the enactment and revision of laws, regulations and rules in respect of investment, trade and other economic areas.

7.2.2. Disseminate in a timely manner information on policies and regulations through various media including newspapers, journals and websites.

7.2.3. Organize and support the organization of various briefings and seminars on economic and trade policies and regulations.

7.2.4. Provide advisory services to commercial and industrial enterprises through channels such as WTO enquiry points and websites of "Invest in China" and "China Business Guide" of the Mainland.

8. Cooperation of Small and Medium Enterprises

The two sides recognize that the development of small and medium enterprises plays an important role in increasing employment, promoting economic development and maintaining social stability. The two sides agree to promote exchanges and cooperation between small and medium enterprises of the two places.

8.1. Cooperation Mechanism

Establish an operational mechanism between relevant government departments of both sides to promote cooperation between small and medium enterprises of the two sides, with a view to fostering their cooperation and seeking mutual development.

8.2. Content of Cooperation

The two sides agree to support and promote cooperation in the following areas:

8.2.1. Explore jointly the strategy and support policy for the development of small and medium enterprises through visits and exchanges.

8.2.2. Organize visits and exchanges on the organizational and operational modes of the intermediaries providing services to small and medium enterprises in the two places, and promote cooperation of the intermediaries.

8.2.3. Establish channels for providing information services to small and medium enterprises in the two places, exchange regularly relevant publications, set up dedicated websites, implement progressively information interchange and the interconnection of information website databases of the two sides.

8.2.4. Organize through different modes direct exchanges and communication between small and medium enterprises of the two places to promote their cooperation.

8.3. Participation of Other Entities

The two sides support and assist semi-official and non-official organizations to play a part in promoting cooperation between small and medium enterprises of the two places.

9. Cooperation in Chinese Traditional Medicine and Medical Products Sector

The two sides recognize that traditional Chinese medicine and medical products, being a fine component of the Chinese culture, bears tremendous market application potential and economic benefits. Both sides have their own competitive edge in areas such as promoting the industrialization of traditional Chinese medicine and medical products and advancing its modernization and internationalization. Cooperation in this area will be of notable significance to economic and social development of both sides. The two sides agree to strengthen cooperation in the development of the traditional Chinese medicine and medical products sector.

9.1. Cooperation Mechanism

The two sides will strengthen and improve the mechanism of liaison and cooperation between their respective government departments so as to promote the development of cooperation in traditional Chinese medicine and medical products sector of the two places.

9.2. Content of Cooperation

Based on the situation and development trend of cooperation in traditional Chinese medicine and medical products sector in the two places, the two sides agree to strengthen cooperation in the following areas:

9.2.1. Communicate on the formulation of their respective regulations on and management of traditional Chinese medicine and medical products with a view to achieving information sharing.

9.2.2. Enhance cooperation in research on traditional Chinese medicine and medical products, exchange and share information on areas such as industry development strategy and development orientation of traditional Chinese medicine and medical products.

9.2.3. Strengthen communication and coordination in registration management of traditional Chinese medical products, implement standardization in the management of traditional Chinese medical products, and facilitate mutual trade in traditional Chinese medical products.

9.2.4. Cooperate in such areas as facility management and regulations and requirements for clinical trials, with a view to achieving mutual recognition of clinical data.

9.2.5. Conduct exchanges and cooperate in quality standardization for traditional Chinese medical products, and jointly promote the enhancement of quality standards for traditional Chinese medical products.

9.2.6. Support cooperation between the traditional Chinese medicine and medical products enterprises of the two places and jointly strive for international market expansion.

9.2.7. Strengthen trade and investment promotion and cooperation in the traditional Chinese medicine and medical products sector.

9.2.8. Conduct exchanges and consultations on ways to solve problems arising from cooperation in traditional Chinese medicine and medical products sector.

9.3. Participation of Other Entities

The two sides will support and assist the participation of semi-official and non-official organizations in cooperation in the traditional Chinese medicine and medical products sector, including the cooperation already established between the National Center for Traditional Chinese Medicine and the Hong Kong Jockey Club Institute of Chinese Medicine Ltd.

10. According to paragraphs 3 and 4 of Article 17 of the "CEPA", any new area or content of trade and investment facilitation agreed by the two sides will be incorporated into this Annex.

11. This Annex will come into effect on the day of signature by the representatives of the two sides.

*

SUPPLEMENT TO THE MAINLAND AND HONG KONG CLOSER ECONOMIC PARTNERSHIP ARRANGEMENT[*]
[excerpts]

> The Supplement to the Mainland and Hong Kong Closer Economic Partnership Arrangement was signed on 27 October 2004.

To further enhance the level of economic and trade exchanges and cooperation between the Mainland[1] and the Hong Kong Special Administrative Region (hereinafter referred to as "Hong Kong"), and pursuant to the requirements of the Mainland and Hong Kong Closer Economic Partnership Arrangement (hereinafter referred to as "CEPA") signed on 29 June 2003 and its Annexes signed on 29 September 2003, the two sides agreed to sign this Supplement to further liberalize trade in goods and trade in services in the Mainland for Hong Kong.

1. Trade in Goods

   (1) From 1 January 2005, the Mainland shall apply zero tariff to imported goods of Hong Kong origin as set out in Annex 1 of this Supplement. Annex 1 of this Supplement is a supplement to Table 1 of Annex 1 of "CEPA"- "List of Hong Kong Origin Products for Implementation of Zero Import Tariff by the Mainland".

   (2) The rules of origin for imported goods of Hong Kong origin listed in Annex 1 of this Supplement, which were drawn up pursuant to Annex 2 of "CEPA" – "Rules of Origin for Trade in Goods", are set out in Annex 2 of this Supplement. Annex 2 of this Supplement is a supplement to Table 1 of Annex 2 of "CEPA"- "Schedule on Rules of Origin of Hong Kong Goods Subject to Tariff Preference for Trade in Goods".

2. Trade in Services

   (1) From 1 January 2005, the Mainland shall further relax the market access conditions for services and service suppliers of Hong Kong in the areas of legal, accounting, medical, audiovisual, construction, distribution, banking, securities, transport, freight forwarding agency, on the basis of Annex 4 of "CEPA" - "Specific Commitments on Liberalization of Trade in Services", and shall expand the geographical and business scope of individually owned stores established in the Mainland by Hong Kong permanent residents with Chinese citizenship. The specific contents are detailed in Annex 3 of this Supplement.

---

[*] *Source*: The Government of the People's Republic of China and Hong Kong (China) (2004). "Supplement to the Mainland and Hong Kong Closer Economic Partnership Arrangement", available on the Internet (http://www.tid.gov.hk/english/cepa/files/sa_main_e.doc). [Note added by the editor.]

[1] In "CEPA", the "Mainland" refers to the entire customs territory of China.

(2)   From 1 January 2005, the Mainland shall liberalize and relax the market access conditions for services and service suppliers of Hong Kong in the areas of patent agency, trademark agency, airport services, cultural entertainment, information technology, job referral agency, job intermediary, and professional qualification examinations. The specific contents are detailed in Annex 3 of this Supplement.

(3)   Commitments in the area of construction and part of the commitments in the area of distribution, as set out in Annex 3 to this Supplement, have already been implemented from 28 August 2004. The specifics are set out in the specific commitments of construction and related engineering services, and distribution services in Annex 3 of this Supplement. The commitment with respect to Mainland branches of Hong Kong banks conducting insurance agents business, as set out in Annex 3 of this Supplement, shall be implemented from 1 November 2004.

(4)   Annex 3 of this Supplement is a supplement and amendment to Table 1 of Annex 4 of "CEPA" – "The Mainland's Specific Commitments on Liberalization of Trade in Services for Hong Kong". In the event of conflict between the provisions of the two instruments, the provisions of Annex 3 of this Supplement shall prevail.

(5)   "Service suppliers" as referred to in Annex 3 of this Supplement should meet the relevant requirements of Annex 5 of "CEPA" – "Definition of "Service Supplier" and Related Requirements".

3. Supplements and Amendments to Annexes to "CEPA"

(1)   Article 5(3)2. of Annex 1 of "CEPA" – "Arrangements for Implementation of Zero Tariff on Trade in Goods" is amended as follows: For goods proposed to be produced, the Mainland shall, in accordance with the consensus reached between the two sides, add the list of goods concerned to Table 1 of Annex 1 of "CEPA" and the rules of origin of the goods concerned to Table 1 of Annex 2 of "CEPA". After the applicant has put the proposed goods into production, the Hong Kong Trade and Industry Department shall conduct verification jointly with the Hong Kong Customs and Excise Department and inform the Ministry of Commerce. The Mainland shall, after confirmation by both sides, release the relevant imports on zero tariff basis in line with "CEPA" upon presentation of the certificates of origin issued by the Hong Kong issuing authorities.

(2)   The following is added to Article 3.1.2(2) of Annex 5 of "CEPA" – "Definition of "Service Supplier" and Related Requirements": A Hong Kong service supplier providing air transport ground services should have obtained the relevant licence in the provision of the relevant air transport ground services in Hong Kong, and have engaged in substantive business operations for 5 years or more.

4.   Annexes

The Annexes to this Supplement form an integral part of this Supplement.

5.   Coming into Effect

This Supplement shall come into effect on the day of signature by the representatives of the two sides.

[...]

Annex 3

Supplements and Amendments to the Mainland's Specific Commitments on Liberalization of Trade in Services for Hong Kong[1]

Sectors or sub-sectors	1. Business services
	A. Professional services
	a. Legal services (CPC861)
Specific commitments	Hong Kong lawyers providing professional assistance at the request of Mainland law firms on the basis of individual cases will not be required to apply for a Hong Kong legal consultant permit.
Sectors or sub-sectors	1. Business services
	A. Professional services
	b. Accounting, auditing and bookkeeping services (CPC862)
Specific commitments	1. To allow consultancy companies in the Mainland established by Hong Kong accountants that have satisfied the requirements of the Mainland's "Provisional Measures for the Administration of the Provision of Bookkeeping Services" to provide bookkeeping services. Hong Kong accountants providing bookkeeping services should have obtained the Mainland's accounting qualification certificate. In addition, the person in charge of the bookkeeping services should hold the relevant Mainland's professional qualification (professional title) of accountant or above. 2. When Hong Kong accountants apply for a practising licence in the Mainland, the length of auditing experience that they have acquired in Hong Kong is equivalent to the length of auditing experience acquired in the Mainland.
Sectors or sub-sectors	1. Business services
	A. Professional services
	h. Medical and dental services (CPC9312)
Specific commitments	1. Hong Kong permanent residents who are legally eligible to practise western medicine, dentistry and Chinese medicine in the Hong Kong Special Administrative Region are not required to sit the Mainland's qualification examination for the purpose of short term practice in the Mainland. 2. To allow Hong Kong permanent residents who are legally eligible to practise western medicine and dentistry in Hong Kong to sit the Mainland's qualification examination (excluding Chinese medicine practitioners). A "medical practitioner's qualification certificate" of the Mainland will be issued to those who pass the examination. 3. To allow Hong Kong permanent residents who are legally eligible to practise in Hong Kong and have practised in Hong Kong for at least 5 years to open clinics in the Mainland on the condition that they have obtained the

---

[1] Sectoral classification is based on WTO's GATS Services Sectoral Classification List□GNS/W/120□. For the contents of the sectors, reference is made to the relevant CPC, United Nations Provisional Central Product Classification.

	"medical practitioner's qualification certificate" of the Mainland. Matters relating to the application for opening and registration of clinics in the Mainland should be handled in accordance with Mainland regulations.
	4. To allow Hong Kong permanent residents who have acquired a Chinese medicine degree from the University of Hong Kong and are legally eligible to practise in Hong Kong to sit the Mainland's qualification examination on the condition that they have completed 1 year's internship in a level III traditional Chinese medicine hospital in the Mainland and have passed the performance test, or that they have been licensed to practise in Hong Kong for more than 1 year. A "medical (Chinese medicine) practitioner's qualification certificate" of the Mainland will be issued to those who pass the examination.
Sectors or sub-sectors	1. Business services
	B. Computer and related services
	Information technology services
Specific commitments	To allow Hong Kong service suppliers to apply for qualification certification of computer information system integration in accordance with the provisions of the relevant regulations and rules of the Mainland.
Sectors or sub-sectors	1. Business services
	F. Other business services
	k. Placement and supply services of personnel (CPC872)
Specific commitments	Job referral agency To allow Hong Kong service suppliers to set up wholly-owned job referral agencies in the Mainland. The minimum registered capital is US$125,000.
	Job intermediary To allow Hong Kong service suppliers to set up joint-venture job intermediaries in the Mainland. The minimum registered capital is US$125,000. The proportion of Hong Kong service suppliers' shareholding should not exceed 70% and the Mainland partner intermediary must have been established for over 1 year.
Sectors or sub-sectors	2. Communications services
	D. Audiovisual services
	Videos distribution services (CPC83202), Sound recording products distribution services Cinema theatre services Chinese language motion pictures and motion pictures jointly produced Technical services of cable television Jointly produced Television dramas
Specific commitments	Cinema theatre services To allow Hong Kong service suppliers to construct or renovate cinema theatres for the operation of film screening business on a wholly-owned basis.
	Chinese language motion pictures and motion pictures jointly produced 1. To allow motion pictures co-produced by Hong Kong and the Mainland to be processed outside the Mainland after obtaining the approval of the relevant authorities in the Mainland. 2. To allow Hong Kong service suppliers to establish wholly owned companies in the Mainland on a pilot basis to engage in the distribution of Mainland produced motion pictures after obtaining the approval of the relevant authorities in the Mainland.

	Technical service of cable television To allow Hong Kong companies engaging in the operation of cable television network to provide professional technical services for cable television networks of Guangdong Province on a pilot basis after obtaining the approval of the relevant Mainland authorities.
	Jointly produced Television dramas Television dramas co-produced by the Mainland and Hong Kong are permitted to be broadcast and distributed in the same way as Mainland produced television dramas after being examined by the relevant Mainland authorities.
Sectors or sub-sectors	3. Construction and related engineering services CPC511, 512, 513[1], 514, 515, 516, 517, 518[2]
Specific commitments	1. For construction enterprises set up in the Mainland by Hong Kong service suppliers, the construction contract performance of the enterprises both in the Mainland and outside the Mainland is taken into account in assessing the qualification of the construction enterprises in the Mainland. However, the number of managerial and technical staff in the construction enterprises in the Mainland will be the actual number of staff working there. 2. There will be no restriction on the proportion of Hong Kong permanent residents being project managers approved by the qualification administration authorities for construction enterprises in the Mainland set up by Hong Kong service suppliers.
	3. Hong Kong service suppliers who have already obtained the certificate of approval for establishment of enterprises with investment of Taiwan, Hong Kong and Macao in the Mainland but have not yet obtained the construction enterprise qualification certificate may apply, before 1 July 2005, for a certificate for undertaking single construction project based on their signed construction contract and "Construction Qualification Certificate for Taiwan, Hong Kong and Macao Enterprise". Subject to the preliminary vetting and agreement of construction administration department at provincial level, the application will be processed by the Ministry of Construction. 4. The residency requirement is waived for Hong Kong permanent residents employed as engineering technical staff and economic managerial staff in construction enterprises in the Mainland set up by Hong Kong service suppliers. 5. The commitments in relation to construction and related engineering services stated above have been implemented from 28 August 2004.
Sectors or sub-sectors	4. Distribution services
	A. Commission agents' services (excluding salt and tobacco) B. Wholesale trade services (excluding salt and tobacco)
Specific commitments	To allow commission agents' services and wholesale trade enterprises, established by Hong Kong service suppliers in the Mainland on a wholly-owned basis, to operate services in respect of books, newspapers, magazines,

---

[1] Including dredging services relating to infrastructure construction.

[2] Coverage is limited only to the rental and leasing services of construction and/or demolition machines (with operators) which are owned and used by foreign construction enterprises in the course of providing services.

	pharmaceutical products, pesticides and mulching films with effect from 28 August 2004[1].
Sectors or sub-sectors	4. Distribution services
	C. Retailing services (excluding tobacco)
Specific commitments	1. To allow retail trade enterprises, established by Hong Kong service suppliers in the Mainland on a wholly-owned basis, to operate services in respect of books, newspapers, magazines, pharmaceutical products, pesticides mulching films and processed oil with effect from 28 August 2004[1].
	2. To allow Hong Kong service suppliers to set up wholly-owned retail enterprises in the Mainland for retailing of motor vehicles in accordance with the relevant motor vehicle distribution rules in the Mainland[2]. To waive the qualification requirement for application for the setting up of the above enterprises for Hong Kong service suppliers[3].
Sectors or sub-sectors	7. Financial services
	B. Banking and other financial services (excluding insurance and securities)

	a. Acceptance of deposits and other repayable funds from the public;
	    b. Lending of all types, including consumer credit, mortgage credit, factoring and financing of commercial transaction;
	    c. Financial leasing;
	    d. All payment and money transmission services, including credit, charge and debit cards, travellers cheques and bankers drafts (including import and export settlement);
	    e. Guarantees and commitments;
	    f. Trading for own account or for account of customers: foreign exchange.

Specific commitments	To allow Mainland branches of Hong Kong banks to conduct insurance agents business after obtaining approval with effect from 1 November 2004.
Sectors or sub-sectors	7. Financial services
	B. Banking and other financial services
	Securities
Specific commitments	To allow intermediaries which are licensed with the Securities and Futures Commission of Hong Kong and which satisfy the requirements of the China Securities Regulatory Commission to set up joint venture futures brokerage companies in the Mainland. The percentage of shareholding owned by Hong Kong licensed intermediaries should not exceed 49% (including shareholding of related parties). Requirements in respect of the scope of business and amount of capital etc. of the joint venture futures brokerage companies shall be the same as those for Mainland enterprises.
Sectors or sub-sectors	10. Recreational, cultural and sporting services

---

[1] Wholesale trade services and commission agents' services provided by Hong Kong service suppliers in the Mainland in respect of chemical fertilizers, processed oil and crude oil remain subject to Mainland's commitments to members of the World Trade Organization.

[1] Chain stores with more than 30 outlets remain subject to Mainland's commitments to members of the World Trade Organization. The retailing services provided by Hong Kong service suppliers in the Mainland in respect of chemical fertilizers, staple food, vegetable oil, edible sugar and cotton remain subject to Mainland's commitments to members of the World Trade Organization.

[2] Chain stores with more than 30 outlets remain subject to Mainland's commitments to members of the World Trade Organization.

[3] Original qualification requirements are "the average annual sales value of a Hong Kong service supplier in the preceding 3 years is not less than US$100 million; the minimum asset in the previous year is US$10 million; the minimum registered capital for setting up a motor vehicle retail commercial enterprise in the Mainland is RMB 10 million. For setting up a motor vehicle retail commercial enterprise in the Central and Western Region, the minimum registered capital is RMB 6 million."

	A. Cultural services (excluding audiovisual services)
Specific commitments	1. To allow Hong Kong service suppliers to set up performing venues in the Mainland on an equity joint venture, contractual joint venture or wholly-owned basis. 2. To allow Hong Kong performing arts agencies to set up branches in the Mainland. 3. To allow Hong Kong service suppliers to set up performance agencies in the Mainland on an equity joint venture or contractual joint venture basis. 4. To allow Hong Kong service suppliers to set up internet culture business units and internet online service business premises in the Mainland with the Mainland party holding majority shareholding. 5. To allow Hong Kong service suppliers to set up art galleries, art shops and art work exhibition units in the Mainland on an equity joint venture, contractual joint venture or wholly-owned basis.
Sectors or sub-sectors	11. Transport services
	A. Maritime transport services H. Auxiliary services
	International transport (freight and passengers) (CPC7211, 7212, less cabotage transport services) Container station and depot services Others
Specific commitments	1 To allow Hong Kong service suppliers to set up wholly-owned shipping companies in the Mainland to provide shipping agency services for vessels owned or operated by the Hong Kong service suppliers themselves, including customs declaration and inspection, and use of common commercial bills of lading or multimodal transport documents for conducting multimodal transport services. 2. To allow Hong Kong service suppliers to set up wholly-owned shipping companies in the Mainland to provide regular business services for feeders that they operate between Hong Kong and ports that are opened to foreign vessels in the Mainland, such as shipping undertaking, issuance of bills of lading, settlement of freight rates, signing of service contracts, etc.[1]
	3. To allow Hong Kong service suppliers to set up wholly-owned companies in the Mainland to provide supplies services other than fuel and water to vessels owned or managed by the Hong Kong service suppliers themselves. 4. To allow Hong Kong service suppliers to set up wholly-owned companies in the Mainland to provide port cargo loading and unloading services.
Sectors or sub-sectors	11. Transport services
	C. Airport services
	Airport operation services (excl. cargo handling) (CPC74610) Other supporting services for air transport (CPC74690)
Specific commitments	1. To allow Hong Kong service suppliers to provide, in the form of cross-border supply, contractual joint venture, equity joint venture or wholly-owned operations, contract management services for small and medium airports. The

---

[1] The requirement that "50% or more of the ships owned by it, calculated in terms of tonnage, should be registered in Hong Kong" as set out in Annex 5 of "CEPA" is not applicable to Hong Kong service suppliers which provide feeder transport services.

	period of validity of the contract should not exceed 20 years. 2. To allow Hong Kong service suppliers to provide, in the form of cross-border supply, consumption abroad, contractual joint venture, equity joint venture or wholly-owned operations, airport management training and consultation services 3. To allow Hong Kong service suppliers to provide, in the form of equity joint venture or wholly-owned operations, the following seven types of air transport ground services in the Mainland: agency services; loading and unloading control, communication, and departure control system;unit load devices management; passenger and baggage services; cargo and mail services; ramp services; and aircraft services.
Sectors or sub-sectors	11. Transport services
	F. Road transport services
	Freight transportation by road in trucks or cars (CPC7123) Road passenger transportation (CPC7121, 7122)
Specific commitments	1. To allow passenger transport companies operating franchised bus services and companies operating non-franchised bus services (Guangdong–Hong Kong cross-boundary coach services) in Hong Kong to set up joint venture enterprises in Guangdong, Guangxi, Hunan, Hainan, Fujian, Jiangxi, Yunnan, Guizhou and Sichuan to provide "direct passenger bus services" between Hong Kong and the above nine provinces[1]. 2. To allow passenger transport companies operating franchised bus services in Hong Kong to set up wholly-owned enterprises in Mainland cities at the municipal level to provide passenger public transport and hire car services at those cities.
Sectors or sub-sectors	11. Transport services
	H. Services auxiliary to all modes of transport
	Freight forwarding agency services (CPC748, 749, excluding freight inspection)
Specific commitments	To allow freight forwarding agency enterprises in the Mainland established by Hong Kong services suppliers to set up branch offices upon full payment of registered capital.
Sectors or sub-sectors	Service sectors (sectors not set out in GNS/W/120)
	Qualification examinations for professionals and technicians
Specific commitments	To allow eligible Hong Kong residents to take the following qualification examinations for professionals and technicians in the Mainland: registered architect, registered structural engineer, registered civil engineer (geotechnical), construction supervising engineer, cost engineer, registered town planner, estate agent, certified safety engineer, registered nuclear safety engineer, constructor, registered public facility engineer, registered chemical engineer, registered civil engineer (harbour and waterway), registered facility supervising engineer, cost evaluator, enterprise legal consultant, cotton quality examiner, auctioneer, pharmacist, environmental impact assessment engineer, real estate appraiser, registered electrical engineer, certified tax accountant, certified public valuer, prosthetist and orthotist, mining rights assessor, registered consulting engineer (investment), international business personnel, land registration agent, gemstone quality examiner; quality, translation, computing technology and software, auditing, health, economic, statistics,

---

[1] "Direct passenger bus services" means direct road transport services between Hong Kong and the Mainland. In this sector, Hong Kong service suppliers supplying "direct passenger bus services" must be enterprise juridical person.

	accountant professional qualification. Certificates of the relevant professional qualifications will be issued to those who pass the examination.
Sectors or sub-sectors	Service sectors (sectors not set out in GNS/W/120)
	Trade mark agency
Specific commitments	To allow Hong Kong service suppliers to conduct, after registering with the Administration for Industry and Commerce at the provincial level and acquiring the statutory operating body qualification, trade mark agency business in the Mainland.
Sectors or sub-sectors	Service sectors (sectors not set out in GNS/W/120)
	Patent agency
Specific commitments	1. To allow eligible Hong Kong permanent residents with Chinese citizenship to take the National Qualification Examination for Patent Agents in the Mainland. A Patent Agent Qualification Certificate will be issued to those who pass the examination. 2. Hong Kong permanent residents with Chinese citizenship who have obtained the Patent Agent Qualification Certificates may practise in patent agencies established with permission in the Mainland. Those who meet the prescribed requirements may become partners or shareholders of patent agencies established with permission in the Mainland.
Sectors or sub-sectors	Service sectors (sectors not set out in GNS/W/120)
	Individually owned stores
Specific commitments	To allow Hong Kong permanent residents with Chinese citizenship to set up, in accordance with the relevant Mainland laws, regulations and administrative regulations, individually owned stores in all provinces, autonomous regions, municipalities directly under the Central Government in the Mainland without being subject to the approval procedures applicable to foreign investments, to provide retailing services; food and beverage services; hair dressing, beauty treatment and health care services, bathing services and repair services of home electrical appliances and other goods for daily uses under residents services and other services; excluding franchising operation. No more than 8 persons should be engaged in the operation of the individually owned stores, and the business area of such stores should not exceed 300 square meters.

*

MAINLAND AND MACAO CLOSER ECONOMIC PARTNERSHIP ARRANGEMENT*
[excerpts]

The Mainland and Macao Closer Economic Partnership Arrangement was signed on 17 October 2003. It entered into force on the day of signature.

Preamble

To promote the joint economic prosperity and development of the Mainland[1] and the Macao Special Administrative Region (hereinafter referred to as the "two sides"), to facilitate the further development of economic links between the two sides and other countries and regions, the two sides decided to sign the Mainland and Macao Closer Economic Partnership Arrangement (hereinafter referred as to the "CEPA").

[…]

CHAPTER 4
TRADE IN SERVICES

Article 11
Market Access

1.   Either side will progressively reduce or eliminate existing restrictive measures against services and service suppliers of the other side in accordance with the content and timetable set out in Annex 4.

2.   At the request of either side, the two sides may, through consultation, pursue further liberalisation of trade in services between them.

3.   Any new measure on liberalization of trade in services implemented pursuant to paragraph 2 of this Article shall be added to Annex 4.

Article 12
Service Suppliers

1.   The definition of and related provisions on "service suppliers" under the "CEPA" are set out in Annex 5.

2.   Service suppliers of other WTO Members that are juridical persons established under the laws of one side will be entitled to preferential treatments granted by the other side under the

---

* *Source*: The Government of the People's Republic of China (2003). "Mainland and Macao Closer Economic Partnership Arrangement", available on the Internet (http://www.economia.gov.mo/page/english/cepa_e.htm). [Note added by the editor.]
[1] In the "CEPA", the "Mainland" refers to the entire customs territory of China.

"CEPA", provided that they are engaged in substantive business operations as stipulated in Annex 5 in the area of the former side.

Article 13
Financial Services Cooperation

The two sides shall adopt the following measures to further strengthen cooperation in the areas of banking, securities and insurance:

1.   Support Mainland financial institutions in establishing business in Macao;

2.   Support Mainland banks in developing network and business activities in Macao through acquisition;

3.   Encourage, assist and support business exchange between Macao and Mainland banks, securities and insurance institutions;

4.   Strengthen cooperation and information sharing between their financial regulators.

Article 14
Cooperation in Tourism

1.   In order to further promote the development of the tourism industry of Macao, the Mainland will allow residents in Beijing, Shanghai and Guangzhou, Shenzhen, Zhuhai, Dongguan, Zhongshan, Jiangmen, Foshan, Huizhou of Guangdong Province to visit Macao individually. This measure will be extended to the entire Guangdong Province no later than 1 July 2004.

2.   The two sides shall strengthen cooperation in tourism promotion, including promotion of tourism between each other and development of external promotion programs centered around the Pearl River Delta.

3.   The two sides shall cooperate to raise the service standards of their tourism industries and protect the legitimate rights and interests of tourists.

Article 15
Mutual Recognition of Professional Qualifications

1.   The two sides shall encourage mutual recognition of professional qualifications and promote the exchange of professional talents between each other.

2.   Competent authorities and professional bodies of both sides will, in consultation with each other, consider and design specific methodologies for mutual recognition of professional qualifications.

CHAPTER 5
TRADE AND INVESTMENT FACILITATION

Article 16
Measures

The two sides shall promote trade and investment facilitation through greater transparency, standards conformity and enhanced information exchange.

Article 17
Areas of Cooperation

1.   The two sides will promote cooperation in the following areas:

    1.   Trade and investment promotion;
    2.   Customs clearance facilitation;
    3.   Commodities Inspection, inspection and quarantine of animals and plants, food safety, sanitary quarantine, certification, accreditation and standardization management;
    4.   Electronic business;
    5.   Transparency in laws and regulations;
    6.   Cooperation of Small and medium sized enterprises;
    7.   Industries cooperation.

2.   Details on the areas of cooperation listed in paragraph 1 of this Article are set out in Annex 6.

3.   At the request of either side, the two sides may expand the scope and content of trade and investment facilitation through consultation.

4.   Any new scope or content concluded under paragraph 3 of this Article shall be added to Annex 6.
[…]

ANNEX 4
Specific Commitments on Liberalization of Trade in Services

1.   Pursuant to the Mainland and Macao Closer Economic Partnership Arrangement (hereinafter referred to as the "CEPA"), the Mainland and Macao Special Administrative Region have concluded this Annex on the specific commitments on liberalization of trade in services.

2.   As from 1 January 2004, the Mainland will apply to services and service suppliers of Macao the specific commitments set out in Table 1 of this Annex. Table 1 forms an integral part of this Annex. The commitments on value-added telecommunications services will apply as from the next day after the date of signature of CEPA.

3.   In respect of the service sectors, sub-sectors or relevant measures not covered by this Annex, the Mainland will apply Annex 9 of the "Schedule of Specific Commitments on Services

List of Article II MFN Exemptions" of the "Protocol on the Accession of the People's Republic of China".

4.   In respect of the implementation of the specific commitments set out in Table 1 of this Annex, apart from applying the provisions of this Annex, the relevant laws and regulations, and administrative regulations of the Mainland shall also be applicable.

5.   As from 1 January 2004, Macao will not impose any new discriminatory measure on Mainland's services and service suppliers in the areas of services covered in this Annex.

6.   The two sides will, through consultations, formulate and implement further liberalization of Macao's service sectors for the Mainland. The relevant specific commitments will be listed in Table 2. Table 2 forms an integral part of this Annex.

7.   The two sides will, through consultations, formulate and implement specific commitments of Macao in relation to Mainland people obtaining professional qualifications of Macao.

8.   In the event that the implementation of this Annex causes substantial impact on the trade and relevant sectors of either side, the two sides will conduct consultations on the relevant provisions of this Annex at the request of either side.

9.   This Annex will come into effect on the day of signature by the representatives of the two sides.

*

Table 1

The Mainland's Specific Commitments on Liberalization of Trade in Services for Macao[1]

Sectors or sub-sectors	1. Business services
	A. Professional services
	a. Legal services (CPC861)
Specific commitments	1. To allow Macao law firms that have set up representative offices in the Mainland to operate in association with Mainland law firms, except in the form of partnership. Macao lawyers participating in such association may not handle matters of Mainland law. 2. To allow Mainland law firms to employ Macao practicing lawyers. Such practicing lawyers who are employed by Mainland law firms must not handle matters of Mainland law. 3. To allow Macao lawyers with Chinese citizenship who have already acquired Mainland lawyer qualifications to intern and practise on non-litigation legal work in the Mainland.

---

[1] Sectoral classification is based on WTO's GATS Services Sectoral Classification List (GNS/W/120). For the contents of the sectors, reference is made to the relevant CPC, United Nations Provisional Central Product Classification.

	4. To allow Macao permanent residents with Chinese citizenship to sit the legal qualifying examination in the Mainland and acquire Mainland legal professional qualification in accordance with the "State Judicial Examination Implementation Measures".
	5. To allow those who have acquired Mainland legal professional qualification under item 4 above to engage in non-litigation legal work in Mainland law firms in accordance with the "Law of the People's Republic of China on Lawyers".
	6. The minimum residency requirement is waived for all Macao representatives stationed in the Mainland representative offices of Macao law firms located in Shenzhen and Guangzhou. For the Macao representatives stationed in the Mainland representative offices of Macao law firms located in places other than Shenzhen and Guangzhou, their minimum residency requirement is 2 months each year.
	7. To confer those Macao lawyers, qualified after training, with Mainland recognized notary qualification.
	8. To allow Macao lawyers that are Macao permanent residents to engage in legal matters of Macao as well as other countries and regions that the lawyers are allowed to practise in the Mainland pursuant to the Mainland laws, regulations and administrative regulations.
Sectors or sub-sectors	1. Business services
	A. Professional services
	b. Accounting, auditing and bookkeeping services (CPC862)
Specific commitments	1. Macao auditors and accountants who have already qualified as Chinese Certified Public Accountants (CPAs) and practised in the Mainland (including partnership) are treated on par with Chinese CPAs in respect of the requirement for annual residency in the Mainland.
	2. The validity period of the "Temporary Auditing Business Permit" applied by Macao auditing firms and auditors to conduct temporary auditing services in the Mainland is 1 year.
Sectors or sub-sectors	1. Business services
	A. Professional services
	d. Architectural services (CPC8671) e. Engineering services (CPC8672) f. Integrated engineering services (CPC8673) g. Urban planning and landscape architectural services (except general urban planning) (CPC8674)
Specific commitments	To allow Macao service suppliers to provide, in the form of wholly-owned operations, architectural services, engineering services, integrated engineering services, urban planning and landscape architectural services in the Mainland.
Sectors or sub-sectors	1. Business services
	A. Professional services
	h. Medical and dental services (CPC9312)
Specific commitments	1. The majority of medical personnel employed by Macao-Mainland joint venture hospitals or clinics can be Macao permanent residents.
	2. The maximum duration of the licence to provide short-term medical, dental and Chinese medicine services in Mainland is 3 years for practitioners who are legally eligible to practise in the Macao Special Administrative Region. On expiry, the licence for short term practice is renewable.

	3. To allow Macao permanent residents in possession of a medical (traditional Chinese medicine and dental) higher degree from a full-time tertiary institution approved by the Education Administration Department of the Mainland State Council to sit the Mainland's medical qualification examination after they have become legally eligible to practise in Macao for over 1 year. They may also sit the Mainland's medical qualification examination after they have completed 1 year of internship in the Mainland and passed an assessment in accordance with the relevant requirements. A "medical (traditional Chinese medicine) practitioner's qualification certificate" of the Mainland will be issued to those who pass the examination. 4. To allow Macao permanent residents who have acquired a Chinese medicine degree from the Macao University of Science and Technology and are legally eligible to practise in Macao to sit the Mainland's qualification examination on the condition that they have completed 1 year's internship in a third-level traditional Chinese medicine hospital in the Mainland and have passed the performance test; or that they have been practising in Macao for more than 1 year. A "medical (traditional Chinese medicine) practitioner's qualification certificate" of the Mainland will be issued to those who pass the examination. 5. The categories of medical qualifications that Macao permanent residents may apply to sit are clinical medicine, traditional Chinese medicine and dental medicine.
Sectors or sub-sectors	1. Business services
	D. Real estate services
	a. Real estate services involving own or leased property (CPC821) b. Real estate services on a fee or contract basis (CPC822)
Specific commitments	1. To allow Macao service suppliers to provide, in the form of wholly-owned operations, high standard real estate project services in the Mainland.[1] 2. To allow Macao service suppliers to provide, in the form of wholly-owned operations, real estate services on a fee or contract basis in the Mainland. 3. To allow Macao service suppliers to provide, in the form of wholly-owned operations, real estate agency services in the Mainland.
Sectors or sub-sectors	1. Business services
	F. Other business services
	a. Advertising services (CPC871)
Specific commitments	To allow Macao service suppliers[1] to set up wholly-owned advertising firms in the Mainland.
Sectors or sub-sectors	1. Business services
	F. Other business services
	c. Management Consulting services (CPC86501, 86502, 86503, 86504, 86505, 86506, 86509)
Specific commitments	1. To allow Macao service suppliers to provide, in the form of wholly-owned operations, management consulting services, including general management consulting services, financial management consulting services (except industrial tax), marketing management consulting services, human resource management

---

[1] High standard real estate projects refer to the real estate projects with construction costs per unit two times over the average construction costs per unit in the same city.

[1] In this sector, a Macao service supplier must be a juridical person engaging in advertising services (but not necessarily as its principal business).

	consulting services, production management consulting services, public relations services and other management consulting services in the Mainland.
	2. The minimum registered capital requirement for Macao service suppliers providing management consulting services in the Mainland follows the requirements in the "Company Law of the People's Republic of China".
Sectors or sub-sectors	1. Business services
	F. Other business services
	Convention services and exhibition services (CPC87909)
Specific commitments	To allow Macao service suppliers to provide, in the form of wholly-owned operations, convention services and exhibition services in the Mainland.[1]
Sectors or sub-sectors	2. Communications services
	C. Telecommunications services
	Valued-added services
Specific commitments	1. As from the day following that of the signing of CEPA, to allow Macao service suppliers to set up joint venture enterprises in the Mainland to provide the following five types of value-added telecommunications services.[1] 1. internet data centre services; 2. store and forward services; 3. call centre services; 4. internet access services; 5. content services. 2. Macao service suppliers' shareholding in the joint venture enterprises engaging in the value-added telecommunications services mentioned in item 1 above should not exceed 50%. 3. There will be no geographic restriction for the joint venture enterprises formed by Macao service suppliers and the Mainland to provide value-added telecommunications services mentioned in item 1 above.
Sectors or sub-sectors	2. Communications services
	D. Audiovisual services
	Video distribution services (CPC83202), Sound recording products distribution services Cinema theatre services Chinese language motion pictures and motion pictures jointly produced
Specific commitments	Videos, sound recording products distribution services 1. To allow Macao service suppliers to provide, in the form of joint venture, videos and sound recording products (including motion picture products) distribution services in the Mainland.[1] 2. To allow majority shareholding, not exceeding 70%, for Macao service suppliers.

---

[1] Excluding exhibitions outside the Mainland.

[1] To implement in accordance with the Mainland's "Telecommunication business classification".

[1] In undertaking distribution services in the Mainland in respect of videos and sound recording products, Macao service suppliers should comply with the relevant laws, regulations and requirements of the review system in the Mainland.

<table>
<tr>
<td></td>
<td>

Cinema theatre services

1. To allow Macao service suppliers to construct/renovate and operate cinema theatres on an equity joint venture or   contractual joint venture basis.

2. To allow majority shareholding, not exceeding 75%, for Macao service suppliers.

</td>
</tr>
<tr>
<td></td>
<td>

Chinese language motion pictures and motion pictures jointly produced.

1. Chinese language motion pictures produced in Macao may be imported for distribution in the Mainland on a quota-free basis, after vetting and approval by the relevant Mainland authority.

2. Chinese language motion pictures produced in Macao refer to those motion pictures made by production companies which are set up or established in accordance with the relevant laws of the Macao Special Administrative Region, and which own more than 75% of the copyright of the motion pictures concerned. Macao residents should comprise more than 50% of the total principal personnel[1] in the motion pictures concerned.

3. Motion pictures jointly produced by Macao and the Mainland are treated as Mainland motion pictures for the purpose of distribution in the Mainland. Translated versions of the motion pictures in languages of other Chinese ethnic groups and Chinese dialects, which are based on the Putonghua version, are allowed to be distributed in the Mainland.

4. For motion pictures jointly produced by Macao and the Mainland, there is no restriction on the percentage of principal creative personnel[1] from Macao, but at least one-third of the leading artists must be from the Mainland; there is no restriction on where the story takes place, but the plots or the leading characters must be related to the Mainland.

</td>
</tr>
<tr>
<td>Sectors or sub-sectors</td>
<td>

3. Construction and related engineering services

CPC511, 512, 513[1], 514, 515, 516, 517, 518[2]

</td>
</tr>
<tr>
<td>Specific commitments</td>
<td>

1. For construction enterprises set up in the Mainland by Macao service suppliers, the performance of both the enterprises in Macao and in the Mainland is taken into account in assessing the qualification of the construction enterprises in the Mainland. However, the number of managerial and technical staff in the construction enterprises in the Mainland will be the actual number of staff working there.

2. To allow Macao service suppliers to wholly acquire construction enterprises in the Mainland.

</td>
</tr>
<tr>
<td></td>
<td>

3. Construction enterprises in the Mainland set up with investment by Macao

</td>
</tr>
</table>

---

[1] Principal personnel includes personnel performing the roles of director, screenwriter, leading actor, leading actress, supporting actor, supporting actress, producer, cinematographer, editor, art director, costume designer, action choreographer, and composer of the original film score.

[1] Major creative personnel refers to personnel performing the roles of director, screenwriter, cinematographer and leading artists. Leading artists refer to leading actor, leading actress, leading supporting actor and leading supporting actress.

[1] Including dredging services relating to infrastructure construction.

[2] Coverage is limited only to the rental and leasing services of construction and/or demolition machines (with operators), which are owned and used by foreign construction enterprises in the course of providing services.

	service suppliers are exempted from foreign investment restrictions when undertaking Chinese-foreign joint construction projects.
	4. Construction enterprises in the Mainland with investment by Macao service suppliers will follow the relevant laws and regulations in the Mainland for application of construction qualification certificates. Those which have acquired such certification are permitted in accordance with laws to bid for construction projects in all parts of the Mainland.
Sectors or sub-sectors	4. Distribution services A. Commission agents' services (excluding salt and tobacco) B. Wholesale trade services (excluding salt and tobacco)
Specific commitments	1. To allow Macao service suppliers to provide, in the form of wholly-owned operations, commission agents' services and wholesale trade services and to set up wholly-owned foreign trading companies in the Mainland.[1] 2. To apply for the setting up of wholesale commercial enterprises in the Mainland on a wholly-owned, equity joint venture, or contractual joint venture basis, Macao service suppliers must fulfil the following conditions:
	The average annual sales value of a Macao service supplier in the preceding 3 years is not less than US$30 million; the assets in the preceding year is not less than US$10 million; the minimum registered capital for setting up an enterprise in the Mainland is RMB 50 million. For setting up a wholesale commercial enterprise in the Central and Western Region[2], the average annual sales value of a Macao service supplier in the preceding 3 years is not less than US$20 million; the minimum registered capital is RMB 30 million. 3. To apply for the setting up of foreign trading companies in the Mainland on a wholly-owned, equity joint venture or contractual joint venture basis, the Macao service suppliers must fulfil the following conditions: The average annual trade value with the Mainland of a Macao service supplier in the preceding 3 years is not less than US$10 million; for setting up an foreign trading company in the Central and Western Region, the average annual trade value with the Mainland of a Macao service supplier in the preceding 3 years is not less than US$5 million; the minimum registered capital for setting up a company in the Mainland is RMB 20 million; for setting up an foreign trading company in the Central and Western Region, the minimum registered capital is RMB 10 million.
	4. There are no geographic restrictions for Macao service suppliers to provide, in the form of wholly-owned operations, commission agents' services and wholesale trade services in the Mainland.
Sectors or sub-sectors	4. Distribution services

---

[1] The wholesale trade services and commission agents' services provided by Macao service suppliers in the Mainland in respect of books, newspapers, magazines, pharmaceutical products, pesticides, mulching film, chemical fertilizers, processed oil and crude oil remain subject to Mainland's commitments to members of the World Trade Organization.

[2] In this Annex, the Central and Western Region include Central Region and Western Region. Western Region refers to 12 provinces/autonomous regions/municipalities including Chongqing, Sichuan, Guizhou, Yunnan, Tibet, Shanxi, Gansu, Qinghai, Ningxia, Xinjiang, Inner Mongolia and Guangxi; and Xianxi Tugia-Miao Autonomous Prefecture of Hunan Province, Enshi Tugia-Miao Autonomous Prefecture of Hubei Province and Yanbian Korean Autonomous Prefecture of Jilin Province. Central Region refers to 8 provinces including Heilongjiang, Jilin, Shanxi, Henan, Hubei, Hunan, Anhui and Jiangxi.

	C. Retailing services (excluding tobacco)
Specific commitments	1. To allow Macao service suppliers to set up wholly-owned retail commercial enterprises in the Mainland.[1]
	2. To apply for the setting up of retail commercial enterprises in the Mainland on a wholly-owned, equity joint venture or contractual joint venture basis, Macao service suppliers must fulfil the following conditions:
	The average annual sales value of a Macao service supplier in the preceding 3 years will not be less than US$100 million; the minimum assets in the previous year will be US$10 million; the minimum registered capital for setting up an enterprise in the Mainland will be RMB 10 million. For setting up a retail commercial enterprise in the Central and Western Region, the minimum registered capital will be RMB 6 million.
	3. To allow Macao service suppliers to set up retailing enterprises in all cities at the prefectural level in the Mainland, and cities at the county level in Guangdong Province.
	4. To allow Macao service suppliers to set up wholly owned retailing enterprises in the Mainland for sale of motor vehicles.[2]
	5. To allow Macao permanent residents with Chinese citizenship to set up, in accordance with the relevant laws, regulations and administrative regulations, individually owned stores in Guangdong to provide retailing services excluding franchising operation, without being subject to the approval procedures applicable to foreign investments. The sales area of such stores will not exceed 300 square metres.
Sectors or sub-sectors	4. Distribution services
	D. Franchising
Specific commitments	To allow Macao service suppliers to engage, in the form of wholly-owned operations, in franchising in the Mainland.[1]
Sectors or sub-sectors	7. Financial services
	A. All insurance and insurance-related services

	a. Life, health and pension/ annuities insurance
	  b. Non-life insurance
	  c. Reinsurance
	  d. Services auxiliary to insurance

Specific commitments	1. To allow groups formed by Macao insurance companies through re-grouping and strategic mergers to enter the Mainland insurance market subject to established market access conditions (total assets held by the group of over US$ 5 thousand million; more than 30 years of establishment experience attributable to one of the Macao insurance companies in the group; and a representative office established in the Mainland for over 2 years by one of the Macao insurance companies in the group).
	2. The maximum limit of capital participation by a Macao insurance company

[1] The retailing services provided by Macao service suppliers in the Mainland in respect of books, newspapers, magazines, pharmaceuticals, pesticides, mulching film, chemical fertilizers, staple food, vegetable oil, edible sugar, cotton and processed oil remain subject to Mainland's commitments to members of the World Trade Organization.

[2] Chain stores with more than 30 outlets remain subject to Mainland's commitments to members of the World Trade Organization.

[1] The respective regulation will be promulgated separately.

	in a Mainland insurance company is 24.9%.
	3. To allow Macao residents with Chinese citizenship, after obtaining the Mainland's professional qualifications in actuarial science, to practise in the Mainland without prior approval. 4. To allow Macao residents, after obtaining the Mainland's insurance qualifications and being employed or appointed by a Mainland insurance institution, to engage in the relevant insurance business.
Sectors or sub-sectors	7. Financial services
	B. Banking and other financial services (excluding insurance and securities)
	a. Acceptance of deposits and other repayable funds from the public; b. Lending of all types, including consumer credit, mortgage credit, factoring and financing of commercial transaction; c. Financial leasing; d. All payment and money transmission services, including credit, charge and debit cards, travellers cheques and bankers drafts (including import and export settlement); e. Guarantees and commitments; f. Trading in foreign exchange for own account or for account of customers.
Specific commitments	1. For Macao banks to set up branches or body corporates in the Mainland, the total asset requirement at the end of the year preceding application is not less than US$ 6 thousand million; for Macao finance companies to set up body corporates, the total asset requirement at the end of the year preceding application is not less than US$ 6 thousand million. 2. There will be no requirement for setting up a representative office in the Mainland before a Macao bank establishes a joint venture bank or joint venture finance company in the Mainland, or before a Macao finance company establishes a joint venture finance company in the Mainland. 3. For Mainland branches of Macao banks to apply to conduct RMB business: (1) they should have been operating in the Mainland for more than 2 years; (2) in conducting profitability assessment, the relevant authorities will base their assessment on the overall profitability position of all branches of the bank in the Mainland instead of the profitability position of its individual branches.
Sectors or sub-sectors	7. Financial services
	B. Banking and other financial services
	Securities
Specific commitments	To allow those Macao securities and futures professionals who are Macao permanent residents to apply for practicing qualification in the Mainland in accordance to relevant procedures.
Sectors or sub-sectors	9. Tourism and travel related services
	A. Hotels (including apartment buildings) and restaurants (CPC641-643 B. Travel agency and tour operator (CPC7471) Others

Specific commitments	1. To allow Macao service suppliers to construct, renovate and operate, on a wholly-owned basis, hotels, apartment buildings and restaurant establishments in the Mainland. 2. There will be no geographic restriction on Macao travel agencies forming joint venture travel agencies in the Mainland where the Mainland agencies have majority shareholding. 3. To allow residents of Beijing, Shanghai, and Guangzhou, Shenzhen, Zhuhai, Dongguan, Zhongshan, Jiangmen, Foshan and Huizhou of the Guangdong Province to visit Macao individually for tourism, and to allow the same in respect of the whole of Guangdong Province not later than 1 July 2004.
Sectors or sub-sectors	11. Transport services
	A. Maritime transport services H. Auxiliary services
	International transport (freight and passengers) (CPC7211, 7212, less cabotage transport services) Container station and depot services Others
Specific commitments	1. To allow Macao service suppliers[1] to set up wholly-owned enterprises in the Mainland to operate international ship management services, storage and warehousing for international maritime freight, container station and depot services, and non-vessel operating common carrying services. 2. To allow Macao service suppliers to set up wholly-owned shipping companies in the Mainland to provide regular business services for vessels that they own or operate, such as shipping undertaking, issuance of bills of lading, settlement of freight rates, signing of service contracts, etc. 3. To allow Macao service suppliers to use liner vessels serving main routes to move, without any restrictions, empty containers that they own or rent, as long as customs procedures are observed.
Sectors or sub-sectors	11. Transport services
	F. Road transport services
	Freight transportation by road in trucks or cars (CPC7123) Road passenger transportation (CPC7121, 7122)
Specific commitments	1. To allow Macao service suppliers to set up wholly-owned enterprises in the Mainland to provide road freight transport services. 2. To allow Macao service suppliers to provide direct non-stop road freight transport services between Macao and individual provinces, cities and autonomous regions in the Mainland.[1] 3. To allow Macao service suppliers to set up wholly-owned enterprises in the Western Region of the Mainland to provide road passenger transport services
Sectors or sub-sectors	11. Transport services
	H. Services auxiliary to all modes of transport
	Storage and warehouse services (CPC742)

---

[1] In this sector, the Macao service suppliers must be enterprise juridical persons.
[1] Non-stop services mean direct road transport services between Macao and the Mainland. In this sector, Macao service suppliers supplying non-stop services must be enterprise juridical persons.

Specific commitments	1. To allow Macao service suppliers to provide, in the form of wholly-owned operations, storage and warehousing services in the Mainland.
	2. The minimum registered capital requirement for storage and warehousing enterprises in the Mainland set up and invested by Macao service suppliers will be the same as that for Mainland enterprises.
Sectors or sub-sectors	11. Transport services
	H. Services auxiliary to all modes of transport
	Freight forwarding agency services (CPC748, 749, excluding freight inspection)
Specific commitments	1. To allow Macao service suppliers to provide, in the form of wholly-owned operations, freight forwarding agency services in the Mainland.[1]
	2. The minimum registered capital requirement for freight forwarding agency enterprise (international freight forwarding) in the Mainland set up and invested by Macao service suppliers will be the same as that for Mainland enterprises.
Sectors or sub-sectors	Service sectors (sectors not set out in GNS/W/120)
	Logistics services
Specific commitments	To allow Macao service suppliers to provide, in the form of wholly-owned operations, logistics services in the Mainland, which include road transport, storage and warehousing, loading and unloading, value adding processing, packaging, delivery and related information and consultancy services for ordinary road freight; freight transport agency services within the Mainland; and the management and operation of logistics services through computer network.

Table 2
Macao's Specific Commitments on Liberalization of Trade in Services for the Mainland[1]

*

[…]

ANNEX 5
Definition of "Service Supplier" and Related Requirements

1.   Pursuant to the Mainland and Macao Closer Economic Partnership Arrangement (hereinafter referred to as the "CEPA"), the Mainland and Macao Special Administrative Region have concluded this Annex on the definition of "service supplier" and related requirements.

2.   Unless otherwise stipulated in the "CEPA" and its Annexes, "service supplier" as used in the "CEPA" and its Annexes refers to any person that supplies a service. In this context:

2.1.   "person" means either a natural person or a juridical person;

2.2.   "natural person":

2.2.1.   in the case of the Mainland, means a citizen of the People's Republic of China;

---

[1] In this sector, the Macao service suppliers must be enterprise juridical persons.
[1] The two sides will, through consultations, formulate and implement further liberalization of Macao's service sectors for the Mainland. The relevant specific commitments will be listed in this table.

2.2.2. in the case of Macao, means a permanent resident of the Macao Special Administrative Region of the People's Republic of China;

2.3. "juridical person" means any legal entity duly constituted or otherwise organised under the applicable laws of the Mainland or the Macao Special Administrative Region, whether for profit or otherwise, and whether privately-owned or governmentally-owned, including any corporation, trust, partnership, joint venture, sole proprietorship or association (business association).

3. The specific criteria for Macao service suppliers who provide services in the form of juridical persons:

3.1. with the exception of the legal services sector, a Macao service supplier, when applying to provide the relevant services under Annex 4 in the Mainland, should:

3.1.1. be registered pursuant to the Macao Commercial Code, Macao Commercial Registration Code or other relevant laws of the Macao Special Administrative Region.[1] If required by law, it should also have obtained the licence or permit for providing such services; and

3.1.2. be engaged in substantive business operations in Macao. The criteria for determination is:

(1) The nature and scope of business

The nature and scope of the services provided by a Macao service supplier in Macao should encompass the nature and scope of the services it intends to provide in the Mainland.

(2) Years of operation required

A Macao service supplier should be registered in Macao, and have engaged in substantive business operations for 3 years or more.[2]

A Macao service supplier providing construction and related engineering services should be registered in Macao, and have engaged in substantive business operations for 5 years or more; there is no limitation on the years of substantive business operations in Macao for Macao service suppliers providing real estate services;

A Macao service supplier providing banking and other financial services (excluding insurance and securities), i.e. a Macao bank or finance company should have engaged in substantive business

---

[1] Any overseas company, representative office, liaison office, "mail box company" and company specifically established for providing certain services to its parent company, which is registered in Macao, is not Macao service supplier under this Annex.

[2] From the day the "CEPA" comes into effect, where more than 50% of the equity interest of a Macao service supplier has been owned for at least one year since a merger or acquisition by a service supplier other than one from either side, the service supplier which has been acquired or merged will be regarded as a Macao service supplier.

operations for 5 years or more pursuant to the Macao Financial System Act;

A Macao service supplier providing insurance and related services, i.e. a Macao insurance company should have engaged in substantive business operations for 5 years or more.

(3)   Complementary tax

During the period of substantive business operations in Macao, a Macao service supplier should have paid complementary tax in accordance with the law.

(4)   Business premises

A Macao service supplier should own or rent premises in Macao to engage in substantive business operations. The scale of its business premises should be commensurate with the scope and the scale of its business.

For a Macao service supplier providing maritime transport services, 50% or more of the ships owned by it, calculated in terms of tonnage, should be registered in Macao.

(5)   Employment of staff

more than 50% of the staff employed in Macao by the Macao service supplier should be residents staying in Macao without limit of stay and persons permitted to reside in Macao in accordance with the relevant regulations of Macao.

3.2.   A Macao law firm of the legal services sector, when applying to provide the relevant services under Annex 4 in the Mainland, should:

3.2.1.   be registered as a Macao law firm pursuant to the relevant legislation of the Macao Special Administrative Region.

3.2.2.   The sole proprietor and all the partners of the law firm should be registered Macao practising lawyer(s).

3.2.3.   The principal scope of business of the law firm should be to provide local legal services in Macao.

3.2.4.   The law firm or its sole proprietor or partners should pay complementary tax or income tax in accordance with the law.

3.2.5.   The law firm should have engaged in substantive business operations in Macao for 3 years or more.

   3.2.6. The law firm should own or rent premises in Macao to engage in substantive business operations.

4. Unless otherwise stipulated in the "CEPA" and its Annexes, Macao service suppliers providing services in the form of natural persons should be permanent residents of the Macao Special Administrative Region of the People's Republic of China.

5. Service suppliers of the Mainland should fulfil the definition of Article 2 of this Annex. Specific criteria will be determined by the two sides through consultation.

6. To obtain the treatment under the "CEPA", a Macao service supplier should provide:

   6.1. In the event that the Macao service supplier is a juridical person, the Macao service supplier should submit the following documents and information, and statutory declaration, which have been verified by relevant institutions (persons) of Macao, as well as the certificate issued by the Macao Special Administrative Region Government:

    6.1.1. Documents and information (if applicable)

     (1) Copy of the Certificate of Commercial and Movable Property Registration issued by the Registry for Commerce and Movable Property of the Macao Special Administrative Region;

     (2) Copies of the Industrial Tax M/1 format Declaration issued by the Macao Finance Services of the Macao Special Administrative Region;

     (3) Annual reports or audited financial statements of the Macao service supplier for the past 3 years (or 5 years);

     (4) Original or copy of document(s) substantiating that the Macao service supplier owns or rents business premises in Macao;[3]

     (5) Copy of the Complementary Tax Declaration Form and proof of tax payments in respect of the Macao service supplier for the past 3 years (or 5 years); in the event of loss, the Macao service supplier should provide copy of the relevant Complementary Tax Declaration Form and proof of tax payments for the past 3 years (or 5 years);

     (6) Copy of the Certificate of Contribution of the Macao service supplier to the Macao Social Security Fund in respect of its employees in Macao, and the original or a copy of other relevant document(s) substantiating that the service supplier fulfils the percentage requirement of Article 3.1.2.(5) of this Annex;

---

[3] A Macao service supplier applying to provide maritime transport services in the Mainland should separately submit document(s) or its copy (attested) to verify that 50% or more of the ships owned by it, calculated in terms of tonnage, is registered in Macao.

(7)   Original or copy of other relevant document(s) that can substantiate the nature and scope of the business in Macao of the Macao service supplier;

(8)   Macao service supplier of logistics, freight forwarding agency and warehousing should obtain certificate, issued by the Macao Special Administrative Region Government, of the right to provide intermodal transport service.

6.1.2. Declaration

For any Macao service supplier applying to obtain treatment under the "CEPA", its authorised representative should make a declaration to the Macao Special Administrative Region Government.[4] The format of the declaration will be determined by the Mainland and the Macao Special Administrative Region through consultation.

6.1.3.   Certificate

A Macao service supplier should submit the documents and information, and the declaration as required under Articles 6.1.1. and 6.1.2. of this Annex to the Macao Economic Services of the Macao Special Administrative Region for examination. The Macao Economic Services may, in the circumstances it considers necessary, entrust other government departments of the Macao Special Administrative Region, bodies, or independent professional institutions (personnel) to conduct verification.[5] Macao Economic Services will issue a certificate to the applicants that it considers to have fulfilled the criteria of Macao service suppliers as required under this Annex. The content and format of the certificate will be determined by the Mainland and the Macao Special Administrative Region through consultation.

6.2.   In the event that a Macao service supplier is a natural person, the Macao service supplier should provide proof of his or her Macao permanent resident status. For Chinese citizens among such service suppliers, their Home Visit Permit for Hong Kong and Macao Residents or Macao Special Administrative Region passport should also be provided.

6.3.   Declarations and copies of the identification documents of natural persons as required under Articles 6.1 and 6.2 of this Annex, as well as the documents and information that in the Macao Economic Services' view should be attested by notary public of the Macao Special Administrative Region Government or by notary recognised by the Mainland. The qualification of attestation and the

---

[4] A person is subject to criminal liability of Macao if he knowingly makes a false or untrue declaration pursuant to the legislation applicable in Macao.

[5] In the telecommunications sector, Macao Economic Services will entrust the authority of the Government of the Macao Special Administrative Region that regulates telecommunications to conduct verification with a view to substantiating the nature and scope of business of the Macao service suppliers providing internet data centre services, store and forwarding services, call centre services, and content services.

examination procedures of the notarization will be determined by the Mainland and the Macao Special Administrative Region through consultation.

7.   When applying to the Mainland's examining authorities to obtain treatment under the "CEPA", Macao service suppliers should follow the following procedures:

    7.1.   When it applies to provide the services under Annex 4 in the Mainland, a Macao service supplier should submit to the Mainland's examining authorities documents and information, declaration and certificate as required under Article 6 of this Annex.

    7.2.   Pursuant to the powers conferred under Mainland laws and regulations, the Mainland examining authorities, in examining the application for supplying Macao services, should at the same time verify the qualifications of the Macao service supplier.

    7.3.   When holding a different view in respect of the qualification of the Macao service supplier, the Mainland examining authority should inform the Macao service supplier within a stipulated period, and notify the Ministry of Commerce. The Ministry of Commerce will in turn inform the Macao Economic Services, giving the reasons for the divergent views. The Macao service supplier may, through the Macao Economic Services and with written justification, request the Ministry of Commerce for reconsideration. The Ministry of Commerce should give a written reply to the Macao Economic Services within a stipulated period.

8.   Macao service suppliers who have already been providing services in the Mainland should apply for obtaining treatment under the "CEPA" in accordance with the requirements of Articles 6 and 7 of this Annex.

9.   This Annex will come into effect on the day of signature by the representatives of the two sides.

*

ANNEX 6
Trade and Investment Facilitation

1.   Pursuant to the Mainland/Macao Closer Economic Partnership Arrangement (hereinafter referred to as the "CEPA"), the Mainland and the Macao Special Administrative Region have concluded this Annex on cooperation in trade and investment facilitation.

2.   The two sides agree to cooperate in trade and investment facilitation in seven areas, namely, trade and investment promotion; customs clearance facilitation; commodity inspection, inspection and quarantine of animals and plants, food safety, sanitary quarantine, certification, accreditation and standardization management; electronic business; transparency in laws and regulations; cooperation of small and medium sized enterprises, and industrial cooperation. Cooperation in these areas will follow the guidance and coordination of the Joint Steering Committee set up in accordance with Article 19 of the "CEPA".

3.   Trade and Investment Promotion

The two sides recognize the importance of mutual trade and investment to their economic and social development. Taking into account the actual development of trade and investment as well as the need for growth, the two sides agree to strengthen cooperation in trade and investment promotion.

> 3.1.   Cooperation Mechanisms
>
> Relevant working groups under the Joint Steering Committee will be made full use of in guiding and coordinating cooperation in trade and investment promotion between the two sides.
>
> 3.2.   Content of Cooperation
>
> Based on past cooperation experience, as well as the development of economic and trade exchanges and cooperation between both sides, the two sides will strengthen cooperation in the following areas:
>
> 3.2.1.   Notify and publicize their respective policies and regulations on foreign trade and foreign investment promotion, with a view to achieving information sharing.
>
> 3.2.2.   Exchange views and conduct consultations to solve common problems relating to trade and investment of both sides.
>
> 3.2.3.   Strengthen communication and cooperation in mutual investment and joint promotion of overseas investment.
>
> 3.2.4.   Strengthen cooperation in organising exhibitions and arranging delegations to participate in overseas exhibitions.
>
> 3.2.5.   Co-initiate economic and trade activities to promote trade and investment between the two sides and the Portuguese-speaking countries.
>
> 3.2.6.   Conduct exchanges on other issues of mutual concern relating to trade and investment promotion.
>
> 3.3.   Participation of Other Entities
>
> The two sides note that the participation of semi-official and non-official organizations in the area of trade and investment promotion has positive effect and significance. The two sides agree to support and assist these organizations in various ways to launch trade and investment promotion activities.

4.   Customs Clearance Facilitation

Recognizing the importance of close and long-term cooperation between the two Customs Administrations and of the implementation of customs clearance facilitation to their economic and social development, the two sides agree to strengthen cooperation in customs clearance facilitation.

4.1.   Cooperation Mechanism

The two sides will steer and coordinate cooperation in customs clearance facilitation through customs administrations of both sides and promote the launch of cooperation in customs clearance facilitation through expert groups of the Customs Administrations and relevant departments of the two sides.

4.2.   Content of Cooperation

Taking into account the need for different customs clearance systems and monitoring modes as well as experience in cooperation, the two sides agree to strengthen cooperation in the following areas:

4.2.1.   Establish a reciprocal notification system to report their respective policies and regulations on customs clearance and management of clearance facilitation.

4.2.2.   Conduct studies and exchanges on the differences between their respective customs clearance systems and on existing problems, with a view to enriching the specific content of cooperation in customs clearance facilitation.

4.2.3.   Explore the expansion of the scope for further cooperation in strengthening control and enhancing efficiency in respect of customs clearance in areas such as sea and land transportation, intermodal operation and logistics.

4.2.4.   Strengthen cooperation in establishing a crisis management mechanism at control points and adopt effective measures to maintain as far as possible smooth clearance on the two sides.

4.2.5.   Establish a regular liaison mechanism to study the feasibility of setting up the "Guangdong and Macao Customs Working Group on Operational Efficiency of Road Control Points" under the Guangdong Branch of the General Administration of Customs and the Macao Customs Service.

4.2.6.   Study the establishment of the "Expert Group on Cargo Data Sharing and Road Cargo Clearance" under the two Customs Administrations, study the feasibility of data interchange and development of electronic customs clearance systems at control points, strengthen the risk management of customs clearance with technical solutions, and enhance its efficiency in customs clearance.

5.   Commodity Inspection, Inspection and Quarantine of Animals and Plants, Food Safety, Sanitary Quarantine, Certification, Accreditation and Standardization Management

Recognizing the importance of protecting the health and safety of Mainland and Macao people in the course of trade in goods and movement of persons, the two sides agree to strengthen cooperation and exchange in the areas of commodity inspection, inspection and quarantine of animals and plants, food safety, sanitary quarantine, certification, accreditation and standardization.

5.1.   Cooperation Mechanisms

The two sides will make use of the existing cooperation channels of relevant departments to promote the launch of cooperation in the relevant areas through reciprocal visits, discussions and other modes of communication.

5.2.   Content of Cooperation

The two sides agree to strengthen cooperation in the following areas:

5.2.1. Inspection and supervision of products

To ensure the safety of consumers of both sides, the two sides will enhance information flow and exchanges through established communication channels, in particular the exchange of intelligence on the safety of goods, so as to jointly prevent safety problems associated with these goods. The two sides will also promote cooperation in the training of inspection and supervisory officers.

The two sides will study the signing of the "Cooperation Arrangement on Goods Safety", establish relevant laws and regulations, safety standards, enforce working procedures of the regulations and communication channels in the event of unsafe products, promote the launch of technical exchanges and strengthen training.

5.2.2. Inspection and quarantine of animals and plants

The two sides will establish coordination mechanisms to step up cooperation in inspection and quarantine of animals and plants as well as in food safety, so as to enable both sides to enforce their respective regulations more effectively.

5.2.3. Sanitary quarantine

The two sides will make use of the existing channels to regularly notify each other of the information on epidemic outbreaks occurred in either side and to step up academic exchanges and joint research on health and quarantine issues; discuss sanitary monitoring issues in respect of small vessels navigating between the control points of Guangdong; enhance cooperation in areas such as investigation and prevention of tropical infectious diseases and live vectors, surveillance and control of special articles and radioactive articles, transportation of biological disease factors and the related inspection, treatment and control measures.

5.2.4. Certification, accreditation and standardization management

The two sides will encourage their respective organizations to strengthen cooperation with a view to promoting conformity assessment (including testing, certification and inspection), accreditation and standardization management.

5.2.5   Increase efficiency in inspection and quarantine

The two sides will strengthen cooperation on customs clearance management on inspection and quarantine; mutually provide customs declaration and inspection information of goods in advance. Simultaneously, in order to increase efficiency in inspection and quarantine at control points, the two sides will study the feasibility of data interchange in mutual customs inspection, electronic monitoring of inspection and quarantine at control points, establishing the electronic data exchange mechanism on inspection and quarantine of products and persons.

6.   Electronic business

The two sides recognize that the application and promotion of electronic commerce will create more trade and investment opportunities for both sides. They agree to step up exchange and cooperation in the area of electronic commerce.

6.1.   Cooperation Mechanism

Under the guidance and coordination of the Joint Steering Committee, the two sides will set up a working group to act as a communication channel as well as a consultation and coordination mechanism for cooperation in electronic commerce, with a view to promoting cooperation and joint development in the area of electronic commerce.

6.2   Content of Cooperation

The two sides agree to cooperate in the following areas:

6.2.1.   Specialized projects in respect of the study and formulation of rules, standards and regulations of electronic commerce, such as feasibility of recognition and intercommunication of a mutual electronic certificate, with a view to creating a favourable environment for promoting and ensuring the healthy development of electronic commerce.

6.2.2.   Strengthen exchange and cooperation in areas such as corporate application, promotion and training. Make full use of the relevant government departments of the two sides in promotion and coordination, enhance promotion for electronic commerce, foster interaction between the enterprises of the two sides, and facilitate the launching of electronic commerce among the enterprises.

6.2.3.   Strengthen cooperation in implementing electronic government, such as feasibility of information interchange; intensify exchange and cooperation in the development planning of electronic government at various levels.

6.2.4.   Cooperate in economic and trade information exchange, and expand the scope and extent of cooperation.

7.   Transparency in Laws and Regulations

The two sides recognize that enhanced transparency in laws and regulations is an important foundation for promoting economic and trade flow of the two sides. In the spirit of serving the commercial and industrial enterprises in the two sides, the two sides agree to strengthen cooperation in the area of enhanced transparency of laws and regulations.

7.1.   Cooperation Mechanisms

The two sides will cooperate through relevant working groups under the Joint Steering Committee as well as their respective representative agencies.

7.2.   Content of Cooperation

The two sides agree to strengthen cooperation in the following areas:

7.2.1.   Exchange information on the enactment and revision of laws, regulations and rules in respect of investment, trade and other economic areas.

7.2.2.   Disseminate in a timely manner information on policies and regulations through various media including newspapers, journals and websites.

7.2.3.   Organize and support the organization of various briefings and seminars on economic and trade policies and regulations.

7.2.4.   Provide advisory services to commercial and industrial enterprises through channels such as WTO enquiry points, websites of "Invest in China" and "China Business Guide" of the Mainland; websites of "Macao Economic Services" and "Macao Trade and Investment Promotion Institute" of the Macao Special Administrative Region.

8.   Cooperation of Small and Medium Sized Enterprises

The two sides recognize that the development of small and medium sized enterprises plays an important role in increasing employment, promoting economic development and maintaining social stability. The two sides agree to promote exchanges and cooperation between small and medium sized enterprises of the two sides.

8.1.   Cooperation Mechanisms

Establish an operational mechanism between relevant government departments of both sides to promote cooperation between small and medium enterprises of the two sides, with a view to fostering their cooperation and seeking mutual development.

8.2.   Content of Cooperation

The two sides agree to support and promote cooperation in the following areas:

      8.2.1. Explore jointly the strategy and support policy for the development of small and medium sized enterprises through visits and exchanges.

      8.2.2. Organize visits and exchanges on the organizational and operational methods of the intermediaries providing services to small and medium sized enterprises in the two sides, and promote cooperation of the intermediaries.

      8.2.3. Establish channels for providing information services to small and medium sized enterprises in the two places, exchange regularly relevant publications, set up dedicated websites, implement progressively information interchange and the interconnection of information website databases of the two sides.

      8.2.4. Organize through different forms of direct exchanges and communication between small and medium sized enterprises of the two sides to promote their cooperation.

      8.2.5. Promote exchange and cooperation between small and medium sized enterprises of the two sides and overseas small and medium sized enterprises with Macao, as their economic and trade cooperation platform.

  8.3. Participation of Other Entities

The two sides support and assist semi-official and non-official organizations to play a part in promoting cooperation between small and medium sized enterprises of the two sides.

9.   Industrial Cooperation

The two sides recognize that, in accordance with the principle of complementarity with each other's advantages, overall industrial, social and economic development will benefit from strengthening industrial cooperation and exchanges. The two sides will promote cooperation on industrialization of Chinese medicine and will consider expanding this cooperation to other industrial projects in due time.

  9.1. Cooperation Mechanism

A special working group will be established under the supervision of the Joint Steering Committee in appropriate time to deal with the relevant matters regarding industrial cooperation.

  9.2. Content of Cooperation

The two sides agree to strengthen cooperation in the following areas:

      9.2.1. Conduct joint dedicated studies on cooperation in specific industries in which both sides have their respective specific advantages with respect to the industrial development objectives and positioning of the two sides.

9.2.2. Communicate on industrial development status, development path and the formulation of respective laws and regulations of both sides.

9.2.3. Strengthen cooperation in industrial scientific research, technology and commercialization of scientific research outcomes.

9.2.4. Promote investment cooperation between the enterprises of the two sides in relevant industries.

9.2.5. Support cooperation between the enterprises in relevant industries of the two sides, facilitate bilateral product trade and jointly explore the international market.

10.   According to paragraphs 3 and 4 of Article 17 of the "CEPA", any new area or content of trade and investment facilitation agreed by the two sides will be incorporated into this Annex.

11.   This Annex will come into effect on the day of signature by the representatives of the two sides.

Signed in duplicate in Macao, this 17th day of October, 2003 in the Chinese language.

*

SUPPLEMENTARY PROTOCOL TO THE MAINLAND AND MACAO CLOSER ECONOMIC PARTNERSHIP ARRANGEMENT*

The Supplementary Protocol to the Mainland and Macao Closer Economic Partnership Arrangement was signed on 29 October 2004.

To further enhance the economic and trade interflow, as well as the cooperation level between the Mainland[1] and the Macao Special Administrative Region (hereinafter referred to as "Macao"), and in accordance with the provisions of the Mainland and Macao Closer Economic Partnership Arrangement (hereinafter referred to as "CEPA") and its annexes, signed on 17 October 2003, on the Mainland's further liberalization to Macao of trade in goods and trade in services, the two sides decided to sign this Protocol.

I.   Trade In Goods

(1)   From 1 January 2005, the Mainland will apply zero tariff to the import of those goods of Macao origin listed in Annex 1 to this Protocol. Annex 1 to this Protocol forms a

---

* *Source*: The Government of the People's Republic of China and Macao (2004). "Supplementary Protocol to the Mainland and Macao Closer Economic Partnership Arrangement", available on the Internet (http://www.economia.gov.mo/page/english/cepa_e.htm). [Note added by the editor.]
[1] In the CEPA, the "Mainland" refers to the entire customs territory of the People's Republic of China.

supplement to Table 1 "List of Macao Origin Products for Implementation of Zero Import Tariff by the Mainland" of Annex 1 to the CEPA.

(2) Annex 2 to this Protocol laid down the rules of origin for those imported goods of Macao origin listed in Annex 1 to this Protocol which was drawn up in pursuance of Annex 2 "Rules of Origin for Trade in Goods" to the CEPA. Annex 2 to this Protocol forms a supplement to Table 1 "Schedule on Rules of Origin for Macao Goods Benefiting from Tariff Preference for Trade in Goods" of Annex 2 to the CEPA.

II. Trade In Services

(1) From 1 January 2005, the Mainland will, on the basis of Annex 4 "Specific Commitments on Liberalization of Trade in Services" to the CEPA, further relax the market access requirements to services and service suppliers of Macao in service areas of legal, accounting, medical and dental, audiovisual, construction and related engineering, distribution, banking, securities, transport, and freight forwarding agency; and expand the geographical and business scopes where and in which Macao permanent residents with Chinese citizenship can set up individually owned stores. Details are set out in Annex 3 to this Protocol.

(2) From 1 January 2005, the Mainland will liberalize and relax market access requirements to services and service suppliers of Macao in service areas of patent agency, trademark agency, airport, cultural entertainment, information technology, job referral agency, job intermediary, as well as professionals and technicians qualification examinations. Details are set out in Annex 3 to this Protocol.

(3) Commitments in the area of construction and related engineering, and part of the commitments in the area of distribution stated in Annex 3 to this Protocol will come into effect from 1 November 2004. Details are set out in the specific commitments for construction and related engineering services and distribution services in Annex 3 to this Protocol. The specific commitment in Annex 3 to this Protocol that allows Mainland branches of Macao banks to conduct insurance agents business will come into effect from 1 November 2004.

(4) Annex 3 to this Protocol forms a supplement and amendment to Table 1 "The Mainland's Specific Commitments on Liberalization of Trade in Services for Macao" of Annex 4 to the CEPA. When clauses in the two annexes contradict each other, those of Annex 3 to this Protocol shall prevail.

(5) "Service supplier" as referred to in Annex 3 to this Protocol shall conform to the criteria set out in Annex 5 'Definition of "Service Supplier" and Related Requirements' to the CEPA.

III. Supplement and Amendment to Annexes to the CEPA

(1) Paragraph 3.2 of Article 5 of Annex 1 "Arrangements for Implementation of Zero Tariff for Trade in Goods" to the CEPA was amended to: For planned production, the Mainland will, in accordance with the consensus reached between the two sides, add the list of goods to Table 1 of Annex 1 to the CEPA and the corresponding rules of origin to Table 1 of Annex 2 to the CEPA. After the applicant enterprise has put the

proposed goods into production, the Macao Economic Services will conduct verification and thereafter inform the Ministry of Commerce. Upon confirmation by the two sides, the Mainland will, based on the certificate of origin issued by the Macao Economic Services, release the relevant imports on zero tariff basis in line with the CEPA.

(2) Paragraph 3.1.2.2 of Article 3 of Annex 5 'Definition of "Service Supplier" and Related Requirements' to the CEPA was amended to add the following contents: Macao service suppliers of air transport ground services shall have obtained the licenses to provide air transport ground services in Macao, and have engaged in substantive business operations for five years or more. In case of a Macao service supplier of airport management services is affiliated with an airline, the Mainland's relevant rules and regulations also apply.

IV.   Annexes

The Annexes to this Protocol form an integral part of this Protocol.

V.   Coming Into Effect

This Protocol will come into effect on the day of signature by the representatives of the two sides.

*

ANNEX 3
Supplements and Amendments to the Mainland's Specific Commitments on Liberalization of Trade in Services for Macao[1]

Sectors or sub-sectors	1. Business services
	A. Professional services
	a. Legal services (CPC861)
Specific commitments	Macao registered lawyers providing legal assistance at the request of Mainland law firms on the basis of individual cases will not be required to apply for a Macao legal consultant permit.
Sectors or sub-sectors	1. Business services
	A. Professional services
	b. Accounting, auditing and bookkeeping services (CPC862)
Specific commitments	1. To allow consultancy companies in the Mainland established by Macao auditors and accountants that have satisfied the requirements of the Mainland's "Provisional Measures for the Administration of the Provision of Bookkeeping Services" to provide bookkeeping services. Macao auditors and accountants providing bookkeeping services should have obtained the Mainland's accounting qualification certificate. In addition, the person in charge of the bookkeeping services should hold the relevant Mainland's professional qualification (professional title) of accountant or above.

---

[1] Sectoral classification is based on WTO's GATS Services Sectoral Classification List (GNS/W/120). For contents of the sectors, refers to the relevant CPC, United Nations Provisional Central Product Classification.

	2. When Macao auditors and accountants apply for practising licence in the Mainland, the length of auditing experience that they have acquired in Macao is equivalent to the length of auditing experience acquired in the Mainland.
Sectors or sub-sectors	1. Business services
	A. Professional services
	h. Medical and dental services (CPC9312)
Specific commitments	1. Macao permanent residents who are legally eligible to practise western medicine, dentistry and Chinese medicine in the Macao Special Administrative Region are not required to sit the Mainland's qualification examinations for the purpose of short-term practice in the Mainland. 2. To allow Macao permanent residents who are legally eligible to practise western medicine, dentistry in Macao and have practised for 1 completed year to sit the Mainland's qualification examinations (excluding Chinese medicine practitioners). A "Medical Practitioner's Qualification Certificate" of the Mainland will be issued to those who pass the examination. 3. To allow Macao permanent residents who are legally eligible to practise in Macao and have practised for 5 completed years to open clinics in the Mainland on the condition that they have obtained the Mainland's "Medical Practitioner's Qualification Certificate" (medicine practitioner). Matters relating to the application for opening and registration of clinics in the Mainland should be handled in accordance with Mainland regulations.
Sectors or sub-sectors	1. Business services
	B. Computer and related services
	Information technology services
Specific commitments	To allow Macao service suppliers to apply for computer information system integration qualification certification in accordance with the provisions of relevant regulations and rules of the Mainland.
Sectors or sub-sectors	1. Business services
	F. Other business services
	k. Placement and supply services of personnel (CPC872)
Specific commitments	Job referral agency To allow Macao service suppliers to set up wholly-owned job referral agencies in the Mainland. The minimum registered capital is US$125,000.
	Job intermediary To allow Macao service suppliers to set up joint venture job intermediaries in the Mainland. The minimum registered capital is US$125,000. The proportion of Macao service suppliers' shareholding should not exceed 70% and the Mainland partner intermediary must have been established for over 1 year.
Sectors or sub-sectors	2. Communications services
	D. Audiovisual services
	Video distribution services (CPC83202), Sound recording products distribution services Cinema theatre services Chinese language motion pictures and motion pictures jointly produced Technical service of cable television Television programmes jointly produced
Specific commitments	Cinema theatre services Macao service suppliers are permitted to construct or renovate cinema theatres for the operation of film screening business on wholly-owned basis.

	Chinese language motion pictures and motion pictures jointly produced 1. Motion pictures co-produced by the Mainland and Macao are permitted to be processed outside the Mainland after obtaining the approval of the competent authorities in the Mainland.
	2. Macao service suppliers are permitted to establish wholly-owned companies in pilot areas in the Mainland to engage in distribution of Mainland produced motion pictures after obtaining the approval of the competent authorities in the Mainland.
	Technical service of cable television Macao companies engaging in the operation of cable television network are permitted to provide professional technical services related to cable television networks in pilot areas of the Guangdong Province after obtaining the approval of the competent authorities in the Mainland.
	Television programmes jointly produced Television programmes co-produced by the Mainland and Macao are permitted to be broadcast and distributed in the same way as Mainland produced television programmes after being examined by the competent authorities in the Mainland.
Sectors or sub-sectors	3. Construction and related engineering services
	CPC511, 512, 513[1], 514, 515, 516, 517, 518[2]
Specific commitments	1. For construction enterprises set up in the Mainland by Macao service suppliers, the construction contract performance of the enterprises both in the Mainland and outside the Mainland is taken into account in assessing the qualification of the construction enterprises in the Mainland. The total managerial and technical staff of the construction enterprises in the Mainland should be based on the actual employed staff in the Mainland for the purpose of proceeding qualification assessment. 2. There will be no restriction on the proportion of Macao permanent residents being project managers approved by the qualification administration authorities for construction enterprises in the Mainland set up by Macao service suppliers.
	3. Macao service suppliers who have already obtained the certificate of approval for establishment of enterprises with investment of Taiwan, Hong Kong and Macao in the Mainland but have not yet obtained the construction enterprise qualification certificate may apply, before 1 July 2005, for a certificate for undertaking single construction project based on their signed construction contract and "Construction Qualification Certificate for Taiwan, Hong Kong and Macao Enterprise". Subject to the preliminary vetting and agreement of construction administration department at provincial level, the application will be processed by the Ministry of Construction. 4. The residency requirement is waived for Macao permanent residents employed as engineering technical staff and financial managerial staff in construction enterprises in the Mainland set up by Macao service suppliers.

---

[1] Including dredging services relating to infrastructure construction.
[2] Coverage is limited only to the rental and leasing services of construction and/or demolition machines (with operators), which are owned and used by foreign construction enterprises in the course of providing services.

	5. The commitments in relation to construction and related engineering services stated above will come into effect from 1 November 2004.
Sectors or sub-sectors	4. Distribution services
	A. Commission agents' services (excluding salt and tobacco) B. Wholesale trade services (excluding salt and tobacco)
Specific commitments	To allow Macao service suppliers to set up, in the form of wholly-owned operations, commission agents' and wholesale trade enterprises in the Mainland in respect of books, newspapers, magazines, pharmaceutical products, pesticides and mulching films with effect from 1 November 2004.[1]
Sectors or sub-sectors	4. Distribution services
	C. Retailing services (excluding tobacco)
Specific commitments	1. To allow Macao service suppliers to set up, in the form of wholly-owned operations, retail trade enterprises in the Mainland in respect of books, newspapers, magazines, pharmaceutical products, pesticides, mulching films and processed oil with effect from 1 November 2004.[1] 2. To allow Macao service suppliers to set up, in the form of wholly-owned operations, retail enterprises in the Mainland for motor vehicles in accordance with the relevant motor vehicle distribution rules in the Mainland.[2] The application conditions for setting up the above enterprises are waived for Macao service suppliers[3].
Sectors or sub-sectors	7. Financial services
	B. Banking and other financial services (excluding insurance and securities)
	a. Acceptance of deposits and other repayable funds from the public; b. Lending of all types, including consumer credit, mortgage credit, factoring and financing of commercial transaction; c. Financial leasing; d. All payment and money transmission services, including credit, charge and debit cards, travellers cheques and bankers drafts (including import and export settlement); e. Guarantees and commitments; f. Trading in foreign exchange for own account or for account of customers.
Specific commitments	To allow Mainland branches of Macao banks to conduct insurance agents business after obtaining approval with effect from 1 November 2004.
Sectors or sub-sectors	7. Financial services
	B. Banking and other financial services
	Securities Futures
Specific commitments	To allow intermediary agencies which are registered with the Monetary Authority of Macao and which satisfy the requirements of the China Securities

---

[1] The commission agents' and wholesale trade enterprises set up by Macao service suppliers in the Mainland in respect of chemical fertilizers, processed oil and crude oil remain subject to Mainland's commitments to members of the World Trade Organization.

[1] Chain stores with more than 30 outlets remain subject to Mainland's commitments to members of the World Trade Organization. The retailing trade enterprises set up by Macao service suppliers in the Mainland in respect of chemical fertilizers, staple food, vegetable oil, edible sugar, and cotton remain subject to Mainland's commitments to members of the World Trade Organization.

[2] Chain stores with more than 30 outlets remain subject to Mainland's commitments to members of the World Trade Organization.

[3] The application conditions are: the average annual sales value of a Macao service supplier in the preceding 3 years is not less than US$100 million; the assets in the previous year is not less than US$10 million; the minimum registered capital for setting up a retail enterprise for motor vehicles in the Mainland is RMB10 million; while the minimum registered capital for setting up a retail enterprise for motor vehicles in the Central and Western Region, is RMB 6 million.

	Regulatory Commission to set up joint venture futures brokerage companies in the Mainland. The percentage of shareholding owned by Macao registered intermediaries should not exceed 49% (including shareholding of related parties). Requirements in respect of the scope of business and amount of capital etc. of the joint venture futures brokerage companies shall be the same as those for Mainland enterprises.
Sectors or sub-sectors	10. Recreational, cultural and sporting services
	A. Recreational services (excluding audiovisual services)
Specific commitments	1. To allow Macao service suppliers to set up performing venues in the Mainland on an equity joint venture, contractual joint venture or wholly-owned basis. 2. To allow Macao performing arts agencies to set up branches in the Mainland. 3. To allow Macao service suppliers to set up performance agencies in the Mainland on an equity joint venture or contractual joint venture basis. 4. To allow Macao service suppliers to set up internet culture business units and internet online service premises in the Mainland with the Mainland party holding majority shares. 5. To allow Macao service suppliers to set up art galleries, art shops and art work exhibition units in the Mainland on an equity joint venture, contractual joint venture or wholly-owned basis.
Sectors or sub-sectors	11. Transport services
	A. Maritime transport services. H. Auxiliary services
	International transport (freight and passengers) (CPC7211, 7212, less cabotage transport services) Container station and depot services Others
Specific commitments	1. To allow Macao service suppliers to set up wholly-owned shipping companies in the Mainland to provide shipping agency services for vessels owned or operated by the Macao service suppliers themselves, including customs declaration and inspection, and use of common commercial bills of lading or multimodal transport documents for conducting multimodal transport services. 2. To allow Macao service suppliers to set up wholly-owned shipping companies in the Mainland to provide regular business services for feeders that they operate between Macao and ports that are opened to foreign vessels in the Mainland, such as shipping undertaking, issuance of bills of lading, settlement of freight rates, signing of service contracts, etc.[1]
	3. To allow Macao service suppliers to set up wholly-owned companies in the Mainland to provide supplies services other than fuel and water to vessels owned or managed by the same Macao service supplier. 4. To allow Macao service suppliers to set up wholly-owned companies in the Mainland to provide port cargo loading and unloading services.
Sectors or sub-sectors	11. Transport services
	C. Air transport services
	Airport operation services (excluding cargo handling) (CPC74610) Other supporting services for air transport (CPC74690)

---

[1] The requirement that "50%" or more of the ships owned by it, calculated in terms of tonnage, should be registered in Macao" stipulated in Annex 5 to the CEPA is not applicable to the feeder transport service provided by Macao service suppliers.

Specific commitments	1. To allow Macao service suppliers to provide, in the form of cross-border supply, contractual joint venture, equity joint venture or wholly-owned operations, contract management services for small and medium airports. The period of validity of the contract should not exceed 20 years.[1]
	2. To allow Macao service suppliers to provide, in the form of cross-border supply, consumption abroad, contractual joint venture, equity joint venture or wholly-owned operations, airport management training and consultation services.[2]
	3. To allow Macao service suppliers to provide, in the form of equity joint venture or wholly-owned operations, seven types of air transport ground services in the Mainland, namely, agency services; loading and unloading control, communication, and departure control system services; unit load devices management services; passenger and baggage services; cargo and mail services; ramp services and aircraft services.
Sectors or sub-sectors	11. Transport services
	F. Road transport services
	Freight transportation by road in trucks or cars (CPC7123) Road passenger transportation (CPC7121, 7122)
Specific commitments	1. To allow passenger transport companies operating franchised bus services and companies operating non-franchised bus services (Guangdong-Macao cross-boundary coach services) in Macao to set up joint venture enterprises in Guangdong, Guangxi, Hunan, Hainan, Fujian, Jiangxi, Yunnan, Guizhou and Sichuan to provide "Direct Passenger Bus Services" between Macao and the above nine provinces.[1]
	2. To allow passenger transport companies operating franchised bus services in Macao to set up wholly-owned enterprises in Mainland cities at the municipal level to provide passenger public transport and car rental services at those cities.
Sectors or sub-sectors	11. Transport services
	H. Services auxiliary to all modes of transport
	Freight forwarding agency services (CPC748, 749, excluding freight inspection)
Specific commitments	To allow freight forwarding agency enterprises in the Mainland established by Macao services suppliers to set up branch offices upon full payment of registered capital.
Sectors or sub-sectors	Service sectors (sectors not elsewhere classified in GNS/W/120)
	Professionals and technicians qualification examinations
Specific commitments	To allow eligible Macao residents to sit the following qualification examinations for professionals and technicians in the Mainland: registered architect, registered structural engineer, registered civil engineer (geotechnical), construction supervising engineer, cost engineer, registered town planner, real estate agent, certified safety engineer, registered nuclear safety engineer, constructor, registered public facility engineer, registered chemical engineer, registered civil engineer (harbour and waterway), registered facility supervising engineer, cost evaluator, enterprise legal consultant, cotton quality examiner, auctioneer, pharmacist, environmental impact assessment

---

[1] In the case if the Macao service suppliers providing airport operation services be affiliated with airlines, the relevant regulations and rules in the Mainland apply.

[2] Same as aforementioned.

[1] "Direct Passenger Bus Services" means direct road transport services between the Mainland and Macao. In this sector, Macao service suppliers supplying direct passenger bus services must be enterprise juridical persons.

	engineer, real estate appraiser, registered electrical engineer, certified tax accountant, certified public valuer, prosthetist and orthotist, mining rights assessor, registered consulting engineer (investment), international business personnel, land registration agent, gemstone quality examiner; and in professional areas of quality, translation computing technology and software, auditing, health, economics, statistics, accounting, etc. A qualification certificate will be issued to those who pass the examination.
Sectors or sub-sectors	Service sectors (sectors not elsewhere classified in GNS/W/120)
	Trade mark agency
Specific commitments	To allow Macao service suppliers to conduct, after registering with the Administration for Industry and Commerce at the provincial level and acquiring the statutory operating body qualification, trade mark agency business in the Mainland.
Sectors or sub-sectors	Service sectors (sectors not elsewhere classified in GNS/W/120)
	Patent agency
Specific commitments	1. To allow eligible Macao permanent residents with Chinese citizenship to sit the National Qualification Examination for Patent Agents in the Mainland. A "Patent Agent Qualification Certificate" will be issued to those who pass the examination. 2. Macao permanent residents with Chinese citizenship who have obtained the "Patent Agent Qualification Certificate" may practise in patent agencies that are approved for establishment in the Mainland. Those who meet the prescribed requirements may join to become partners or shareholders of patent agencies that are approved for establishment in the Mainland.
Sectors or sub-sectors	Service sectors (sectors not elsewhere classified in GNS/W/120)
	Individually owned stores
Specific commitments	To allow Macao permanent residents with Chinese citizenship to set up, in accordance with the relevant Mainland laws, regulations and administrative regulations, individually owned stores in all provinces, autonomous regions, municipalities directly under the Central Government in the Mainland, without being subject to the approval procedures applicable to foreign investments. The scope of business for individually owned stores, excluding franchising, includes retailing services, food and beverage services, as well as hair dressing services, beauty and health treatment services, bathing services, repair services for household electric appliances and goods for daily uses under the category of residents services and other services. The number of employees for each store shall not exceed 8 persons and the business area shall not exceed 300 square metres.

*

TRATADO DE LIBRE COMERCIO
ENTRE EL GOBIERNO DE LA REPÚBLICA ORIENTAL DEL URUGUAY Y EL GOBIERNO DE LOS ESTADOS UNIDOS MEXICANOS*
[excerpts]

The Free Trade Agreement Between the Government of the Republic of Uruguay and the Government of the United Mexican States was signed on 15 November 2003. It entered into force on 15 July 2004.

[…]

CAPÍTULO X
COMERCIO TRANSFRONTERIZO DE SERVICIOS

Artículo 10-01: Definiciones.

Para efectos de este capítulo, se entenderá por:

servicios: todo servicio de cualquier sector, comprendido en la clasificación de uso de cada Parte, excepto los servicios suministrados en ejercicio de facultades gubernamentales;

servicios suministrados en ejercicio de facultades gubernamentales: todo servicio que no se suministre en condiciones comerciales ni en competencia con uno o varios proveedores de servicios;

empresa: significa una "empresa" como está definida en el Artículo 2-01 (Definiciones Generales), y la sucursal de una empresa;

empresa de una Parte: una empresa constituida u organizada de conformidad con las leyes de una Parte, incluidas las sucursales localizadas en el territorio de una Parte y realizando actividades económicas en ese territorio;

comercio transfronterizo de servicios o prestación transfronteriza de un servicio: la prestación de un servicio:

a)   del territorio de una Parte al territorio de otra Parte;

b)   en territorio de una Parte, por personas de esa Parte, a personas de otra Parte; o

c)   por un nacional de una Parte en territorio de otra Parte, pero no incluye la prestación de un servicio en el territorio de una Parte mediante una inversión, tal como está definida en el Artículo 13-01 (Definiciones), en ese territorio;

---

* *Source*: The Organization of the American States (2003). "Tratado de Libre Comercio entre el Gobierno de la República Oriental del Uruguay y el Gobierno de los Estados Unidos Mexicanos", available on the Internet (http://www.sice.oas.org/Trade/mexurufta_s/mexuruind_s.asp). [Note added by the editor.]

prestador de servicios de una Parte: una persona de la Parte que pretenda prestar o presta un servicio;

restricción cuantitativa: una medida no discriminatoria que impone limitaciones sobre:

a)   el número de prestadores de servicios, sea a través de una cuota, monopolio o una prueba de necesidad económica o por cualquier otro medio cuantitativo; o

b)   las operaciones de cualquier prestador de servicios, sea a través de una cuota o de una prueba de necesidad económica, o por cualquier otro medio cuantitativo;

servicios aéreos especializados: cartografía aérea; topografía aérea; fotografía aérea; control de incendios forestales; extinción de incendios; publicidad aérea; remolque de planeadores; servicios de paracaidismo; servicios aéreos para la construcción; transporte aéreo de troncos; vuelos panorámicos; vuelos de entrenamiento; inspección y vigilancia aéreas y rociamiento aéreo; y

servicios profesionales: sujeto a la legislación de cada Parte, la realización a título oneroso o gratuito de todo acto o la prestación de cualquier servicio propio de cada profesión y cuyo ejercicio profesional es autorizado o restringido por una Parte, pero no incluye los servicios prestados por personas que practican un oficio o a los tripulantes de barcos mercantes y aeronaves.

Artículo 10-02: Ámbito de aplicación.

1.   Este capítulo se refiere a las medidas que una Parte adopte o mantenga y que afecten al comercio transfronterizo de servicios, incluidas las relativas a:

a)   la producción, distribución, comercialización, venta y prestación de un servicio;

b)   la compra, o uso o el pago de un servicio;

c)   el acceso a servicios que se ofrezcan al público en general, y la utilización de los mismos, con motivo de la prestación de un servicio;

d)   la presencia en su territorio de un prestador de servicios de la otra Parte; y

e)   el otorgamiento de una fianza u otra forma de garantía financiera, como condición para la prestación de un servicio.

2.   Este capítulo no se refiere a:

a)   los servicios financieros,

b)   los servicios aéreos, incluidos los de transporte aéreo nacional e internacional, regulares y no regulares, así como las actividades auxiliares de apoyo a los servicios aéreos, salvo:

i.   los servicios de reparación y mantenimiento de aeronaves durante el periodo en que se retira una aeronave de servicio;

ii. los servicios aéreos especializados;

iii. la venta y comercialización de los servicios de transporte aéreo; y

iv. los servicios de reserva informatizados;

c) las compras gubernamentales hechas por una Parte o empresa del Estado; ni a

d) los subsidios o donaciones otorgados por una Parte o una empresa del Estado, incluidos los préstamos, garantías y seguros apoyados por el gobierno. Las Partes tomarán en cuenta los resultados del tratamiento de este tema en el seno del Grupo de Trabajo sobre las Normas del AGCS de la OMC, en el marco de la ronda Doha.

3. Ninguna disposición de este capítulo se interpretará en el sentido de:

a) imponer a una Parte ninguna obligación respecto a un nacional de otra Parte que pretenda ingresar a su mercado de trabajo o que tenga empleo permanente en su territorio, ni de conferir ningún derecho a ese nacional, respecto a dicho acceso o empleo; o

b) impedir a una Parte prestar servicios o llevar a cabo funciones tales como la ejecución de las leyes y servicios de readaptación social, pensión o seguro de desempleo o servicios de seguridad social, las relativas al bienestar social, educación pública, capacitación pública, salud y protección de la niñez, cuando se desempeñen de manera que no sea incompatible con este capítulo.

Artículo 10-03: Trato nacional.

1. Cada Parte otorgará a los servicios y prestadores de servicios de la otra Parte, con respecto a todas las medidas que afecten a la prestación de servicios, un trato no menos favorable que el que otorgue, en circunstancias similares, a sus prestadores de servicios.

2. El trato otorgado por una Parte de conformidad con el párrafo 1 significa, respecto a un estado o departamento, un trato no menos favorable que el trato más favorable que ese estado o departamento otorgue, en circunstancias similares, a los servicios o prestadores de servicios de la Parte a la que pertenece.

3. Lo establecido en el párrafo 1, no obliga a las Partes a compensar desventajas competitivas intrínsecas que resulten del carácter extranjero de los servicios o prestadores de servicios pertinentes.

Artículo 10-04: Trato de nación más favorecida.

Cada Parte otorgará inmediata e incondicionalmente a los servicios y prestadores de servicios de la otra Parte un trato no menos favorable que el que otorgue, en circunstancias similares, a servicios y prestadores de servicios de un país que no sea Parte.

Artículo 10-05: Presencia local.

Ninguna Parte exigirá a un prestador de servicios de la otra Parte que establezca o mantenga una oficina de representación ni ningún tipo de empresa, o que sea residente en su territorio como condición para la prestación transfronteriza de un servicio.

Artículo 10-06: Reservas y excepciones.

1.　　Los artículos 10-03, 10-04 y 10-05 no se aplicarán a:

　　a)　　cualquier medida disconforme existente que sea adoptada o mantenida por:

　　　　i.　　una Parte a nivel nacional o federal, o estatal o departamental, según corresponda, como se establece en su lista del Anexo I (Reservas y Excepciones), o

　　　　ii.　　un gobierno municipal; ni a

　　b)　　la continuación o la pronta renovación de cualquier medida disconforme a la que se refiere el literal a);

　　c)　　la reforma de cualquier medida disconforme a que se refiere el literal a), siempre que dicha reforma o renovación no disminuya el grado de conformidad de la medida, tal como estaba en vigor inmediatamente antes de la reforma, con los artículos 10-03, 10-04 y 10-05.

2.　　A partir de la entrada en vigor de este Tratado, ninguna Parte incrementará el grado de disconformidad de sus medidas existentes respecto a los artículos 10-03, 10-04 y 10-05. Las Partes listarán sus medidas disconformes en el Anexo I (Reservas y Excepciones), el cual deberá ser completado por las Partes a más tardar en un plazo de un plazo de un año a partir de la entrada en vigor de este Tratado.

Artículo 10-07: Restricciones cuantitativas no discriminatorias.

1.　　Cada Parte indicará en su lista del Anexo II (Restricciones Cuantitativas no Discriminatorias), en un plazo de un año a partir de la entrada en vigor de este Tratado, cualesquier restricción cuantitativa que mantenga a nivel nacional o federal y estatal o departamental.

2.　　Cada Parte notificará a la otra Parte cualquier restricción cuantitativa, diferente a las de nivel de gobierno local, que adopte después de la fecha de entrada en vigor de este Tratado, e indicará la restricción en su lista del Anexo II (Restricciones Cuantitativas no Discriminatorias).

3.　　Las Partes se esforzarán periódicamente, pero en cualquier caso cuando menos cada 2 (dos) años, para negociar la liberalización o la remoción de las restricciones cuantitativas indicadas en su lista del Anexo II (Restricciones Cuantitativas no Discriminatorias), de conformidad con lo establecido en los párrafos 1 y 2.

Artículo 10-08: Liberalización futura.

Con el objeto de lograr a un nivel de liberalización progresiva, la Comisión podrá convocar negociaciones tendientes a eliminar las restricciones remanentes inscritas de conformidad con el artículo 10-06.

Artículo 10-09: Procedimientos.

La Comisión establecerá procedimientos para:

a) que una Parte notifique a las otras Partes e incluya en su lista pertinente:

i. las restricciones cuantitativas, de conformidad con el artículo 10-07;

ii. las reformas o renovaciones a medidas a las cuales se hace referencia en el artículo 10-06 (1)(b); y

b) la celebración de consultas sobre reservas, restricciones cuantitativas o compromisos, tendientes a lograr una mayor liberalización.

Artículo 10-10: Reglamentación Nacional.

1. Cada Parte se asegurará que todas las medidas de aplicación general que afecten al comercio de servicios sean administradas de manera razonable, objetiva e imparcial.

2. Cada Parte tendrán derecho a reglamentar el suministro de servicios en su territorio, y a establecer nuevas reglamentaciones al respecto, con el fin de realizar los objetivos de su política nacional, incluidas reglamentaciones en materia pro-competitiva y defensa del consumidor.

Artículo 10-11: Otorgamiento de licencias y certificados.

1. Cuando se exija licencia, matrícula, certificado u otro tipo de autorización para la prestación de un servicio, las autoridades competentes de la Parte de que se trate, en un plazo prudencial a partir de la presentación de una solicitud:

a) resolverán sobre la misma informando al interesado cuando la solicitud estuviese completa; o

b) informarán al interesado, cuando la solicitud no estuviese completa, sin atrasos innecesarios sobre el estado de la solicitu

2. Con el objeto de garantizar que toda medida que una Parte adopte o mantenga en relación con los requisitos y procedimientos para el otorgamiento de licencias o certificaciones a los nacionales de la otra Parte no constituya una barrera innecesaria al comercio, cada Parte procurará garantizar que dichas medidas:

a) se sustenten en criterios objetivos y transparentes, tales como la capacidad y la aptitud para prestar un servicio;

b) no sean más gravosas de lo necesario para asegurar la calidad de un servicio; y

c) no constituyan una restricción encubierta a la prestación transfronteriza de un servicio.

3. Cuando una Parte reconozca, de manera unilateral o por acuerdo con otro país no Parte, la educación, la experiencia, las licencias o los certificados obtenidos en el territorio de la otra Parte o de cualquier país que no sea Parte:

a) nada de lo dispuesto en el artículo 10-04 se interpretará en el sentido de exigir a esa Parte que reconozca la educación, la experiencia, las licencias o los certificados obtenidos en el territorio de la otra Parte; y

b) la Parte proporcionará a la otra Parte, oportunidad adecuada para demostrar que la educación, la experiencia, las licencias o los certificados obtenidos en territorio de esa otra Parte también deberán reconocerse, o para celebrar un arreglo o acuerdo que tenga efectos equivalentes.

4. Cada Parte, en un plazo de 2 (dos) años a partir de la fecha de entrada en vigor de este Tratado, eliminará todo requisito de nacionalidad o de residencia permanente, indicado en su lista del Anexo I (Reservas y Excepciones), que mantenga para el otorgamiento de licencias o certificados a prestadores de servicios profesionales de la otra Parte. Cuando una Parte no cumpla con esta obligación con respecto de un sector en particular, la otra Parte podrá, en el mismo sector y durante el mismo tiempo que la Parte en incumplimiento mantenga su requisito, mantener, como único recurso, un requisito equivalente indicado en su lista del Anexo I (Reservas y Excepciones) o restablecer:

a) cualquiera de tales requisitos a nivel federal que hubiere eliminado conforme a este artículo; o

b) mediante notificación a la Parte en incumplimiento, cualquiera de tales requisitos a nivel estatal que hubieren estado existentes a la fecha de entrada en vigor de este Tratado.

5. Las Partes consultarán entre ellas periódicamente con el objeto de examinar la posibilidad de eliminar los requisitos restantes de nacionalidad o de residencia permanente para el otorgamiento de licencias o certificados a los prestadores de servicios de cada Parte.

6. El Anexo 10-11(6) se aplica a las medidas adoptadas o mantenidas por una Parte relacionadas con el otorgamiento de licencias o certificados a prestadores de servicios profesionales.

Artículo 10-12: Denegación de beneficios.

Previa notificación y consulta de conformidad con los Artículos 16-03 (Notificación y suministro de información), y 18-03 (Consultas), una Parte podrá denegar los beneficios de este capítulo a un prestador de servicios de la otra Parte, cuando la Parte determine que el servicio está siendo prestado por una empresa que no realiza actividades de operaciones comerciales sustantivas en territorio de cualquiera de las Partes, y que es propiedad o está bajo control de personas de un país que no es Parte.
[...]

ANEXOS

Se acordó la elaboración de los siguientes Anexos:

Anexo I   Reservas y Excepciones

Anexo II Restricciones Cuantitativas no Discriminatorias

Anexo III Exenciones a la Cláusula de Nación más Favorecida

Anexo IV Actividades Reservadas al Estado

Anexo 10-11(6)
Servicios profesionales

Objetivo.

1.   Este anexo tiene por objeto establecer las reglas que observarán las Partes para armonizar, ente ellas, las medidas que normarán el reconocimiento mutuo de títulos o grados académicos para la prestación de servicios profesionales, mediante el otorgamiento de la autorización para el ejercicio profesional.

Trámite de solicitudes para el otorgamiento de licencias y certificados.

2.   Cada Parte se asegurará que sus autoridades competentes, en un plazo razonable a partir de la presentación de una solicitud de licencias o certificados por un nacional de la otra Parte:

a)   si la solicitud está completa, resuelvan sobre ella y notifiquen al solicitante la resolución; o

b)   si está incompleta, informen al solicitante, sin demora injustificada, sobre la situación que guarda la solicitud y la información adicional que se requiera conforme a su legislación.

Elaboración de normas profesionales.

3.   Las Partes alentarán a los organismos pertinentes en sus respectivos territorios a elaborar normas y criterios mutuamente aceptables para el otorgamiento de licencias y certificados a los prestadores de servicios profesionales, así como a presentar a la Comisión recomendaciones sobre su reconocimiento mutuo.

4.   Las normas y criterios a que se refiere el párrafo 3 podrán elaborarse con relación a los siguientes aspectos:

a)   educación: acreditación de escuelas o de programas académicos;

b) exámenes: exámenes de calificación para la obtención de licencias, inclusive métodos alternativos de evaluación, tales como exámenes orales y entrevistas;

c) experiencia: duración y naturaleza de la experiencia requerida para obtener una licencia;

d) conducta y ética: normas de conducta profesional y la naturaleza de las medidas disciplinarias en caso de que los prestadores de servicios profesionales las contravengan;

e) desarrollo profesional y renovación de la certificación: educación continua y los requisitos correspondientes para conservar el certificado profesional;

f) ámbito de acción: extensión y límites de las actividades autorizadas;

g) conocimiento local: requisitos sobre el conocimiento de aspectos tales como las leyes y reglamentos, el idioma, la geografía o el clima locales; y

h) protección al consumidor: requisitos alternativos al de residencia, tales como fianzas, seguros sobre responsabilidad profesional y fondos de reembolso al cliente para asegurar la protección de los consumidores.

5.   Al recibir una recomendación mencionada en el párrafo 3, la Comisión la revisará en un plazo razonable para decidir si es congruente con las disposiciones de este Tratado. Con fundamento en la revisión que lleve a cabo la Comisión, cada Parte alentará a sus respectivas autoridades competentes, a poner en práctica esa recomendación, en los casos que correspondan, dentro de un plazo mutuamente acordado.

Otorgamiento de licencias temporales.

6.   Cuando las Partes lo convengan, cada una de ellas alentará a los organismos pertinentes en sus respectivos territorios a elaborar procedimientos para la expedición de licencias temporales a los prestadores de servicios profesionales de la otra Parte.

Revisión.

7.   La Comisión revisará periódicamente, al menos una vez cada 3 (tres) años, la aplicación de las disposiciones de este Anexo.

CAPÍTULO XI
TELECOMUNICACIONES

Artículo 11-01: Definiciones.

Para efectos de este capítulo, se entenderá por:

comunicaciones intracorporativas: las telecomunicaciones mediante las cuales una empresa se comunica:

a) internamente, con sus subsidiarias, sucursales y filiales o éstas entre sí, según las defina cada Parte; o

b) de una manera no comercial y sujeto a la legislación vigente de cada Parte, con todas las personas de importancia fundamental para la actividad económica de la empresa, y que sostienen una relación contractual continua con ella;

pero no incluye los servicios de telecomunicaciones que se suministren a personas distintas a las descritas en esta definición;

equipo autorizado: el equipo terminal o de otra clase que ha sido aprobado para conectarse a la red pública de telecomunicaciones de acuerdo con los procedimientos de evaluación de la conformidad de la Parte donde el mismo se instale;

equipo terminal: cualquier dispositivo digital o analógico capaz de procesar, recibir, conmutar, señalizar o transmitir señales a través de medios electromagnéticos y que se conecta a la red pública de telecomunicaciones, mediante conexiones de radio o cable, en un punto terminal; medidas relativas a la normalización: "medidas relativas a la normalización", tal como se define en el artículo 9-01(Definiciones);

procedimiento de evaluación de la conformidad: "procedimiento de evaluación de la conformidad", tal como se define en el artículo 9-01 (Definiciones);

protocolo: un conjunto de reglas y formatos que rigen el intercambio de información entre dos entidades pares, para efectos de la transferencia de información de señales o datos;

proveedor principal u operador dominante: un proveedor u operador que tiene la capacidad de afectar de manera importante las condiciones de participación (desde el punto de vista de los precios y del suministro) en un mercado dado de servicios de telecomunicaciones como resultado del control de las instalaciones esenciales o la utilización de su posición en el mercado;

punto terminal de la red: la demarcación final de la red pública de telecomunicaciones en las instalaciones del usuario;

red privada de telecomunicaciones: la red de telecomunicaciones internas de una empresa o entre personas, para satisfacer sus propias necesidades de telecomunicación, sin comercializar ningún servicio a terceros;

red pública de telecomunicaciones: la red de telecomunicaciones que se utiliza para explotar comercialmente servicios de telecomunicaciones destinados a satisfacer las necesidades del público en general, sin incluir los equipos terminales de telecomunicaciones de los usuarios, ni las redes privadas de telecomunicaciones que se encuentren mas allá del punto terminal de la red;

servicios mejorados o de valor agregado: los servicios de telecomunicaciones que emplean sistemas de procesamiento computarizado que:

a)   actúan sobre el formato, contenido, código, protocolo o aspectos similares de la información transmitida del usuario[1];

b)   proporcionan al cliente información adicional, diferente o reestructurada; o

c)   implican la interacción del usuario con información almacenada;

servicio de telecomunicaciones: cualquier servicio de telecomunicaciones que una Parte obligue explícitamente o de hecho a que se ofrezca al público en general, incluidos el telégrafo, teléfono, telex y transmisión de datos y que, por lo general, conlleva la transmisión en tiempo real de información suministrada por el cliente entre dos o más puntos, sin cambio "de punto a punto" en la forma o contenido de la información del usuario; y

telecomunicación: toda transmisión, emisión, recepción de signos, señales, escritos, imágenes, sonidos e informaciones de cualquier naturaleza, por hilo, radioelectricidad, medios ópticos u otros sistemas electromagnéticos.

Artículo 11-02: Ámbito de aplicación y extensión de las obligaciones.

1.   Reconociendo el doble papel de los servicios de telecomunicaciones, como sector específico de actividad económica y como medio de prestación de servicios para otras actividades económicas, este capítulo se aplica a:

a)   las medidas que adopte o mantenga una Parte, relacionadas con el acceso a y el uso continuo de redes públicas o servicios de telecomunicaciones por personas de otra Parte, incluyendo su acceso y uso cuando operen redes privadas para llevar a cabo las comunicaciones intracorporativas;

b)   las medidas que adopte o mantenga una Parte sobre la prestación de servicios mejorados o de valor agregado por personas de otra Parte en el territorio de la primera o a través de sus fronteras; y

c)   las medidas relativas a la normalización respecto de conexión de equipo terminal u otro equipo a las redes públicas de telecomunicaciones.

2.   Salvo para garantizar que las personas que operen estaciones de radiodifusión y sistemas por cable tengan acceso y uso continuos de las redes públicas y de los servicios de telecomunicaciones, este capítulo no se aplica a ninguna medida que una Parte adopte o mantenga en relación con la radiodifusión o la distribución por cable de programación de radio o televisión.

3.   Ninguna disposición de este capítulo se interpretará en el sentido de:

a) obligar a cualquier Parte a autorizar a una persona de otra Parte a que establezca, construya, adquiera, arriende, opere o suministre redes o servicios de telecomunicaciones;

b) obligar a cualquier Parte o a que ésta, a su vez, exija a alguna persona a que establezca, construya, adquiera, arriende, opere o suministre redes públicas o servicios de telecomunicaciones que no se ofrezcan al público en general;

c) impedir a cualquier Parte que prohiba a las personas que operen redes privadas el uso de tales redes para suministrar redes públicas o servicios de telecomunicaciones a terceras personas; ni

d) obligar a una Parte a exigir a cualquier persona involucrada en la radiodifusión o distribución por cable de programación de radio o de televisión, a que proporcione su infraestructura de distribución por cable o de radiodifusión como red pública de telecomunicaciones.

Artículo 11-03: Acceso a redes públicas y servicios de telecomunicaciones y su uso.

1. Cada Parte garantizará que cualquier persona de la otra Parte tenga acceso a cualquier red pública o servicio de telecomunicaciones y pueda hacer uso de ellos, así como a los circuitos privados arrendados, ofrecidos en su territorio o de manera transfronteriza en términos y condiciones razonables y no discriminatorios, para la conducción de sus negocios, según se especifica en los párrafos 2 al 7.

2. Sujeto a lo dispuesto en los párrafos 6 y 7, cada Parte garantizará que a las personas de la otra Parte se les permita:

a) comprar o arrendar y conectar el equipo terminal u otro equipo que haga interfaz, con la red pública de telecomunicaciones;

b) interconectar circuitos privados, arrendados o propios, con redes públicas de telecomunicaciones en territorio de esa Parte o con circuitos arrendados o propios de otra persona, en términos y condiciones mutuamente aceptadas por dichas personas;

c) realizar funciones de conmutación, señalización y procesamiento; y

d) utilizar los protocolos de operación que ellas elijan siempre que no vaya en detrimento de la calidad de servicio.

3. Sin perjuicio de lo establecido en su legislación vigente, cada Parte procurará que la fijación de precios para los servicios de telecomunicaciones esté orientada por los costos económicos directamente relacionados con la prestación de dichos servicios.

4. Cada Parte garantizará que las personas de la otra Parte puedan emplear las redes públicas o los servicios de telecomunicaciones para transmitir la información en su territorio o a través de sus fronteras, incluso para las comunicaciones intracorporativas, y para el acceso a la información contenida en bases de datos o almacenada en cualquier otra forma que sea legible por una máquina en territorio de cualquiera de las Partes.

5.   Cada Parte podrá adoptar cualquier medida necesaria para asegurar la confidencialidad y seguridad de los mensajes y la protección de la intimidad de los suscriptores de redes o servicios públicos de telecomunicaciones.

6.   Cada Parte garantizará que no se impongan más condiciones al acceso a redes públicas o servicios de telecomunicaciones y a su uso, que las necesarias para:

a)   salvaguardar las responsabilidades del servicio, de los proveedores de redes públicas o servicios de telecomunicaciones, en particular su capacidad para poner sus redes o servicios a disposición del público en general; o

b)   proteger la integridad técnica de las redes públicas o los servicios de telecomunicaciones.

7.   Siempre que las condiciones para el acceso a redes públicas o servicios de telecomunicaciones y su uso cumplan los lineamientos establecidos en el párrafo 6, dichas condiciones podrán incluir:

a)   restricciones a la reventa o al uso compartido de tales servicios;

b)   requisitos para utilizar interfaces técnicas determinadas, inclusive protocolos de interfaz, para la interconexión con las redes o los servicios mencionados;

c)   restricciones en la interconexión de circuitos privados, arrendados o propios, con las redes o los servicios mencionados, o con circuitos arrendados o propios de otra persona, cuando éstos se utilicen para el suministro de redes públicas o servicios de telecomunicaciones; y

d)   procedimientos para otorgar licencias, permisos, registros, autorizaciones o notificaciones que, de adoptarse o mantenerse, sean transparentes y cuyo trámite de solicitudes se resuelva conforme a los plazos establecidos en la legislación de cada Parte.

Artículo 11-04: Condiciones para la prestación de servicios mejorados o de valor agregado.

1.   Cada Parte garantizará que:

a)   cualquier procedimiento que adopte o mantenga para otorgar licencias, permisos, registros, autorizaciones o notificaciones referentes a la prestación de servicios mejorados o de valor agregado sea transparente y no discriminatorio y que las solicitudes se tramiten conforme a los plazos establecidos en la legislación de cada Parte; y

b)   la información requerida conforme a tales procedimientos se limite a la necesaria para acreditar que el solicitante tiene la solvencia financiera para iniciar la prestación del servicio, o que los servicios, el equipo terminal u otro equipo del solicitante cumplen con las normas técnicas o reglamentaciones técnicas aplicables de la Parte.

2.   Sin perjuicio de lo establecido en su legislación vigente, ninguna Parte exigirá a un prestador de servicios mejorados o de valor agregado:

a)   prestarlos al público en general;

b)   justificar sus tarifas de acuerdo a sus costos;

c)   registrar una tarifa;

d)   interconectar sus redes con cualquier cliente o red en particular; o

e)   satisfacer alguna norma o reglamentación técnica en particular, para una interconexión distinta a la interconexión con una red pública de telecomunicaciones.

3.   No obstante lo dispuesto en el literal c) del párrafo 2, cada Parte podrá requerir el registrar una tarifa a:

a)   un prestador de servicios mejorados o de valor agregado, con el fin de corregir una práctica de este prestador que la Parte, de conformidad con su legislación, haya considerado, en un caso particular, como contraria a la competencia; o

b)   un proveedor principal u operador dominante, al que se apliquen las disposiciones del artículo 11-06.

Artículo 11-05: Medidas relativas a la normalización.

1.   Cada Parte garantizará que sus medidas relativas a la normalización que se refieren a la conexión del equipo terminal u otro equipo a las redes públicas de telecomunicaciones, incluso aquellas medidas que se refieren al uso del equipo de prueba y medición para el procedimiento de evaluación de la conformidad, se adopten o mantengan solamente en la medida que sean necesarias para:

a)   evitar daños técnicos a las redes públicas de telecomunicaciones;

b)   evitar la interferencia técnica con los servicios de telecomunicaciones o su deterioro;

c)   evitar la interferencia electromagnética y asegurar la compatibilidad con otros usos del espectro electromagnético;

d)   evitar el mal funcionamiento del equipo de facturación; o

e)   garantizar la seguridad del usuario y su acceso a las redes públicas o servicios de telecomunicaciones.

2.   Cada Parte podrá establecer el requisito de aprobación para la conexión del equipo terminal u otro equipo que no esté autorizado a la red pública de telecomunicaciones, siempre que los criterios de aprobación sean compatibles con lo dispuesto en el párrafo 1.

3.   Cada Parte garantizará que los puntos terminales de las redes públicas de telecomunicaciones se definan a partir de una base razonable y transparente.

4.   Ninguna Parte exigirá autorización adicional al equipo que se conecte del lado del consumidor, una vez que el equipo haya sido autorizado, ya que este equipo autorizado sirve como protección a la red, cumpliendo con los criterios del párrafo 1.

5.   Cada Parte:

a)   asegurará que sus procedimientos de evaluación de la conformidad sean transparentes y no discriminatorios y que las solicitudes que se presenten al efecto se tramiten conforme a los plazos establecidos en su legislación;

b)   permitirá que cualquier entidad técnicamente calificada realice la prueba requerida al equipo terminal o a otro equipo que vaya a ser conectado a la red pública de telecomunicaciones, de acuerdo con los procedimientos de evaluación de la conformidad de la Parte, a reserva del derecho de la misma de revisar la exactitud y la integridad de los resultados de las pruebas; y

c)   garantizará que no sean discriminatorias las medidas que adopte o mantenga para autorizar a las personas que actúan como agentes de proveedores de equipo de telecomunicaciones ante los organismos competentes para la evaluación de la conformidad de la Parte.

6.   A más tardar un año después de la entrada en vigor de este tratado, cada Parte adoptará entre sus procedimientos de evaluación de la conformidad, las disposiciones necesarias para aceptar los resultados de las pruebas que realicen, con base en sus normas y procedimientos establecidos, los laboratorios que se encuentran en territorio de la otra Parte.

7.   Las Partes establecerán, de conformidad con el capítulo IX (Normas, Reglamentos Técnicos y Procedimientos de Evaluación de la Conformidad), un Subcomité de Medidas Relativas a la Normalización de Telecomunicaciones.

Artículo 11-06: Prácticas contrarias a la competencia.

1.   Cuando una Parte mantenga o establezca un proveedor principal u operador dominante para proveer redes públicas y servicios de telecomunicaciones, y éste compita, directamente o a través de una filial, en la prestación de servicios mejorados o de valor agregado u otros bienes o servicios vinculados con las telecomunicaciones, la Parte se asegurará que el proveedor principal u operador dominante no utilice su posición para incurrir en prácticas contrarias a la competencia en esos mercados, ya sea de manera directa o a través de los tratos con sus filiales, de modo tal que afecte desventajosamente a una persona de la otra Parte.

2.   Cada Parte procurará introducir o mantener medidas eficaces para impedir la conducta contraria a la competencia a que se refiere el párrafo 1, tales como:

a)   requisitos de contabilidad;

b)   requisitos de separación estructural;

c) reglas para asegurar que el monopolio, proveedor principal u operador dominante otorgue a sus competidores acceso a sus redes o sus servicios de telecomunicaciones y al uso de los mismos, en términos y condiciones no menos favorables que los que se conceda a sí mismo o a sus filiales; o

d) reglas para asegurar la divulgación oportuna de los cambios técnicos de las redes públicas de telecomunicaciones y sus interfaces.

Artículo 11-07: Relación con organizaciones y acuerdos internacionales.

1. Las Partes harán su mejor esfuerzo para estimular el papel de los organismos a nivel regional y subregional e impulsarlos como foros para promover el desarrollo de las telecomunicaciones de la región.

2. Las Partes, reconociendo la importancia de las normas internacionales para lograr la compatibilidad e interoperabilidad global de las redes o servicios de telecomunicaciones, promoverán dichas normas mediante la labor de los organismos internacionales competentes, tales como la Unión Internacional de Telecomunicaciones y la Organización Internacional de Normalización.

Artículo 11-08: Cooperación técnica y otras consultas.

1. Con el fin de estimular el desarrollo de la infraestructura de servicios de telecomunicaciones interoperables, las Partes cooperarán en el intercambio de información técnica en el desarrollo de programas intergubernamentales de entrenamiento, así como en otras actividades afines. En cumplimiento de esta obligación, las Partes pondrán especial énfasis en los programas de coordinación e intercambio existentes.

2. Las Partes consultarán entre ellas para determinar la posibilidad de liberalizar aún más el comercio de todos los servicios de telecomunicaciones.

Artículo 11-09: Transparencia.

Además de lo dispuesto en el capítulo XVI (Transparencia), cada Parte pondrá a disposición del público las medidas relativas al acceso a redes públicas o servicios de telecomunicaciones y su uso, incluyendo las medidas referentes a:

a) tarifas y otros términos y condiciones del servicio;

b) especificaciones de las interfaces técnicas con dichos servicios y redes;

c) información sobre los órganos responsables de la elaboración y adopción de medidas relativas a normalización que afecten dicho acceso y uso;

d) condiciones aplicables a la conexión de equipo terminal o de otra clase, a la red pública de telecomunicaciones; y

e) cualquier requisito de notificación, permiso, registro, licencia o contrato.

Artículo 11-10: Relación con otros capítulos.

En caso de incompatibilidad entre las disposiciones de este capítulo y cualquier otra disposición de este Tratado, prevalecerán las de este capítulo en la medida de la incompatibilidad.

CAPÍTULO XII
ENTRADA TEMPORAL DE PERSONAS DE NEGOCIOS

Artículo 12-01: Definiciones.

Para efectos del presente capítulo, se entenderá por:

entrada temporal significa la entrada de una persona de negocios de una Parte a territorio de la otra Parte, sin la intención de establecer residencia permanente;

persona de negocios significa el nacional de una Parte que participa en el comercio de bienes o prestación de servicios, o en actividades de inversión;

temporal: incluye la expresión "temporaria"; y

vigente: la calidad de obligatoriedad de los preceptos legales de las Partes en el momento de entrada en vigor de este Tratado.

Artículo 12-02: Principios generales.

Las disposiciones de este capítulo reflejan la relación comercial preferente entre las Partes, la conveniencia de facilitar la entrada temporal conforme al principio de reciprocidad y de establecer criterios y procedimientos transparentes para tal efecto. Así mismo, refleja la necesidad de garantizar la seguridad de las fronteras, y de proteger la fuerza de trabajo nacional y el empleo permanente en sus respectivos territorios.

Artículo 12-03: Obligaciones generales.

1.   Cada Parte aplicará las medidas relativas a las disposiciones de este capítulo de conformidad con el artículo 12-02 y, en particular, las aplicará de manera expedita para evitar demoras o perjuicios indebidos en el comercio de bienes y de servicios, o en las actividades de inversión comprendidas en este Tratado.

2.   Las Partes procurarán desarrollar y adoptar criterios, definiciones e interpretaciones comunes para la aplicación de este capítulo.

Artículo 12-04: Autorización de entrada temporal.

1.   De acuerdo con las disposiciones de este capítulo, incluso las contenidas en el Anexo 12-04, cada Parte autorizará la entrada temporal a personas de negocios que cumplan con las medidas migratorias aplicables, y las relativas a salud y seguridad públicas, así como con las referentes a seguridad nacional.

2.	Cada Parte limitará el importe de los derechos que cause el trámite de solicitudes de entrada temporal de personas de negocios al costo aproximado de los servicios que se presten.

Artículo 12-05: Suministro de información.

1.	Además de lo dispuesto en el Artículo 16-02, (Publicación), cada Parte:

a)	proporcionará a la otra Parte los materiales que les permitan conocer las medidas relativas a este capítulo; y

b)	a más tardar un año después de la fecha de entrada en vigor del Tratado, preparará, publicará y pondrá a disposición de los interesados, tanto en su territorio como en el de la otra Parte, un documento consolidado con material que explique los requisitos para la entrada temporal conforme a este capítulo, de manera que puedan conocerlos las personas de negocios de la otra Parte.

2.	Cada Parte recopilará, mantendrá y pondrá a disposición de la otra Parte, de conformidad con su legislación, la información relativa al otorgamiento de autorizaciones de entrada temporal, de acuerdo con este capítulo, a personas de negocios de la otra Parte a quienes se les haya expedido documentación migratoria. Esta recopilación incluirá información específica para cada ocupación, profesión o actividad.

Artículo 12-06: Comité sobre entrada temporal.

1.	Las Partes establecen un Comité sobre Entrada Temporal de Personas de Negocios, integrado por representantes de cada una de ellas, que incluya funcionarios de migración.

2.	El Comité se reunirá cuando menos una vez cada año para examinar:

a)	la aplicación y administración de este capítulo;

b)	la elaboración de medidas que faciliten aún más la entrada temporal de personas de negocios conforme al principio de reciprocidad; o

c)	las propuestas de modificaciones o adiciones a este capítulo.

Artículo 12-07: Solución de controversias.

1.	Las Partes no podrán iniciar los procedimientos previstos en el capítulo XVIII (Solución de Controversias), respecto a una negativa de autorización de entrada temporal conforme a este capítulo, ni respecto de ningún caso particular comprendido en el artículo 12-03 (1), salvo que:

a)	el asunto se refiera a una práctica recurrente; y

b)	la persona de negocios afectada haya agotado los recursos administrativos a su alcance respecto a ese asunto en particular.

2.	Los recursos mencionados en el párrafo (1)(b) se considerarán agotados cuando la autoridad competente no haya emitido una resolución definitiva en un año, contado a partir del inicio del procedimiento administrativo, y la resolución no se haya demorado por causas imputables a la persona de negocios afectada.

Artículo 12-08: Relación con otros capítulos.

Salvo lo dispuesto en este capítulo y en los capítulos I (Disposiciones Iniciales), XVI (Transparencia), XVII (Solución de Controversias), y XX (Disposiciones Finales), ninguna disposición de este Tratado impondrá obligación alguna a las Partes respecto a sus medidas migratorias.

Anexo 12-04
Entrada temporal de personas de negocios

Sección A - Visitantes de negocios

1.   Cada Parte autorizará la entrada temporal a la persona de negocios que pretenda llevar a cabo alguna actividad de negocios mencionada en el Apéndice 12-04(A)(1), siempre que, además de cumplir con las medidas migratorias vigentes, aplicables a la entrada temporal, exhiba:

    a)   prueba de nacionalidad de una Parte;

    b)   documentación que acredite que emprenderá tales actividades y señale el propósito de su entrada; y

    c)   prueba del carácter internacional de la actividad de negocios que se propone realizar y de que la persona no pretende ingresar en el mercado local de trabajo.

2.   Cada Parte estipulará que una persona de negocios pueda cumplir con los requisitos señalados en el literal c) del párrafo 1, cuando demuestre que:

    a)   la fuente principal de remuneración correspondiente a esa actividad se encuentra fuera del territorio de la Parte que autoriza la entrada temporal; y

    b)   el lugar principal del negocio y donde se obtiene la mayor parte de las ganancias se encuentran fuera de este territorio.

3.   Cada Parte autorizará la entrada temporal a la persona de negocios que pretenda llevar a cabo alguna actividad distinta a las señaladas en el Apéndice 12-04(A)(1), en términos no menos favorables que los previstos en las disposiciones existentes de las medidas señaladas en el Apéndice 12-04(A)(2), siempre que dicha persona de negocios cumpla además con las medidas migratorias vigentes, aplicables a la entrada temporal.

4.   Ninguna Parte podrá:

    a)   exigir como condición para autorizar la entrada temporal conforme al párrafo 1 ó 3, procedimientos previos de aprobación, peticiones, pruebas de certificación laboral, permiso de trabajo u otros procedimientos de efecto similar; o

b) imponer ni mantener ninguna restricción numérica a la entrada temporal de conformidad con el párrafo 1 ó 3.

Sección B - Comerciantes e inversionistas

1. Cada Parte autorizará la entrada temporal y expedirá documentación comprobatoria a la persona de negocios que pretenda:

a) desarrollar un intercambio de actividades comerciales sustantivas de bienes o servicios, principalmente entre el territorio de la Parte de la cual es nacional y el territorio de la Parte a la cual se solicita la entrada; o

b) establecer, desarrollar, administrar o prestar asesoría o servicios técnicos clave para administrar una inversión en la cual la persona o su empresa hayan comprometido, o estén en vías de comprometer, un monto importante de capital, y que ejerza funciones de supervisión, ejecutivas o que conlleven habilidades esenciales, siempre que la persona cumpla además con las medidas migratorias vigentes, aplicables a la entrada temporal.

2. Ninguna Parte podrá:

a) exigir pruebas de certificación laboral, permiso de trabajo u otros procedimientos de efecto similar, como condición para autorizar la entrada temporal conforme al párrafo 1; ni

b) imponer ni mantener restricciones numéricas en relación con la entrada temporal conforme al párrafo 1.

Sección C - Transferencias de personal dentro de una empresa

1. Cada Parte autorizará la entrada temporal y expedirá documentación comprobatoria a la persona de negocios empleada por una empresa legalmente constituida y en operación en su territorio que pretenda desempeñar funciones gerenciales, ejecutivas o que conlleven conocimientos especializados, en esa empresa o en una de sus subsidiarias o filiales, siempre que cumpla con las medidas migratorias vigentes aplicables a la entrada temporal. La Parte podrá exigir que la persona haya sido empleada de la empresa, de manera continua, durante un año dentro de los 3 (tres) años inmediatamente anteriores a la fecha de presentación de la solicitud.

2. Ninguna de las Partes podrá:

a) exigir pruebas de certificación laboral, permiso de trabajo u otros procedimientos de efecto similar como condición para autorizar la entrada temporal conforme al párrafo 1; ni

b) imponer ni mantener restricciones numéricas en relación con la entrada temporal conforme al párrafo 1.

Sección D - Profesionales

1.   Cada Parte autorizará la entrada temporal y expedirá documentación comprobatoria a la persona de negocios que pretenda llevar a cabo actividades a nivel profesional en el ámbito de una profesión señalada en el Apéndice 12-04(D)(1)a la sección D del Anexo al artículo 3, cuando la persona, además de cumplir con los requisitos migratorios vigentes, aplicables a la entrada temporal, exhiba:

   a)   prueba de nacionalidad de una Parte; y

   b)   documentación que acredite que la persona emprenderá tales actividades y que señale el propósito de su entrada.

2.   Ninguna Parte podrá:

   a)   exigir procedimientos previos de aprobación, peticiones, pruebas de certificación laboral, permiso de trabajo u otros de efecto similar, como condición para autorizar la entrada temporal conforme al párrafo 1; ni

   b)   imponer ni mantener restricciones numéricas en relación con la entrada temporal conforme al párrafo 1.

Apéndice 12-04(A)(1)
Visitantes de negocios

I.   Investigación y actividades científicas

- Investigadores, técnicos, y científicos que realicen actividades de manera independiente o para una empresa ubicada en territorio de la otra Parte.

II.   Docencia y actividades académicas

- Personas que, contando con una capacitación especial, realizan de la docencia una actividad habitual o aquellas que, sin poseer título docente, dicten seminarios, cursos o conferencias.

III.   Cultivo, manufactura y producción

- Personal de compras y de producción, a nivel gerencial, que lleve a cabo operaciones comerciales para una empresa ubicada en territorio de la otra Parte.

IV.   Consultoría

- Personas expertas en una materia sobre la que asesoran profesionalmente, entre otras, en áreas técnicas, científicas o sociales.

V.   Comercialización

- Investigadores y analistas de mercado que efectúen investigaciones o análisis de manera independiente o para una empresa ubicada en territorio de la otra Parte

- Personal de ferias y de promoción que asista a convenciones comerciales.

VI. Ventas

- Representantes y agentes de ventas que levanten pedidos o negocien contratos sobre bienes y servicios para una empresa ubicada en territorio de la otra Parte, pero que no entreguen los bienes ni presten los servicios.

- Compradores que hagan adquisiciones para una empresa ubicada en territorio de la otra Parte.

VII. Distribución

-Operadores de transporte que efectúen operaciones de transporte de bienes o de pasajeros a territorio de una Parte desde territorio de la otra Parte, o efectúen operaciones de carga y transporte de bienes o de pasajeros desde territorio de una Parte a territorio de la otra, sin realizar operaciones de descarga, al territorio de la otra Parte.

-Agentes aduanales que brinden servicios de asesoría en lo tocante a facilitar la importación o exportación de bienes.[1]

VIII. Servicios posteriores a la venta

- Personal de instalación, reparación, mantenimiento y supervisión que cuente con los conocimientos técnicos especializados esenciales para cumplir con la obligación contractual del vendedor; y que preste servicios, o capacite a trabajadores para que presten esos servicios, de conformidad con una garantía u otro contrato de servicios conexo a la venta de equipo o maquinaria comercial o industrial, incluidos los programas de computación comprados a una empresa ubicada fuera del territorio de la Parte a la cual se solicita entrada temporal, durante la vigencia del contrato de garantía o de servicio.

IX. Servicios generales

- Profesionales que realicen actividades de negocios a nivel profesional en el ámbito de una profesión señalada en el Apéndice 12-04(D)(1).

- Personal gerencial y de supervisión que intervenga en operaciones comerciales para una empresa ubicada en territorio de la otra Parte.

- Personal de servicios financieros (agentes de seguros, personal bancario o corredores de inversiones) que intervenga en operaciones comerciales para una empresa ubicada en territorio de la otra Parte.

- Personal de relaciones públicas y de publicidad que brinde asesoría a clientes o que asista o participe en convenciones.

---

[1] Para México, Agente Aduanal es la persona física autorizada por la Secretaría de Hacienda y Crédito Público, mediante una patente, para promover por cuenta ajena el despacho de las mercancías, en los diferentes regímenes aduaneros previstos en la Ley Aduanera.

- Personal de turismo (agentes de excursiones y de viajes, guías de turistas u operadores de viajes) que asista o participe en convenciones o conduzca alguna excursión que se haya iniciado en territorio de la otra Parte.

- Traductores o intérpretes que presten servicios como empleados de una empresa ubicada en territorio de la otra Parte.

Apéndice 12-04(A)(2)
Medidas Migratorias Vigentes

1.   Para el caso de México, Ley General de Población, 1974, con sus reformas y reglamentos, y Manual de Trámites Migratorios, 21 de septiembre 2000.

2.   Para el caso de Uruguay, Decreto del 28 de febrero de 1947 y Decreto 441/01.

Apéndice12-04(D)(1)[2]
Profesionales

PROFESIÓN[3]	REQUISITOS ACADÉMICOS MÍNIMOS Y TÍTULOS ALTERNATIVOS
Científico	
Agrónomo	Grado de Licenciatura
Apicultor	Grado de Licenciatura
Astrónomo	Grado de Licenciatura
Biólogo	Grado de Licenciatura
Bioquímico	Grado de Licenciatura
Científico en Animales	Grado de Licenciatura
Científico en Aves de Corral	Grado de Licenciatura
Científico en Lácteos	Grado de Licenciatura
Criador de Animales	Grado de Licenciatura
Edafólogo	Grado de Licenciatura
Entomólogo	Grado de Licenciatura
Epidemiólogo	Grado de Licenciatura
Farmacólogo	Grado de Licenciatura
Físico	Grado de Licenciatura
Fitocultor	Grado de Licenciatura
Genetista	Grado de Licenciatura
Geofísico	Grado de Licenciatura
Geólogo	Grado de Licenciatura
Geoquímico	Grado de Licenciatura
Horticultor	Grado de Licenciatura

---

[2] Las Partes establecerán la lista definitiva de profesionales, a más tardar sesenta (60) días después de la firma del presente Tratado.

[3] La persona de negocios que solicite entrada temporal conforme a este Apéndice podrá desempeñar funciones de adiestramiento relacionadas con su profesión, incluida la impartición de seminarios.

Meteorólogo	Grado de Licenciatura
Químico	Grado de Licenciatura
Zoólogo	Grado de Licenciatura

General

Abogado	Grado de Licenciatura
Administrador de fincas (Conservador de fincas)	Grado de Licenciatura
Administrador Hotelero	Grado de Licenciatura en administración de hoteles/restaurantes; Certificado Post achillerato"[4] en administración de hoteles/restaurantes y tres años de experiencia en administración de hoteles/restaurantes.
Ajustador de Seguros contra Desastres (empleado por una compañía ubicada en el territorio de una Parte, o un ajustador independiente)	Grado de Licenciatura y haber completado exitosamente el entrenamiento en las áreas apropiadas del ajuste de seguros correspondientes a demandas de reparación de daños causados por desastres; o tres años de experiencia en ajustes y haber completado exitosamente el entrenamiento en las áreas correspondientes del ajuste de demandas por daños ocasionados por desastres
Analista de Sistemas	Grado de Licenciatura o "Diploma o Certificado Post-bachillerato" y tres años de experiencia
Arquitecto	Grado de Licenciatura
Arquitecto del Paisaje	Grado de Licenciatura
Asistente de Investigación (que trabaje en una institución educativa Post-bachillerato)	Grado de Licenciatura
Bibliotecario	Grado de Licenciatura
Consultor en Administración	Grado de Licenciatura o experiencia profesional equivalente, según lo determine una declaración o título profesional que haga constar cinco años de experiencia como consultor en administración o cinco años de experiencia en un campo de especialidad relacionado con la consultoría en administración
Contador	Grado de Licenciatura
Diseñador de Interiores	Grado de Licenciatura o "Diploma o Certificado Post-bachillerato" y tres años de experiencia
Diseñador Gráfico	Grado de Licenciatura o "Diploma o Certificado Post-bachillerato" y tres años de experiencia

---

[4] El término "Certificado post-bachillerato" significa un certificado expedido, una vez completados dos o más años de educación post-bachillerato en una institución académica por el gobierno federal o un gobierno estatal mexicano, una institución académica reconocida por el gobierno federal o estatal, o una institución académica creada por ley federal o estatal.

Diseñador Industrial	Grado de Licenciatura o "Diploma o Certificado Post-bachillerato" y tres años de experiencia
Economista	Grado de Licenciatura
Escritor de Publicaciones Técnicas	Grado de Licenciatura o Diploma o Certificado Post- bachillerato y tres años de experiencia
Ingeniero	Grado de Licenciatura o licencia estatal
Ingeniero Forestal	Grado de Licenciatura o licencia estatal
Matemático (incluye a los estadígrafos)	Grado de Licenciatura
Orientador Vocacional	Grado de Licenciatura
Planificador Urbano (incluye "Geógrafo")	Grado de Licenciatura
Silvicultor (Incluye Especialista Forestal)	Grado de Licenciatura
Técnico/Tecnólogo Científico[5]	Poseer:

(a) conocimiento teórico en cualquiera de las siguientes disciplinas: ciencias agrícolas, astronomía, biología, química, ingeniería, silvicultura, geología, geofísica, meteorología o física; y

(b) capacidad para resolver problemas prácticos en cualquiera de tales disciplinas, o aplicar los principios de las disciplinas a la investigación básica o aplicada

Topógrafo	Grado de Licenciatura ; o licencia estatal/ federal
Trabajador Social	Grado de Licenciatura

Profesionales Médicos/ Asociados

Dentista	Doctor en Odontología o Doctor en Cirugía Dental
Dietista	Grado de Licenciatura
Enfermera Registrada	Grado de Licenciatura
Farmacéutico	Grado de Licenciatura
Médico (sólo enseñanza o investigación)	Doctor en Medicina
Médico Veterinario Zootécnico	Doctor en Veterinaria
Nutriólogo	Grado de Licenciatura
Sicólogo	Grado de Licenciatura
Tecnólogo Médico[6]	Certificado Post-bachillerato y tres años de experiencia

---

[5] Una persona de negocios en esta categoría solicitará entrada temporal para trabajar apoyando directamente a profesionales en ciencias agrícolas, astronomía, biología, química, ingeniería, silvicultura, geología, geofísica, meteorología o física.

Terapeuta Fisiológico y Físico	Grado de Licenciatura
Terapeuta Ocupacional	Grado de Licenciatura
Terapeuta Recreativo	Grado de Licenciatura

Profesor

| Seminario | Grado de Licenciatura |
| Universidad | Grado de Licenciatura |

CAPÍTULO XIII
INVERSIÓN

SECCIÓN A. Definiciones

Artículo 13-01: Definiciones.

Para efectos de este capítulo, se entenderá por:

acciones de capital u obligaciones: incluyen acciones con o sin derecho a voto, bonos o instrumentos de deuda convertibles, opciones sobre acciones y garantías;

CIADI: el Centro Internacional de Arreglo de Diferencias Relativas a Inversiones;

Convenio del CIADI: el Convenio sobre Arreglo de diferencias Relativas a Inversiones entre Estados y Nacionales de otros Estados, celebrado en Washington el 18 de marzo de 1965;

Convención Interamericana: la Convención Interamericana sobre Arbitraje Comercial Internacional, celebrada en Panamá el 30 de enero de 1975;

Convención de Nueva York: la Convención de Naciones Unidas sobre el Reconocimiento y ejecución de las Sentencias Arbitrales Extranjeras, celebrada en Nueva York, el 10 de junio de 1958;

empresa: cualquier entidad constituida u organizada conforme a la legislación vigente de alguna de las Partes, tenga o no fines de lucro y sea de propiedad privada o gubernamental, incluidas las sociedades, sucursales, fideicomisos, participaciones, empresas de propietario único, coinversiones u otras asociaciones que realizan o que tengan contemplado realizar, directa o indirectamente, actividades necesarias para la producción de un bien o la prestación de un servicio en el país receptor de la inversión;

empresa de una Parte: una empresa constituida u organizada de conformidad con la ley de una Parte; y una sucursal ubicada en territorio de una Parte y que desempeñe actividades comerciales en el mismo;

---

[6] La persona de negocios en esta categoría solicitará entrada temporal para desempeñar actividades en un laboratorio de pruebas y análisis químicos, biológicos, hematológicos, inmunológicos, microscópicos o bacteriológicos para el diagnóstico, tratamiento o prevención de enfermedades.

---

inversión: significa los siguientes activos

    a)   una empresa;

    b)   acciones representativas del capital de una empresa;

    c)   instrumentos de deuda de una empresa:

        i)   cuando la empresa es una filial del inversionista, o

        ii)   cuando la fecha de vencimiento original del instrumento de deuda sea por lo menos de (3) tres años,

pero no incluye un instrumento de deuda del Estado o de una empresa del Estado, independientemente de la fecha original del vencimiento

    d)   un préstamo a una empresa:

        i)   cuando la empresa es una filial del inversionista, o

        ii)   cuando la fecha de vencimiento original del préstamo sea por lo menos de (3) tres años,

pero no incluye un préstamo a una empresa del Estado, independientemente de la fecha original del vencimiento;

    e)   una participación en una empresa, que le permita al propietario participar en los ingresos o en las utilidades de la empresa;

    f)   una participación en una empresa que otorgue derecho al propietario para participar del haber social de esa empresa en una liquidación, siempre que éste no derive de un instrumento de deuda o un préstamo excluidos conforme los literales c) o d);

    g)   bienes raíces u otra propiedad, tangibles o intangibles,[1] adquiridos con la expectativa de, o utilizados con el propósito de obtener un beneficio económico, o con el propósito de la producción de un bien o la prestación de un servicio, o para otros fines empresariales; y

    h)   la participación que resulte del capital u otros recursos comprometidos para el desarrollo de una actividad económica o productiva en territorio de la otra Parte, entre otros, conforme a:

        i)   contratos que involucran la presencia de la propiedad de un inversionista en territorio de la otra Parte, incluidos, las concesiones, los contratos de construcción y de llave en mano, o

---

[1] Para mayor certeza, éstos incluyen los derechos de propiedad intelectual de acuerdo a las categorías de propiedad intelectual que son objeto de protección conforme al capítulo XV (Propiedad Intelectual).

      ii)   contratos donde la remuneración depende sustancialmente de la producción, ingresos o ganancias de una empresa;

pero no se entenderá por inversión:

    i)   reclamaciones pecuniarias derivadas exclusivamente de:

      i)   contratos comerciales para la venta de bienes o servicios por un nacional o empresa en territorio de una Parte a una empresa en territorio de la otra Parte, o

      ii)   el otorgamiento de crédito en relación con una transacción comercial, como el financiamiento al comercio, salvo un préstamo cubierto por las disposiciones del literal d); o

    j)   cualquier otra reclamación pecuniaria;

que no conlleve los tipos de interés dispuestos en los literales a) a h).

institución financiera: cualquier intermediario financiero u otra empresa que esté autorizada para hacer negocios y esté regulada o supervisada como una institución financiera conforme a la legislación de la Parte en cuyo territorio se encuentre ubicada;

inversión de un inversionista de una Parte: la inversión propiedad o bajo control directo o indirecto de un inversionista de dicha Parte;

inversionista de una Parte: una Parte o una empresa de la misma, o un nacional o empresa de dicha parte, que pretenda realizar, realiza o ha realizado una inversión;

inversión de un país que no es Parte: un inversionista que no es inversionista de una Parte, que pretende realizar, realiza, o ha realizado una inversión,

inversionista contendiente: un inversionista que formula una reclamación en los términos de la sección C;

Parte contendiente: la Parte contra la cual se hace una reclamación en los términos de la Sección C;

parte contendiente: el inversionista contendiente o la Parte contendiente;

partes contendientes: el inversionista contendiente y la Parte contendiente;

Reglas de Arbitraje de CNUDMI: las Reglas de Arbitraje de la Comisión de Naciones Unidas sobre Derecho Mercantil Internacional (CNUDMI), aprobadas por la Asamblea General de las Naciones Unidas, el 15 de diciembre de 1976;

Secretario General: el Secretario General del CIADI;

transferencias: transferencia y pagos internacionales; y

tribunal: un tribunal arbitral establecido conforme al artículo 13-20 o 13-26.

SECCIÓN B. Inversión

Artículo 13-02: Ámbito de aplicación.

1.   Este capítulo se aplica a las medidas que adopte o mantenga una Parte relativas a:

   a)   los inversionistas de la otra Parte;

   b)   las inversiones de inversionistas de otra Parte realizadas en territorio de la Parte; y

   c)   en lo relativo al artículo 13-07, todas las inversiones en el territorio de la Parte.

2.   Este capítulo cubre tanto las inversiones existentes a la fecha de entrada en vigor de este Tratado como las inversiones hechas o adquiridas con posterioridad. Las disposiciones de este Tratado no se aplicarán a controversia, reclamo o diferendo alguno que haya surgido con anterioridad a su entrada en vigor.

3.   Una Parte tiene el derecho de desempeñar exclusivamente las actividades económicas señaladas en el Anexo IV (Actividades Reservadas al Estado), y de negarse a autorizar el establecimiento de inversiones en tales actividades.

4.   Este capítulo no se aplica a las medidas que adopte o mantenga una Parte en relación a inversionistas de la otra Parte e inversiones de tales inversionistas en instituciones financieras en el territorio de la Parte.

5   Ninguna disposición en este capítulo se interpretará en el sentido de impedir a una Parte prestar servicios sociales o llevar a cabo funciones, tales como la ejecución y aplicación de las leyes, servicios de readaptación social, pensión o seguro de desempleo o servicios de seguridad social, bienestar social, educación pública, capacitación pública, salud, y protección a la infancia, cuando se desempeñen de manera que no sea incompatible con este capítulo.

Artículo 13-03: Trato nacional.

1.   Cada Parte otorgará a los inversionistas de la otra Parte un trato no menos favorable que el que otorgue, en circunstancias similares, a sus propios inversionistas en lo referente al establecimiento, adquisición, expansión, administración, conducción, operación, venta u otra disposición de las inversiones.

2.   Cada Parte otorgará a las inversiones de inversionistas de la otra Parte un trato no menos favorable que el que otorga, en circunstancias similares, a las inversiones de sus propios inversionistas en el establecimiento, adquisición, expansión, administración, conducción, operación, venta u otra disposición de las inversiones.

3.   El trato otorgado por una Parte, de conformidad con los párrafos 1 y 2, significa, respecto a un estado o un departamento, un trato no menos favorable que el trato más favorable que ese estado o departamento otorgue, en circunstancias similares, a los inversionistas e inversiones de la Parte de la que forman parte integrante.

4.   Para mayor certeza, ninguna Parte podrá:

a)   imponer a un inversionista de otra Parte un requisito de que un nivel mínimo de participación accionaria en una empresa establecida en territorio de la Parte, esté en manos de sus nacionales, salvo que se trate de acciones nominativas para directivos o miembros fundadores de sociedades; o

b)   requerir que un inversionista de otra Parte, por razón de su nacionalidad, venda o disponga de cualquier otra manera de una inversión en territorio de una Parte.

Artículo 13-04: Trato de nación más favorecida.

1.   Cada Parte otorgará a los inversionistas de la otra Parte, trato no menos favorable que el que otorgue, en circunstancias similares, a los inversionistas de la otra Parte o de un país que no sea Parte, en lo referente al establecimiento, adquisición, expansión, administración, conducción, operación, venta u otra disposición de inversiones.

2.   Cada Parte otorgará a las inversiones de inversionistas de la otra Parte un trato no menos favorable que el que otorgue, en circunstancias similares, a las inversiones de inversionistas de la otra Parte o de un país que no sea Parte, en lo referente al establecimiento, adquisición, expansión, administración, conducción, operación, venta u otra disposición de inversiones.

Artículo 13-05: Nivel de trato.

Cada Parte otorgará a los inversionistas y a las inversiones de inversionistas de otra Parte el mejor de los tratos, requeridos por los artículos 13-03 y 13-04.

Artículo 13-06: Nivel mínimo de trato.

1.   Sujeto a lo dispuesto en el Anexo 13-06(1), cada Parte otorgará a las inversiones de los inversionistas de la otra Parte, trato acorde con el derecho internacional, incluido trato justo y equitativo, así como protección y seguridad plenas.

2.   Sin perjuicio por lo dispuesto en el párrafo 1 y no obstante lo dispuesto en el artículo 13-09, cada Parte otorgará a los inversionistas de la otra Parte y a las inversiones de inversionistas de la otra Parte, cuyas inversiones sufran pérdidas en su territorio debidas a conflictos armados o contiendas civiles, trato no discriminatorio respecto de cualquier medida que adopte o mantenga en relación con esas pérdidas.

3.   El párrafo segundo no se aplica a las medidas existentes relacionadas con subsidios o ventajas que pudieran ser incompatibles con el artículo 13-03, salvo por lo dispuesto por el artículo 13-09.

Artículo 13-07: Requisitos de desempeño.

1.   Ninguna Parte podrá imponer ni hacer cumplir cualquiera de los siguientes requisitos o hacer cumplir ningún compromiso o iniciativa, en relación con el establecimiento, adquisición, expansión, administración, conducción u operación de una inversión de un inversionista de una Parte o de un país no Parte en su territorio para:

a) exportar un determinado nivel o porcentaje de bienes o servicios;

b) alcanzar un determinado grado o porcentaje de contenido nacional;

c) adquirir o utilizar u otorgar preferencia a bienes producidos o a servicios prestados en su territorio, o adquirir bienes de productores o servicios de prestadores de servicios en su territorio;

d) relacionar en cualquier forma el volumen o valor de las importaciones con el volumen o valor de las exportaciones, o con el volumen de los ingresos de divisas extranjeras relacionadas con dicha inversión;

e) restringir las ventas en su territorio de los bienes o servicios que tal inversión produce o presta, relacionando de cualquier manera dichas ventas al volumen o valor de sus exportaciones o a ganancias que generen en divisas; o

f) transferir a una persona en su territorio, tecnología, un proceso productivo u otro conocimiento reservado, salvo cuando el requisito se imponga o el compromiso o iniciativa se hagan cumplir por un tribunal judicial o administrativo o autoridad competente para reparar una supuesta violación a las leyes en materia de competencia o para actuar de una manera que no sea incompatible con otras disposiciones de este Tratado.

2. La medida que exija que una inversión emplee una tecnología para cumplir en lo general con requisitos aplicables a salud, seguridad o medio ambiente, no se considerará incompatible con el párrafo 1(f). Para brindar mayor certeza, los artículos 13-03 y 13-04 se aplican a la citada medida.

3. Ninguna Parte podrá condicionar la recepción de una ventaja o que se continúe recibiendo la misma, en relación con una inversión en su territorio por parte de un inversionista de un país Parte o no Parte, al cumplimiento de cualquiera de los siguientes requisitos:

a) alcanzar un determinado grado o porcentaje de contenido nacional;

b) comprar, utilizar u otorgar preferencia a bienes producidos en su territorio, o a comprar bienes de productores en su territorio;

c) relacionar, en cualquier forma, el volumen o valor de las importaciones con el volumen o valor de las exportaciones, o con el monto de las entradas de divisas asociadas con dicha inversión; o

d) restringir las ventas en su territorio de los bienes o servicios que tal inversión produce o presta, relacionando de cualquier manera dichas ventas al volumen o valor de sus exportaciones o a las ganancias que generen en divisas.

4. Nada de lo dispuesto en el párrafo 3 se interpretará como impedimento para que una Parte condicione la recepción de una ventaja o la continuación de su recepción, en relación con una inversión en su territorio por parte de un inversionista de un país Parte o no Parte, al requisito de que ubique la producción, preste servicios, capacite o emplee trabajadores, construya o amplíe instalaciones particulares, o lleve a cabo investigación y desarrollo, en su territorio.

5.   Los párrafos 1 y 3 no se aplican a ningún otro requisito distinto a los señalados en esos párrafos.

6.   Siempre que dichas medidas no se apliquen de manera arbitraria o injustificada, o no constituyan una restricción encubierta al comercio o inversión internacionales, nada de lo dispuesto en los párrafos 1 b) o c) o 3 a) o b) se interpretará en el sentido de impedir a una Parte adoptar o mantener medidas, incluidas las de naturaleza ambiental, competencia, defensa del consumidor y demás necesarias para:

a)   asegurar el cumplimiento de leyes y reglamentaciones que no sean incompatibles con las disposiciones de este Tratado;

b)   proteger la vida o salud humana, animal o vegetal; o

c)   la preservación de recursos naturales no-renovables vivos o no.

Artículo 13-08: Altos ejecutivos y consejos de administración.

1.   Ninguna de las Partes podrá exigir que una empresa de esa Parte, que sea una inversión de un inversionista de la otra Parte, designe a individuos de alguna nacionalidad en particular para ocupar puestos de alta dirección.

2.   Una Parte podrá exigir que la mayoría de los miembros de un consejo de administración o de cualquier comité de tal consejo, de una empresa de esa Parte que sea una inversión de un inversionista de la otra Parte, sea de una nacionalidad en particular o sea residente en territorio de la Parte, siempre que el requisito no menoscabe significativamente la capacidad del inversionista para ejercer el control de su inversión.

Artículo 13-09: Reservas y excepciones.

1.   Los artículos 13-03, 13-04, 13-07 y 13-08 no se aplicarán a:

a)   cualquier medida disconforme existente que sea mantenida por:

i)   una Parte a nivel nacional o federal, o estatal o departamental, según corresponda, como se estipula en su lista del Anexo I (Reservas y Excepciones) o IV (Actividades Reservadas al Estado); o

ii)   un gobierno municipal; ni a

b)   la continuación o pronta renovación de cualquier medida disconforme a la que se refiere el literal a); o

c)   la reforma de cualquier medida disconforme a la cual se refiere en el literal a) siempre que dicha reforma no disminuya el grado de conformidad de la medida, tal y como estaba en vigor antes de la reforma, con los artículos 13-03, 13-04, 13-07 y 13-08.

2.   A partir de la entrada en vigor de este Tratado, ninguna de las Partes incrementará el grado de disconformidad de sus medidas existentes respecto a los artículos 13-03, 13-04 y 13-07

y 13-08. Las Partes listarán sus medidas disconformes en el Anexo I (Reservas y Excepciones), el cual deberá ser completado por las Partes a más tardar en un plazo de un plazo de un año a partir de la entrada en vigor de este Tratado.

3.   Cada Parte tendrá un año a partir de la fecha de entrada en vigor de este Tratado para indicar en su lista del Anexo I (Reservas y Excepciones) cualquier medida disconforme que, no incluyendo a los gobiernos locales mantenga un gobierno estatal o departamental.

4.   Los artículos 13-03 y 13-04 no se aplican a cualquier medida que constituya una excepción o derogación a las obligaciones, conforme al Artículo 15-04 (Trato nacional), como expresamente se señala en ese artículo.

5.   El artículo 13-04, no es aplicable al trato otorgado por una de las Partes de conformidad con los tratados, o con respecto a los sectores, estipulados en su lista del Anexo III (Excepciones al Trato de Nación más Favorecida).

6.   Los artículos 13-03, 13-04 y 13-08 no se aplican a:

   a)   las compras realizadas por una Parte o por una empresa del Estado; o

   b)   subsidios o aportaciones, incluyendo los préstamos, garantías y seguros respaldados por el gobierno, otorgados por una Parte o por una empresa del Estado.

7.   Las disposiciones contenidas en:

   a)   los párrafos 1 a), b) y c), y 3 a) y b) del artículo 13-07 no se aplicarán a los requisitos para calificación de los bienes y servicios con respecto a programas de promoción a las exportaciones y de ayuda externa;

   b)   los párrafos 1 b), c), f) y g), y 3 a) y b) del artículo 13-07 no se aplicarán a las compras realizadas por una Parte o por una empresa del Estado; y

   c)   los párrafos 3 a) y b) del artículo 13-07 no se aplicarán a los requisitos impuestos por una Parte importadora a los bienes que en virtud de su contenido, califiquen para aranceles o cuotas preferenciales.

Artículo 13-10: Transferencias.

1.   Cada Parte permitirá que todas las transferencias relacionadas con la inversión de un inversionista de la otra Parte en territorio de la Parte, se hagan en moneda libremente convertible sin restricciones y sin demora.

Dichas transferencias incluyen entre otras:

   a)   ganancias, dividendos, intereses, ganancias de capital, pagos por regalías, gastos por administración, asistencia técnica y otros cargos, ganancias en especie y otros montos derivados de la inversión;

   b)   productos derivados de la venta o liquidación, total o parcial, de la inversión;

c) pagos realizados conforme a un contrato del que sea parte un inversionista o su inversión, incluidos pagos efectuados conforme a un convenio de préstamo;

d) pagos efectuados de conformidad con el artículo 13-11; y

e) pagos que provengan de la aplicación de la Sección C.

2. En lo referente a las transacciones al contado (spot) de la divisa que vaya a transferirse, cada Parte permitirá que las transferencias se realicen en divisa de libre uso al tipo de cambio vigente en el mercado en la fecha de la transferencia.

3. Ninguna Parte podrá exigir a sus inversionistas, que efectúen transferencias de sus ingresos, ganancias, o utilidades u otros montos derivados de, o atribuibles a inversiones llevadas a cabo en territorio de otra Parte, ni los sancionará en caso de que no realicen la transferencia.

4. No obstante lo dispuesto en los párrafos 1 y 2, las Partes podrán impedir la realización de transferencias, por medio de la aplicación equitativa, no discriminatoria y de buena fe de sus leyes en los siguientes casos:

a) quiebra, insolvencia o protección de los derechos de los acreedores;

b) emisión, comercio y operaciones de valores;

c) infracciones penales;

d) informes de transferencias de divisas u otros instrumentos monetarios; o

e) garantía del cumplimiento de los fallos en procedimientos contenciosos.

5. El párrafo 3 no se interpretará como un impedimento para que una Parte, a través de la aplicación de sus leyes de manera equitativa, no discriminatoria y de buena fe, imponga cualquier medida relacionada con los literales a) al e) del párrafo 4.

6. No obstante lo dispuesto en el párrafo 1, una Parte podrá restringir las transferencias de ganancias en especie, en circunstancias en donde pudiera, de otra manera, restringir dichas transferencias conforme a lo dispuesto en este Tratado, incluyendo lo señalado en el párrafo 4.

Artículo 13-11: Expropiación e indemnización.

1. Ninguna Parte podrá nacionalizar ni expropiar, directa o indirectamente, una inversión de un inversionista de la otra Parte en su territorio, ni adoptar ninguna medida equivalente a la expropiación o nacionalización de esa inversión (expropiación), salvo que sea: a) por causa de utilidad pública; b) sobre bases no discriminatorias; c) con apego al principio de legalidad y al artículo 13-06; y d) mediante indemnización conforme a los párrafos 2 al 6.

2. La indemnización será equivalente al valor de mercado que tenga la inversión expropiada inmediatamente antes de que la medida expropiatoria se haya llevado a cabo (fecha de expropiación), y no reflejará ningún cambio en el valor debido a que la intención de expropiar se conoció con antelación a la fecha de expropiación. Los criterios de valuación incluirán en el

valor corriente, el valor del activo (incluyendo el valor fiscal declarado de bienes tangibles), así como otros criterios que resulten apropiados para determinar el valor de mercado.

3.   El pago de la indemnización se hará sin demora y será completamente liquidable.

4.   La cantidad pagada no será inferior a la cantidad equivalente que por indemnización se hubiese pagado en la fecha de expropiación en una divisa de libre conversión en el mercado financiero internacional y dicha divisa se hubiese convertido a la cotización de mercado vigente en la fecha de valuación, más los intereses correspondientes a una tasa comercial razonable para dicha divisa hasta la fecha de pago.

5.   Una vez pagada, la indemnización podrá transferirse libremente de conformidad con el artículo 13-10.

6.   Este artículo no se aplica a la expedición de licencias obligatorias otorgadas en relación a derechos de propiedad intelectual, o a la revocación, limitación o creación de dichos derechos en la medida que dicha expedición revocación, limitación o creación sea conforme con el capítulo XV (Propiedad Intelectual).

Artículo 13-12: Formalidades especiales y requisitos de información.

1.   Nada de lo dispuesto en el artículo 13-03 se interpretará en el sentido de impedir a una Parte adoptar o mantener una medida que prescriba formalidades especiales conexas al establecimiento de inversiones por inversionistas de otra Parte, tales como el requisito de que los inversionistas sean residentes de la Parte o que las inversiones se constituyan conforme a las leyes y reglamentos de la Parte, siempre que dichas formalidades no menoscaben significativamente la protección otorgada por una Parte a inversionistas de la otra Parte y a inversiones de inversionistas de la otra Parte de conformidad con este capítulo.

2.   No obstante lo dispuesto en los artículos 13-03 y 13-04, una Parte podrá exigir de un inversionista de la otra Parte o de su inversión, en su territorio, que proporcione información rutinaria referente a esa inversión exclusivamente con fines de información o estadística. La Parte protegerá de cualquier divulgación la información que sea confidencial, que pudiera afectar negativamente la situación competitiva de la inversión o del inversionista. Nada de lo dispuesto en este párrafo se interpretará como un impedimento para que una Parte obtenga o divulgue información referente a la aplicación equitativa y de buena fe de su legislación.

Artículo 13-13: Relación con otros capítulos.

1.   En caso de incompatibilidad entre este capítulo y otro capítulo prevalecerá la de este último en la medida de la incompatibilidad.

2.   Si una Parte requiere a un prestador de servicios de la otra Parte que deposite una fianza u otra forma de garantía financiera como condición para prestar un servicio en su territorio; ello, por sí mismo no hace aplicable este capítulo a la prestación transfronteriza de ese servicio. Este capítulo se aplica al trato que otorgue esa Parte a la fianza depositada o garantía financiera.

Artículo 13-14: Denegación de beneficios.

Previa notificación y consulta, de conformidad con los artículos 16-03 (Notificación y suministro de información) y 18-03 (Consultas), una Parte podrá denegar los beneficios de este capítulo a un inversionista de la otra Parte que sea una empresa de dicha Parte y a las inversiones de tal inversionista, si inversionistas de un país que no sea Parte, son propietarios o controlan la empresa y ésta no tiene actividades empresariales sustanciales en el territorio de la Parte conforme a cuya ley está constituida u organizada.

SECCION C. Solución de controversias entre una Parte y un inversionista de otra Parte.

Artículo 13-15: Objetivo.

Sin perjuicio de los derechos y obligaciones de las Partes establecidos en el capítulo XVIII, (Solución de Controversias), esta sección establece un mecanismo para la solución de controversias en materia de inversión que asegura el trato igual entre inversionistas de las Partes de acuerdo con el principio de reciprocidad internacional, asegurando el debido proceso legal y la imparcialidad de los tribunales.

Artículo 13-16: Reclamación del inversionista de una Parte por cuenta propia, en virtud de los daños y perjuicios sufridos por él mismo.

1.   De conformidad con esta sección el inversionista de una Parte podrá someter a arbitraje una reclamación en el sentido de que la otra Parte ha violado una obligación establecida en:

   a)   la Sección B o el artículo 14-04, párrafo 2, (Empresas del Estado); o

   b)   el artículo 14-03, párrafo 4, literal a) (Monopolios), cuando el monopolio ha actuado de manera incompatible con las obligaciones de la Parte de conformidad con la Sección B;

   y que el inversionista ha sufrido pérdidas o daños en virtud de la violación o a consecuencia de ella.

2.   El inversionista no podrá presentar una reclamación si han transcurrido más de 3 (tres) años a partir de la fecha en la cual tuvo conocimiento por primera vez o debió haber tenido conocimiento de la presunta violación, y de que sufrió pérdidas o daños.

Artículo 13-17: Reclamación del inversionista de una Parte en representación de una empresa, en virtud de daños sufridos por una empresa de la otra Parte que sea una persona jurídica propiedad del inversionista o que esté bajo su control directo o indirecto.

1.   El inversionista de una Parte podrá someter a arbitraje, de conformidad con esta sección, una reclamación en el sentido de que la otra Parte ha violado una obligación establecida en:

   (a)   la Sección B o el artículo 14-04, párrafo 2, (Empresas del Estado); o

(b)   el Artículo 14-03, párrafo 4, literal a) (Monopolios), cuando el monopolio haya actuado de manera incompatible con las obligaciones de la Parte de conformidad con la Sección B,

y que una empresa de la otra Parte que sea una persona jurídica propiedad del inversionista o que esté bajo su control directo o indirecto ha sufrido pérdidas o daños en virtud de esa violación o a consecuencia de ella.

2.   Un inversionista no podrá presentar una reclamación conforme el párrafo 1, si han transcurrido más de 3 (tres) años a partir de la fecha en la cual la empresa tuvo conocimiento por primera vez, o debió tener conocimiento de la presunta violación y de que sufrió pérdidas o daños.

3.   Cuando un inversionista presente una reclamación de conformidad con este artículo y de manera paralela el inversionista o un inversionista que no tenga el control de una empresa, presente una reclamación en los términos del artículo 13-16 como consecuencia de los mismos actos que dieron lugar a la presentación de una reclamación de acuerdo con este artículo, y dos o más demandas se sometan a arbitraje en los términos del artículo 13-20, el Tribunal establecido conforme al artículo 13-26, examinará conjuntamente dichas demandas, salvo que el Tribunal determine que los intereses de una parte contendiente se verían perjudicados.

4.   Una inversión no podrá presentar una reclamación conforme a esta sección.

Artículo 13-18: Solución de una reclamación mediante consulta y negociación.

Las partes contendientes intentarán primero dirimir la controversia por vía de consulta o negociación.

Artículo 13-19: Notificación de la intención de someter la reclamación a arbitraje.

El inversionista contendiente notificará por escrito a la Parte contendiente su intención de someter una reclamación a arbitraje, cuando menos 90 días antes de que se presente formalmente la reclamación, y la notificación señalará lo siguiente:

a)   el nombre y domicilio del inversionista contendiente; y cuando la reclamación se haya realizado conforme el artículo 13-17, incluirá el nombre y la dirección de la empresa;

b)   las disposiciones de este Tratado presuntamente incumplidas y cualquier otra disposición aplicable;

c)   las cuestiones de hecho y de derecho en que se funda la reclamación; y

d)   la reparación que se solicita y el monto aproximado de los daños reclamados.

Artículo 13-20: Sometimiento de la reclamación al arbitraje.

1.   Siempre que hayan transcurrido 6 (seis) meses desde que tuvieron lugar los actos que motivan la reclamación, un inversionista contendiente podrá someter la reclamación a arbitraje de acuerdo con:

a)	el Convenio del CIADI, siempre que tanto la Parte contendiente como la Parte del inversionista, sean Estados parte del mismo;

b)	las Reglas del Mecanismo Complementario del CIADI, cuando la Parte contendiente o la Parte del inversionista, pero no ambas, sea Parte del Convenio del CIADI; o

c)	las Reglas de Arbitraje de CNUDMI.

2.	Si un inversionista contendiente o una empresa de la otra Parte que sea una persona jurídica propiedad del inversionista o que esté bajo su control directo o indirecto, inician procedimientos ante un tribunal nacional respecto a una medida que constituya un supuesto incumplimiento de conformidad con los artículos 13-16 ó 13-17, la controversia no podrá someterse a arbitraje, de acuerdo con esta sección. Asimismo, en caso de que un inversionista haya sometido la controversia a arbitraje internacional, la elección de ese procedimiento será definitiva.

3.	En caso de que un inversionista de una Parte someta una reclamación a arbitraje, la inversión – la empresa de la otra Parte que sea una persona jurídica propiedad del inversionista o que esté bajo su control directo o indirecto-, no podrán iniciar o continuar procedimientos ante un tribunal nacional o cualquier otro procedimiento de solución de controversias reclamando la misma medida.

4.	Las reglas de arbitraje aplicables al procedimiento de solución de controversias seguirán ese procedimiento salvo en la medida de lo modificado en esta sección.

Artículo 13-21: Presupuestos del sometimiento de una reclamación al procedimiento arbitral.

1.	Un inversionista contendiente podrá someter una reclamación al procedimiento arbitral de conformidad con el artículo 13-16, sólo si:

a)	consiente someterse al arbitraje en los términos de los procedimientos establecidos en este Tratado; y

b)	el inversionista y la empresa, cuando la reclamación se refiera a pérdida o daño de una participación de una empresa de otra Parte que sea una persona moral propiedad del inversionista o que esté bajo su control directo o indirecto, renuncian a su derecho a iniciar o continuar cualquier procedimiento ante un tribunal administrativo o judicial conforme al derecho de cualquiera de las Partes u otros procedimientos de solución de controversias respecto a la medida presuntamente violatoria de las disposiciones a las que se refiere el artículo 13-16. Lo anterior, salvo los procedimientos en que se solicite la aplicación de medidas precautorias de carácter suspensivo, declaratorio o extraordinario, que no impliquen el pago de daños ante el tribunal administrativo o judicial, conforme a la legislación de la Parte contendiente.

2.	Un inversionista contendiente podrá someter una reclamación al procedimiento arbitral de conformidad con el artículo 13-17, sólo si tanto el inversionista como la empresa:

a) consienten en someterse al arbitraje en los términos de los procedimientos establecidos en este Tratado; y

b) renuncian a su derecho de iniciar o continuar cualquier procedimiento con respecto a la medida de la Parte contendiente que presuntamente sea una de las violaciones a las que se refiere el artículo 13-17 ante cualquier tribunal administrativo o judicial conforme al derecho de cualquiera de las Partes u otros procedimientos de solución de controversias. Lo anterior, salvo los procedimientos en que se solicite la aplicación de medidas precautorias de carácter suspensivo, declarativo o extraordinario, que no impliquen el pago de daños ante el tribunal administrativo o judicial, conforme al derecho de la Parte contendiente.

3.   El consentimiento y la renuncia requeridos por este artículo se manifestarán por escrito, se entregarán a la Parte contendiente y se incluirán en el sometimiento de la reclamación a arbitraje.

4.   Solo en el caso que la Parte contendiente haya privado al inversionista contendiente del control en una empresa:

a) no se requerirá la renuncia de la empresa conforme al párrafo 1 b) o 2 b); y

b) no será aplicable, en lo conducente los párrafos 2 y 3 del artículo 13-20.

Artículo 13-22: Consentimiento al arbitraje.

1.   Cada Parte consiente en someter reclamaciones a arbitraje de conformidad a los procedimientos establecidos en este Tratado.

2.   El consentimiento a que se refiere el párrafo 1 y el sometimiento de una reclamación a arbitraje por parte de un inversionista contendiente cumplirá con los requisitos señalados en:

a) el Capítulo II del Convenio del CIADI (Jurisdicción del Centro) y las Reglas del Mecanismo Complementario que exigen el consentimiento por escrito de las Partes;

b) el Artículo II de la Convención de Nueva York, que exige un acuerdo por escrito; y

c) el Artículo I de la Convención Interamericana, que requiere un acuerdo.

Artículo 13-23: Número de árbitros y método de nombramiento.

Con excepción de lo que se refiere al tribunal establecido conforme al artículo 13-26, y a menos que las Partes contendientes acuerden otra cosa, el tribunal estará integrado por 3 (tres) árbitros. Cada Parte contendientes nombrará a uno. El tercer arbitro, quien será el presidente del tribunal arbitral, será designado por acuerdo de las partes contendientes.

Artículo 13-24: Integración del tribunal en caso de que una Parte no designe árbitro o las partes contendientes no logren un acuerdo en la designación del presidente del tribunal arbitral.

1.   El Secretario General del CIADI, (en adelante el Secretario General) nombrará a los árbitros en los procedimientos de arbitraje, de conformidad con esta sección.

2.   Cuando un tribunal, que no sea el establecido de conformidad con el artículo 13-26, no se integre en un plazo de noventa días a partir de la fecha en que la reclamación se someta al arbitraje, el Secretario General, a petición de cualquiera de las Partes contendientes, nombrará, a su discreción, al árbitro o árbitros no designados todavía, pero no al presidente del tribunal quién será designado conforme a lo dispuesto en el párrafo 3.

3.   El Secretario General designará al presidente del tribunal de entre los árbitros de la lista a la que se refiere el párrafo 4, asegurándose que el Presidente del Tribunal no sea nacional de la Parte contendiente o nacional de la Parte del inversionista contendiente. En caso de que no se encuentre en la lista un árbitro disponible para presidir el tribunal, el Secretario General designará, del Panel de árbitros del CIADI, al Presidente del tribunal arbitral, siempre que sea de nacionalidad distinta a la de cualquiera de las Partes.

4.   A la fecha de entrada en vigor de este Tratado, las Partes establecerán y mantendrán una lista de 10 árbitros como posibles presidentes de tribunal arbitral, que reúnan las cualidades establecidas en el Convenio y en las reglas contempladas en el artículo 13-20 y que cuenten con experiencia en derecho internacional y en asuntos en materia de inversión. Los miembros de la lista serán designados por consenso sin importar su nacionalidad.

Artículo 13-25: Consentimiento para la designación de árbitros.

Para los propósitos del Artículo 39 del Convenio del CIADI y del Artículo 7 de la Parte C de las Reglas del Mecanismo Complementario, y sin perjuicio de objetar a un árbitro de conformidad con el artículo 13-24(3) o sobre base distinta a la nacionalidad:

a)   la Parte contendiente acepta la designación de cada uno de los miembros de un tribunal establecido de conformidad con el Convenio del CIADI o con las Reglas del Mecanismo Complementario;

b)   un inversionista contendiente al que se refiere el artículo 13-16, podrá someter una reclamación a arbitraje o continuar el procedimiento conforme al Convenio de CIADI o a las Reglas del Mecanismo Complementario, únicamente a condición de que el inversionista contendiente manifieste su consentimiento por escrito sobre la designación de cada uno de los miembros del tribunal; y

c)   el inversionista contendiente al que se refiere el artículo 13-17 (1) podrá someter una reclamación a arbitraje o continuar el procedimiento conforme al Convenio del CIADI o las Reglas del Mecanismo Complementario, únicamente a condición de que el inversionista contendiente y la empresa manifiesten su consentimiento por escrito sobre la designación de cada uno de los miembros del Tribunal.

Artículo 13-26: Acumulación de procedimientos.

1.   Un tribunal establecido conforme a este artículo se instalará con apego a las Reglas de Arbitraje de CNUDMI y procederá de conformidad con lo contemplado en dichas Reglas, salvo lo que disponga esta sección.

2.   Cuando un tribunal establecido conforme a este artículo determine que las reclamaciones sometidas a arbitraje de acuerdo con el artículo 13-20 planteen cuestiones en común de hecho o de derecho, el tribunal, en interés de una resolución justa y eficiente, y habiendo escuchado a las Partes contendientes, podrá ordenar que:

      a)   asuma jurisdicción, sustancie y resuelva todas o parte de las reclamaciones, de manera conjunta; o

      b)   asuma jurisdicción, sustancie y resuelva una o más de las reclamaciones sobre la base de que ello contribuirá a la resolución de las otras.

3.   Una parte contendiente que pretenda se determine la acumulación en los términos del párrafo 2, solicitará al Secretario General que instale un tribunal y especificará en su solicitud:

      a)   el nombre de la Parte contendiente o de los inversionistas contendientes contra los cuales se pretenda obtener la orden de acumulación;

      b)   la naturaleza de la orden de acumulación solicitada; y

      c)   el fundamento en que se apoya la solicitud.

4.   Una parte contendiente entregará copia de su solicitud a la otra Parte contendiente o a los inversionistas contendientes contra quienes se pretende obtener la orden de acumulación.

5.   En un plazo de 60 días a partir de la fecha de la recepción de la solicitud, el Secretario General instalará un tribunal integrado por tres árbitros. El Secretario General nombrará al Presidente del tribunal de la lista de árbitros a la que se refiere el artículo 13-24 (4). En caso de que no se encuentre en la lista un árbitro disponible para presidir el tribunal, el Secretario General designará, de la lista de Árbitros del CIADI, al presidente del tribunal quien no será nacional de ninguna de las Partes. El Secretario General designará a los otros dos integrantes del tribunal; de la lista a la que se refiere el Artículo 13-24 (4) y, cuando no estén disponibles en dicha lista los seleccionará de la lista de Árbitros de CIADI; de no haber disponibilidad de árbitros en esta lista, el Secretario General hará discrecionalmente los nombramientos faltantes. Uno de los miembros será nacional de la Parte contendiente y el otro miembro del tribunal será nacional de una Parte de los inversionistas contendientes.

6.   Cuando se haya establecido un tribunal conforme a este artículo, el inversionista contendiente que haya sometido una reclamación a arbitraje conforme al artículo 13-16 ó 13-17 y no haya sido mencionado en la solicitud de acumulación hecha de acuerdo con el párrafo 3, podrá solicitar por escrito al Tribunal que se le incluya en una orden formulada de acuerdo con el párrafo 2, y especificará en dicha solicitud:

      a)   el nombre y domicilio del inversionista contendiente;

b) la naturaleza de la orden de acumulación solicitada; y

c) los fundamentos en que se apoya la solicitud.

7. Un inversionista contendiente al que se refiere el párrafo 6, entregará copia de su solicitud a las Partes contendientes señaladas en una solicitud hecha conforme al párrafo 3.

8. Un tribunal establecido conforme al artículo 13-20 no tendrá jurisdicción para resolver una reclamación, o parte de ella, respecto de la cual haya asumido jurisdicción un tribunal establecido conforme a este artículo.

9. A solicitud de una parte contendiente, un tribunal establecido de conformidad con este artículo podrá, en espera de su decisión conforme al párrafo 2, disponer que los procedimientos de un tribunal establecido de acuerdo al artículo 13-20 se aplacen, a menos que ese último tribunal haya suspendido sus procedimientos.

10. Una Parte contendiente entregará al Secretariado en un plazo de 15 días a partir de la fecha en que se reciba por la Parte contendiente:

a) una solicitud de arbitraje hecha conforme al párrafo 1 del Artículo 36 del Convenio del CIADI;

b) una notificación de arbitraje en los términos del Artículo 2 de la Parte C de las Reglas del Mecanismo Complementario del CIADI; o

c) una notificación de arbitraje en los términos previstos por las Reglas de Arbitraje de CNUDMI.

11. Una Parte contendiente entregará al Secretariado copia de la solicitud formulada en los términos del párrafo 3:

a) en un plazo de 15 días a partir de la recepción de la solicitud, en el caso de una petición hecha por el inversionista contendiente; o

b) en un plazo de 15 días a partir de la fecha de la solicitud, en el caso de una petición hecha por la Parte contendiente.

12. Una Parte contendiente entregará al Secretariado, copia de una solicitud formulada en los términos del párrafo 6 en un plazo de 15 días a partir de la fecha de recepción de la solicitud.

13. El Secretariado conservará un registro público de los documentos a los que se refieren los párrafos 10, 11- y 12.

Artículo 13-27: Notificación.

La Parte contendiente entregará a la otra Parte:

a) notificación escrita de una reclamación que se haya sometido a arbitraje a más tardar 30 días después de la fecha de sometimiento de la reclamación a arbitraje; y

b)   copias de todos los escritos presentados en el procedimiento arbitral.

Artículo 13-28: Participación de una Parte.

Previa notificación escrita a las partes contendientes, una Parte podrá comunicar a un tribunal su interpretación jurídica sobre cuestiones vinculadas a la interpretación de las disposiciones de este tratado, en el marco de la controversia de que se trate.

Artículo 13-29: Documentación.

1.   Una Parte tendrá, a su costa, derecho a recibir de la Parte contendiente una copia de:

a)   las pruebas ofrecidas al tribunal; y

b)   los argumentos escritos presentados por las Partes contendientes.

2.   Una Parte que reciba información conforme a lo dispuesto en el párrafo 1, dará tratamiento a la información como si fuera una Parte contendiente.

Artículo 13-30: Sede del procedimiento arbitral.

Salvo que las partes contendientes acuerden otra cosa, un tribunal llevará a cabo el procedimiento arbitral en territorio de una Parte que sea parte de la Convención de Nueva York, el cual será elegido de conformidad con:

a)   las Reglas del Mecanismo Complementario del CIADI, si el arbitraje se rige por esas reglas o por el Convenio del CIADI; o

b)   las Reglas de Arbitraje de CNUDMI, si el arbitraje se rige por esas reglas.

Artículo 13-31: Derecho aplicable.

1.   Un tribunal establecido conforme a esta sección decidirá las controversias que se sometan a su consideración de conformidad con este Tratado y con las reglas y principios del derecho internacional aplicables.

2.   La interpretación que formule la Comisión sobre una disposición de este Tratado, será obligatoria para un tribunal establecido de conformidad con esta sección.

Artículo 13-32: Interpretación de los anexos.

1.   Cuando una Parte alegue como defensa que una medida presuntamente violatoria cae en el ámbito de una reserva o excepción consignada en el Anexo I (Reservas y Excepciones), Anexo III (Excepciones al Trato de Nación más Favorecida) o Anexo IV (Actividades Reservadas al Estado), a petición de la Parte contendiente, el tribunal solicitará a la Comisión una interpretación sobre ese asunto. La Comisión, en un plazo de 60 días a partir de la entrega de la solicitud, presentará por escrito al tribunal su interpretación.

2.   De conformidad con el artículo 13-31(2), la interpretación de la Comisión sometida conforme al párrafo 1 será obligatoria para el Tribunal. Si la Comisión no somete una interpretación dentro de un plazo de 60 días, el Tribunal decidirá sobre el asunto.

Artículo 13-33: Dictámenes de expertos.

Sin perjuicio de la designación de otro tipo de expertos cuando lo autoricen las reglas de arbitraje aplicables, el tribunal, a petición de una parte contendiente, o por iniciativa propia a menos que las partes contendientes no lo acepten, podrá designar uno o más expertos para dictaminar por escrito cualquier cuestión de hecho relativa a asuntos ambientales, de salud, seguridad u otros asuntos científicos que haya planteado una parte contendiente en un procedimiento, de acuerdo a los términos y condiciones que acuerden las partes contendientes.

Artículo 13-34: Medidas provisionales de protección.

Un tribunal podrá ordenar o recomendar una medida provisional de protección para preservar los derechos de la parte contendiente o para asegurar que la jurisdicción del tribunal surta plenos efectos, incluso una orden para preservar las pruebas que estén en posesión o control de una parte contendiente, u ordenes para proteger la jurisdicción del tribunal. Un tribunal no podrá ordenar el embargo, ni la suspensión de la aplicación de la medida presuntamente violatoria a la que se refiere el artículo 13-16 ó 13-17.

Artículo 13-35: Laudo definitivo.

1.   Cuando un tribunal dicte un laudo definitivo desfavorable a la Parte, el tribunal sólo podrá otorgar, por separado o en combinación:

a)   reparación de daños pecuniarios y los intereses correspondientes;

b)   la restitución de la propiedad, en cuyo caso el laudo dispondrá que la Parte contendiente podrá pagar daños pecuniarios, más los intereses que proceda, en lugar de la restitución.

2.   Un tribunal podrá también disponer el pago de costas de acuerdo con las reglas de arbitraje aplicables.

3.   De conformidad con en el párrafo 1, cuando la reclamación se haga con base en el artículo 13-17(1):

a)   el laudo que prevea la restitución de la propiedad, dispondrá que la restitución se otorgue a la empresa;

b)   el laudo que conceda daños pecuniarios e intereses correspondientes, dispondrá que la suma de dinero se pague a la empresa; y

c)   el laudo dispondrá que el mismo se dicte sin perjuicio de cualquier derecho que cualquier persona tenga sobre la reparación conforme al derecho interno aplicable.

4.   Un tribunal no podrá ordenar que una Parte pague daños que tengan carácter punitivo.

Artículo 13-36: Carácter definitivo y ejecución del laudo.

1.   El laudo dictado por un tribunal será obligatorio sólo para las partes contendientes y únicamente respecto del caso concreto.

2.   Conforme a lo dispuesto en el párrafo 3 y al procedimiento de revisión aplicable a un laudo provisional, una parte contendiente acatará y cumplirá el laudo sin demora.

3.   Una parte contendiente no podrá solicitar la ejecución de un laudo definitivo en tanto:

   a)   en el caso de un laudo definitivo dictado conforme al Convenio del CIADI:

      i)   no hayan transcurrido 120 días desde la fecha en que se dictó el laudo y ninguna parte contendiente haya solicitado la revisión o anulación del mismo; o

      ii)   no hayan concluido los procedimientos de revisión o anulación; y

   b)   en el caso de un laudo definitivo conforme a las Reglas del Mecanismo Complementario del CIADI o las Reglas de Arbitraje de CNUDMI;

      i)   hayan transcurrido 3 (tres) meses desde la fecha en que se dictó el laudo y ninguna parte contendiente haya iniciado un procedimiento para revisarlo, desecharlo o anularlo; o

      ii)   un Tribunal haya desechado o admitido una solicitud de reconsideración, desechamiento o anulación del laudo y esta resolución no pueda recurrirse.

4.   Cada Parte dispondrá la debida ejecución de un laudo en su territorio.

5.   Cuando una Parte contendiente incumpla o no acate un laudo definitivo, la Comisión, a la entrega de una solicitud de una Parte cuyo inversionista fue parte en el procedimiento de arbitraje, integrará un panel conforme al artículo 18-04 (Solicitud de integración de un Tribunal Arbitral). La Parte solicitante podrá invocar dichos procedimientos para:

   a)   una determinación en el sentido de que el incumplimiento o desacato de los términos del laudo definitivo es contrario a las obligaciones de este Tratado; y

   b)   una recomendación en el sentido de que la Parte cumpla y acate el laudo definitivo.

6.   El inversionista contendiente podrá recurrir a la ejecución de un laudo arbitral conforme al Convenio del CIADI, la Convención de Nueva York o la Convención Interamericana, independientemente de que se hayan iniciado o no los procedimientos contemplados en el párrafo 5.

7.   Para los efectos del Artículo I de la Convención de Nueva York y del Artículo I de la Convención Interamericana, se considerará que la reclamación que se somete a arbitraje conforme a esta sección, surge de una relación u operación comercial.

Artículo 13-37: Disposiciones generales.

A. **Momento en que la reclamación se considera sometida al procedimiento arbitral.**

1. Una reclamación se considera sometida a arbitraje en los términos de esta sección cuando:

    a) la solicitud para un arbitraje conforme al párrafo 1 del Artículo 36 del Convenio del CIADI ha sido recibida por el Secretario General;

    b) la notificación de arbitraje de conformidad con el Artículo 2 de la Parte C de las Reglas del Mecanismo Complementario del CIADI ha sido recibida por el Secretario General; o

    c) la notificación de arbitraje contemplada en las Reglas de Arbitraje de CNUDMI se ha recibido por la Parte contendiente.

B. **Entrega de documentos.**

2. La entrega de la notificación y otros documentos a una Parte se hará en el lugar designado por ella en el Anexo 13-37.2.

C. **Pagos conforme a Contratos de Seguro o Garantía.**

3. En un procedimiento arbitral conforme a lo previsto en esta sección, una Parte no aducirá como defensa, contrademanda, derecho de compensación, u otros, que el inversionista contendiente ha recibido o recibirá, de acuerdo a un contrato de seguro o garantía, indemnización u otra compensación por todos o por parte de los presuntos daños.

D. **Publicación de laudos.**

4. El Anexo 13-37.4 se aplica a las Partes señaladas en ese anexo en lo referente a la publicación de laudos.

Artículo 13-38: Exclusiones.

1. Sin perjuicio de la aplicación o no aplicación de las disposiciones de solución de controversias de esta sección o del capítulo XVIII (Solución de Controversias), a otras acciones acordadas por una Parte de conformidad con el Artículo 19-03, (Seguridad Nacional), la resolución de una Parte que prohiba o restrinja la adquisición de una inversión en su territorio por un inversionista de la otra Parte o su inversión, de acuerdo con aquel artículo, no estará sujeta a dichas disposiciones.

2. Las disposiciones de solución de controversias de esta sección y las del capítulo XVIII (Solución de Controversias) no se aplicarán a las cuestiones a que se refiere el Anexo 13-38.2.

Anexo 13-06(1)
Nivel Mínimo de Trato conforme al Derecho Internacional

1.   El artículo 13-06(1) establece el nivel mínimo de trato a los extranjeros propio del derecho internacional consuetudinario, como el nivel mínimo de trato que debe otorgarse a las inversiones de los inversionistas de otra Parte.

2.   Los conceptos de "trato justo y equitativo" y "protección y seguridad plenas" no requieren un trato adicional al requerido por el nivel mínimo de trato a los extranjeros propio del derecho internacional consuetudinario, ni que vaya más allá de éste.

3.   Una resolución en el sentido de que se ha violado otra disposición de este Tratado o de un acuerdo internacional distinto no establece que se ha violado el artículo 13-06(1).

Anexo 13-37.2
Entrega de documentos a una Parte de conformidad con la Sección C

Para efectos del artículo 13-37 (2), el lugar para entrega de notificaciones y otros documentos bajo la sección C será:

1.   Para el caso de México:
Dirección General de Inversión Extranjera
Secretaría de Economía
Insurgentes Sur 1940, Piso 8,
Colonia Florida, C.P. 01030, México, D.F.

2.   Para el caso de Uruguay:
Ministerio de Economía y Finanzas
Colonia 1089
C.P. 11100, Montevideo, Uruguay

Anexo 13-37.4
Publicación de laudos

México

Cuando México sea la Parte contendiente, las reglas de procedimiento correspondientes se aplicarán con respecto a la publicación de un laudo.

Anexo 13-38.2

Exclusiones de las disposiciones de solución de controversias

México

Las disposiciones relativas al mecanismo de solución de controversias previsto en el capítulo XVIII (Solución de Controversias), no se aplicarán a una decisión de la Comisión Nacional de Inversiones Extranjeras que resulte de someter a revisión una inversión conforme a las disposiciones del Anexo I (Reservas y Excepciones) relativa a si debe o no permitirse una adquisición que esté sujeta a dicha revisión.

[...]

CAPÍTULO XV
PROPIEDAD INTELECTUAL

Sección A - Definiciones y disposiciones generales

Artículo 15-01: Definiciones.

Para efectos de este capítulo, se entenderá por:

Acuerdo sobre los ADPIC: el Acuerdo sobre los Aspectos de los Derechos de Propiedad Intelectual Relacionados con el Comercio, de fecha 15 de abril de 1994;

Convenio de Berna: el Convenio de Berna para la Protección de las Obras Literarias y Artísticas, conforme al Acta de París, de fecha 24 de julio de 1971;

Convenio de Ginebra: el Convenio para la Protección de los Productores de Fonogramas contra la Reproducción no Autorizada de sus Fonogramas, adoptado en la ciudad de Ginebra el 29 de octubre de 1971;

Convenio de París: el Convenio de París para la Protección de la Propiedad Industrial, conforme al Acta de Estocolmo, de fecha 14 de julio de 1967;

Convención de Roma: la Convención Internacional sobre Protección de los Artistas Intérpretes o Ejecutantes, de los Productores de Fonogramas y los Organismos de Radiodifusión, adoptada en la ciudad de Roma el 26 de octubre de 1961;

Convenio UPOV: el Convenio Internacional para la Protección de las Obtenciones Vegetales de 2 de diciembre de 1961, revisado en Ginebra el 10 de noviembre de 1972, conforme al Acta de 23 de octubre de 1978; y

derechos de propiedad intelectual: comprende todas las categorías de propiedad intelectual que son objeto de protección mediante este capítulo, en los términos que en este se indican.

Artículo 15-02: Protección de los derechos de propiedad intelectual

1.   Cada Parte otorgará en su territorio protección y defensa adecuada y eficaz para los derechos de propiedad intelectual a los que se refiere este capítulo y asegurará que las medidas destinadas a defender esos derechos no se conviertan, a su vez, en obstáculos al comercio legítimo.

2.   Cada Parte podrá prever en su legislación, una protección más amplia que la exigida en este capítulo, a condición de que tal protección no infrinja las disposiciones del mismo.

Artículo 15-03: Relación con otros convenios sobre propiedad intelectual.

1.   Ninguna disposición de este capítulo, referida a los derechos de propiedad intelectual, irá en detrimento de las obligaciones que las Partes puedan tener entre sí en virtud del Convenio de París, el Convenio de Berna, la Convención de Roma, el Convenio de Ginebra y el Convenio UPOV, ni perjudicará ningún derecho u obligación en virtud de otros tratados.

2.   Con objeto de otorgar protección y defensa adecuada y eficaz a los derechos de propiedad intelectual a los que se refiere este capítulo, las Partes aplicarán, cuando menos, las disposiciones sustantivas del Convenio de París, el Convenio de Berna, la Convención de Roma, el Convenio de Ginebra y el Convenio UPOV.

3.   Las Partes harán todo lo posible para adherirse al Tratado de la OMPI sobre Derecho de Autor de 1996 y al Tratado de la OMPI sobre Interpretación o Ejecución y Fonogramas de 1996, si aún no son parte de ellos a la fecha de entrada en vigor de este Tratado.

Artículo 15-04: Trato nacional.

1.   Cada Parte concederá a los nacionales de la otra Parte un trato no menos favorable que el que otorgue a sus nacionales con respecto a la protección de los derechos de propiedad intelectual previstos en este capítulo, a reserva de las excepciones ya previstas en, el Convenio de París, el Convenio de Berna, la Convención de Roma, Convenio de Ginebra y el Convenio de UPOV.

2.   Cada Parte podrá recurrir a las excepciones permitidas en el párrafo 1 en relación con los procedimientos judiciales y administrativos, para la protección de los derechos de propiedad intelectual incluida la designación de un domicilio legal o el nombramiento de un agente dentro de la jurisdicción de una Parte, solamente cuando tales excepciones:

      a)   sean necesarias para conseguir el cumplimiento de leyes y reglamentos que no sean incompatibles con las disposiciones de este capítulo; y

      b)   cuando tales prácticas no se apliquen de manera que constituyan una restricción encubierta del comercio.

3.   Ninguna Parte podrá exigir a los titulares de derechos de propiedad intelectual referidos en este capítulo, que cumplan con formalidad o condición alguna para adquirir derechos de autor y derechos conexos, como condición para el otorgamiento del trato nacional conforme a este artículo.

Artículo 15-05: Trato de la nación más favorecida.

Con respecto a la protección de los derechos de propiedad intelectual a los que se refiere este capítulo, toda ventaja, favor, privilegio o inmunidad que conceda una Parte a los nacionales de cualquier otro país no Parte, se otorgará inmediatamente y sin condiciones a los nacionales de la otra Parte. Quedan exentos de esta obligación toda ventaja, favor, privilegio o inmunidad concedidos por una Parte que:

a) se deriven de acuerdos internacionales sobre asistencia judicial u observancia de la ley de carácter general y no limitados en particular a la protección de la propiedad intelectual;

b) se hayan otorgado de conformidad con las disposiciones del Convenio de Berna o de la Convención de Roma que autorizan que el trato concedido no esté en función del trato nacional sino del trato dado en otro país; o

c) se refieran a los derechos de los artistas intérpretes o ejecutantes, los productores de fonogramas y los organismos de radiodifusión, que no estén previstos en este capítulo.

Artículo 15-06: Control de prácticas y condiciones abusivas o contrarias a la competencia.

Cada Parte podrá aplicar, siempre que sea compatible con lo dispuesto en este capítulo, medidas apropiadas para prevenir el abuso de los derechos de propiedad intelectual por sus titulares o el recurso a prácticas que limiten de manera injustificable el comercio o redunden en detrimento de la transferencia de tecnología.

Artículo 15-07: Cooperación para eliminar el comercio de bienes objeto de infracciones.

Las Partes cooperarán entre sí con objeto de eliminar el comercio de bienes que infrinjan los derechos de propiedad intelectual.

Sección B - Derechos de Autor

Artículo 15-08: Derechos de autor.

1. Cada Parte protegerá las obras comprendidas en el Artículo 2 del Convenio de Berna, incluyendo cualesquiera otras que incorporen una expresión original en el sentido que confiere a ese término dicho Convenio.

2. Cada Parte otorgará a los autores o a sus causahabientes los derechos que se enuncian en el Convenio de Berna con respecto a las obras contempladas en el párrafo 1.

3. Los programas de computación, sean programas fuente o programas objeto, serán protegidos como obras literarias en virtud del Convenio de Berna.

4. Las compilaciones de datos o de otros materiales, en forma legible por máquina o en otra forma, que por razones de la selección o disposición de sus contenidos constituyan creaciones de carácter intelectual, serán protegidas como tales. Esa protección no abarcará los datos o materiales en sí mismos y se entenderá sin perjuicio de cualquier derecho de autor que subsista respecto de dichos datos o materiales.

5. Al menos respecto de los programas de computación y de las obras cinematográficas, las Partes conferirán a los autores, causahabientes y demás titulares, el derecho de autorizar o prohibir el arrendamiento comercial al público de los originales o copias de sus obras amparadas por el derecho de autor. Se exceptuará a una Parte de esa obligación con respecto a las obras cinematográficas, a menos que, el arrendamiento haya dado lugar a una realización muy

extendida de copias de esas obras que menoscabe en medida importante el derecho exclusivo de reproducción conferido en dicha Parte a los autores, causahabientes y demás titulares. En lo referente a los programas de computación, esa obligación no se aplica a los arrendamientos cuyo objeto esencial no sea el programa en sí.

Artículo 15-09: Artistas intérpretes o ejecutantes.

1. Cada Parte otorgará a los artistas intérpretes o ejecutantes los derechos a que se refiere la Convención de Roma.

2. No obstante lo anterior, una vez que un artista intérprete o ejecutante haya consentido que se incorpore su actuación en una fijación visual o audiovisual, dejará de ser aplicable el Artículo 7 de la Convención de Roma.

Artículo 15-10: Productores de fonogramas.

1. Cada Parte otorgará a los productores de fonogramas, los derechos a que se refiere la Convención de Roma y el Convenio de Ginebra, incluyendo el derecho de autorizar o prohibir la primera distribución pública del original y de cada copia del fonograma mediante venta, arrendamiento o cualquier otro medio.

2. Cada Parte conferirá a los productores de fonogramas, conforme a su legislación, el derecho de autorizar o prohibir el arrendamiento comercial al público de los originales o copias de los fonogramas protegidos.

Artículo 15-11: Protección de señales de satélite portadoras de programas.

Dentro de los cinco años siguientes a la entrada en vigor de este Tratado, las Partes se comprometen a establecer que incurrirá en responsabilidad civil todo aquel que fabrique, importe, venda, de en arrendamiento, o realice un acto con un fin comercial, que permita tener dispositivos que sean de ayuda primordial para descifrar una señal de satélite cifrada portadora de programas, o use de éstos con fines comerciales, sin autorización del prestador o distribuidor legítimo del servicio, dependiendo de la legislación de cada Parte.

Artículo 15-12: Facultades conferidas a las Partes con respecto a derechos de autor y derechos conexos.

1. Cada Parte dispondrá que para los derechos de autor y derechos conexos, cualquier persona que adquiera o detente derechos económicos o patrimoniales:

   a) pueda libremente y por separado, transferirlos a cualquier título; y

   b) tenga la capacidad de ejercitar esos derechos en nombre propio y de disfrutar plenamente los beneficios derivados de los mismos.

2. Cada Parte circunscribirá las limitaciones y excepciones a los derechos de autor y derechos conexos a casos especiales determinados que no impidan su explotación normal, ni ocasionen perjuicios injustificados a los legítimos intereses del titular del derecho.

Artículo 15-13: Duración de los derechos de autor y de los derechos conexos.

1.   El derecho de autor dura toda la vida de éste y se extiende, como mínimo, hasta 50 años después de su muerte.

2.   Cuando la duración de la protección de una obra se calcule sobre una base distinta de la vida de una persona física o natural, esa duración será de no menos de 50 años contados desde el final del año calendario de la publicación autorizada o, a falta de tal publicación autorizada, dentro de un plazo de 50 años a partir de la realización de la obra, contados a partir del final del año calendario de su realización.

3.   La duración de la protección concedida a los artistas intérpretes o ejecutantes y los productores de fonogramas no podrá ser inferior a 50 años, contados a partir del final del año calendario en que se haya realizado la fijación o haya tenido lugar la interpretación o ejecución.

4.   La duración de la protección concedida a los organismos de radiodifusión será otorgada por cada Parte conforme a su legislación vigente.

Sección C – Marcas

Artículo 15-14: Materia objeto de la protección.

1.   Podrá constituir una marca cualquier signo o combinación de signos que sean capaces de distinguir los bienes o servicios de una persona física o jurídica de los de otra persona física o jurídica. Tales signos podrán registrarse como marcas, en particular las palabras, incluidos los nombres de personas, las letras, los números, los elementos figurativos y las combinaciones de colores, así como cualquier combinación de estos signos.

2.   Cuando los signos no sean intrínsecamente capaces de distinguir los bienes o servicios pertinentes, cada Parte podrá supeditar la posibilidad de registro de los mismos al carácter distintivo que hayan adquirido mediante su uso.

3.   Las marcas incluirán las de servicio y las colectivas, y dependiendo de la legislación de cada Parte incluirán las de certificación.

4.   Cada Parte podrá exigir como condición para el registro que los signos sean perceptibles visualmente.

5.   Cada Parte podrá establecer prohibiciones para el registro de marcas conforme a lo dispuesto en su legislación sobre la materia.

6.   La naturaleza del bien o servicio al que la marca ha de aplicarse no será en ningún caso obstáculo para el registro de la marca.

7.   De conformidad con su legislación, cada Parte publicará las marcas antes de su registro o prontamente después de él, y ofrecerá una oportunidad razonable de pedir la anulación del registro. Además cada Parte podrá ofrecer la oportunidad de oponerse al registro de una marca.

Artículo 15-15: Derechos conferidos.

El titular de una marca registrada gozará del derecho exclusivo de impedir que terceros, sin su consentimiento, utilicen en el curso de operaciones comerciales signos idénticos o similares para bienes o servicios que sean idénticos o similares a aquellos para los que se ha registrado la marca, cuando ese uso de lugar a probabilidad de confusión. Se presumirá que existe probabilidad de confusión en caso de que se use un signo idéntico o similar para bienes o servicios idénticos o similares. Los derechos antes mencionados se entenderán sin perjuicio de los derechos existentes con anterioridad y no afectarán la posibilidad de las Partes de reconocer derechos basados en el uso.

Artículo 15-16: Marcas notoriamente conocidas.

1.   Se entenderá que una marca es notoriamente conocida en una Parte, cuando un sector determinado del público o de los círculos comerciales de la Parte conozca la marca, como consecuencia de las actividades comerciales desarrolladas en esa Parte o fuera de ella, por una persona que emplea esa marca en relación con sus bienes o servicios, así como cuando se tenga conocimiento de la marca en el territorio de la Parte, como consecuencia de la promoción o publicidad de la misma.

2.   Cada Parte establecerá en su legislación los medios necesarios para impedir o anular el registro como marca de aquellos signos, iguales o similares a una marca notoriamente conocida, para ser aplicada a cualquier bien o servicio.

3.   Cada Parte aplicará el Artículo 16.3 del Acuerdo ADPIC.

4.   A efectos de demostrar la notoriedad de la marca, podrán emplearse todos los medios probatorios admitidos por la Parte en la cual se desea probar la notoriedad de la misma.

Artículo 15-17: Excepciones.

Las Partes podrán establecer excepciones limitadas a los derechos conferidos por una marca, por ejemplo, el uso leal de términos descriptivos, a condición de que en las excepciones se tengan en cuenta los intereses legítimos del titular de la marca y de terceros.

Artículo 15-18: Duración de la protección.

El registro inicial de una marca tendrá, por lo menos, una duración de diez años contados a partir de la fecha de la presentación de la solicitud o de la fecha de su concesión, según la legislación de cada Parte, y podrá renovarse indefinidamente por períodos sucesivos no menores de diez años, siempre que se satisfagan las condiciones para su renovación.

Artículo 15-19: Requisito de uso de la marca.

1.   Si para mantener el registro de una marca una Parte exige el uso, el registro sólo podrá anularse después de un período ininterrumpido de 3 (tres) años como mínimo de falta de uso, a menos que el titular de la marca demuestre que hubo para ello razones válidas basadas en la existencia de obstáculos a dicho uso. Se reconocerán como razones válidas de falta de uso las circunstancias que surjan independientemente de la voluntad del titular de la marca y que

constituyan un obstáculo al uso de la misma, como las restricciones a la importación u otros requisitos oficiales impuestos a los bienes o servicios protegidos por la marca.

2.   Cada Parte, de conformidad con la legislación nacional, determinará cuando una marca se encuentra en uso.

3.   Cuando esté controlada por el titular, se considerará que la utilización de una marca por otra persona, constituye uso de la marca a los efectos de mantener el registro.

Artículo 15-20: Otros requisitos.

No se complicará injustificadamente el uso de una marca en el curso de operaciones comerciales con exigencias especiales, como por ejemplo el uso con otra marca, el uso en una forma especial o el uso de una manera que menoscabe la capacidad de la marca para distinguir los bienes o servicios de una persona física o empresa de los de otras personas físicas o empresas.

Artículo 15-21: Licencias y cesión de marcas.

Cada Parte podrá establecer las condiciones para las licencias y la cesión de las marcas, quedando entendido que no se permitirán las licencias obligatorias de marcas y que el titular de una marca registrada tendrá derecho a cederla con o sin la transferencia de la empresa a que pertenezca la marca.

Sección D - Indicaciones geográficas y Denominaciones de origen

Artículo 15-22: Protección de las indicaciones geográficas y de las denominaciones de origen.

1.   Cada Parte protegerá las denominaciones de origen y las indicaciones geográficas según lo prevea su legislación, a solicitud de las autoridades competentes o de los interesados de la Parte donde esa indicación geográfica o denominación de origen esté protegida.

2.   Las denominaciones de origen o las indicaciones geográficas protegidas en una Parte no serán consideradas comunes o genéricas para distinguir un bien, mientras subsista su protección en el país de origen.

3.   En relación con las denominaciones de origen y las indicaciones geográficas, cada Parte establecerá medios legales para que las partes interesadas puedan impedir:

   a)   el uso de cualquier medio que, en la designación o presentación del bien, indique o sugiera que el bien de que se trate proviene de un territorio, región o localidad geográfica distinta del verdadero lugar de origen, de modo que induzca al público a error en cuanto al origen geográfico del bien; y

   b)   cualquier otra utilización que constituya un acto de competencia desleal en el sentido del Artículo 10 bis del Convenio de París.

4.   Cada Parte, de oficio si su legislación lo permite, o a petición de parte interesada, negará o anulará el registro de una marca que contenga o consista en una indicación geográfica o

denominación de origen respecto a bienes que no se originen en el territorio, región o localidad indicado, si el uso de esa indicación en la marca para esos bienes es de naturaleza tal, que induzca al público a error en cuanto al verdadero lugar de origen de los bienes.

5.   Los párrafos 4 y 5 se aplican a toda denominación de origen o indicación geográfica que, aunque indique de manera correcta el territorio, región o localidad en que se originan los bienes, proporcione al público una idea falsa de que éstos se originan en otro territorio, región o localidad.

6.   Uruguay reconocerá las denominaciones de origen "Tequila" y "Mezcal", para su uso exclusivo en bienes originarios de México siempre que éstos sean elaborados y certificados en México, conforme a las leyes, reglamentaciones y normativa de México aplicables a esos bienes.

Sección E - Patentes

Artículo 15-23: Materia Patentable.

1.   Sujeto a lo dispuesto en los párrafos 2 y 3, las patentes se otorgarán para invenciones, ya sean de productos o de procedimientos, en todos los campos de la tecnología, siempre que sean nuevas, resulten de una actividad inventiva y sean susceptibles de aplicación industrial.

2.   Sujeto a lo dispuesto en el párrafo 3, no habrá discriminación en el otorgamiento de las patentes, ni en el goce de los derechos respectivos, en función del campo de la tecnología del territorio del país en que la invención fue realizada o de si los productos son importados o producidos localmente.

3.   Cada Parte podrá excluir de la patentabilidad las invenciones cuya explotación comercial en su territorio deba impedirse para proteger el orden público o la moral, inclusive para proteger la salud o la vida humana, animal o para preservar los vegetales, o para evitar daño grave a la naturaleza o al ambiente, siempre que esa exclusión no se fundamente únicamente en que la Parte prohiba en su territorio la explotación comercial de la materia que sea objeto de la patente.

4.   Así mismo, cada Parte podrá excluir de la patentabilidad:

   a)   los métodos de diagnóstico, terapéuticos y quirúrgicos para el tratamiento de personas o animales;

   b)   las plantas y los animales excepto los microorganismos, y los procedimientos esencialmente biológicos para la producción de plantas o animales, con excepción de los procedimientos no biológicos o microbiológicos; o

   c)   el material biológico y genético, como existe en la naturaleza.

Artículo 15-24: Derechos conferidos.

1.   Una patente conferirá a su titular los siguientes derechos exclusivos:

a) cuando la materia de la patente sea un producto, el de impedir que terceros, sin su consentimiento, realicen actos de: fabricación, uso, oferta para la venta, venta o importación para estos fines del producto objeto de la patente; o

b) cuando la materia de la patente sea un procedimiento, el de impedir que terceros, sin su consentimiento, realicen el acto de utilización del procedimiento y los actos de: uso, oferta para la venta, venta o importación para estos fines de, por lo menos, el producto obtenido directamente por medio de dicho procedimiento.

2.   Así mismo, los titulares de las patentes tendrán el derecho de ceder o transferir la patente y de concertar contratos de licencia.

Artículo 15-25: Excepciones.

Cada Parte podrá prever excepciones limitadas a los derechos exclusivos conferidos por una patente, a condición de que esas excepciones no atenten la explotación normal de la patente de manera injustificable, ni causen un perjuicio injustificado a los intereses del titular de la patente, teniendo en cuenta los intereses legítimos de terceros.

Artículo 15-26: Otros usos sin autorización del titular del derecho.

Cuando la legislación de una Parte permita otros usos de la materia de una patente, distintos a los permitidos conforme al artículo 15-25, sin autorización del titular del derecho, incluido el uso por el gobierno o por terceros autorizados por el gobierno, se observarán las disposiciones del Artículo 31 del Acuerdo sobre los ADPIC.

Artículo 15-27: Nulidad o caducidad.

Cada Parte de conformidad con su legislación dispondrá de la posibilidad de revisión de toda decisión de nulidad o caducidad de una patente.

Artículo 15-28: Pruebas en casos de infracción de procesos patentados.

1.   A efectos de los procedimientos civiles o administrativos, en el caso de que la legislación de cada Parte lo establezca, en materia de infracción de los derechos del titular a los que se refiere el párrafo 1 b) del artículo 15-24, cuando el objeto de una patente sea un procedimiento para obtener un producto, las autoridades judiciales o administrativas estarán facultadas para ordenar que el demandado pruebe que el procedimiento para obtener un producto es diferente del procedimiento patentado. Por consiguiente, cada Parte establecerá que, salvo prueba en contrario, todo producto idéntico producido por cualquier parte sin el consentimiento del titular de la patente ha sido obtenido mediante el procedimiento patentado, por lo menos en una de las circunstancias siguientes:

a) si el producto obtenido por el procedimiento patentado es nuevo;

b) si existe una probabilidad sustancial de que el producto idéntico haya sido fabricado mediante el procedimiento y el titular de la patente no puede establecer mediante esfuerzos razonables cuál ha sido el procedimiento efectivamente utilizado.

2.	En la recopilación y valoración de las pruebas se tomará en cuenta el interés legítimo del demandado para la protección de sus secretos industriales y comerciales.

Artículo 15-29: Duración de la protección.

Cada Parte establecerá un período de protección para las patentes de por lo menos 20 años, contados a partir de la fecha de presentación de la solicitud.

Sección F - Modelos de Utilidad

Artículo 15-30: Protección a los Modelos de Utilidad.

Cada Parte protegerá los modelos de utilidad de conformidad con su legislación, por un plazo de por lo menos diez años contados a partir de la fecha de presentación de la solicitud.

Sección G - Diseños industriales

Artículo 15-31: Condiciones para la protección.

1.	Cada Parte otorgará protección a los diseños industriales nuevos u originales que sean de creación independiente.

2.	Cada Parte podrá establecer que los diseños no se consideren nuevos u originales si no difieren en grado significativo de diseños conocidos o de combinaciones de características de diseños conocidos.

3.	Cada Parte podrá establecer que esa protección no se extienda a los diseños basados esencialmente en consideraciones funcionales o técnicas.

Artículo 15-32: Duración de la protección.

Cada Parte otorgará un período de protección para los diseños industriales de por lo menos diez años, contados a partir de la fecha de presentación de la solicitud.

Artículo 15-33: Derechos conferidos.

1.	El titular de un diseño industrial tendrá el derecho de impedir que terceros que no cuenten con el consentimiento del titular, fabriquen, importen o vendan productos que ostenten o incorporen su diseño o que fundamentalmente copien el mismo, cuando esos actos se realicen con fines comerciales.

2.	Cada Parte podrá prever excepciones limitadas a la protección de los diseños industriales, a condición de que esas excepciones no interfieran la explotación normal de los diseños industriales de manera indebida, ni ocasionen un perjuicio injustificado a los legítimos intereses del titular del diseño, tomando en cuenta los intereses legítimos de terceros.

Sección H - Protección de los Derechos de los Obtentores Vegetales

Artículo 15-34: Protección de los Derechos de los Obtentores Vegetales.

De conformidad con su legislación, cada Parte reconocerá y otorgará protección a las variedades vegetales, mediante derechos de obtentor otorgados de conformidad con el Convenio UPOV.

Sección I - Protección a la información no divulgada

Artículo 15-35: Protección de los secretos industriales y de negocios.

1.   Al garantizar una protección efectiva contra la competencia desleal, de conformidad con lo establecido en el Artículo 10 bis del Convenio de París (1967), cada Parte protegerá los secretos industriales y de negocios, de conformidad con el párrafo 2.

2.   Las personas físicas y jurídicas tendrán la posibilidad de impedir que la información que esté legítimamente bajo su control se divulgue a terceros o sea adquirida o utilizada por terceros sin su consentimiento de manera contraria a los usos comerciales honestos, en la medida en que dicha información:

a)   sea secreta en el sentido de que no sea, como cuerpo o en la configuración y reunión precisas de sus componentes, generalmente conocida ni fácilmente accesible para personas introducidas en los círculos en que normalmente se utiliza el tipo de información en cuestión; y

b)   tenga un valor comercial por ser secreta; y

c)   haya sido objeto de medidas razonables, en las circunstancias, para mantenerla secreta, tomadas por la persona que legítimamente la controla.

3.   Para otorgar la protección a que se refiere este artículo, cada Parte exigirá que un secreto industrial y de negocios conste en documentos, medios electrónicos o magnéticos, discos ópticos, microfilmes, películas u otros instrumentos similares.

4.   Ninguna Parte podrá limitar la duración de la protección para los secretos industriales y de negocios, en tanto existan las condiciones descritas en los literales a), b) y c) del párrafo 2.

5.   Ninguna Parte desalentará ni impedirá el licenciamiento voluntario de secretos industriales y de negocios imponiendo condiciones excesivas o discriminatorias a esas licencias, o condiciones que diluyan el valor de los secretos industriales y de negocios.

Sección J - Control de las prácticas anticompetitivas en las licencias contractuales

Artículo 15-36: Control de las prácticas anticompetitivas en las licencias contractuales.

1.   Las Partes convienen en que ciertas prácticas o condiciones relativas a la concesión de las licencias de los derechos de propiedad intelectual a los que se refiere este capítulo, que

restringen la competencia, pueden tener efectos perjudiciales para el comercio y pueden impedir la transferencia y la divulgación de la tecnología.

2.   Ninguna disposición de este capítulo impedirá que las Partes especifiquen en su legislación las prácticas o condiciones relativas a la concesión de licencias que puedan constituir, en determinados casos, un abuso de los derechos de propiedad intelectual que tenga un efecto negativo sobre la competencia en el mercado correspondiente. Como se establece en el párrafo 1, una Parte podrá adoptar, en forma compatible con las restantes disposiciones de este capítulo, medidas apropiadas para impedir o controlar dichas prácticas que puedan incluir las condiciones exclusivas de retrocesión, las condiciones que impidan la impugnación de la validez y las licencias conjuntas obligatorias, a la luz de las leyes y reglamentos pertinentes de esa Parte.

Sección K - Observancia de los derechos de propiedad intelectual.

Artículo 15-37: Obligaciones generales.

1.   Las Partes se asegurarán que en su legislación se establezcan procedimientos de observancia de los derechos de propiedad intelectual a los que se refiere este capítulo conforme a lo previsto en esta sección que permitan la adopción de medidas eficaces contra cualquier acción infractora a estos derechos, con inclusión de recursos ágiles para prevenir las infracciones, y de recursos que constituyan un medio eficaz de disuasión de nuevas infracciones. Estos procedimientos se aplicarán de forma que se evite la creación de obstáculos al comercio legítimo y deberán prever salvaguardias contra su abuso.

2.   Los procedimientos relativos a la observancia de los derechos de propiedad intelectual serán justos y equitativos. No serán innecesariamente complicados o gravosos, ni implicarán plazos injustificados o retrasos innecesarios.

3.   Las decisiones sobre el fondo de un caso se formularán, preferentemente, por escrito y serán razonadas. Se pondrán a disposición, al menos de las partes en el procedimiento, sin retrasos indebidos. Sólo se basarán en pruebas acerca de las cuales se haya dado a las partes la oportunidad de ser oídas.

4.   Se dará a las partes en el procedimiento la oportunidad de una revisión por una autoridad judicial de las decisiones administrativas finales y, con sujeción a las disposiciones en materia de competencia jurisdiccional previstas en la legislación de cada Parte relativa a la importancia de un caso, de al menos los aspectos jurídicos de las decisiones judiciales iniciales sobre el fondo del caso. Sin embargo, no será obligatorio darles la oportunidad de revisión de las sentencias absolutorias dictadas en casos penales.

5.   Queda entendido que la presente sección no impone ninguna obligación de instaurar un sistema judicial para la observancia de los derechos de propiedad intelectual distinto del ya existente para la aplicación de la legislación en general, ni afecta a la capacidad de las Partes para hacer observar su legislación en general. Ninguna disposición de la presente sección crea obligación alguna con respecto a la distribución de los recursos entre los medios destinados a lograr la observancia de los derechos de propiedad intelectual y los destinados a la observancia de la legislación en general.

Artículo 15-38: Procedimientos justos y equitativos.

Las Partes pondrán al alcance de los titulares de derechos, procedimientos judiciales civiles para lograr la observancia de todos los derechos de propiedad intelectual a que se refiere el presente capítulo. Los demandados tendrán derecho a recibir aviso por escrito en tiempo oportuno y con detalles suficientes, con inclusión del fundamento de la reclamación. Se autorizará a las partes a estar representadas por un abogado independiente y los procedimientos no impondrán exigencias excesivamente gravosas en cuanto a las comparecencias personales obligatorias. Todas las partes en estos procedimientos estarán debidamente facultadas para sustanciar sus alegatos y presentar todas las pruebas pertinentes. El procedimiento deberá prever medios para identificar y proteger la información confidencial, salvo que ello sea contrario a prescripciones constitucionales existentes.

Artículo 15-39: Pruebas.

1.   Las autoridades judiciales estarán facultadas para ordenar que, cuando una parte haya presentado las pruebas de que razonablemente disponga y que basten para sustentar sus alegatos, y haya identificado alguna prueba pertinente para sustanciar sus alegatos que se encuentre bajo el control de la parte contraria, ésta aporte dicha prueba, con sujeción, en los casos procedentes, a condiciones que garanticen la protección de la información confidencial.

2.   En caso de que una de las partes en el procedimiento deniegue voluntariamente y sin motivos sólidos el acceso a información necesaria o de otro modo no facilite tal información en un plazo razonable u obstaculice de manera sustancial un procedimiento relativo a una medida adoptada para asegurar la observancia de un derecho, las Partes podrán facultar a las autoridades judiciales para formular determinaciones preliminares y definitivas, afirmativas o negativas, sobre la base de la información que les haya sido presentada, con inclusión de la reclamación o del alegato presentado por la parte afectada desfavorablemente por la denegación del acceso a la información, a condición de que se de a las partes la oportunidad de ser oídas respecto de los alegatos o las pruebas.

Artículo 15-40: Mandamientos judiciales.

1.   Las autoridades judiciales estarán facultadas para ordenar a una parte que desista de una infracción, entre otras cosas para impedir que los bienes importados que infrinjan un derecho de propiedad intelectual entren en los circuitos comerciales de su jurisdicción, inmediatamente después del despacho de aduana de los mismos. Las Partes no tienen la obligación de conceder esa facultad en relación con una materia protegida que haya sido adquirida o pedida por una persona antes de saber o tener motivos razonables para saber que operar con esa materia implicaría una infracción de un derecho de propiedad intelectual.

2.   A pesar de las demás disposiciones de esta sección, y siempre que se respeten las disposiciones de este capítulo específicamente referidas a la utilización por el gobierno, o por terceros autorizados por el gobierno, sin el consentimiento del titular de los derechos, las Partes podrán limitar los recursos disponibles contra tal utilización al pago de una compensación adecuada al titular de los derechos, según las circunstancias propias de cada caso, habida cuenta del valor económico de la autorización. En los demás casos se aplicarán los recursos previstos en esta sección o, cuando éstos sean incompatibles con la legislación nacional, podrán obtenerse sentencias declarativas y una compensación adecuada.

Artículo 15-41: Perjuicios.

1.   Las autoridades judiciales estarán facultadas para ordenar al infractor que pague al titular del derecho un resarcimiento adecuado para compensar el daño que éste haya sufrido debido a una infracción de su derecho de propiedad intelectual, causada por un infractor que sabiéndolo o teniendo motivos razonables para saberlo, haya desarrollado una actividad infractora.

2.   Las autoridades judiciales estarán asimismo facultadas para ordenar al infractor que pague los gastos del titular del derecho, que pueden incluir los honorarios de los abogados, que sean procedentes. Cuando así proceda, las Partes podrán facultar a las autoridades judiciales para que concedan reparación por concepto de beneficios y/o resarcimiento por daños reconocidos previamente, aun cuando el infractor no sabiéndolo o no teniendo motivos razonables para saberlo, haya desarrollado una actividad infractora.

Artículo 15-42: Otros recursos.

Para establecer un medio eficaz de disuasión de las infracciones, las autoridades judiciales estarán facultadas para ordenar que las mercancías que se hayan determinado que son mercancías infractoras sean, sin indemnización alguna, apartadas de los circuitos comerciales, de forma que se evite causar daños al titular del derecho, o que sean destruidas, siempre que ello no sea incompatible con disposiciones constitucionales vigentes. Las autoridades judiciales estarán además facultadas para ordenar que los materiales e instrumentos que se hayan utilizado predominantemente para la producción de los bienes infractores, sean, sin indemnización alguna, apartados de los circuitos comerciales, de forma que se reduzcan al mínimo los riesgos de nuevas infracciones. Se tendrán en cuenta, al dar curso a las correspondientes solicitudes, tanto la necesidad de que haya proporción entre la gravedad de la infracción y las medidas ordenadas como los intereses de terceros. En cuanto a las mercancías de marcas falsificadas, la simple retirada de la marca puesta ilícitamente no bastará, salvo en casos excepcionales, para que se permita la colocación de los bienes en los circuitos comerciales.

Artículo 15-43: Derecho de información.

Las Partes podrán disponer que, salvo que resulte desproporcionado con la gravedad de la infracción, las autoridades judiciales puedan ordenar al infractor que informe al titular del derecho sobre la identidad de los terceros que hayan participado en la producción y distribución de los bienes o servicios infractores, y sobre sus circuitos de distribución.

Artículo 15-44: Indemnización al demandado.

1.   Las autoridades judiciales estarán facultadas para ordenar a una parte, a cuya instancia se hayan adoptado medidas y que haya abusado del procedimiento de observancia, que indemnice adecuadamente a la parte a que se haya impuesto indebidamente una obligación o una restricción, por el daño sufrido a causa de tal abuso. Las autoridades judiciales estarán asimismo facultadas para ordenar al demandante que pague los gastos del demandado, que pueden incluir los honorarios de los abogados, que sean procedentes.

2.   En relación con la administración de cualquier legislación relativa a la protección o a la observancia de los derechos de propiedad intelectual, las Partes eximirán tanto a las autoridades como a los funcionarios públicos de las responsabilidades que darían lugar a las medidas

correctoras adecuadas sólo en el caso de actuaciones llevadas a cabo o proyectadas de buena fe para la administración de dicha legislación.

Artículo 15-45: Procedimientos administrativos.

En la medida en que puedan ordenarse remedios civiles derivados de procedimientos administrativos referentes al fondo de un caso, esos procedimientos se atendrán a principios sustancialmente equivalentes a los enunciados en los Artículos 15-38 al 15-44.

Artículo 15-46: Medidas provisionales.

1.   Las autoridades judiciales estarán facultadas para ordenar la adopción de medidas provisionales rápidas y eficaces destinadas a:

   a)   evitar que se produzca la infracción de cualquier derecho de propiedad intelectual comprendido en este capítulo y, en particular, evitar que las mercancías ingresen en los circuitos comerciales de la jurisdicción de aquéllas, inclusive las mercancías importadas, inmediatamente después del despacho de aduana; y

   b)   preservar las pruebas pertinentes relacionadas con la presunta infracción.

2.   Las autoridades judiciales estarán facultadas para adoptar medidas provisionales, cuando ello sea conveniente, sin haber oído a la otra parte, en particular cuando haya probabilidad de que cualquier retraso cause daño irreparable al titular de los derechos, o cuando haya un riesgo demostrable de destrucción de pruebas.

3.   Las autoridades judiciales estarán facultadas para exigir al demandante que presente las pruebas de que razonablemente disponga, con el fin de establecer a su satisfacción con un grado suficiente de certidumbre que el demandante es el titular del derecho y que su derecho es objeto o va a ser objeto inminentemente de infracción, y para ordenar al demandante que aporte una fianza o garantía equivalente que sea suficiente para proteger al demandado y evitar abusos.

4.   Cuando se hayan adoptado medidas provisionales sin haber oído a la otra parte, éstas se notificarán sin demora a la parte afectada a más tardar inmediatamente después de aplicarlas. A petición del demandado, en un plazo razonable contado a partir de esa notificación se procederá a una revisión, en la que se le reconocerá el derecho a ser oído, con objeto de decidir si deben modificarse, revocarse o confirmarse esas medidas.

5.   La autoridad encargada de la ejecución de las medidas provisionales podrá exigir al demandante que presente cualquier otra información necesaria para la identificación de las mercancías de que se trate.

6.   Sin perjuicio de lo dispuesto en el párrafo 4, las medidas provisionales adoptadas al amparo de los párrafos 1 y 2 se revocarán o quedarán de otro modo sin efecto, a petición del demandado, si el procedimiento conducente a una decisión sobre el fondo del asunto no se inicia en un plazo razonable que habrá de ser establecido cuando la legislación de una Parte lo permita, por determinación de la autoridad judicial que haya ordenado las medidas, y que a falta de esa determinación no será superior a 20 días hábiles o 31 días naturales, si este plazo fuera mayor.

7.   En los casos en que las medidas provisionales sean revocadas o caduquen por acción u omisión del demandante, o en aquellos casos en que posteriormente se determine que no hubo infracción o amenaza de infracción de un derecho de propiedad intelectual, las autoridades judiciales estarán facultadas para ordenar al demandante, previa petición del demandado, que pague a éste una indemnización adecuada por cualquier daño causado por esas medidas.

8.   En la medida en que puedan ordenarse medidas provisionales derivadas de procedimientos administrativos, esos procedimientos se atenderán a principios sustancialmente equivalentes a los enunciados en este artículo.

Sección L - Prescripciones especiales relacionadas con las medidas en frontera

Artículo 15-47: Suspensión del despacho de aduana por las autoridades aduaneras.

1.   Las Partes de conformidad con las disposiciones de ésta sección, adoptarán procedimientos para que el titular de un derecho, que tenga motivos válidos para sospechar que se prepara la importación de mercancías de marcas falsificadas o mercancías piratas que lesionan el derecho de autor, pueda presentar a las autoridades competentes, administrativas o judiciales, una demanda por escrito con objeto de que las autoridades de aduanas suspendan el despacho de esas mercancías para libre circulación.

2.   Las Partes podrán autorizar para que se haga dicha demanda también respecto de mercancías que supongan otras infracciones de los derechos de propiedad intelectual, siempre que se cumplan las prescripciones de los artículos 15-47 al 15-56. Las Partes podrán establecer también procedimientos análogos para que las autoridades de aduanas suspendan el despacho de esas mercancías destinadas a la exportación desde su territorio.

Artículo 15-48: Demanda.

Se exigirá a todo titular de un derecho que inicie un procedimiento de conformidad con el artículo 15-47 que presente pruebas suficientes que demuestren a satisfacción de las autoridades competentes que, de acuerdo con la legislación del país de importación, existe presunción de infracción de su derecho de propiedad intelectual y que ofrezca una descripción suficientemente detallada de las mercancías, de modo que puedan ser reconocidas con facilidad por las autoridades de aduanas. Las autoridades competentes comunicarán al demandante, dentro de un plazo razonable, si han aceptado la demanda y, cuando sean ellas mismas quienes lo establezcan, el plazo de actuación de las autoridades de aduanas.

Artículo 15-49: Fianza o garantía equivalente.

1.   Las autoridades competentes estarán facultadas para exigir al demandante que aporte una fianza o garantía equivalente que sea suficiente para proteger al demandado y a las autoridades competentes e impedir abusos. Esa fianza o garantía equivalente no deberá disuadir indebidamente del recurso a estos procedimientos.

2.   Cuando a consecuencia de una demanda presentada en el ámbito de la presente sección, las autoridades aduaneras hayan suspendido el despacho para libre circulación de mercancías que comporten diseños industriales, patentes o información no divulgada, sobre la base de una decisión no tomada por una autoridad judicial u otra autoridad independiente, y el plazo

estipulado en el artículo 15-51 haya vencido sin que la autoridad debidamente facultada al efecto dicte una medida precautoria provisional, y si se han cumplido todas las demás condiciones requeridas para la importación, el propietario, el importador o el consignatario de esas mercancías tendrá derecho a obtener que se proceda al despacho de aduana de las mismas previo depósito de una fianza por un importe que sea suficiente para proteger al titular del derecho en cualquier caso de infracción. El pago de tal fianza se entenderá sin perjuicio de ningún otro recurso a disposición del titular del derecho, y se entenderá asimismo que la fianza se devolverá si éste no ejerce el derecho de acción en un plazo razonable.

Artículo 15-50: Notificación de la suspensión.

Se notificará prontamente al importador y al demandante la suspensión del despacho de aduana de las mercancías, de conformidad con el artículo 15-47.

Artículo 15-51: Duración de la suspensión.

En caso de que en un plazo no superior a 10 días hábiles contados a partir de la comunicación de la suspensión al demandante mediante aviso, las autoridades de aduanas no hayan sido informadas de que una parte, que no sea el demandado, ha iniciado el procedimiento conducente a una decisión sobre el fondo de la cuestión o de que la autoridad debidamente facultada al efecto ha adoptado medidas provisionales que prolonguen la suspensión del despacho de aduana de las mercancías, se procederá al despacho de las mismas si se han cumplido todas las demás condiciones requeridas para su importación o exportación. En los casos en que proceda, el plazo mencionado podrá ser prorrogado por otros 10 días hábiles. Si se ha iniciado el procedimiento conducente a una decisión sobre el fondo del asunto a petición del demandado, se procederá en un plazo razonable a una revisión, que incluirá el derecho de éste a ser oído, con objeto de decidir si esas medidas deben modificarse, revocarse o confirmarse. No obstante, cuando la suspensión del despacho de aduana se efectúe o se continúe en virtud de una medida judicial provisional, se aplicarán las disposiciones del párrafo 6 del artículo 15-46.

Artículo 15-52: Indemnización al importador y al propietario de las mercancías.

Las autoridades pertinentes estarán facultadas para ordenar al demandante que pague al importador, al consignatario y al propietario de las mercancías una indemnización adecuada por todo daño a ellos causado por la retención infundada de las mercancías o por la retención de las que se hayan despachado de conformidad con lo dispuesto en el artículo 15-51.

Artículo 15-53: Derecho de inspección e información.

Sin perjuicio de la protección de la información confidencial, las Partes facultarán a las autoridades competentes para dar al titular del derecho oportunidades suficientes para que haga inspeccionar, con el fin de fundamentar sus reclamaciones, cualesquiera mercancías retenidas por las autoridades de aduanas. Las autoridades competentes estarán asimismo facultadas para dar al importador oportunidades equivalentes para que haga inspeccionar esas mercancías. Las Partes podrán facultar a las autoridades competentes para que, cuando se haya adoptado una decisión positiva sobre el fondo del asunto, comuniquen al titular del derecho el nombre y dirección del consignador, el importador y el consignatario, así como la cantidad de las mercancías de que se trate.

Artículo 15-54: Actuación de oficio.

Cuando las Partes pidan a las autoridades competentes que actúen por propia iniciativa y suspendan el despacho de aquellas mercancías respecto de las cuales tengan la presunción de que infringen un derecho de propiedad intelectual:

a)   las autoridades competentes podrán pedir en cualquier momento al titular del derecho toda información que pueda serles útil para ejercer esa potestad;

b)   la suspensión deberá notificarse sin demora al importador y al titular del derecho. Si el importador recurre contra ella ante las autoridades competentes, la suspensión quedará sujeta, *mutatis mutandis*, a las condiciones previstas en el artículo 15-51; y

c)   las Partes eximirán tanto a las autoridades como a los funcionarios públicos de las responsabilidades, que darían lugar a las medidas correctoras adecuadas sólo en el caso de actuaciones realizadas o intentadas de buena fe.

Artículo 15-55: Recursos.

Sin perjuicio de las demás acciones que correspondan al titular del derecho y a reserva del derecho del demandado a apelar ante una autoridad judicial, las autoridades competentes estarán facultadas para ordenar la destrucción o eliminación de las mercancías infractoras, de conformidad con los principios establecidos en el artículo 15-42. En cuanto a las mercancías de marcas falsificadas, las autoridades no permitirán, salvo en circunstancias excepcionales, que las mercancías infractoras se reexporten en el mismo estado ni las someterán a un procedimiento aduanero distinto.

Artículo 15-56: Importaciones insignificantes.

Las Partes podrán excluir de la aplicación de las disposiciones precedentes las cantidades pequeñas de mercancías que no tengan carácter comercial y formen parte del equipaje personal de los viajeros o se envíen en pequeñas partidas.

Sección M – Disposiciones Penales

Artículo 15-57: Procedimientos penales.

1.   Las Partes establecerán procedimientos y sanciones penales al menos para los casos de falsificación dolosa de marcas o de piratería lesiva del derecho de autor a escala comercial. Los recursos disponibles comprenderán la pena de prisión y/o la imposición de sanciones pecuniarias suficientemente disuasivas que sean coherentes con el nivel de las sanciones aplicadas por delitos de gravedad correspondiente.

2.   Cuando proceda, entre los recursos disponibles figurarán también la confiscación, el decomiso y la destrucción de las mercancías infractoras y de todos los materiales y accesorios utilizados predominantemente para la comisión del delito. Las Partes podrán prever la aplicación de procedimientos y sanciones penales en otros casos de infracción de derechos de propiedad intelectual, en particular cuando se cometan con dolo y a escala comercial.

Sección N - Disposiciones finales

Artículo 15-58: Aplicación de las normas de este capítulo.

1.   Las normas contenidas en este capítulo no generan obligaciones relativas a actos realizados antes de la fecha de entrada en vigor de este Tratado.

2.   Salvo disposición en contrario, las normas contenidas en este capítulo generan obligaciones relativas a toda la materia existente en la fecha de entrada en vigor de este Tratado y que esté protegida en esa Parte en dicha fecha. En lo concerniente a este párrafo y al párrafo 3, las obligaciones de protección mediante el derecho de autor relacionadas con las obras existentes se determinarán únicamente con arreglo al Artículo 18 del Convenio de Berna.

3.   No habrá obligación de restablecer la protección a la materia que, en la fecha de entrada en vigor de este Tratado, haya pasado al dominio público.

[...]

CAPÍTULO XIX
EXCEPCIONES

Artículo 19-01: Definiciones.

Para efectos de este capítulo, se entenderá por:

convenio tributario: un convenio para evitar la doble tributación u otro convenio o arreglo internacional en materia tributaria;

Fondo: el Fondo Monetario Internacional; e

impuestos y medidas tributarias no incluyen:

   a)   un "arancel aduanero", tal como se define en el Artículo 2-01 (Definiciones generales); ni

   b)   las medidas listadas en las excepciones b), c) y d) de esa definición; pagos por transacciones internacionales corrientes: los "pagos por transacciones corrientes internacionales", tal como se define en los Artículos del Convenio del Fondo; transacciones internacionales de capital: las "transacciones internacionales de capital", tal como se define en los Artículos del Convenio del Fondo; y transferencias: las transacciones internacionales y transferencias internacionales y pagos conexos.

Artículo 19-02: Excepciones generales.

1.   Se incorporan a este Tratado y forman parte integrante del mismo, el Artículo XX del GATT de 1994 y sus notas interpretativas, para efectos de:

   a)   los capítulos III (Trato Nacional y Acceso de Bienes al Mercado), IV (Régimen de Origen), V (Procedimientos Aduaneros para el Manejo de Origen de los

Bienes), VI (Salvaguardias), VII (Prácticas Desleales de Comercio), salvo en la medida en que alguna de sus disposiciones se aplique a servicios o a inversión;

b)   el capítulo VIII (Medidas Sanitarias y Fitosanitarias), salvo en la medida en que alguna de sus disposiciones se aplique a servicios o a inversión; y

el capítulo IX (Normas, Reglamentos Técnicos y Procedimientos Evaluación de la Conformidad), salvo en la medida que alguna de sus disposiciones se aplique a servicios.

2.   Se incorporan a este Tratado y forman parte integrante del mismo, el Artículo XIV del GATS, para efectos de:

a)   los capítulos III (Trato Nacional y Acceso de Bienes al Mercado), IV (Régimen de Origen), V (Procedimientos Aduaneros para el Manejo de Origen de los Bienes), VI (Salvaguardias), VII (Prácticas Desleales de Comercio) y Capítulo VIII (Medidas Sanitarias y Fitosanitarias), salvo en la medida en que alguna de sus disposiciones se aplique a servicios;

b)   el capítulo IX (Normas, Reglamentos Técnicos y Procedimientos Evaluación de la Conformidad);

c)   el capítulo X (Comercio Transfronterizo de Servicios); y

d)   el capítulo XI (Telecomunicaciones).

Artículo 19-03: Seguridad nacional.

Ninguna disposición de este Tratado se interpretará en el sentido de:

a)   obligar a una Parte a proporcionar ni a dar acceso a información cuya divulgación considere contraria a sus intereses esenciales en materia de seguridad;

b)   impedir a una Parte que adopte cualquier medida que considere necesaria para proteger sus intereses esenciales en materia de seguridad:

    i)   relativa al comercio de armamento, municiones y pertrechos de guerra y al comercio y las operaciones sobre bienes, materiales, servicios y tecnología que se lleven a cabo con la finalidad directa o indirecta de proporcionar suministros a una institución militar o a otro establecimiento de defensa,

    ii)   adoptada en tiempo de guerra o de otras emergencias en las relaciones internacionales, o

    iii)   referente a la aplicación de políticas nacionales o de acuerdos internacionales en materia de no proliferación de armas nucleares o de otros dispositivos explosivos nucleares; ni

c)   impedir a cualquier Parte adoptar medidas de conformidad con sus obligaciones derivadas de la Carta de las Naciones Unidas para el Mantenimiento de la Paz y la Seguridad Internacionales.

Artículo 19-04: Excepciones a la divulgación de información confidencial.

Ninguna disposición de este Tratado se interpretará en el sentido de obligar a una Parte a proporcionar o a dar acceso a información confidencial cuya divulgación pueda impedir el cumplimiento o ser contraria a su Constitución Política o a sus leyes.

Artículo 19-05: Tributación.

1.   Salvo lo dispuesto en este artículo, ninguna disposición de este Tratado se aplicará a medidas tributarias.

2.   Nada de lo dispuesto en el presente Tratado afectará los derechos y las obligaciones de cualquiera de las Partes que se deriven de cualquier convenio tributario. En caso de incompatibilidad entre este Tratado y cualquiera de estos convenios, el convenio prevalecerá en la medida de la incompatibilidad.

3.   No obstante lo dispuesto en el párrafo 2:

   a)   el Artículo 3-02 (Trato nacional), y aquellas otras disposiciones en este Tratado necesarias para hacer efectivo dicho artículo, se aplicarán a las medidas tributarias en el mismo grado que el Artículo III del GATT de 1994; y

   b)   el Artículo 3-10 (Impuestos a la exportación), se aplicará a las medidas tributarias.

4.   El Artículo 13-11 (Expropiación e indemnización), se aplicará a las medidas tributarias, salvo que ningún inversionista podrá invocar ese artículo como fundamento de una reclamación, hecha en virtud del Artículo 13-16 (Reclamación del inversionista de una Parte por cuenta propia, en virtud de los daños y perjuicios sufridos por él mismo) o del Artículo 13-17 (Reclamación del inversionista de una Parte en representación de una empresa, en virtud de daños sufridos por una empresa de la otra Parte que sea una persona jurídica propiedad del inversionista o que esté bajo su control directo o indirecto). Si las autoridades competentes de las Partes no acuerdan examinar el asunto o si, habiendo acordado examinarlo no convienen en estimar que la medida no constituye una expropiación, dentro de un plazo de 6 (seis) meses después de que se les haya sometido el asunto, el inversionista podrá someter una reclamación a arbitraje, de conformidad con el Artículo 13- 20 (Sometimiento de la reclamación a arbitraje).

Artículo 19-06: Balanza de pagos.

1.   Ninguna disposición de este Tratado se interpretará en el sentido de impedir que una Parte adopte ni mantenga medidas que restrinjan las transferencias cuando la Parte afronte dificultades serias en su balanza de pagos, o amenaza de las mismas, siempre que las restricciones sean compatibles con este artículo.

2.   Tan pronto sea factible después de que una Parte aplique una medida conforme a este artículo, la Parte deberá:

   a)   someter a revisión del Fondo todas las restricciones a las operaciones de cuenta corriente de conformidad con el Artículo VIII de los Artículos del Convenio del Fondo Monetario Internacional;

b)   iniciar consultas de buena fe con el Fondo respecto a las medidas de ajuste económico encaminadas a afrontar los problemas económicos fundamentales que subyacen en las dificultades; y

c)   adoptar o mantener políticas económicas compatibles con dichas consultas.

3.   Las medidas que se apliquen o mantengan de conformidad con este artículo deberán:

a)   evitar daños innecesarios a los intereses comerciales, económicos o financieros de la otra Parte;

b)   no ser más onerosas de lo necesario para afrontar las dificultades en la balanza de pagos, o la amenaza de las mismas;

c)   ser temporales y eliminarse progresivamente a medida que mejore la situación de la balanza de pagos;

d)   ser compatibles con las del párrafo 2(c), así como con los Artículos del Convenio del Fondo; y

e)   aplicarse de acuerdo con el más favorable, entre los principios de trato nacional y de nación más favorecida.

4.   Una Parte podrá adoptar o mantener una medida conforme a este artículo que otorgue prioridad a los objetivos esenciales para su programa económico, siempre que la Parte no aplique la medida con el fin de proteger a una industria o sector en particular, salvo que la medida sea compatible con el párrafo 2(c), y con el Artículo VIII (3) de los Artículos del Convenio del Fondo.

5.   Las restricciones impuestas a transferencias:

a)   deberán ser compatibles con el Artículo VIII (3) de los Artículos del Convenio del Fondo, cuando se apliquen a los pagos por transacciones internacionales corrientes;

b)   deberán ser compatibles con el Artículo VI de los Artículos del Convenio del Fondo y aplicarse sólo en conjunción con medidas sobre los pagos por transacciones internacionales corrientes de conformidad con el párrafo 2(a), cuando se apliquen a las transacciones internacionales de capital;

c)   no podrán impedir sustancialmente que las transferencias se realicen en moneda de libre uso a un tipo de cambio de mercado, cuando se apliquen a las transferencias previstas en el Artículo 13-10 (Transferencias) y a transferencias relativas al comercio de bienes; y

d)   no podrán tomar la forma de sobretasas arancelarias, cuotas, licencias o medidas similares.

[...]

*

AGREEMENT BETWEEN THE GOVERNMENT OF THE UNITED STATES OF AMERICA AND THE GOVERNMENT OF THE KINGDOM OF SAUDI ARABIA CONCERNING THE DEVELOPMENT OF TRADE AND INVESTMENT RELATIONS *

> The Agreement Between the Government of the United States of America and the Government of the Kingdom of Saudi Arabia Concerning the Development of Trade and Investment Relations was signed on 31 July 2003.

The Government of the United States of America and the Government of the Kingdom of Saudi Arabia (individually a "Party" and collectively the "Parties"):

1)   Desiring to enhance the historical bonds of friendship and spirit of cooperation between the two countries;

2)   Desiring to develop further both countries' international trade and economic interrelationship;

3)   Recognizing the importance of fostering an open and predictable environment for international trade and investment and economic cooperation;

4)   Recognizing the benefits to each Party resulting from increased international trade and investment, and that trade-distorting investment measures and protectionism would deprive the Parties of such benefits;

5)   Recognizing the essential role of private sector investment, both domestic and foreign, in furthering growth, creating jobs, expanding trade, enhancing economic development, and improving technology;

6)   Recognizing that foreign direct investment confers positive benefits on each Party;

7)   Desiring to encourage and facilitate private sector contacts between the two countries;

8)   Recognizing the desirability of resolving trade and investment problems as expeditiously as possible;

9)   Acknowledging prior bilateral Agreements signed by the Parties, including the Provisional Agreement Between the United States of America and the Kingdom of Saudi Arabia in Regard to Diplomatic and Consular Representation, Juridical Protection, Commerce and Navigation, signed November 7, 1933 and the Joint Statement on Saudi Arabian-United States Cooperation signed June 8, 1974;

Source: The Government of the United States and the Government of the Kingdom of Saudi Arabia (2003). "Agreement Between the Government of the United States of America and the Government of the Kingdom of Saudi Arabia Concerning the Development of Trade and Investment Relations", available on the Internet (http://www.ustr.gov/assets/Trade_Agreements/Regional/MEFTA/asset_upload_file304_3532.pdf). [Note added by the editor.]

10)   Noting that this agreement is without prejudice to the rights and obligations of the Parties under the agreements cited in the precedent paragraph 9;

11)   Recognizing the increased importance of services in their economies and in their bilateral relations;

12)   Taking into account the need to eliminate non-tariff barriers in order to facilitate greater access to the markets of both countries and the mutual benefits thereof;

13)   Recognizing the importance of providing adequate and effective protection and enforcement of intellectual property rights and the importance of adherence to international intellectual property rights standards;

14)   Recognizing the importance of protecting and enforcing worker rights in accordance with each nation's own labor laws and of working toward the respect and promotion of internationally recognized core labor standards;

15)   Desiring to ensure that trade and environmental policies are mutually supportive in furtherance of sustainable development; and

16)   Considering that it would be in their mutual interest to establish an additional bilateral mechanism between the Parties for encouraging the liberalization of trade and investment between them.

To this end, the Parties agree as follows:

ARTICLE ONE

The Parties will seek to:

1.   Expand trade in goods and services between them, within the framework and terms of this Agreement.

2.   Take appropriate measures to encourage and facilitate the exchange of goods and services and to secure favorable conditions for long-term development and diversification of trade between the two countries.

3.   Promote an attractive trade and investment climate between the two countries and facilitate expanded contacts between their respective private sectors.

ARTICLE TWO

Without prejudice to the work of the United States-Saudi Arabia Joint Commission on Economic Cooperation, the Parties shall establish a United States-Saudi Arabia Council on Trade and Investment ("the Council"), which shall be composed of representatives of both Parties. The Saudi Arabian side will be chaired by the Ministry of Commerce and Industry; and the U.S. side will be chaired by the Office of the U.S. Trade Representative ("USTR"). Both Parties may be assisted by officials of other government entities as circumstances require. The Council will meet at least once a year and at such times as agreed by the two Parties.

ARTICLE THREE

The objectives of the Council are as follows:

1.   To monitor trade and investment relations, to identify opportunities for expanding trade and investment, and to identify issues appropriate for negotiation.

2.   To hold consultations on specific trade and investment matters of interest to the Parties.

3.   To identify and work toward the removal of impediments to trade and investment flows.

4.   To facilitate expanded contacts between and seek the advice of the private sector in their respective countries on matters related to the work of the Council where the Parties deem it appropriate. Private sector representatives may be asked to participate in Council meetings whenever both Parties agree it is appropriate.

5.   To promote an attractive trade and investment climate between the two countries as a means of furthering growth, creating jobs, expanding trade, enhancing economic development, and improving technology.

ARTICLE FOUR

F or the purpose of further developing bilateral trade and providing for a steady increase in the exchange of products and services and promoting an attractive investment climate in the two countries, the Parties shall consider whether further agreements relating to trade, intellectual property, investment, vocational training, labor, environmental issues, and any other matters agreed upon by the Parties would be desirable.

ARTICLE FIVE

1.   Either Party may raise for consultation any trade or investment matter between the Parties.

Requests for consultation shall be accompanied by a written explanation of the subject to be discussed and consultations shall be held within 60 days of the request, unless the requesting Party agrees to a later date.

2.   Each party shall endeavor to provide for an opportunity for consultations before taking actions that could affect adversely the trade or investment interests of the other Party.

ARTICLE SIX

This Agreement is without prejudice to the rights and obligations of either Party under its domestic law or under any other agreements, conventions, or other instruments to which either country is a party. This Agreement may be amended through an exchange of notes between the Parties through diplomatic channels.

ARTICLE SEVEN

This Agreement shall enter into force on the date of its signature by both Parties.

ARTICLE EIGHT

This Agreement shall remain in force unless terminated by mutual consent of the Parties or by either Party upon six months written notice to the other Party.

IN WITNESS WHEREOF, the undersigned, being duly authorized by their respective governments, have signed this Agreement.

DONE at Washington this 31st day of July 2003, in duplicate in the English and Arabic languages, both texts being equally authentic.

*

UNITED STATES - AUSTRALIA FREE TRADE AGREEMENT*
[excerpts]

The United States - Australia Free Trade Agreement was signed on 18 May 2004.

[...]

CHAPTER TEN
CROSS-BORDER TRADE IN SERVICES

ARTICLE 10.1: SCOPE AND COVERAGE

1.   This Chapter applies to measures adopted or maintained by a Party affecting cross-border trade in services by service suppliers of the other Party. Such measures include measures affecting:

(a)   the production, distribution, marketing, sale, and delivery of a service;

(b)   the purchase or use of, or payment for, a service;

(c)   the access to and use of distribution, transport, or telecommunications networks and services in connection with the supply of a service;

(d)   the presence in its territory of a service supplier of the other Party; and

(e)   the provision of a bond or other form of financial security as a condition for the supply of a service.

2.   For the purposes of this Chapter, **measures adopted or maintained by a Party** means measures adopted or maintained by:

(a)   central, regional, or local governments and authorities; and

(b)   non-governmental bodies in the exercise of powers delegated by central, regional, or local governments or authorities.

3.   Articles 10.4, 10.7, and 10.8 shall also apply to measures by a Party affecting the supply of a service in its territory by a covered investment.

4.   This Chapter does not apply to:

---

* *Source*: The Government of the United States and the Government of Australia (2004). "United States - Australia Free Trade Agreement", available on the Internet (http://www.ustr.gov/Trade_Agreements/Bilateral/Australia_FTA/Final_Text/Section_Index.html). [Note added by the editor.]

(a)   financial services as defined in Article 13.19 (Definitions), except that paragraph 3 shall apply where the financial service is supplied by a covered investment that is not a covered investment in a financial institution (as defined in Article 13.19) in the Party's territory;

(b)   government procurement;

(c)   air services, including domestic and international air transportation services, whether scheduled or non-scheduled, and related services in support of air services, other than:

   (i)   aircraft repair and maintenance services during which an aircraft is withdrawn from service; and

   (ii)   specialty air services;

(d)   subsidies or grants provided by a Party, including government-supported loans, guarantees, and insurance; or

(e)   services supplied in the exercise of governmental authority within the territory of each respective Party, as defined in Article 1.2.22.

5.   This Chapter does not impose any obligation on a Party with respect to a national of the other Party seeking access to its employment market, or employed on a permanent basis in its territory, and does not confer any right on that national with respect to that access or employment.

ARTICLE 10.2: NATIONAL TREATMENT

Each Party shall accord to service suppliers of the other Party treatment no less favourable than that it accords, in like circumstances, to its own service suppliers.

ARTICLE 10.3: MOST-FAVOURED-NATION TREATMENT

Each Party shall accord to service suppliers of the other Party treatment no less favourable than that it accords, in like circumstances, to service suppliers of a non-Party.

ARTICLE 10.4: MARKET ACCESS

Neither Party may adopt or maintain, either on the basis of a regional subdivision or on the basis of its entire territory, measures that:

(a)   impose limitations on:

   (i)   the number of service suppliers, whether in the form of numerical quotas, monopolies, exclusive service suppliers, or the requirement of an economic needs test;

   (ii)   the total value of service transactions or assets in the form of numerical quotas or the requirement of an economic needs test;

(iii) the total number of service operations or the total quantity of services output expressed in terms of designated numerical units in the form of quotas or the requirement of an economic needs test;[10-1] or

(iv) the total number of natural persons that may be employed in a particular service sector or that a service supplier may employ and who are necessary for, and directly related to, the supply of a specific service in the form of numerical quotas or the requirement of an economic needs test; or

(b) restrict or require specific types of legal entity or joint venture through which a service supplier may supply a service.

ARTICLE 10.5: LOCAL PRESENCE

Neither Party may require a service supplier of the other Party to establish or maintain a representative office or any form of enterprise, or to be resident, in its territory as a condition for the cross-border supply of a service.

ARTICLE 10.6: NON-CONFORMING MEASURES

1. Articles 10.2, 10.3, 10.4, and 10.5 do not apply to:

(a) any existing non-conforming measure that is maintained by a Party at:

(i) the central level of government, as set out by that Party in its Schedule to Annex I;

(ii) a regional level of government, as set out by that Party in its Schedule to Annex I; or

(iii) a local level of government;

(b) the continuation or prompt renewal of any non-conforming measure referred to in subparagraph (a); or

(c) an amendment to any non-conforming measure referred to in subparagraph (a) to the extent that the amendment does not decrease the conformity of the measure, as it existed immediately before the amendment, with Articles 10.2, 10.3, 10.4, or 10.5.

2. Articles 10.2, 10.3, 10.4, and 10.5 do not apply to any measure that a Party adopts or maintains with respect to sectors, sub-sectors, or activities as set out in its Schedule to Annex II.

ARTICLE 10.7: DOMESTIC REGULATION

1. Where a Party requires authorization for the supply of a service, the Party's competent authorities shall, within a reasonable time after the submission of an application considered complete under its laws and regulations, inform the applicant of the decision concerning the

---

[10-1] 1This paragraph does not cover measures of a Party which limit inputs for the supply of services.

application. At the request of the applicant, the competent authorities of the Party shall provide, without undue delay, information concerning the status of the application. This obligation shall not apply to authorization requirements that a Party adopts or maintains with respect to sectors, sub-sectors, or activities as set out in its Schedule to Annex II.

2.   With a view to ensuring that measures relating to qualification requirements and procedures, technical standards, and licensing requirements do not constitute unnecessary barriers to trade in services, each Party shall endeavour to ensure, as appropriate for individual sectors, that such measures are:

(a)   based on objective and transparent criteria, such as competence and the ability to supply the service;

(b)   not more burdensome than necessary to ensure the quality of the service; and

(c)   in the case of licensing procedures, not in themselves a restriction on the supply of the service.

3.   If the results of the negotiations related to Article VI:4 of GATS (or the results of any similar negotiations undertaken in other multilateral fora in which both Parties participate) enter into effect, this Article shall be amended, as appropriate, after consultations between the Parties, to bring those results into effect under this Agreement. The Parties shall coordinate on such negotiations, as appropriate.

ARTICLE 10.8: TRANSPARENCY IN DEVELOPMENT AND APPLICATION OF REGULATIONS

Further to Chapter Twenty (Transparency):

1.   Each Party shall maintain or establish appropriate mechanisms for responding to inquiries from interested persons regarding its regulations relating to the subject matter of this Chapter.

2.   If a Party does not provide advance notice and opportunity for comment pursuant to Article 20.2 (Publication), it shall, to the extent possible, address in writing the reasons therefore.

3.   At the time it adopts final regulations relating to the subject matter of this Chapter, each Party shall, to the extent possible, including on request, address in writing substantive comments received from interested persons with respect to the proposed regulations.

4.   To the extent possible, each Party shall provide notice of the requirements of final regulations prior to their effective date.

ARTICLE 10.9: RECOGNITION

1.   For the purposes of fulfilment, in whole or in part, of its standards or criteria for the authorisation, licensing, or certification of services suppliers, and subject to the requirements of paragraph 4, a Party may recognise the education or experience obtained, requirements met, or licences or certifications granted in a particular country. Such recognition, which may be achieved through harmonisation or otherwise, may be based on an agreement or arrangement with the country concerned or may be accorded autonomously.

2.   Where a Party recognizes, autonomously or by agreement or arrangement, the education or experience obtained, requirements met, or licenses or certifications granted in the territory of a non-Party, nothing in Article 10.3 shall be construed to require the Party to accord such recognition to the education or experience obtained, requirements met, or licenses or certifications granted in the territory of the other Party.

3.   A Party that is a party to an agreement or arrangement of the type referred to in paragraph 1, whether existing or future, shall afford adequate opportunity for the other Party, if the other Party is interested, to negotiate accession to such an agreement or arrangement or to negotiate a comparable one with it. Where a Party accords recognition autonomously, it shall afford adequate opportunity for the other Party to demonstrate that education, experience, licenses, or certifications obtained or requirements met in that other Party's territory should be recognized.

4.   A Party shall not accord recognition in a manner which would constitute a means of discrimination between countries in the application of its standards or criteria for the authorization, licensing, or certification of services suppliers, or a disguised restriction on trade in services.

5.   Annex 10-A (Professional Services) applies to measures adopted or maintained by a Party relating to the licensing or certification of professional service suppliers as set out in that Annex.

ARTICLE 10.10: TRANSFERS AND PAYMENTS

1.   Each Party shall permit all transfers and payments relating to the cross-border supply of services to be made freely and without delay into and out of its territory.

2.   Each Party shall permit such transfers and payments relating to the cross-border supply of services to be made in a freely usable currency at the market rate of exchange prevailing on the date of transfer.

3.   Notwithstanding paragraphs 1 and 2, a Party may prevent or delay a transfer or payment through the equitable, non-discriminatory, and good faith application of its laws relating to:

   (a)   bankruptcy, insolvency, or the protection of the rights of creditors;

   (b)   issuing, trading, or dealing in securities, futures, options, or derivatives;

   (c)   financial reporting or record keeping of transfers when necessary to assist law enforcement or financial regulatory authorities;

   (d)   criminal or penal offences; or

   (e)   ensuring compliance with orders or judgments in judicial or administrative proceedings.

ARTICLE 10.11: DENIAL OF BENEFITS

1.   A Party may deny the benefits of this Chapter to a service supplier of the other Party if the service supplier is an enterprise owned or controlled by persons of a non-Party, and the denying Party:

(a)   does not maintain diplomatic relations with the non-Party; or

(b)   adopts or maintains measures with respect to the non-Party or a person of the non-Party that prohibit transactions with the enterprise or that would be violated or circumvented if the benefits of this Chapter were accorded to the enterprise.

2.   A Party may deny the benefits of this Chapter to a service supplier of the other Party if the service supplier is an enterprise owned or controlled by persons of a non-Party or of the denying Party that has no substantial business activities in the territory of the other Party.

ARTICLE 10.12: SPECIFIC COMMITMENTS

Express Delivery Services

1.   For the purposes of this Chapter, **express delivery services** means the collection, transport, and delivery, of documents, printed matter, parcels, or other items on an expedited basis, while tracking and maintaining control of these items throughout the supply of the service.

Express delivery services do not include (i) air transport services, (ii) services supplied in the exercise of governmental authority, as defined in Article 1.2.22, or (iii) maritime transport services.[10-2]

2.   The Parties confirm their desire to maintain at least the level of market openness for express delivery services that is in existence on the date this Agreement is signed. If a Party considers that the other Party is not maintaining such level of access, it may request consultations. The other Party shall afford adequate opportunity for consultations and, to the extent possible, shall provide information in response to inquiries regarding the level of access and any related matter.

3.   Each Party confirms its intention to prevent the direction of revenues derived from monopoly postal services to confer an advantage to its own or any other competitive supplier's express delivery services in a manner inconsistent with that Party's laws and practices applicable to the monopoly supply of postal services.

4.   For greater certainty, this Agreement, including Articles 14.3 (Designated Monopolies) and 14.5 (State Enterprises and Related Matters), applies to express delivery services.

[10-2] For greater clarity, express delivery services do not include:
(a) for the United States, delivery of letters subject to the Private Express Statutes (18 U.S.C. 1693 et seq., 39 U.S.C. 601 et seq.), but do include delivery of letters subject to the exceptions to, or suspensions promulgated under, those statutes, which permit private delivery of extremely urgent letters; and
(b) for Australia, services reserved for exclusive supply by Australia Post as set out in the Australian Postal Corporation Act 1989 and its subordinate legislation and regulations.

ARTICLE 10.13: IMPLEMENTATION

The Parties shall meet annually, or as otherwise agreed, on issues related to implementation of this Chapter and any other issues of mutual interest affecting trade in services.

ARTICLE 10.14: DEFINITIONS

For the purposes of this Chapter:

1.   **cross-border trade in services** or **cross-border supply of services** means the supply of a service:

(a)   from the territory of one Party into the territory of the other Party;

(b)   in the territory of one Party by a person of that Party to a person of the other Party; or

(c)   by a national of a Party in the territory of the other Party;

but does not include the supply of a service in the territory of a Party by a covered investment;

2.   **enterprise** means an enterprise as defined in Article 1.2.7 (General Definitions), and a branch of an enterprise;

3.   **enterprise of a Party** means an enterprise organized or constituted under the laws of a Party, and a branch located in the territory of a Party and carrying out business activities there;

4.   **freely usable currency** means a currency determined by the International Monetary Fund under its *Articles of Agreement* to be a currency that is, in fact, widely used to make payments for international transactions and is widely traded in the principal exchange markets;

5.   **professional services** means services, the supply of which requires specialized postsecondary education, or equivalent training or experience, and for which the right to practice is granted or restricted by a Party, but does not include services supplied by trades-persons or vessel and aircraft crew members;

6.   **service supplier of a Party** means a person of that Party that seeks to supply or supplies a service;[10-3] and

7.   **specialty air services** means any non-transportation air services, such as aerial firefighting, sightseeing, spraying, surveying, mapping, photography, parachute jumping, glider towing, and helicopter-lift for logging and construction, and other airborne agricultural, industrial, and inspection services.

[10-3] 10-3For the purposes of Articles 10.2 and 10.3, service suppliers has the same meaning as "services and service suppliers" as used in Articles II and XVII of GATS.

ANNEX 10-A
PROFESSIONAL SERVICES

DEVELOPMENT OF PROFESSIONAL SERVICES

1. The Parties shall encourage the relevant bodies in their respective territories to develop mutually acceptable standards and criteria for licensing and certification of professional services suppliers and to provide recommendations on mutual recognition to the Joint Committee.

2. The standards and criteria referred to in paragraph 1 may be developed with regard to the following matters:

    (a)   education – accreditation of schools or academic programs;

    (b)   examinations – qualifying examinations for licensing, including alternative methods of assessment, such as oral examinations and interviews;

    (c)   experience – length and nature of experience required for licensing;

    (d)   conduct and ethics – standards of professional conduct and the nature of disciplinary action for non-conformity with those standards;

    (e)   professional development and re-certification – continuing education and ongoing requirements to maintain professional certification;

    (f)   scope of practice – extent of, or limitations on, permissible activities;

    (g)   local knowledge – requirements for knowledge of such matters as local laws, regulations, geography, or climate; and

    (h)   consumer protection – alternatives to residency requirements, including bonding, professional liability insurance, and client restitution funds, to provide for the protection of consumers.

3. On receipt of a recommendation referred to in paragraph 1, the Joint Committee shall review the recommendation within a reasonable time to determine whether it is consistent with this Agreement. Based on the Joint Committee's review, each Party shall encourage its respective competent authorities, where appropriate, to implement the recommendation within a mutually agreed time.

TEMPORARY LICENSING

4. Where the Parties agree, each Party shall encourage the relevant bodies in its territory to develop procedures for the temporary licensing of professional services suppliers of the other Party.

WORKING GROUP ON PROFESSIONAL SERVICES

5. The Parties shall establish a Professional Services Working Group, comprising representatives of each Party, to facilitate the activities listed in paragraph 1.

6.   In pursuing this objective, the Working Group shall consider, as appropriate, relevant bilateral, plurilateral and multilateral agreements relating to professional services.

7.   The issues that the Working Group should consider, for professional services generally and, as appropriate, for individual professional services, include:

   (a)   procedures for fostering the development of mutual recognition arrangements between their relevant professional bodies;

   (b)   the feasibility of developing model procedures for the licensing and certification of professional services suppliers; and

   (c)   other issues of mutual interest relating to the supply of professional services.

8.   To facilitate the efforts of the Working Group, each Party shall consult with the relevant bodies in its territory to seek to identify professional services to which the Working Group should give consideration.

9.   The Working Group shall report to the Joint Committee on its progress, including with respect to any recommendations for initiatives to promote mutual recognition of standards and criteria, and on the further direction of its work, within two years of the entry into force of the Agreement.

REVIEW

10.   The Joint Committee shall, at least once every three years, review the implementation of this Annex.

CHAPTER ELEVEN
INVESTMENT

ARTICLE 11.1: SCOPE AND COVERAGE

1.   This Chapter applies to measures adopted or maintained by a Party relating to:

   (a)   investors of the other Party;

   (b)   covered investments; and

   (c)   with respect to Articles 11.9 and 11.11, all investments in the territory of the Party.

2.   For greater certainty, nothing in this Chapter imposes an obligation on a Party to privatise.

ARTICLE 11.2: RELATION TO OTHER CHAPTERS

1.   In the event of any inconsistency between this Chapter and another Chapter, the other Chapter shall prevail to the extent of the inconsistency.

2.   A requirement by a Party that a service supplier of the other Party post a bond or other form of financial security as a condition of the cross-border supply of a service does not of itself make this Chapter applicable to measures adopted or maintained by the Party relating to such cross-border supply of the service. This Chapter applies to measures adopted or maintained by the Party relating to the posted bond or financial security, to the extent that such bond or financial security is a covered investment.

3.   This Chapter does not apply to measures adopted or maintained by a Party to the extent that they are covered by Chapter Thirteen (Financial Services).

ARTICLE 11.3: NATIONAL TREATMENT

1.   Each Party shall accord to investors of the other Party treatment no less favourable than that it accords, in like circumstances, to its own investors with respect to the establishment, acquisition, expansion, management, conduct, operation, and sale or other disposition of investments in its territory.

2.   Each Party shall accord to covered investments treatment no less favourable than that it accords, in like circumstances, to investments in its territory of its own investors with respect to the establishment, acquisition, expansion, management, conduct, operation, and sale or other disposition of investments.

ARTICLE 11.4: MOST-FAVOURED NATION TREATMENT

1.   Each Party shall accord to investors of the other Party treatment no less favourable than that it accords, in like circumstances, to investors of any non-Party with respect to the establishment, acquisition, expansion, management, conduct, operation, and sale or other disposition of investments in its territory.

2.   Each Party shall accord to covered investments treatment no less favourable than that it accords, in like circumstances, to investments in its territory of investors of any non-Party with respect to the establishment, acquisition, expansion, management, conduct, operation, and sale or other disposition of investments.

ARTICLE 11.5: MINIMUM STANDARD OF TREATMENT[11-1]

1.   Each Party shall accord to covered investments treatment in accordance with the customary international law minimum standard of treatment of aliens, including fair and equitable treatment and full protection and security.

[11-1] Article 11.5 shall be interpreted in accordance with Annex 11-A.

2.   For greater certainty, the concepts of "fair and equitable treatment" and "full protection and security" do not require treatment in addition to or beyond that which is required by that standard, and do not create additional substantive rights. The obligation in paragraph 1 to provide:

(a)   "fair and equitable treatment" includes the obligation not to deny justice in criminal, civil, or administrative adjudicatory proceedings in accordance with the principle of due process embodied in the principal legal systems of the world; and

(b)   "full protection and security" requires each Party to provide the level of police protection required under customary international law.

3.   A determination that there has been a breach of another provision of this Agreement, or of a separate international agreement, does not establish that there has been a breach of this Article.

ARTICLE 11.6: TREATMENT IN CASE OF STRIFE

1.   Notwithstanding Article 11.13.5(b), each Party shall accord to investors of the other Party, and to covered investments, with respect to measures it adopts or maintains relating to losses suffered by investments in its territory owing to armed conflict or civil strife, treatment no less favourable than that it accords, in like circumstances, to:

(a)   its own investors and their investments; and

(b)   investors of any non-Party and their investments.

2.   Notwithstanding paragraph 1, if an investor of a Party, in the situations referred to in paragraph 1, suffers a loss in the territory of the other Party resulting from:

(a)   requisitioning of its covered investment or part thereof by the latter's forces or authorities; or

(b)   destruction of its covered investment or part thereof by the latter's forces or authorities, which was not required by the necessity of the situation,

the latter Party shall provide the investor with restitution, compensation, or both, as appropriate, for such loss. Any compensation shall be prompt, adequate, and effective in accordance with Article 11.7.2 through 11.7.4, *mutatis mutandis*.

3.   Paragraph 1 does not apply to existing measures relating to subsidies or grants that would be inconsistent with Article 11.3 but for Article 11.13.5(b).

ARTICLE 11.7: EXPROPRIATION AND COMPENSATION[11-2]

1.   Neither Party may expropriate or nationalise a covered investment either directly or indirectly through measures equivalent to expropriation or nationalisation ("expropriation"), except:

[11-2] Article 11.7 shall be interpreted in accordance with Annexes 11-A and 11-B.

    (a)   for a public purpose;

    (b)   in a non-discriminatory manner;

    (c)   on payment of prompt, adequate, and effective compensation; and

    (d)   in accordance with due process of law.

2.   The compensation referred to in paragraph 1(c) shall:

    (a)   be paid without delay;

    (b)   be equivalent to the fair market value of the expropriated investment immediately before the expropriation took place ("the date of expropriation");

    (c)   not reflect any change in value occurring because the intended expropriation had become known earlier; and

    (d)   be fully realisable and freely transferable.

3.   If the fair market value is denominated in a freely usable currency or the Australian dollar, the compensation referred to in paragraph 1(c) shall be no less than the fair market value on the date of expropriation, plus interest at a commercially reasonable rate for that currency, accrued from the date of expropriation until the date of payment.

4.   However, if the fair market value is denominated in the Australian dollar and the Australian dollar is not transferable on the date of payment at the market rate of exchange, or if it is denominated in another currency that is not freely usable, the compensation referred to in paragraph 1(c) – converted into the currency of payment at the market rate of exchange prevailing on the date of payment – shall be no less than:

    (a)   the fair market value on the date of expropriation, converted into a freely usable currency at the market rate of exchange prevailing on that date, plus

    (b)   interest, at a commercially reasonable rate for that freely usable currency, accrued from the date of expropriation until the date of payment.

5.   This Article does not apply to the issuance of compulsory licenses granted in relation to intellectual property rights in accordance with the TRIPS Agreement, or to the revocation, limitation, or creation of intellectual property rights, to the extent that such issuance, revocation, limitation, or creation is consistent with Chapter Seventeen (Intellectual Property Rights).[11-3]11-3

ARTICLE 11.8: TRANSFERS

1.   Each Party shall permit all transfers relating to a covered investment to be made freely and without delay into and out of its territory. Such transfers include:

    (a)   contributions to capital, including the initial contribution;

[11-3] For greater certainty, the reference to the "TRIPS Agreement" in paragraph 5 includes any waiver in force between the Parties of any provision of that Agreement granted by WTO Members in accordance with the WTO Agreement.

(b)   profits, dividends, capital gains, and proceeds from the sale of all or any part of the covered investment or from the partial or complete liquidation of the covered investment;

(c)   interest, royalty payments, management fees, and technical assistance and other fees;

(d)   payments made under a contract, including a loan agreement;

(e)   payments made pursuant to Articles 11.6.1 and 11.6.2 and Article 11.7; and

(f)   payments arising out of a dispute.

2.   Each Party shall permit transfers relating to a covered investment to be made in a freely usable currency at the market rate of exchange prevailing at the time of transfer.

3.   Each Party shall permit returns in kind relating to a covered investment to be made as authorised or specified in a written agreement between the Party and a covered investment or an investor of the other Party that takes effect on or after the date of entry into force of this Agreement.

4.   Notwithstanding paragraphs 1 through 3, a Party may prevent or delay a transfer through the equitable, non-discriminatory, and good faith application of its laws relating to:

(a)   bankruptcy, insolvency, or the protection of the rights of creditors;

(b)   issuing, trading, or dealing in securities, futures, options, or derivatives;

(c)   criminal or penal offences;

(d)   financial reporting or record keeping of transfers when necessary to assist law enforcement or financial regulatory authorities; or

(e)   ensuring compliance with orders or judgments in judicial or administrative proceedings.

ARTICLE 11.9: PERFORMANCE REQUIREMENTS

1.   Neither Party may, in connection with the establishment, acquisition, expansion, management, conduct, operation, or sale or other disposition of an investment of an investor of a Party or of a non-Party in its territory, impose or enforce any requirement, or enforce any commitment or undertaking, to:[11-4]

(a)   export a given level or percentage of goods or services;

(b)   achieve a given level or percentage of domestic content;

[11-4] For greater certainty, a condition for the receipt or continued receipt of an advantage referred to in paragraph 2 does not constitute a "commitment or undertaking" for the purposes of paragraph 1.

(c)   purchase, use, or accord a preference to goods produced in its territory, or to purchase goods from persons in its territory;

(d)   relate in any way the volume or value of imports to the volume or value of exports or to the amount of foreign exchange inflows associated with such investment;

(e)   restrict sales of goods or services in its territory that such investment produces or supplies by relating such sales in any way to the volume or value of its exports or foreign exchange earnings;

(f)   transfer a particular technology, a production process, or other proprietary knowledge to a person in its territory; or

(g)   supply exclusively from the territory of the Party the goods that such investment produces or the services that such investment supplies to a specific regional market or to the world market.

2.   Neither Party may condition the receipt or continued receipt of an advantage, in connection with the establishment, acquisition, expansion, management, conduct, operation, or sale or other disposition of an investment in its territory of an investor of a Party or of a non-Party, on compliance with any requirement to:

(a)   achieve a given level or percentage of domestic content;

(b)   purchase, use, or accord a preference to goods produced in its territory, or to purchase goods from persons in its territory;

(c)   relate in any way the volume or value of imports to the volume or value of exports or to the amount of foreign exchange inflows associated with such investment; or

(d)   restrict sales of goods or services in its territory that such investment produces or supplies by relating such sales in any way to the volume or value of its exports or foreign exchange earnings.

3.   (a)   Nothing in paragraph 2 shall be construed to prevent a Party from conditioning the receipt or continued receipt of an advantage, in connection with an investment in its territory of an investor of a Party or of a non-Party, on compliance with a requirement to locate production, supply a service, train or employ workers, construct or expand particular facilities, or carry out research and development, in its territory.

(b)   Paragraph 1(f) does not apply:

(i)   when a Party authorises use of an intellectual property right in accordance with Article 17.9.7 (Patents), or to measures requiring the disclosure of proprietary information that fall within the scope of, and are consistent with, Article 39 of the TRIPS Agreement; or

(ii) when the requirement is imposed or the commitment or undertaking is enforced by a court, administrative tribunal, or competition authority to remedy a practice determined after judicial or administrative process to be anticompetitive under a Party's laws relating to the prevention of anticompetitive behaviour.[11-5]

(c) Provided that such measures are not applied in an arbitrary or unjustifiable manner, and provided that such measures do not constitute a disguised restriction on investment or international trade, paragraphs 1(b), (c), and (f), and 2(a) and (b), shall not be construed to prevent a Party from adopting or maintaining measures, including environmental measures:

(i) necessary to secure compliance with laws and regulations that are not inconsistent with this Agreement;

(ii) necessary to protect human, animal, or plant life or health; or

(iii) related to the conservation of living or non-living exhaustible natural resources.

(d) Paragraphs 1(a), (b), and (c), and 2(a) and (b), do not apply to qualification requirements for goods or services with respect to export promotion and foreign aid programs.

(e) Paragraphs 1(b), (c), (f), and (g), and 2(a) and (b), do not apply to government procurement.

(f) Paragraphs 2(a) and (b) do not apply to requirements imposed by an importing Party relating to the content of goods necessary to qualify for preferential tariffs or preferential quotas.

4. For greater certainty, paragraphs 1 and 2 do not apply to any requirement other than the requirements set out in those paragraphs.

5. This Article does not preclude enforcement of any commitment, undertaking, or requirement between private parties, where a Party did not impose or require the commitment, undertaking, or requirement.

ARTICLE 11.10: SENIOR MANAGEMENT AND BOARDS OF DIRECTORS

1. Neither Party may require that an enterprise of that Party that is a covered investment appoint to senior management positions natural persons of any particular nationality.

2. A Party may require that a majority or less of the board of directors, or any committee thereof, of an enterprise of that Party that is a covered investment, be of a particular nationality, or resident in the territory of the Party, provided that the requirement does not materially impair the ability of the investor to exercise control over its investment.

[11-5] The Parties recognize that a patent does not necessarily confer market power.

ARTICLE 11.11: INVESTMENT AND ENVIRONMENT

Nothing in this Chapter shall be construed to prevent a Party from adopting, maintaining, or enforcing any measure otherwise consistent with this Chapter that it considers appropriate to ensure that investment activity in its territory is undertaken in a manner sensitive to environmental concerns.

ARTICLE 11.12: DENIAL OF BENEFITS

1.   A Party may deny the benefits of this Chapter to an investor of the other Party that is an enterprise of such other Party and to investments of that investor if persons of a non-Party own or control the enterprise and the denying Party:

(a)   does not maintain diplomatic relations with the non-Party; or

(b)   adopts or maintains measures with respect to the non-Party or a person of the non-Party that prohibit transactions with the enterprise or that would be violated or circumvented if the benefits of this Chapter were accorded to the enterprise or its investments.

2.   A Party may deny the benefits of this Chapter to an investor of the other Party that is an enterprise of such other Party and to investments of that investor if the enterprise has no substantial business activities in the territory of the other Party and persons of a non-Party, or of the denying Party, own or control the enterprise.

ARTICLE 11.13: NON-CONFORMING MEASURES

1.   Articles 11.3, 11.4, 11.9, and 11.10 do not apply to:

(a)   any existing non-conforming measure that is maintained by a Party at:

(i)   the central level of government, as set out by that Party in its Schedule to Annex I,

(ii)   a regional level of government, as set out by that Party in its Schedule to Annex I, or

(iii)   a local level of government;

(b)   the continuation or prompt renewal of any non-conforming measure referred to in sub-paragraph (a); or

(c)   an amendment to any non-conforming measure referred to in subparagraph (a) to the extent that the amendment does not decrease the conformity of the measure, as it existed immediately before the amendment, with Article 11.3, 11.4, 11.9, or

2.   Articles 11.3, 11.4, 11.9, and 11.10 do not apply to any measure that a Party adopts or maintains with respect to sectors, sub-sectors, or activities, as set out in its Schedule to Annex II.

3.   Neither Party may, under any measure adopted after the date of entry into force of this Agreement and covered by its Schedule to Annex II, require an investor of the other Party, by reason of its nationality, to sell or otherwise dispose of an investment existing at the time the measure becomes effective.

4.   Articles 11.3 and 11.4 do not apply to any measure that is an exception to, or derogation from, the obligations under Article 17.1.6 (National Treatment) as specifically provided in that Article.

5.   Articles 11.3, 11.4, and 11.10 do not apply to:

(a)   government procurement; or

(b)   subsidies or grants provided by a Party, including government-supported loans, guarantees, and insurance.

ARTICLE 11.14: SPECIAL FORMALITIES AND INFORMATION REQUIREMENTS

1.   Nothing in Article 11.3 shall be construed to prevent a Party from adopting or maintaining a measure that prescribes special formalities in connection with covered investments, such as a requirement that investors be residents of the Party or that covered investments be legally constituted under the laws or regulations of the Party, provided that such formalities do not materially impair the protections afforded by a Party to investors of the other Party and covered investments pursuant to this Chapter.

2.   Notwithstanding Articles 11.3 and 11.4, a Party may require an investor of the other Party, or a covered investment, to provide information concerning that investment solely for informational or statistical purposes. The Party shall protect any confidential information from any disclosure that would prejudice the competitive position of the investor or the covered investment. Nothing in this paragraph shall be construed to prevent a Party from otherwise obtaining or disclosing information in connection with the equitable and good faith application of its law.

ARTICLE 11.15: IMPLEMENTATION

The Parties shall meet annually, or as agreed otherwise, to discuss the implementation of this Chapter and other issues of mutual interest, including the operation of their respective investment regimes.

ARTICLE 11.16: CONSULTATIONS ON INVESTOR-STATE DISPUTE SETTLEMENT

1.   If a Party considers that there has been a change in circumstances affecting the settlement of disputes on matters within the scope of this Chapter and that, in light of such change, the Parties should consider allowing an investor of a Party to submit to arbitration with the other Party a claim regarding a matter within the scope of this Chapter, the Party may request consultations with the other Party on the subject, including the development of procedures that may be appropriate. On such a request, the Parties shall promptly enter into consultations with a view towards allowing such a claim and establishing such procedures.

2.   For greater certainty, nothing in this Article prevents a Party from raising any matter arising under this Chapter pursuant to the procedures set out in Chapter 21 (Institutional Arrangements and Dispute Settlement). Nor does anything in this Article prevent an investor of a Party from submitting to arbitration a claim against the other Party to the extent permitted under that Party's law.

ARTICLE 11.17: DEFINITIONS

For the purposes of this Chapter:

1.   **enterprise** means an enterprise as defined in Article 1.2.7 (General Definitions), and a branch of an enterprise;

2.   **enterprise of a Party** means an enterprise constituted or organized under the law of a Party, and a branch located in the territory of a Party and carrying out business activities there;

3.   **freely usable currency** means a currency determined by the International Monetary Fund under its *Articles of Agreement* to be a currency that is, in fact, widely used to make payments for international transactions and is widely traded in the principal exchange markets;

4.   **investment** means every asset that an investor owns or controls, directly or indirectly, that has the characteristics of an investment, including such characteristics as the commitment of capital or other resources, the expectation of gain or profit, or the assumption of risk. Forms that an investment may take include:

(a)   an enterprise;

(b)   shares, stock, and other forms of equity participation in an enterprise;

(c)   bonds, debentures, other debt instruments, and loans;[11-6]

(d)   futures, options, and other derivatives;

(e)   turnkey, construction, management, production, concession, revenue-sharing, and other similar contracts;

(f)   intellectual property rights;

(g)   licenses, authorisations, permits, and similar rights conferred pursuant to the applicable domestic law;[11-7,11-8] and

---

[11-6]Some forms of debt, such as bonds, debentures, and long-term notes, are more likely to have the characteristics of an investment, while other forms of debt, such as claims to payment that are immediately due and result from the sale of goods or services, are less likely to have such characteristics.

[11-7]Whether a particular type of license, authorisation, permit, or similar instrument (including a concession, to the extent that it has the nature of such an instrument) has the characteristics of an investment depends on such factors as the nature and extent of the rights that the holder has under the applicable domestic law. Among the licenses, authorisations, permits, and similar instruments that do not have the characteristics of an investment are those that do not create any rights protected under domestic law. For greater certainty, the foregoing is without prejudice to whether any asset associated with the license, authorisation, permit, or similar instrument has the characteristics of an investment.

[11-8] The term **investment** does not include an order or judgment entered in a judicial or administrative action.

(h)   other tangible or intangible, movable or immovable property, and related property rights, such as leases, mortgages, liens, and pledges;

5.   **investor of a non-Party** means, with respect to a Party, an investor that seeks to make, is making, or has made an investment in the territory of that Party, that is not an investor of either Party;

6.   **investor of a Party** means a Party, or a national or an enterprise of a Party, that seeks to make, is making, or has made an investment in the territory of the other Party; provided, however, that a natural person who is a citizen of both Parties or of a Party and a non-Party shall be deemed to be exclusively a citizen of the State of his or her dominant and effective nationality.

ANNEX 11-A
CUSTOMARY INTERNATIONAL LAW

The Parties confirm their shared understanding that "customary international law" generally and as specifically referenced in Article 11.5 and Annex 11-B results from a general and consistent practice of States that they follow from a sense of legal obligation. With regard to Article 11.5, the customary international law minimum standard of treatment of aliens refers to all customary international law principles that protect the economic rights and interests of aliens.

ANNEX 11-B
EXPROPRIATION

1.   The Parties confirm their shared understanding that Article 11.7.1 is intended to reflect customary international law concerning the obligation of States with respect to expropriation.

2.   An action or a series of actions by a Party cannot constitute an expropriation unless it interferes with a tangible or intangible property right or property interest in an investment.

3.   Article 11.7.1 addresses two situations. The first is direct expropriation, where an investment is nationalized or otherwise directly expropriated through formal transfer of title or outright seizure.

4.   The second situation addressed by Article 11.7.1 is indirect expropriation, where an action or series of actions by a Party has an effect equivalent to direct expropriation without formal transfer of title or outright seizure.

(a)   The determination of whether an action or series of actions by a Party, in a specific fact situation, constitutes an indirect expropriation, requires a case-bycase, fact-based inquiry that considers, among other factors:

(i)   the economic impact of the government action, although the fact that an action or series of actions by a Party has an adverse effect on the economic value of an investment, standing alone, does not establish that an indirect expropriation has occurred;

(ii) the extent to which the government action interferes with distinct, reasonable investment-backed expectations; and

(iii) the character of the government action.

(b) Except in rare circumstances, nondiscriminatory regulatory actions by a Party that are designed and applied to achieve legitimate public welfare objectives, such as the protection of public health, safety, and the environment, do not constitute indirect expropriations.

CHAPTER TWELVE
TELECOMMUNICATIONS

ARTICLE 12.1: SCOPE AND COVERAGE

1. This Chapter applies to measures affecting trade in telecommunications services.

2. Except to ensure that enterprises operating broadcast stations and cable systems have continued access to and use of public telecommunications services, this Chapter does not apply to measures that a Party adopts or maintains relating to broadcast or cable distribution of radio or television programming.

3. Nothing in this Chapter shall be construed as:

(a) requiring a Party to compel any enterprise to establish, construct, acquire, lease, operate, or provide telecommunications networks or services where such networks or services are not offered to the public generally; or

(b) requiring a Party to compel any enterprise exclusively engaged in the broadcast or cable distribution of radio or television programming to make available its broadcast or cable facilities as a public telecommunications network.

Section A: Access To And Use Of Public Telecommunications Services

ARTICLE 12.2: ACCESS AND USE

1. Each Party shall ensure that enterprises of the other Party have access to and use of any public telecommunications service, including leased circuits, offered in its territory or across its borders, on terms and conditions that are reasonable and non-discriminatory (including with respect to timeliness), such as those set out in paragraphs 2 through 5.

2. Each Party shall ensure that such enterprises are permitted to:

(a) purchase or lease, and attach terminal or other equipment that interfaces with a public telecommunications network;

(b) provide services to individual or multiple end-users over leased or owned circuits;

(c)   connect owned or leased circuits with public telecommunications networks and services in the territory, or across the borders, of that Party, or with circuits leased or owned by another enterprise;

(d)   perform switching, signalling, processing, and conversion functions; and

(e)   use operating protocols of their choice.

3.   Each Party shall ensure that enterprises of the other Party may use public telecommunications services for the movement of information in its territory or across its borders and for access to information contained in databases or otherwise stored in machine-readable form in the territory of either Party or any WTO Member.

4.   Notwithstanding paragraph 3, a Party may take such measures as are necessary to ensure the security and confidentiality of messages subject to the requirement that such measures are not applied in a manner that would constitute a means of arbitrary or unjustifiable discrimination or a disguised restriction on trade in services.

5.   Each Party shall ensure that no condition is imposed on access to and use of public telecommunications networks or services, other than as necessary to:

(a)   safeguard the public service responsibilities of suppliers of public telecommunications networks or services, in particular their ability to make their networks or services available to the public generally; or

(b)   protect the technical integrity of public telecommunications networks or services.

Section B: Suppliers Of Public Telecommunications Services[12-1]

ARTICLE 12.3: INTERCONNECTION

1.   Each Party shall ensure suppliers of public telecommunications services in its territory provide, directly or indirectly, interconnection with the suppliers of public telecommunications services of the other Party.

2.   In carrying out paragraph 1, each Party shall ensure that suppliers of public telecommunications services in its territory take reasonable steps to protect the confidentiality of commercially sensitive information of, or relating to, suppliers and end-users of public telecommunications services and only use such information for the purpose of providing those services.

[12-1] For the purposes of this Chapter, Articles 12.4 and 12.5 do not apply to suppliers of commercial mobile services. In addition, a state regulatory authority may exempt a rural local exchange carrier, as defined in section 251(f)(2) of the United States Communications Act of 1934, as amended by the Telecommunications Act of 1996, from the obligations contained in Articles 12.4 and 12.5.

ARTICLE 12.4: NUMBER PORTABILITY

Each Party shall ensure that suppliers of public telecommunications services in its territory provide number portability for fixed telephony and any other service designated by that Party to the extent technically feasible, and on terms and conditions that are reasonable and nondiscriminatory (including with respect to timeliness).

ARTICLE 12.5: DIALING PARITY

Each Party shall ensure that suppliers of public telecommunications services in its territory provide dialing parity to suppliers of public telecommunications services of the other Party, and afford suppliers of public telecommunications services of the other Party non-discriminatory access to telephone numbers and related services.

ARTICLE 12.6: SUBMARINE CABLE SYSTEMS

Each Party shall ensure reasonable and non-discriminatory treatment for access to submarine cable systems (including landing facilities) in its territory, where a supplier is authorized to operate a submarine cable system as a public telecommunications service.

Section C: Conduct Of Major Suppliers Of Public Telecommunications Services[12-2,12-3]

ARTICLE 12.7: TREATMENT BY MAJOR SUPPLIERS

Each Party shall ensure that major suppliers in its territory accord suppliers of public telecommunications services of the other Party treatment no less favourable than such major suppliers accord in like circumstances to their subsidiaries, their affiliates, or non-affiliated service suppliers, regarding:

(a)   the availability, provisioning, rates, or quality of like public telecommunications services; and

(b)   the availability of technical interfaces necessary for interconnection.

ARTICLE 12.8: COMPETITIVE SAFEGUARDS

Each Party shall maintain appropriate measures for the purpose of preventing suppliers who, alone or together, are a major supplier in its territory from engaging in or continuing anticompetitive practices, including in particular:

(a)   engaging in anti-competitive cross-subsidization;

[12-2]For greater clarity, the obligations imposed under this Section only apply with respect to those public telecommunications services that result in a supplier of public telecommunications services being a major supplier.

[12-3] For the purposes of this Chapter, Section C does not apply to suppliers of commercial mobile services. In addition, with respect to the United States, Section C does not apply to rural telephone companies, as defined in section 3(37) of the U.S. Communications Act of 1934, as amended by the Telecommunications Act of 1996, unless a state regulatory authority orders otherwise. A state regulatory authority may also exempt a rural local exchange carrier, as defined in section 251(f)(2) of the U.S. Communications Act of 1934, as amended by the Telecommunications Act of 1996, from the obligations contained in Section C.

(b)   using information obtained from competitors with anti-competitive results; and

(c)   not making available, on a timely basis, to suppliers of public telecommunications services, technical information about essential facilities and commercially relevant information that are necessary for them to provide services.

ARTICLE 12.9: RESALE

1.   Each Party shall ensure that major suppliers in its territory:

(a)   offer for resale, at reasonable rates,[12-4] to suppliers of public telecommunications services of the other Party, public telecommunications services that such major supplier provides at retail to end users that are not suppliers of public telecommunications services; and

(b)   do not impose unreasonable or discriminatory conditions or limitations on the resale of such services.[12-5]

2.   Each Party may determine in accordance with its law and regulations which public telecommunications services must be offered for resale by major suppliers in accordance with paragraph 1, based on the need to promote competition or such other factors as the Party considers relevant.

ARTICLE 12.10: UNBUNDLING OF NETWORK ELEMENTS

Each Party shall provide its telecommunications regulatory body with the authority to require that major suppliers in its territory provide suppliers of public telecommunications services of the other Party access to network elements for the provision of public telecommunications services on an unbundled basis, and on terms and conditions, and at cost-oriented rates that are reasonable, non-discriminatory, and transparent.

ARTICLE 12.11: INTERCONNECTION

General Terms and Conditions

1.   Each Party shall ensure that major suppliers in its territory provide interconnection for the facilities and equipment of suppliers of public telecommunications services of the other Party:

(a)   at any technically feasible point in the major supplier's network;

(b)   under non-discriminatory terms, conditions (including technical standards and specifications), and rates;

[12-4] For the purposes of subparagraph (a): 1) a Party may determine reasonable rates through any methodology it considers appropriate; and 2) wholesale rates, set pursuant to a Party's law and regulations, shall be considered reasonable.

[12-5] Where provided in its laws or regulations, a Party may prohibit a reseller that obtains, at wholesale rates, a public telecommunications service available at retail to only a limited category of subscribers from offering the service to a different category of subscribers.

(c) of a quality no less favourable than that provided by such major suppliers for their own like services, for like services of non-affiliated service suppliers, or for their subsidiaries or other affiliates;

(d) in a timely fashion, on terms, conditions (including technical standards and specifications), and cost-oriented rates, that are transparent, reasonable, having regard to economic feasibility, and sufficiently unbundled so that suppliers seeking interconnection need not pay for network components or facilities that they do not require for the service to be provided; and

(e) on request, at points in addition to the network termination points offered to the majority of users, subject to charges that reflect the cost of construction of necessary additional facilities.

Options for Interconnecting with Major Suppliers

2. Each Party shall ensure that suppliers of public telecommunications services of the other Party may interconnect their facilities and equipment with those of major suppliers in its territory pursuant to at least one of the following options:

(a) a reference interconnection offer or another standard interconnection offer containing the rates, terms, and conditions that the major supplier offers generally to suppliers of public telecommunications services;

(b) the terms and conditions of an existing interconnection agreement;

(c) through negotiation of a new interconnection agreement; or

(d) arbitration.

Public Availability of Interconnection Offers

3. Each Party shall ensure that major suppliers in its territory make publicly available reference interconnection offers or other standard interconnection offers containing the rates, terms, and conditions that the major suppliers offer generally to suppliers of public telecommunications services.

Public Availability of Procedures for Interconnection Negotiations

4. Each Party shall ensure that applicable procedures for interconnection negotiations with major suppliers in its territory are made publicly available.

Public Availability of Terms and Conditions for Interconnection with Major Suppliers

5. Each Party shall ensure that the rates, terms, and conditions for interconnection with major suppliers:

(a) contained in reference interconnection offers or other standard interconnection offers approved by a telecommunications regulatory body; or

(b)   determined by a telecommunications regulatory body through arbitration are made publicly available.

ARTICLE 12.12: PROVISIONING AND PRICING OF LEASED CIRCUIT SERVICES

1.   Each Party shall ensure that major suppliers in its territory provide suppliers of public telecommunications services of the other Party leased circuit services that are public telecommunications services on terms and conditions, and at rates, that are reasonable, nondiscriminatory (including with respect to timeliness), and transparent.

2.   In carrying out paragraph 1, each Party shall provide its telecommunications regulatory body the authority to require major suppliers in its territory to offer such leased circuit services that are public telecommunications services to public telecommunications services suppliers of the other Party at capacity-based, cost-oriented prices.

ARTICLE 12.13: CO-LOCATION

1.   Subject to paragraphs 2 and 3, each Party shall ensure that major suppliers in its territory provide to suppliers of public telecommunications services of the other Party physical collocation of equipment necessary for interconnection or access to unbundled network elements on terms and conditions, and at cost-oriented rates, that are reasonable, non-discriminatory (including with respect to timeliness), and transparent.

2.   Where physical co-location is not practical for technical reasons or because of space limitations, each Party shall ensure that major suppliers facilitate alternative solutions, which may include:

(a)   conditioning additional equipment space or providing virtual co-location, on terms and conditions, and at cost-oriented rates, that are reasonable, nondiscriminatory (including with respect to timeliness), and transparent;

(b)   permitting facilities-based suppliers to locate equipment in a nearby building and to connect such equipment to the major supplier's network;

(c)   optimising the use of existing space; or

(d)   finding adjacent space.

3.   Each Party may determine, in accordance with its law and regulations, which premises in its territory are subject to paragraphs 1 and 2.

ARTICLE 12.14: ACCESS TO POLES, DUCTS, CONDUITS, AND RIGHTS OF WAY

1.   Each Party shall ensure that major suppliers in its territory provide access to poles, ducts, conduits, and rights of way owned or controlled by such major suppliers to suppliers of public telecommunications services of the other Party on terms and conditions, and at cost-oriented[12-6]

[12-6] In the United States, the obligation to provide cost-oriented rates does not apply to those states that regulate such rates as a matter of state law.

rates, that are reasonable, non-discriminatory (including with respect to timeliness), and transparent.

2.   Nothing in this Chapter shall prevent a Party from determining, under its law and regulations, which particular structures owned or controlled by major suppliers in its territory are required to be made available in accordance with paragraph 1, provided that this determination is based on a conclusion that such structures cannot feasibly be economically or technically substituted in order to provide a competing service.

Section D: Other Measures

ARTICLE 12.15: FLEXIBILITY IN THE CHOICE OF TECHNOLOGY

Neither Party may prevent suppliers of public telecommunications services or suppliers of valueadded services from choosing the technologies they wish to use to supply their services, including packet-based services and commercial mobile wireless services, subject to requirements necessary to satisfy legitimate public policy interests.

ARTICLE 12.16: CONDITIONS FOR THE SUPPLY OF VALUE-ADDED SERVICES

1.   Neither Party may require an enterprise in its territory that supplies value-added services over facilities that it does not own to:

    (a)   supply such services to the public generally;

    (b)   cost-justify its rates for such services;

    (c)   file a tariff for such services;

    (d)   interconnect its networks with any particular customer for the supply of such services; or

    (e)   conform with any particular standard or technical regulation for interconnection other than for interconnection to a public telecommunications network, except to remedy a practice that the Party has found in a particular case to be anti-competitive under its law or regulations or to otherwise promote competition or safeguard the interests of consumers.

2.   For greater clarity, nothing in this Article shall exempt a Party from complying with the obligations in Articles 12.2 through 14.

ARTICLE 12.17: INDEPENDENT REGULATORY BODIES AND DIVESTMENT

1.   Each Party shall ensure that any telecommunications regulatory body that it establishes or maintains is independent and separate from, and not accountable to, any supplier of public telecommunications service.

2.   Each Party shall ensure that the decisions and procedures of its telecommunications regulatory body are impartial with respect to all interested persons. To this end, each Party shall

ensure that its regulatory body does not hold a financial interest in any supplier of public telecommunications services, and that any financial interest that the Party holds in a supplier of a public telecommunications services does not influence the decisions and procedures of its telecommunications regulatory body.

3.   Where a Party has an ownership interest in a supplier of a public telecommunications service and it intends to reduce or eliminate that interest, it shall notify the other Party as soon as feasible.

ARTICLE 12.18: UNIVERSAL SERVICE

Each Party shall administer any universal service obligation that it maintains in a transparent, non-discriminatory, and competitively neutral manner and shall ensure that its universal service obligation is not more burdensome than necessary for the kind of universal service that it has defined.

ARTICLE 12.19: REGULATORY PROCEDURES

1.   Each Party shall ensure that rules, including the basis for such rulemaking, of its telecommunications regulatory body are promptly published or otherwise made available to all interested persons.

2.   When a Party requires a supplier of public telecommunications services to have a license, the Party shall make publicly available:

(a)   all the licensing criteria and procedures it applies, including any standard terms and conditions of the license;

(b)   the time it normally requires to reach a decision concerning an application for a license; and

(c)   the terms and conditions of all licenses it has issued.

3.   Each Party shall ensure that, on request, an applicant receives the reasons for the denial of a license.

4.   Each Party shall ensure that tariffs filed with its telecommunications regulatory body are promptly published or otherwise made available to all interested parties.

ARTICLE 12.20: ALLOCATION AND USE OF SCARCE TELECOMMUNICATIONS RESOURCES

1.   Each Party shall administer its procedures for the allocation and use of scarce telecommunications resources, including frequencies, numbers, and rights of way, in an objective, timely, transparent, and non-discriminatory manner.[12-7]

[12-7] For greater clarity, telecommunications resources do not include spectrum allocated and used for the broadcast of radio and television programming.

2.   Each Party shall make publicly available the current state of allocated frequency bands but shall not be required to provide detailed identification of frequencies assigned for specific government uses.

3.   For greater clarity, measures regarding the allocation and assignment of spectrum and regarding frequency management are not measures that are *per se* inconsistent with Article 10.4 (Market Access), which is applied to Chapter Eleven (Investment) through Article 10.1.3 (Scope and Coverage). Accordingly, each Party retains the right to establish and apply its spectrum and frequency management policies, which may limit the number of suppliers of public telecommunications services, provided that it does so in a manner that is consistent with this Agreement. Each Party also retains the right to allocate frequency bands taking into account current and future needs.

4.   When making a spectrum allocation for non-government telecommunications services, each Party shall endeavour to rely on an open and transparent public comment process that considers the overall public interest. Each Party shall endeavour to rely generally on market-based approaches in assigning spectrum for terrestrial non-government telecommunications services.

ARTICLE 12.21: ENFORCEMENT

1.   Each Party shall provide its relevant regulatory body with the authority to enforce compliance with the Party's measures relating to the obligations set out in Articles 12.2 through 12.7 and Articles 12.9 through 12.14.[12-8]

2.   Such authority shall include the ability to impose, or seek from administrative or judicial bodies, effective sanctions, which may include financial penalties, injunctive relief (on an interim or final basis), or the modification, suspension, and revocation of licenses.

ARTICLE 12.22: RESOLUTION OF TELECOMMUNICATIONS DISPUTES AND APPEAL PROCESSES

Further to Articles 20.4 (Administrative Agency Processes) and 20.5 (Review and Appeal), each Party shall ensure that:

(a)   enterprises of the other Party may seek timely review by a telecommunications regulatory body or other relevant body to resolve disputes regarding the Party's measures relating to a matter set out in Articles 12.2 through 12.7 and Articles 12.9 through 12.14;

(b)   suppliers of public telecommunications of the other Party that have requested interconnection with a major supplier in the Party's territory will have recourse to a telecommunications regulatory body:[12-9]

(i)   at any time; or

[12-8] For the purpose of Australia's obligations under this Chapter, notwithstanding this paragraph, a supplier of public telecommunications services may be required to apply to a judicial body for the enforcement of a determination by a regulatory body in relation to the resolution of a dispute under a domestic measure relating to the obligations in Article 12.11.

[12-9] In the United States, this body may be a state regulatory authority.

(ii)   after a reasonable and publicly specified period, to review disputes regarding appropriate terms, conditions, and rates for interconnection;

(c)   any enterprise that is aggrieved or whose interests are adversely affected by a determination or decision of the Party's telecommunications regulatory body may obtain judicial review of such determination or decision by an impartial and independent judicial authority. An application for judicial review shall not constitute grounds for non-compliance with such a determination or decision unless stayed by the relevant judicial body.

ARTICLE 12.23: FORBEARANCE[12-10]

1.   The Parties recognize the importance of relying on market forces to achieve wide choices in the supply of telecommunications services. To this end, each Party may forebear from applying a regulation or other measure, to the extent provided for in the Party's law, to a service that the Party classifies as a public telecommunications service if its telecommunications regulatory body determines that:

(a)   enforcement of such regulation is not necessary to prevent unreasonable or discriminatory practices;

(b)   enforcement of such regulation is not necessary for the protection of consumers; and

(c)   forbearance is consistent with the public interest, including promoting and enhancing competition among suppliers of public telecommunications services.

2.   Each Party shall provide interested persons of the other Party adequate public notice and opportunity to comment before the Party's telecommunication regulatory body makes any decision regarding forbearance.

3.   Each Party shall ensure that any enterprise aggrieved by a decision of the Party's regulatory body regarding forbearance may obtain judicial review of such decision by an independent and impartial judicial authority.

ARTICLE 12.24: RELATIONSHIP TO OTHER CHAPTERS

In the event of any inconsistency between this Chapter and another Chapter, this Chapter shall prevail to the extent of the inconsistency.

ARTICLE 12.25: DEFINITIONS

For the purposes of this Chapter:

1.   **commercial mobile services** means public telecommunications services supplied through mobile wireless means;

[12-10]For the purposes of this Agreement, the extent to which the United States telecommunications regulatory body may forbear is governed by section 10 of the U.S. Communications Act of 1934, as amended by the Telecommunications Act of 1996.

2.   **cost-oriented** means based on cost, and may include a reasonable profit, and may involve different cost methodologies for different facilities or services;

3.   **dialing parity** means the ability of an end-user to use an equal number of digits to access a like public telecommunications service, regardless of the public telecommunications service supplier chosen by such end-user and in a way that involves no unreasonable dialing delays;

4.   **end-user** means a final consumer of or subscriber to a public telecommunications service, including a service supplier other than a supplier of public telecommunications services;

5.   **essential facilities** means facilities of a public telecommunications network or service that:

(a)   are exclusively or predominantly provided by a single or limited number of suppliers, and

(b)   cannot feasibly be economically or technically substituted in order to provide a service;

6.   **interconnection** means linking with suppliers providing public telecommunications services in order to allow the users of one supplier to communicate with the users of another supplier and to access services provided by another supplier;

7.   **leased circuit** means telecommunications facilities between two or more designated points that are set aside for the dedicated use of, or availability to, a particular customer or other users;

8.   **major supplier** means a supplier of a public telecommunications service that has the ability to materially affect the terms of participation (having regard to price and supply) in the relevant market for public telecommunications services as a result of control over essential facilities or use of its position in the market;

9.   **network element** means a facility or equipment used in supplying a public telecommunications service, including features, functions, and capabilities provided by means of such a facility or equipment;

10.   **non-discriminatory** means treatment no less favourable than that accorded to any other user of like public telecommunications services in like circumstances;

11.   **number portability** means the ability of end-users of public telecommunications services to retain, at the same location, existing telephone numbers when switching between suppliers of like public telecommunications services;

12.   **physical co-location** means physical access to space in order to install, maintain, or repair equipment, at premises owned or controlled and used by a major supplier to supply public telecommunications services;

13.   **public telecommunications service** means any telecommunications service that a Party requires, explicitly or in effect, to be offered to the public generally. Such services may include, *inter alia*, telephone and data transmission typically involving customer-supplied information

between two or more points without any end-to-end change in the form or content of the customer's information;[12-11]

14.   **telecommunications** means the transmission and reception of signals by any electromagnetic means;

15.   **telecommunications regulatory body** means a central level body responsible for the regulation of telecommunications;

16.   **user** means an end-user or a supplier of public telecommunications services; and

17.   **value-added services** means services that add value to telecommunications services through enhanced functionality. More specifically, with respect to the obligations of the United States under this Chapter, these are services as defined in 47 USC § 153(20), and with respect to the obligations of Australia under this Chapter, value-added services are telecommunications services for which suppliers "add value" to customer information by enhancing its form or content or by providing for its storage and retrieval.

CHAPTER THIRTEEN
FINANCIAL SERVICES

ARTICLE 13.1: SCOPE AND COVERAGE

1.   This Chapter applies to measures adopted or maintained by a Party relating to:

   (a)   financial institutions of the other Party;

   (b)   investors of the other Party, and investments of such investors, in financial institutions in the Party's territory; and

   (c)   cross-border trade in financial services.

2.   Chapters Ten (Cross-Border Trade in Services) and Eleven (Investment) apply to measures described in paragraph 1 only to the extent that such Chapters or Articles of such Chapters are incorporated into this Chapter.

   (a)   Articles 10.11 (Denial of Benefits), 11.7 (Expropriation and Compensation), 11.8 (Transfers), 11.11 (Investment and the Environment), 11.12 (Denial of Benefits), and 11.14 (Special Formalities and Information Requirements) are hereby incorporated into and made a part of this Chapter.

   (b)   Article 10.10 (Transfers and Payments) is incorporated into and made a part of this Chapter to the extent that cross-border trade in financial services is subject to obligations pursuant to Article 13.5.

[12-11]Because the United States does not classify services described in 47 USC § 153(20) as public telecommunications services, these services are not considered public telecommunications services for the purposes of this Agreement. This does not prejudice either Party's position in the WTO on the scope and definition of these services.

3.   This Chapter does not apply to measures adopted or maintained by a Party relating to:

(a)   activities or services forming part of a public retirement plan or statutory system of social security; or

(b)   activities or services conducted for the account or with the guarantee or using the financial resources of the Party, including its public entities,

except that if a Party allows any of the activities or services referred to in subparagraphs (a) or (b) to be conducted by its financial institutions in competition with a public entity or a financial institution, this Chapter shall apply to measures of that Party relating to such activities or services.

ARTICLE 13.2: NATIONAL TREATMENT

1.   Each Party shall accord to investors of the other Party treatment no less favourable than that it accords to its own investors, in like circumstances, with respect to the establishment, acquisition, expansion, management, conduct, operation, and sale or other disposition of financial institutions and investments in financial institutions in its territory.

2.   Each Party shall accord to financial institutions of the other Party and to investments of investors of the other Party in financial institutions treatment no less favourable than that it accords to its own financial institutions, and to investments of its own investors in financial institutions, in like circumstances, with respect to the establishment, acquisition, expansion, management, conduct, operation, and sale or other disposition of financial institutions and investments.

ARTICLE 13.3: MOST-FAVOURED-NATION TREATMENT

Each Party shall accord to investors of the other Party, financial institutions of the other Party, investments of investors in financial institutions, and cross-border financial service suppliers of the other Party treatment no less favourable than that it accords to the investors, financial institutions, investments of investors in financial institutions, and cross-border financial service suppliers of a non-Party, in like circumstances.

ARTICLE 13.4: MARKET ACCESS FOR FINANCIAL INSTITUTIONS

A Party shall not adopt or maintain, with respect to investors of the other Party, either on the basis of a regional subdivision or on the basis of its entire territory, measures that:

(a)   impose limitations on

(i)   the number of financial institutions, whether in the form of numerical quotas, monopolies, exclusive service suppliers, or the requirement of an economic needs test;

(ii)   the total value of financial service transactions or assets in the form of numerical quotas or the requirement of an economic needs test;

(iii)   the total number of financial service operations or on the total quantity of financial services output expressed in terms of designated numerical units in the form of quotas or the requirement of an economic needs test;[13-1] or

(iv)   the total number of natural persons that may be employed in a particular financial service sector or that a financial institution may employ and who are necessary for, and directly related to, the supply of a specific financial service in the form of numerical quotas or the requirement of an economic needs test; or

(b)   restrict or require specific types of legal entity or joint venture through which a financial institution may supply a service.

ARTICLE 13.5: CROSS-BORDER TRADE

1.   Each Party shall permit, under terms and conditions that accord national treatment, crossborder financial service suppliers of the other Party to supply the services specified in Annex 13-A. National treatment requires that a Party shall accord to cross-border financial service suppliers of the other Party treatment no less favourable than that which it accords to its own financial service suppliers, in like circumstances, with respect to the supply of the relevant service.

2.   Each Party shall permit persons located in its territory, and its nationals wherever located, to purchase financial services from cross-border financial service suppliers of the other Party located in the territory of the other Party. This obligation does not require a Party to permit such suppliers to do business or solicit in its territory. Each Party may define "doing business" and "solicitation" for the purposes of this obligation, provided that those definitions are not inconsistent with paragraph 1.

3.   Without prejudice to other means of prudential regulation of cross-border trade in financial services, a Party may require the registration of cross-border financial service suppliers of the other Party and of financial instruments.

ARTICLE 13.6: NEW FINANCIAL SERVICES

Each Party shall permit a financial institution of the other Party to supply any new financial service that the Party would permit its own financial institutions, in like circumstances, to supply without additional legislative action by the first Party. Notwithstanding Article 13.4(b), a Party may determine the institutional and juridical form through which the new financial service may be supplied and may require authorisation for the supply of the service. Where a Party requires authorisation to supply a new financial service, a decision shall be made within a reasonable time and the authorisation may only be refused for prudential reasons.[13-2]

[13-1] This clause does not cover measures of a Party which limit inputs for the supply of financial services.

[13-2] The Parties understand that nothing in Article 13.6 prevents a financial institution of a Party from applying to the other Party to consider authorising the supply of a financial service that is supplied in neither Party's territory. Such application shall be subject to the law of the Party to which the application is made and, for greater certainty, shall not be subject to the obligations of Article 13.6.

ARTICLE 13.7: TREATMENT OF CERTAIN INFORMATION

Nothing in this Chapter requires a Party to furnish or allow access to information related to the financial affairs and accounts of individual customers of financial institutions or cross-border financial service suppliers.

ARTICLE 13.8: SENIOR MANAGEMENT AND BOARDS OF DIRECTORS

1.   A Party may not require financial institutions of the other Party to engage individuals of any particular nationality as senior managerial or other essential personnel.

2.   A Party may not require that more than a minority of the board of directors of a financial institution of the other Party be composed of nationals of the Party, persons residing in the territory of the Party, or a combination thereof.

ARTICLE 13.9: NON-CONFORMING MEASURES

1.   Articles 13.2 through 13.5 and 13.8 do not apply to:

   (a)   any existing non-conforming measure that is maintained by a Party at

      (i)   the central level of government, as set out by that Party in Section A of its Schedule to Annex III,

      (ii)   a regional level of government, as set out by that Party in Section A of its Schedule to Annex III, or

      (iii)   a local level of government;

   (b)   the continuation or prompt renewal of any non-conforming measure referred to in sub-paragraph (a); or

   (c)   an amendment to any non-conforming measure referred to in sub-paragraph (a) to the extent that the amendment does not decrease the conformity of the measure, as it existed

      (i)   immediately before the amendment, with Articles 13.2, 13.3, 13.4, or 13.8; or

      (ii)   on the date of entry into force of the Agreement, with Article 13.5.

2.   Articles 13.2 through 13.5 and 13.8 do not apply to any measure that a Party adopts or maintains with respect to sectors, sub-sectors, or activities, as set out in Section B of its Schedule to Annex III.

3.   Annex 13-B sets out certain specific commitments by each Party.

4.   A non-conforming measure set out in a Party's Schedule to Annex I or II as not subject to Articles 10.2, 10.3, 11.3, 11.4, or 11.10 shall be treated as a non-conforming measure not subject

to Articles 13.2, 13.3, 13.5.1, or 13.8.2, as the case may be, to the extent that the measure, sector, sub-sector, or activity set out in the non-conforming measure is covered by this Chapter.

ARTICLE 13.10: EXCEPTIONS

1.   Notwithstanding any other provision of this Chapter or Chapters Eleven (Investment), Twelve (Telecommunications), or Sixteen (Electronic Commerce), including specifically Article 12.24 (Relationship to Other Chapters), and Article 10.1 (Scope and Coverage) with respect to the supply of financial services in the territory of a Party by an investor of the other Party or a covered investment, a Party shall not be prevented from adopting or maintaining measures for prudential reasons, including for the protection of investors, depositors, policy holders, or persons to whom a fiduciary duty is owed by a financial institution or cross-border financial service supplier, or to ensure the integrity and stability of the financial system. Where such measures do not conform to the provisions of this Agreement referred to in this paragraph, they shall not be used as a means of avoiding the Party's commitments or obligations under such provisions.

2.   Nothing in this Chapter or Chapters Eleven, Twelve, or Sixteen, including specifically Article 12.24, and Article 10.1 with respect to the supply of financial services in the territory of a Party by an investor of the other Party or a covered investment, applies to non-discriminatory measures of general application taken by any public entity in pursuit of monetary and related credit policies or exchange rate policies. This paragraph shall not affect a Party's obligations under Article 11.9 (Performance Requirements) with respect to measures covered by Chapter Eleven, or under Articles 10.10 or 11.8.

3.   Notwithstanding Articles 10.10 and 11.8, as incorporated into this Chapter, a Party may prevent or limit transfers by a financial institution or cross-border financial service supplier to, or for the benefit of, an affiliate of or person related to such institution or supplier, through the equitable, non-discriminatory, and good faith application of measures relating to maintenance of the safety, soundness, integrity, or financial responsibility of financial institutions or cross-border financial service suppliers. This paragraph does not prejudice any other provision of this Agreement that permits a Party to restrict transfers.

4.   For greater certainty, nothing in this Chapter shall be construed to prevent the adoption or enforcement by a Party of measures necessary to secure compliance with laws or regulations that are not inconsistent with this Chapter, including those relating to the prevention of deceptive and fraudulent practices or to deal with the effects of a default on financial services contracts, subject to the requirement that such measures are not applied in a manner which would constitute a means of arbitrary or unjustifiable discrimination between countries where like conditions prevail, or a disguised restriction on investment in financial institutions or cross-border trade in financial services.

ARTICLE 13.11: REGULATORY TRANSPARENCY

1.   The Parties recognize that transparent regulations and policies governing the activities of financial institutions and cross-border financial service suppliers are important in facilitating their ability to gain access to and operate in each other's market. Each Party commits to promote regulatory transparency in financial services.

2.   Each Party shall ensure that all measures of general application to which this Chapter applies are administered in a reasonable, objective, and impartial manner.

3.   In lieu of Article 20.2.2 (Publication), each Party shall, to the extent practicable,

(a)   publish in advance any regulations of general application relating to the subject matter of this Chapter that it proposes to adopt and the purpose of the regulation; and

(b)   provide interested persons and the other Party a reasonable opportunity to comment on such proposed regulations.

4.   At the time it adopts final regulations, a Party should, to the extent practicable, address in writing substantive comments received from interested persons with respect to the proposed regulations.

5.   To the extent practicable, each Party should provide notice of the requirements of final regulations a reasonable time prior to their effective date.

6.   Each Party shall ensure that the rules of general application adopted or maintained by self-regulatory organisations of the Party are promptly published or otherwise made available in such a manner as to enable interested persons to become acquainted with them.

7.   Each Party shall maintain or establish appropriate mechanisms for responding to inquiries from interested persons regarding measures of general application covered by this Chapter.

8.   Each Party's regulatory authorities shall make publicly available their requirements, including any documentation required, for completing applications relating to the supply of financial services.

9.   On the request of an applicant, a Party's regulatory authority shall inform the applicant of the status of its application. If the authority requires additional information from the applicant, it shall notify the applicant without undue delay.

10.   A Party's regulatory authority shall make an administrative decision on a completed application of an investor in a financial institution, a financial institution, or a cross-border financial service supplier of the other Party relating to the supply of a financial service within 120 days, and shall promptly notify the applicant of the decision. An application shall not be considered complete until all relevant hearings are held and all necessary information is received.

Where it is not practicable for a decision to be made within 120 days, the regulatory authority shall notify the applicant without undue delay and shall endeavour to make the decision within a reasonable time thereafter.

11.   On the request of an unsuccessful applicant, a regulatory authority that has denied an application shall, to the extent practicable, inform the applicant of the reasons for denial of the application.

ARTICLE 13.12: SELF-REGULATORY ORGANISATIONS

Where a Party requires a financial institution or a cross-border financial service supplier of the other Party to be a member of, participate in, or have access to, a self-regulatory organisation to provide a financial service in or into its territory, the Party shall ensure observance of the obligations of Articles 13.2 and 13.3 by such self-regulatory organisation.

ARTICLE 13.13: PAYMENT AND CLEARING SYSTEMS

Under terms and conditions that accord national treatment, each Party shall grant financial institutions of the other Party access to payment and clearing systems operated by public entities, and to official funding and refinancing facilities available in the normal course of ordinary business. This paragraph is not intended to confer access to the Party's lender of last resort facilities.

ARTICLE 13.14: EXPEDITED AVAILABILITY OF INSURANCE SERVICES

The Parties recognise the importance of maintaining and developing regulatory procedures to expedite the offering of insurance services by licensed suppliers.

ARTICLE 13.15: RECOGNITION

1.   A Party may recognise prudential measures of a non-Party in the application of measures covered by this Chapter. Such recognition may be:

(a)   accorded autonomously;

(b)   achieved through harmonisation or other means; or

(c)   based upon an agreement or arrangement with the non-Party.

2.   A Party according recognition of prudential measures under paragraph 1 shall provide adequate opportunity to the other Party to demonstrate that circumstances exist in which there are or would be equivalent regulation, oversight, implementation of regulation, and, if appropriate, procedures concerning the sharing of information between the Parties.

3.   Where a Party accords recognition of prudential measures under paragraph 1(c) and the circumstances set out in paragraph 2 exist, the Party shall provide adequate opportunity to the other Party to negotiate accession to the agreement or arrangement, or to negotiate a comparable agreement or arrangement.

ARTICLE 13.16: FINANCIAL SERVICES COMMITTEE

1.   The Parties hereby establish a Financial Services Committee. The principal representative of each Party shall be an official of the Party's authority responsible for financial services set out in Annex 13-C.

2.   The Committee shall:

(a)   supervise the implementation of this Chapter and its further elaboration; and

(b) consider issues regarding financial services that are referred to it by a Party, including ways to further integrate financial services sectors between the Parties.

3. The Committee shall meet annually, or as otherwise agreed, to assess the functioning of this Agreement as it applies to financial services. The Committee shall inform the Joint Committee established under Article 21.1 (Joint Committee) of the results of each meeting.

ARTICLE 13.17: CONSULTATIONS

1. A Party may request consultations with the other Party regarding any matter arising under this Agreement that affects financial services. The other Party shall give sympathetic consideration to the request. The Parties shall report the results of their consultations to the Committee.

2. Consultations under this Article shall include officials of the authorities specified in Annex 13-C.

ARTICLE 13.18: DISPUTE SETTLEMENT

1. Section B of Chapter Twenty-One (Dispute Settlement) applies as modified by this Article to the settlement of disputes arising under this Chapter.

2. When a Party claims that a dispute arises under this Chapter, Article 21.7 shall apply, except that:

(a) where the Parties so agree, the panel shall be composed entirely of panellists meeting the qualifications in paragraph 3; and

(b) in any other case,

(i) each Party may select panellists meeting the qualifications set out in paragraph 3 or in Article 21.7.3, and

(ii) if the Party complained against invokes Article 13.10, the chair of the panel shall meet the qualifications set out in paragraph 3, unless the Parties agree otherwise.

3. Financial services panellists shall:

(a) have expertise or experience in financial services law or practice, which may include the regulation of financial institutions;

(b) be chosen strictly on the basis of objectivity, reliability, and sound judgment;

(c) be independent of, and not be affiliated with or take instructions from, either Party; and not have a conflict of interest or appearance thereof, as set forth in a code of conduct to be established by the Joint Committee; and

(d) comply with the code of conduct.

4.   Further to Article 21.11 (Non-implementation), where a panel finds a measure to be inconsistent with this Agreement and the measure under dispute affects:

(a)   only a sector other than the financial services sector, the complaining Party may not suspend benefits in the financial services sector; or

(b)   the financial services sector and any other sector, the complaining Party may suspend benefits in the financial services sector that have an effect equivalent to the effect of the measure in the Party's financial services sector.

ARTICLE 13.19: DEFINITIONS

For the purposes of this Chapter:

1.   **cross-border financial service supplier of a Party** means a person of a Party that is engaged in the business of supplying a financial service within the territory of the Party and that seeks to supply or supplies a financial service through the cross-border supply of such services;

2.   **cross-border trade in financial services** or **cross-border supply of financial services** means the supply of a financial service:

(a)   from the territory of one Party into the territory of the other Party,

(b)   in the territory of one Party by a person of that Party to a person of the other Party, or

(c)   by a national of one Party in the territory of the other Party,

but does not include the supply of a financial service in the territory of a Party by an investment in that territory;

3.   **financial institution** means any financial intermediary or other enterprise that is authorised to do business and regulated or supervised as a financial institution under the law of the Party in whose territory it is located;

4.   **financial institution of the other Party** means a financial institution, including a branch, located in the territory of a Party that is controlled by persons of the other Party;

5.   **financial service** means any service of a financial nature. Financial services include all insurance and insurance-related services, and all banking and other financial services (excluding insurance), as well as services incidental or auxiliary to a service of a financial nature. Financial services include the following activities:

insurance and insurance-related services

(a)   Direct insurance (including co-insurance):

(i)   life,
(ii)   non-life;

(b)   Reinsurance and retrocession;

(c)   Insurance intermediation, such as brokerage and agency; and

(d)   Services auxiliary to insurance, such as consultancy, actuarial, risk assessment, and claim settlement services.

banking and other financial services (excluding insurance)

(e)   Acceptance of deposits and other repayable funds from the public;

(f)   Lending of all types, including consumer credit, mortgage credit, factoring, and financing of commercial transactions;

(g)   Financial leasing;

(h)   All payment and money transmission services, including credit, charge, and debit cards, travellers checks, and bankers drafts;

(i)   Guarantees and commitments;

(j)   Trading for own account or for account of customers, whether on an exchange, in an over-the-counter market, or otherwise, the following:

     (i)   money market instruments (including checks, bills, certificates of deposits);

     (ii)   foreign exchange;

     (iii)   derivative products including, but not limited to, futures and options;

     (iv)   exchange rate and interest rate instruments, including products such as swaps, forward rate agreements;

     (v)   transferable securities; and

     (vi)   other negotiable instruments and financial assets, including bullion;

(k)   Participation in issues of all kinds of securities, including underwriting and placement as agent (whether publicly or privately) and provision of services related to such issues;

(l)   Money broking;

(m)   Asset management, such as cash or portfolio management, all forms of collective investment management, pension fund management, custodial, depository, and trust services;

(n)   Settlement and clearing services for financial assets, including securities, derivative products, and other negotiable instruments;

    (o)   Provision and transfer of financial information, and financial data processing and related software by suppliers of other financial services;

    (p)   Advisory, intermediation, and other auxiliary financial services on all the activities listed in clauses (e) through (o), including credit reference and analysis, investment and portfolio research and advice, advice on acquisitions and on corporate restructuring and strategy;

6.   **financial service supplier of a Party** means a person of a Party that is engaged in the business of supplying a financial service within the territory of that Party;

7.   **investment** means "investment" as defined in Article 11.17.4 (Definitions), except that, with respect to "loans" and "debt instruments" referred to in that Article:

    (a)   a loan to or debt instrument issued by a financial institution is an investment only where it is treated as regulatory capital by the Party in whose territory the financial institution is located; and

    (b)   a loan granted by or debt instrument owned by a financial institution, other than a loan to or debt instrument of a financial institution referred to in sub-paragraph (a), is not an investment.

For greater certainty, a loan granted by or debt instrument owned by a cross-border financial service supplier, other than a loan to or debt instrument issued by a financial institution, is an investment for the purposes of Chapter Eleven, if such loan or debt instrument meets the criteria for investments set out in Article 11.17.4;

8.   **investor of a Party** means a Party, or a person of a Party, that seeks to make, is making, or has made an investment in the territory of the other Party; provided, however, that a natural person who is a citizen of both Parties or a Party and a non-Party shall be deemed to be exclusively a citizen of the State of his or her dominant and effective nationality;

9.   **new financial service** means a financial service not supplied in the Party's territory that is supplied within the territory of the other Party, and includes any new form of delivery of a financial service or the sale of a financial product that is not sold in the Party's territory;

10.   **person of a Party** means "person of a Party" as defined in Article 1.2 (Establishment of a Free Trade Area and General Definitions) and, for greater certainty, does not include a branch of an enterprise of a non-Party;

11.   **public entity** means a central bank or monetary authority of a Party, or any financial institution owned or controlled by a Party; for greater certainty, a public entity[13-3] shall not be considered a designated monopoly or a state enterprise for the purposes of Chapter Fourteen (Competition); and

12.   **self-regulatory organisation** means any non-governmental body, including any securities or futures exchange or market, clearing agency, or other organisation or association,

---

[13-3] The Federal Deposit Insurance Corporation of the United States shall be deemed to be within the definition of public entity for purposes of Chapter Fourteen (Competition).

that exercises its own or delegated regulatory or supervisory authority over financial service suppliers or financial institutions; for greater certainty, a self-regulatory organisation shall not be considered a designated monopoly for the purposes of Chapter Fourteen (Competition).

ANNEX 13-A
Cross-Border Trade

UNITED STATES

Insurance and insurance-related services

For the United States, Article 13.5.1 applies to the cross-border supply of or trade in financial services as defined in Article 13.19.2(a) with respect to:

(a)   insurance of risks relating to:

(i)   maritime shipping and commercial aviation and space launching and freight (including satellites), with such insurance to cover any or all of the following: the goods being transported, the vehicle transporting the goods, and any liability arising therefrom; and

(ii)   goods in international transit;

(b)   reinsurance and retrocession, services auxiliary to insurance as referred to in Article 13.19.5(d), and insurance intermediation such as brokerage and agency as referred to in Article 13.9.5(c).

2.   For the United States, Article 13.5.1 applies to the cross-border supply of or trade in financial services as defined in Article 13.19.2(c) with respect to insurance services.

Banking and other financial services (excluding insurance)

For the United States, Article 13.5.1 applies with respect to the provision and transfer of financial information and financial data processing and related software as referred to in Article 13.19.5(o), and advisory and other auxiliary services, excluding intermediation, relating to banking and other financial services as referred to in Article 13.19.5(p).

AUSTRALIA

Insurance and insurance-related services

1.   For Australia, Article 13.5.1 applies to the cross-border supply of or trade in financial services as defined in Article 13.19.2(a) with respect to:

(a)   insurance of risks relating to:

(i)   maritime shipping and commercial aviation and space launching and freight (including satellites), with such insurance to cover any or all of the following: the goods being transported, the vehicle transporting the goods, and any liability arising therefrom; and

    (ii)   goods in international transit;

(b)   reinsurance and retrocession, and services auxiliary to insurance as referred to in Article 13.1.5(d); and

(c)   insurance intermediation, such as brokerage and agency as referred to in Article 13.19.5(c) in relation to the services in sub-paragraphs (a) and (b).

Banking and other financial services (excluding insurance)

2.   For Australia, Article 13.5.1 applies with respect to the provision and transfer of financial information and financial data processing and related software as referred to in Article 13.19.5(o), and advisory and other auxiliary services, excluding intermediation, relating to banking and other financial services as referred to in Article 13.19.5(p).

ANNEX 13-B
Specific Commitments

Portfolio Management

1.   A Party shall allow a financial institution (other than a trust company), organized outside its territory, to provide investment advice and portfolio management services, excluding (1) custodial services, (2) trustee services, and (3) execution services that are not related to managing a collective investment scheme, to a collective investment scheme located in its territory. This commitment is subject to Articles 13.1 and 13.5.3.

2.   For the purposes of paragraph 1, **collective investment scheme** means:

(a)   in Australia, a managed investment scheme as defined under section 9 of the Corporations Act 2001, other than a managed investment scheme operated in contravention of subsection 601ED(5) of the Corporations Act 2001, or an entity that:

    (i)   carries on a business of investment in securities, interests in land, or other investments; and

    (ii)   in the course of carrying on that business, invests funds subscribed, whether directly or indirectly, after an offer or invitation to the public (within the meaning of section 82) made on terms that the funds subscribed would be invested; and

(b)   in the United States, an investment company registered with the Securities and Exchange Commission under the Investment Company Act of 1940.

Related to Article 13.14 (Expedited Availability of Insurance Services)

3.   Recognising the principles of federalism under the U.S. Constitution, the history of state regulation of insurance in the United States, and the McCarran-Ferguson Act, the United States welcomes the efforts of the National Association of Insurance Commissioners ("NAIC") relating to the availability of insurance services as expressed in the NAIC's "Statement of Intent: the Future of Insurance Regulation", including the initiatives on speed-to-market intentions and regulatory re-engineering (under Part II of the Statement of Intent). Regarding the speed-to-market initiative, those U.S. states maintaining product filing requirements for particular lines of insurance shall operate their review process on an expeditious basis. All U.S. states are implementing mechanisms to allow electronic filing; in addition, many U.S. states also allow file-and-use of products.

4.   In Australia, insurance is currently regulated by authorising and supervising insurers and not by approving products. In the event that Australia's system of insurance regulation was modified to include product approval, such approval would be done expeditiously.

ANNEX 13-C
Authorities Responsible for Financial Services

The authority of each Party responsible for financial services is:

(a)   for Australia, the Department of the Treasury; and

(b)   for the United States, the Department of the Treasury for banking and other financial services and the Office of the United States Trade Representative, in coordination with the Department of Commerce and other agencies, for insurance services.

[...]

CHAPTER FIFTEEN
GOVERNMENT PROCUREMENT

ARTICLE 15.1: SCOPE AND COVERAGE

Application of Chapter

1.   This Chapter applies to any measure regarding covered procurement.

2.   For the purposes of this Chapter, **covered procurement** means a procurement of goods, services, or both:

(a)   by any contractual means, including purchase, rental, or lease, with or without an option to buy, build-operate-transfer contracts, and public works concessions contracts;

(b)   for which the value, as estimated in accordance with paragraphs 6, 7, or 8, as appropriate, equals or exceeds the relevant threshold specified in Annex 15-A;

(c) that is conducted by a procuring entity; and

(d) is not excluded from coverage by this Agreement.

3. This Chapter does not apply to:

(a) non-contractual agreements or any form of assistance that a Party or a government enterprise provides, including grants, loans, equity infusions, fiscal incentives, subsidies, guarantees, cooperative agreements, and sponsorship arrangements;

(b) procurement of goods and services by a Party from its own entities and provision of goods or services by or between a procuring entity of a Party and a regional or local government of that Party;

(c) purchases funded by international grants, loans, or other assistance, where the provision of such assistance is subject to conditions inconsistent with this Chapter;

(d) purchases funded by grants and sponsorship payments from persons not listed in Annex 15-A;

(e) procurement for the direct purpose of providing foreign assistance;

(f) procurement of research and development services;

(g) procurement of goods and services (including construction) outside the territory of the procuring Party, for consumption outside the territory of the procuring Party; and

(h) acquisition of fiscal agency or depository services, liquidation and management services for regulated financial institutions, and sale and distribution services for government debt.

4. (a) The Parties acknowledge and reaffirm the commitments made in the *Memorandum of Agreement Between the Government of Australia and the Government of the United States Concerning Reciprocal Defense Procurement*, dated April 19, 1995 (the "MOA") and acknowledge that the MOA, and any extension thereof, applies to certain defence procurements that are outside the scope of this Chapter.

(b) The Parties will continue discussions on improving and expanding the relationship established by the MOA, recognising that this Agreement will have no application to, or impact on, the MOA or any of the rights and responsibilities established under the MOA.

Compliance

5. Each Party shall ensure that its procuring entities comply with this Chapter in conducting covered procurements.

Valuation

6.   In estimating the value of a procurement for the purpose of ascertaining whether it is a covered procurement, a procuring entity shall:

(a)   neither divide a procurement into separate procurements nor use a particular method for estimating the value of the procurement for the purpose of avoiding the application of this Chapter;

(b)   take into account all forms of remuneration, including any premiums, fees, commissions, interest, other revenue streams that may be provided for under the contract, and, where the procurement provides for the possibility of option clauses, the total maximum value of the procurement, inclusive of optional purchases; and

(c)   without prejudice to paragraph 7, where the procurement is to be conducted in multiple parts, with contracts to be awarded at the same time or over a given period to one or more suppliers, base its calculation on the total maximum value of the procurement over its entire duration.

7.   In the case of procurement by lease or rental or procurement that does not specify a total price, the basis for estimating the value of the procurement shall be, with respect to:

(a)   a fixed-term contract,

(i)   where the term is 12 months or less, the total estimated contract value for the contract's duration, or

(ii)   where the term exceeds 12 months, the total estimated contract value, including the estimated residual value, or

(b)   a contract for an indefinite period, the estimated monthly instalment multiplied by 48. Where there is doubt as to whether the contract is to be a fixed-term contract, a procuring entity shall use the basis for estimating the value of the procurement described in this subparagraph.

8.   Where the total estimated maximum value of a procurement over its entire duration is not known, the procurement shall be a covered procurement, unless otherwise excluded under this Agreement

9.   All orders under contracts awarded for covered procurements shall be subject to Articles 15.2.1 and 15.2.2.

ARTICLE 15.2: GENERAL PRINCIPLES

National Treatment and Non-Discrimination

1.   Each Party and its procuring entities shall accord unconditionally to the goods and services of the other Party and to the suppliers of the other Party offering the goods or services of

that Party, treatment no less favourable than the most favourable treatment the Party or the procuring entity accords to domestic goods, services and suppliers.

2.   A procuring entity of a Party may not:

    (a)   treat a locally established supplier less favourably than other locally established suppliers on the basis of degree of foreign affiliation or ownership; nor

    (b)   discriminate against a locally established supplier on the basis that the goods or services offered by that supplier for a particular procurement are goods or services of the other Party.

Procurement Methods

3.   A procuring entity may use:

    (a)   open tendering procedures;

    (b)   selective tendering procedures, in accordance with Article 15.7.6; and

    (c)   limited tendering procedures, in accordance with Article 15.8.

Rules of Origin

4.   Each Party shall apply to covered procurement of goods the rules of origin that it applies in the normal course of trade to those goods.

Offsets

5.   A procuring entity may not seek, take account of, impose, or enforce offsets in the qualification and selection of suppliers, goods, or services, in the evaluation of tenders or in the award of contracts, before or in the course of a covered procurement.

Measures Not Specific to Procurement

6.   Paragraphs 1 and 2 shall not apply to customs duties and charges of any kind imposed on or in connection with importation, the method of levying such duties and charges, other import regulations or formalities, and measures affecting trade in services other than measures governing covered procurements.

Non-Disclosure of Information

7.   Nothing in this Chapter shall be construed as requiring a Party or its procuring entities to disclose, furnish, or allow access to confidential information furnished by a person where such disclosure might prejudice fair competition between suppliers, without the authorization of the person that furnished the information.

ARTICLE 15.3: PUBLICATION OF PROCUREMENT INFORMATION

1.   Each Party shall promptly publish the following information relating to covered procurements, and any changes or additions to this information, in electronic or paper media that are widely disseminated and remain readily accessible to the public:

(a)   laws, regulations, procedures, and policy guidelines; and

(b)   judicial decisions and administrative rulings of general application.

2.   Each Party shall, on request, provide an explanation relating to such information to the requesting Party.

ARTICLE 15.4: PUBLICATION OF NOTICE OF INTENDED PROCUREMENT

1.   For each covered procurement, except in the circumstances described in Articles 15.7.7(a) and (d) and 15.7.8, a procuring entity shall publish a notice inviting interested suppliers to submit tenders ("notice of intended procurement") or, where appropriate, applications for participation in a procurement. The notice shall be published in electronic or paper media that are widely disseminated and remain readily accessible to the public for the entire period established for tendering.

2.   A procuring entity shall include the following information in each notice of intended procurement:

(a)   the name and address of the procuring entity and other information necessary to contact the procuring entity and obtain all relevant documents relating to the procurement;

(b)   a description of the procurement and any conditions for participation; and

(c)   the address and the time limit for the submission of tenders and, where appropriate, any time limit for the submission of an application for participation in a procurement, and the time frame for the delivery of goods or services.

Notice of Planned Procurement

3.   Each Party shall encourage its procuring entities to publish as early as possible in each fiscal year a notice regarding their procurement plans. The notice should include the subject matter of any planned procurement and the estimated date of the publication of the notice of intended procurement. Where the notice is published in accordance with Article 15.5.3(a), a procuring entity may apply Article 15.5.3 for the purpose of establishing shorter time limits for tendering for covered procurements.

ARTICLE 15.5: TIME LIMITS

1.   A procuring entity shall prescribe time limits for tendering that allow suppliers adequate time to submit applications or requests to participate in a covered procurement, including pursuant to Article 15.7.7(b) and (c), and to prepare and submit responsive tenders, taking into account the nature and complexity of the procurement.

2.   Except as provided for in paragraphs 3 and 4, a procuring entity shall establish that the final date for the submission of tenders shall not be less than 30 days:

(a)   from the date on which the notice of intended procurement is published; or

(b)   where the entity has used selective tendering, from the date on which the entity invites suppliers to submit tenders.

3.   Under the following circumstances, a procuring entity may establish a time limit for tendering that is less than 30 days, provided that such time limit is sufficiently long to enable suppliers to prepare and submit responsive tenders and is in no case less than ten days:

(a)   where the procuring entity published a separate notice, including a notice of planned procurement under Article 15.4.3 at least 30 days and not more than 12 months in advance, and such separate notice contains a description of the procurement, the time limits for the submission of tenders or, where appropriate, applications for participation in a procurement, and the address from which documents relating to the procurement may be obtained;

(b)   where the procuring entity procures commercial goods or services;

(c)   in the case of second or subsequent publication of notices for procurement of a recurring nature; or

(d)   where a state of urgency duly substantiated by the procuring entity renders impracticable the time limits specified in paragraph 1.

4.   When a procuring entity publishes a notice of intended procurement in accordance with Article 15.4 in an electronic medium, or, in the case of selective tendering, issues an invitation to tender via an electronic medium and provides, to the extent practicable, the tender documentation via an electronic medium, the procuring entity may reduce the time limit for submission of a tender by up to five days. In no case shall the procuring entity reduce either time limit to less than ten days from the date on which the notice of intended procurement is published.

5.   Where a procuring entity intends to limit the submission of tenders to all suppliers that the entity has determined have satisfied the conditions for participation, except where a notice of a multi-use list has been readily accessible in electronic form for a reasonable period, the entity shall include in an invitation to tender the time limit for submitting applications. Any conditions for participation in a tendering procedure shall be published sufficiently in advance to enable interested suppliers of the other Party to initiate and, to the extent that it is compatible with the efficient operation of the procurement process, complete the registration and qualification procedures within the time allowed for tendering.

6.   A procuring entity shall require all participating suppliers to submit tenders in accordance with a common deadline. For greater certainty, this requirement also applies where:

(a)   as a result of a need to amend information provided to suppliers during the procurement process, the procuring entity extends the time limit for qualification or tendering procedures; or

(b) negotiations are terminated and suppliers are permitted to submit new tenders.

ARTICLE 15.6: INFORMATION ON INTENDED PROCUREMENTS

Tender Documentation

1. A procuring entity shall promptly provide, on request, to any supplier participating in a covered procurement, tender documentation that includes all information necessary to permit suppliers to prepare and submit responsive tenders. Unless already provided in the notice of intended procurement, such documentation shall include a complete description of:

  (a) the procurement, including the nature, scope and, where known, the quantity of the goods or services to be procured and any requirements to be fulfilled, including any technical specifications, conformity certification, plans, drawings, or instructional materials;

  (b) any conditions for participation, including any financial guarantees, information, and documents that suppliers are required to submit;

  (c) all criteria to be considered in the awarding of the contract;

  (d) where there will be a public opening of tenders, the date, time, and place for the opening of tenders; and

  (e) any other terms or conditions relevant to the evaluation of tenders.

2. A procuring entity shall promptly reply to any reasonable request for relevant information by a supplier participating in the covered procurement, provided that the procuring entity may not make available information with regard to a specific procurement in a manner that would give a supplier or group of suppliers an advantage over its competitors in the procurement.

Technical Specifications

3. A procuring entity may not prepare, adopt, or apply any technical specification or prescribe any conformity assessment procedure with the purpose or the effect of creating unnecessary obstacles to trade between the Parties.

4. In prescribing the technical specifications for the good or service being procured, a procuring entity shall:

  (a) specify the technical specifications, wherever appropriate, in terms of performance and functional requirements, rather than design or descriptive characteristics; and

  (b) base the technical specifications on international standards, where such exist and are applicable to the procuring entity, except where the use of an international standard would fail to meet the procuring entity's program requirements or would impose greater burdens than the use of a recognized national standard.

5.   A procuring entity may not prescribe technical specifications that require or refer to a particular trademark or trade name, patent, copyright, design or type, specific origin, producer, or supplier, unless there is no other sufficiently precise or intelligible way of describing the procurement requirements and provided that, in such cases, words such as "or equivalent" are included in the tender documentation.

6.   A procuring entity may not seek or accept, in a manner that would have the effect of precluding competition, advice that may be used in the preparation or adoption of any technical specification for a specific procurement from a person that may have a commercial interest in the procurement.

7.   Notwithstanding paragraph 6, a procuring entity may:

   (a)   conduct market research in developing specifications for a particular procurement; or

   (b)   allow a supplier that has been engaged to provide design or consulting services to participate in procurements related to such services, provided it would not give the supplier an unfair advantage over other suppliers.

8.   For greater clarity, this Article is not intended to preclude a procuring entity from preparing, adopting, or applying technical specifications to promote the conservation of natural resources and the environment.

Modifications

9.   Where, during the course of a covered procurement, a procuring entity modifies the criteria or technical requirements set out in a notice or tender documentation provided to participating suppliers, or amends or reissues a notice or tender documentation, it shall transmit all such modifications or amended or re-issued notice or tender documentation:

   (a)   to all the suppliers that are participating at the time the information is amended, if known, and in all other cases, in the same manner as the original information; and

   (b)   in adequate time to allow such suppliers to modify and re-submit their initial tenders, as appropriate.

ARTICLE 15.7: TENDERING PROCEDURES

Conditions for Participation

1.   A Party, and its procuring entities, shall limit any conditions for participation in a covered procurement to those that ensure that a supplier has the legal, commercial, technical, and financial abilities to fulfill the requirements of the procurement.

2.   In assessing whether a supplier satisfies the conditions for participation, a procuring entity:

(a)   shall evaluate the financial, commercial, and technical abilities of a supplier on the basis of that supplier's business activities both inside and outside the territory of the Party of the procuring entity;

(b)   may not impose the condition that, in order for a supplier to participate in a procurement, the supplier has previously been awarded one or more contracts by a procuring entity of that Party or that the supplier has prior work experience in the territory of that Party;

(c)   shall base its determination of whether a supplier has satisfied the conditions for participation solely on the conditions that the procuring entity has specified in advance in notices or tender documentation; and

(d)   may require relevant prior experience where essential to meet the requirements of the procurement.

3.   Nothing in this Article shall preclude the exclusion of a supplier on grounds such as:

(a)   bankruptcy;

(b)   false declarations; or

(c)   significant deficiencies in performance of any substantive requirement or obligation under a prior contract.

Multi-Use Lists

4.   A Party, and its procuring entities, may establish a multi-use list provided that the procuring entity or other government agency annually publishes or otherwise makes available continuously in electronic form a notice inviting interested suppliers to apply for inclusion on the list. The notice shall include:

(a)   a description of the goods and services, or categories thereof, for which the list may be used;

(b)   the conditions for participation to be satisfied by suppliers and the methods that the procuring entity or other government agency will use to verify a supplier's satisfaction of the conditions;

(c)   the name and address of the procuring entity or other government agency and other information necessary to contact the entity and obtain all relevant documents relating to the list; and

(d)   any deadlines for submission of applications for inclusion on that list.

5.   A procuring entity or other government agency that maintains a multi-use list shall include on the list all suppliers that satisfy the conditions for participation within a reasonably short time.

Selective Tendering

6.　　To ensure optimum effective competition under selective tendering procedures, procuring entities shall, for each intended covered procurement, invite tenders from the largest number of domestic suppliers and suppliers of the other Party that is consistent with the efficient operation of the procurement system.

7.　　A procuring entity applying selective tendering procedures shall use, in accordance with paragraph 6:

(a)　　a multi-use list, provided such a list is compiled in accordance with the provisions of this Chapter and is appropriate to the type of procurement being undertaken;

(b)　　a list of suppliers that have responded to a notice inviting suppliers to submit applications for participation in a procurement;

(c)　　a list of suppliers that have responded to a notice requesting all interested suppliers to express their interest in the procurement, provided that the procuring entity:

(i)　　publishes a notice requesting any interested supplier to submit an expression of its interest in the procurement and any information requested in the notice; the notice may be the notice of planned procurement under Article 15.4.3 where that notice invited suppliers to express their interest in the procurement; and

(ii)　　sends an invitation to submit tenders to all the suppliers that expressed an interest in the procurement, unless it has stated in the notice that it may limit the suppliers that it will invite, in accordance with paragraph 8; or

(d)　　a list of all the suppliers that have been granted a license or that have been determined by the appropriate agency, authority, or organization to comply with specific legal requirements that exist independent of the procurement process, provided that:

(i)　　the requirement for a license or compliance with specific legal requirements is essential to the conduct of the procurement;

(ii)　　the complete list of such suppliers is maintained by the appropriate agency, authority, or organization and is available to the procuring entity; and

(iii)　　the entity invites all the suppliers on the list to submit tenders in the procurement.

8.　　Provided that relevant requirements and criteria have been specified in advance in a notice or in tender documentation, a procuring entity, in determining the suppliers that will be invited to tender, under paragraphs 7(b) and (c) may:

    (a)   in assessing technical ability, assess the extent to which the suppliers' proposals or responses meet the technical and performance specifications of the procurement; and

    (b)   limit the number of suppliers that it invites to tender based on the rating of the supplier proposals or responses.

9.   A procuring entity shall apply the time limits set out in Article 15.5 for responses to the notices referred to in paragraphs 7(b) and (c).

Information on Procuring Entity Decisions

10.   Where a supplier applies for participation in a covered procurement, including through a procedure described in paragraphs 7(b) or (c), or for inclusion on a list referred to in paragraph 4, a procuring entity shall promptly advise such supplier of its decision with respect to its application.

11.   Where a procuring entity:

    (a)   rejects an application for participation in a covered procurement, including an application through a procedure described in paragraph 7(b) or (c);

    (b)   rejects a request for inclusion on a list, referred to in paragraph 4, or

    (c)   ceases to recognize a supplier as having satisfied the conditions for participation; the procuring entity shall promptly inform the supplier and, on request of such supplier, promptly provide the supplier with a written explanation of the reasons for its decision.

ARTICLE 15.8: LIMITED TENDERING

1.   Provided that it does not use this provision for the purpose of avoiding competition, to protect domestic suppliers, or in a manner that discriminates against suppliers of the other Party, a procuring entity may contact a supplier or suppliers of its choice and may choose not to apply Articles 15.4 through 15.7, 15.9.1, and 15.9.3 through 15.9.7 in relation to a covered procurement in any of the following circumstances:

    (a)   where, in response to a prior notice, invitation to participate, or invitation to tender,

        (i)   no tenders were submitted,

        (ii)   no tenders were submitted that conform to the essential requirements in the tender documentation, or

        (iii)   no suppliers satisfied the conditions for participation, and the entity does not substantially modify the essential requirements of the procurement;

(b)   where the goods or services can be supplied only by a particular supplier and no reasonable alternative or substitute goods or services exist for the following reasons:

    (i)   the requirement is for works of art;

    (ii)   the protection of patents, copyrights, or other exclusive rights, or proprietary information; or

    (iii)   due to an absence of competition for technical reasons;

(c)   for additional deliveries of goods or services by the original supplier or authorized representative that are intended either as replacement parts, extensions, or continuing services for existing equipment, software, services, or installations, where a change of supplier would compel the procuring entity to procure goods or services that do not meet requirements of interchangeability with existing equipment;

(d)   for goods purchased on a commodity market;

(e)   where a procuring entity procures a prototype or a first good or service that is intended for limited trial or that is developed at its request in the course of, and for, a particular contract for research, experiment, study, or original development;

(f)   in so far as is strictly necessary where, for reasons of extreme urgency brought about by events unforeseen by the procuring entity, the goods or services could not be obtained in time under tendering procedures consistent with Article 15.4 through 15.7;

(g)   for new construction services consisting of the repetition of similar construction services that conform to a basic project for which an initial contract was awarded following use of open tendering or selective tendering in accordance with this Chapter and for which the entity has indicated in the notice of intended procurement concerning the initial construction service, that limited tendering procedures might be used in awarding contracts for those construction services;

(h)   or purchases made under exceptionally advantageous conditions that only arise in the very short term, such as from unusual disposals, unsolicited innovative proposals, liquidation, bankruptcy, or receivership and not for routine purchases from regular suppliers; or

    (i)   in the case of a contract awarded to the winner of a design contest provided that:

    (i)   the contest has been organized in a manner that is consistent with this Chapter, and

    (ii)   the contest is judged by an independent jury with a view to a design contract being awarded to the winner.

2.   For each contract awarded under paragraph 1, a procuring entity shall prepare a written report that includes:

(a)   the name of the procuring entity;

(b)   the value and kind of goods or services procured; and

(c)   a statement indicating the circumstances and conditions described in paragraph 1 that justify the use of a procedure other than open or selective tendering procedures.

ARTICLE 15.9: TREATMENT OF TENDERS AND AWARDING OF CONTRACTS

Receipt and Opening of Tenders

1.   A procuring entity shall receive and open all tenders under procedures that guarantee the fairness and impartiality of the procurement process.

2.   A procuring entity shall treat tenders in confidence. In particular, it shall not provide information to particular suppliers that might prejudice fair competition between suppliers.

3.   A procuring entity shall not penalize any supplier whose tender is received after the time specified for receiving tenders if the delay is due solely to mishandling on the part of the procuring entity.

4.   Where a procuring entity provides suppliers with opportunities to correct unintentional errors of form between the opening of tenders and the awarding of the contract, the procuring entity shall provide the same opportunities to all participating suppliers.

Awarding of Contracts

5.   A procuring entity may not consider a tender for award unless, at the time of opening, the tender conforms to the essential requirements of all notices issued during the course of a covered procurement or tender documentation.

6.   Unless a procuring entity determines that it is not in the public interest to award a contract, it shall award a contract to the supplier that the entity has determined satisfies the conditions for participation and is fully capable of undertaking the contract and whose tender is determined to be the lowest price, the best value, or the most advantageous, in accordance with the essential requirements and evaluation criteria specified in the notices and tender documentation.

7.   A procuring entity may not cancel a covered procurement, nor terminate or modify awarded contracts so as to circumvent the requirements of this Chapter.

Information Provided to Suppliers

8.   A procuring entity shall promptly inform suppliers that have submitted tenders of the contract award decision. Subject to Article 15.2.7, a procuring entity shall, on request, provide an unsuccessful supplier with the reasons that the entity did not select its tender.

Publication of Award Information

9.   Not later than 60 days after the award of a contract for a covered procurement, a procuring entity shall publish a notice in an officially designated publication, which may be in an electronic or paper medium. The notice shall include at least the following information about the contract:

    (a)   the name and address of the procuring entity;

    (b)   a description of the goods or services procured;

    (c)   the date of award or the contract date;

    (d)   the contract value;

    (e)   the name and address of the successful supplier; and

    (f)   the procurement method used.

Provision of Information to the Other Party

10.   On request of the other Party, a Party shall provide information on the tender and evaluation procedures used in the conduct of a covered procurement sufficient to demonstrate that the particular procurement was conducted fairly, impartially, and in accordance with this Chapter. The information shall include, at a minimum, the information specified in Article 15.8.2, and, to the extent necessary and without disclosing confidential information, information on the characteristics and relative advantages of the successful tender and on the contract price.

Maintenance of Records

11.   A procuring entity shall maintain records and reports of tendering procedures relating to covered procurements, including the reports provided for in Article 15.8, and shall retain such records and reports for a period of at least three years after the award of a contract.

ARTICLE 15.10: ENSURING INTEGRITY IN PROCUREMENT PRACTICES

1.   Each Party shall ensure that criminal or administrative penalties exist to sanction:

    (a)   a procurement official of that Party who solicits or accepts, directly or indirectly, any article of monetary value or other benefit, for that procurement official or for another person, in exchange for any act or omission in the performance of that procurement official's procurement functions;

    (b)   any person who offers or grants, directly or indirectly, to a procurement official of that Party, any article of monetary value or other benefit, for that procurement official or for another person, in exchange for any act or omission in the performance of his or her procurement functions; and

    (c)   any person intentionally offering, promising or giving any undue pecuniary or other advantage, whether directly or through intermediaries, to a foreign procurement official, for that foreign procurement official or a third party, in order that the foreign procurement official act or refrain from acting in relation to the performance of procurement duties, in order to obtain or retain business or other improper advantage.

ARTICLE 15.11: DOMESTIC REVIEW OF SUPPLIER CHALLENGES

1.   In the event of a complaint by a supplier of a Party that there has been a breach of the other Party's measures implementing this Chapter in the context of a covered procurement in which the supplier has or had an interest, the Party of the procuring entity shall encourage the supplier to seek resolution of its complaint in consultation with the procuring entity. In such instances the procuring entity shall accord timely and impartial consideration to any such complaint.

2.   Each Party shall maintain at least one impartial administrative or judicial authority that is independent of its procuring entities to receive and review challenges that suppliers submit, in accordance with the Party's law, relating to a covered procurement. Each Party shall ensure that any such challenge not prejudice the supplier's participation in ongoing or future procurement activities.

3.   Where a body other than an authority referred to in paragraph 2 initially reviews a challenge, the Party shall ensure that the supplier may appeal the initial decision to an impartial administrative or judicial authority that is independent of the procuring entity that is the subject of the challenge.

4.   Each Party shall ensure that the authorities referred to in paragraph 2 have the power to take prompt interim measures, pending the resolution of a challenge, to preserve the supplier's opportunity to participate in the procurement and to ensure that the procuring entities of the Party comply with its measures implementing this Chapter. Such interim measures may include, where appropriate, suspending the contract award or the performance of a contract that has already been awarded.

5.   Each Party shall ensure that its review procedures are conducted in accordance with the following:

(a)   a supplier shall be allowed sufficient time to prepare and submit a written challenge, which in no case shall be less than ten days from the time when the basis of the complaint became known or reasonably should have become known to the supplier;

(b)   a procuring entity shall respond in writing to a supplier's complaint and provide all relevant documents to the review authority;

(c)   a supplier that initiates a complaint shall be provided an opportunity to reply to the procuring entity's response before the review authority takes a decision on the complaint; and

(d)   the review authority shall provide its decision on a supplier's challenge in a timely fashion, in writing, with an explanation of the basis for the decision.

ARTICLE 15.12: EXCEPTIONS

1.   Subject to the requirement that such measures are not applied in a manner that would constitute a means of arbitrary or unjustifiable discrimination between Parties where the same conditions prevail, or a disguised restriction on international trade, nothing in this Chapter shall be construed to prevent a Party from adopting or maintaining measures:

    (a)   necessary to protect public morals, order or safety;

    (b)   necessary to protect human, animal, or plant life or health;

    (c)   necessary to protect intellectual property; or

    (d)   relating to the goods or services of handicapped persons, of philanthropic or not for profit institutions, or of prison labour.

2.   The Parties understand that subparagraph 1(b) includes environmental measures necessary to protect human, animal or plant life or health.

ARTICLE 15.13: MODIFICATIONS AND RECTIFICATIONS TO COVERAGE

1.   The Joint Committee shall modify the relevant section of Annex 15-A to reflect any agreed modification, rectification, or minor amendment in the following circumstances:

    (a)   each Party may make rectifications of a purely formal nature to its coverage under this Chapter, or minor amendments to its Schedules to Section 1, 2, or 3 of Annex 15-A, provided that it notifies the other Party in writing and the other Party does not object in writing within 30 days of the notification. A Party that makes such a rectification or minor amendment need not provide compensatory adjustments.

    (b)   each Party may otherwise modify its coverage under this Chapter provided that it:

        (i)   notifies the other Party in writing and that Party does not object in writing within 30 days of the notification; and

        (ii)   offers within 30 days of the notification compensatory adjustments acceptable to the other Party to maintain a level of coverage comparable to that existing prior to the modification, where necessary.

2.   A Party need not provide compensatory adjustments where the Parties agree that the proposed modification covers a procuring entity over which a Party has effectively eliminated its control or influence in respect of procurement by that entity. Where a Party objects to the assertion that such government control or influence has been effectively eliminated, the objecting Party may request further information or consultations with a view to clarifying the nature of any government control or influence and reaching agreement on the procuring entity's status under this Chapter.

3.   Each Party shall continue to encourage increased participation under this Chapter by its regional government entities.

ARTICLE 15.14: COOPERATION

1.   The Parties recognize their shared interest in promoting international liberalization of government procurement markets in the context of the rules-based international trading system, including in the WTO and Asia Pacific Economic Cooperation.

2.   Not later than 24 months after the date of entry into force of this Agreement, and at least biennially thereafter, the Joint Commission shall review the operation and implementation of this Chapter.

ARTICLE 15.15: DEFINITIONS

For the purposes of this Chapter:

1.   **build-operate-transfer contract** and **public works concession contract** mean any contractual arrangement the primary purpose of which is to provide for the construction or rehabilitation of physical infrastructure, plant, buildings, facilities, or other government owned works and under which, as consideration for a supplier's execution of a contractual arrangement, a procuring entity grants the supplier, for a specified period of time, temporary ownership or a right to control and operate, and demand payment for the use of such works for the duration of the contract;

2.   **commercial goods and services** mean goods and services of a type of goods and services that are sold or offered for sale to, and customarily purchased by, non-governmental buyers for non-governmental purposes; it includes goods and services with modifications customary in the commercial marketplace, as well as minor modifications not customarily available in the commercial marketplace;

3.   **conditions for participation** means registration, qualification, and other pre-requisites for participation in a procurement;

4.   **in writing** or **written** means any worded or numbered expression that can be read, reproduced, and later communicated. It may include electronically transmitted and stored information;

5.   **measure**, as defined in Article 1.2.15, includes any guidelines;

6.   **multi-use list** means a list of suppliers that a procuring entity has determined satisfy the conditions for participation in that list, and that the procuring entity intends to use more than once;

7.   **offsets** means any conditions or undertakings that require use of domestic content, domestic suppliers, the licensing of technology, technology transfer, investment, counter-trade, or similar actions to encourage local development or to improve a Party's balance-of-payments accounts;

8.   **open tendering** means a procurement method where all interested suppliers may submit a tender;

9.   **procurement official** means any person who performs procurement functions;

10.   **procuring entity** means an entity listed in Sections 1 through 3 of Annex 15-A;

11.   **selective tendering** means a procurement method where the procuring entity determines the suppliers that it will invite to submit tenders;

12.   **services** includes construction services, unless otherwise specified;

13.   **supplier** means a person that provides or could provide goods or services to a procuring entity; and

14.   **technical specification** means a tendering requirement that:

(a)   sets out the characteristics of:

(i)   goods to be procured, including quality, performance, safety and dimensions, or the processes and methods for their production; or

(ii)   services to be procured, or the processes or methods for their provision, including any applicable administrative provisions; or

(b)   addresses terminology, symbols, packaging, marking, or labelling requirements, as they apply to a good or service.

[…]

CHAPTER SEVENTEEN
INTELLECTUAL PROPERTY RIGHTS

ARTICLE 17.1: GENERAL PROVISIONS

1.   Each Party shall, at a minimum, give effect to this Chapter. A Party may provide more extensive protection for, and enforcement of, intellectual property rights under its law than this Chapter requires, provided that the additional protection and enforcement is not inconsistent with this Agreement.

International Agreements

2.   Each Party affirms that it has ratified or acceded to the following agreements, as revised and amended:

(a)   the *Patent Cooperation Treaty* (1970);

(b)   the *Convention Relating to the Distribution of Programme-Carrying Signals Transmitted by Satellite* (1974);

(c)   the *Protocol Relating to the Madrid Agreement Concerning the International Registration of Marks* (1989);

(d)   the *Budapest Treaty on the International Recognition of the Deposit of Microorganisms for the Purposes of Patent Procedure* (1980);

(e)   the *International Convention for the Protection of New Varieties of Plants* (1991);

(f)   the *Trademark Law Treaty* (1994);

(g)   the *Paris Convention for the Protection of Industrial Property* (1967) (the Paris Convention); and

(h)   the *Berne Convention for the Protection of Literary and Artistic Works* (1971) (the Berne Convention).

3.   Further to Article 1.1.2 (General), the Parties affirm their rights and obligations with respect to each other under the TRIPS Agreement.

4.   Each Party shall ratify or accede to the *WIPO Copyright Treaty* (1996) and the *WIPO Performances and Phonograms Treaty* (1996) by the date of entry into force of this Agreement, subject to the fulfilment of their necessary internal requirements.

5.   Each Party shall make its best efforts to comply with the provisions of the Geneva Act of the *Hague Agreement Concerning the International Registration of Industrial Designs* (1999), and the *Patent Law Treaty* (2000), subject to the enactment of laws necessary to apply those provisions in its territory.

National Treatment

6.   In respect of all categories of intellectual property covered in this Chapter, each Party shall accord to nationals1[17-1] of the other Party treatment no less favourable than it accords to its own nationals with regard to the protection[17-2] and enjoyment of such intellectual property rights and any benefits derived from such rights. With respect to secondary uses of phonograms by means of analogue communications and free over-the-air radio broadcasting, however, a Party may limit the rights of the performers and producers of the other Party to the rights its persons are accorded in the territory of the other Party.

7.   A Party may derogate from paragraph 6 in relation to its judicial and administrative procedures, including requiring a national of the other Party to designate an address for service of process in its territory, or to appoint an agent in its territory, provided that such derogation is:

(a)   necessary to secure compliance with laws and regulations that are not inconsistent with this Chapter; and

(b)   not applied in a manner that would constitute a disguised restriction on trade.

[17-1] For the purposes of Articles 17.1.6, 17.1.7, 17.2.12(b), and 17.6.1, a **national of a Party** also means, in respect of the relevant right, an entity of that Party that would meet the criteria for eligibility for protection provided for in the agreements listed in Articles 17.1.2 and 17.1.4, and the TRIPS Agreement

[17-2] For the purposes of this paragraph, **protection** includes matters affecting the availability, acquisition, scope, maintenance, and enforcement of intellectual property rights, as well as those matters affecting the use of intellectual property rights specifically covered by this Chapter. Further, for the purposes of this paragraph, **protection** also includes the prohibition on circumvention of effective technological measures specified in Article 17.4.7 and the rights and obligations concerning rights management information specified in Article 17.4.8.

8.   Paragraph 6 does not apply to procedures provided in multilateral agreements concluded under the auspices of World Intellectual Property Organization (WIPO) in relation to the acquisition or maintenance of intellectual property rights.

Application of Agreement to Existing Subject Matter

9.   Except as it provides otherwise, including Article 17.4.5, this Chapter gives rise to obligations in respect of all subject matter existing at the date of entry into force of this Agreement, that is protected on that date in the territory of the Party where protection is claimed, or that meets or comes subsequently to meet the criteria for protection under this Chapter.

10.   Except as otherwise provided in this Chapter, including Article 17.4.5, a Party shall not be required to restore protection to subject matter that on the date of entry into force of this Agreement has fallen into the public domain in the territory of the Party where the protection is claimed.

Application of Agreement to Prior Acts

11.   This Chapter does not give rise to obligations in respect of acts that occurred before the date of entry into force of this Agreement.

Transparency

12.   Further to Article 20.2 (Publication), and with the object of making its protection and enforcement of intellectual property rights as transparent as possible, each Party shall ensure that all laws, regulations, and procedures concerning the protection or enforcement of intellectual property rights shall be in writing and shall be published,[17-3] or where such publication is not practicable, made publicly available, in a national language in such a manner as to enable governments and right holders to become acquainted with them.

ARTICLE 17.2: TRADEMARKS, INCLUDING GEOGRAPHICAL INDICATIONS

1.   Each Party shall provide that marks[17-4] shall include marks in respect of goods and services, collective marks, and certification marks. Each Party shall also provide that geographical indications are eligible for protection as marks.[17-5]

2.   Neither Party may require, as a condition of registration, that marks be visually perceptible, nor may a Party deny registration of a mark solely on the ground that the sign of which it is composed is a sound or a scent.[17-6]

[17-3] A Party may satisfy the requirement for publication by making the law, regulation, or procedure available to the public on the Internet.

[17-4] For the purposes of this Article, in respect of the law of Australia, **marks** means "trademarks".

[17-5] A geographical indication shall be capable of constituting a mark to the extent that the geographical indication consists of any sign, or any combination of signs (such as words, including geographic and personal names, as well as letters, numerals, figurative elements and colours, including single colours), capable of identifying a good as originating in the territory of a Party, or a region or locality in that territory, where a given quality, reputation, or other characteristic of the good is essentially attributable to its geographical origin. For the purposes of this Chapter, **originating** does not have the meaning ascribed to that term in Article 1.2 (General Definitions).

[17-6] A Party may require an adequate description, which can be represented graphically, of the mark.

3.   Each Party shall ensure that its measures mandating the use of the term customary in common language as the common name for a good or service ("common name") including, *inter alia*, requirements concerning the relative size, placement, or style of use of the mark in relation to the common name, do not impair the use or effectiveness of marks used in relation to such goods or services.

4.   Each Party shall provide that the owner of a registered mark shall have the exclusive right to prevent all third parties not having the owner's consent from using in the course of trade identical or similar signs, including geographical indications, for goods or services that are related to those goods or services in respect of which the owner's mark is registered, where such use would result in a likelihood of confusion. In case of the use of an identical sign, including a geographical indication, for identical goods or services, a likelihood of confusion shall be presumed.

5.   Each Party may provide limited exceptions to the rights conferred by a mark, such as fair use of descriptive terms, provided that such exceptions take account of the legitimate interest of the owner of the mark and of third parties.

6.   Article 6*bis* of the *Paris Convention* shall apply, *mutatis mutandis*, to goods or services that are not identical or similar to those identified by a well-known mark,[17-7] whether registered or not, provided that use of that mark in relation to those goods or services would indicate a connection between those goods or services and the owner of the mark, and provided that the interests of the owner of the mark are likely to be damaged by such use.

7.   Recognising the importance of registration systems for marks that provide rights of presumptive validity, through the conduct of examination as to substance as well as to formalities, and through opposition and cancellation procedures, each Party shall provide a system for the registration of marks, which shall include:

   (a)   providing to the applicant a communication in writing, which may be electronic, of the reasons for any refusal to register a mark;

   (b)   an opportunity for the applicant to respond to communications from the authorities responsible for registration of marks, to contest an initial refusal, and to appeal judicially any final refusal to register;

   (c)   an opportunity for interested parties to oppose the registration of a mark or to seek cancellation of a mark after it has been registered; and

   (d)   a requirement that decisions in opposition or cancellation proceedings be reasoned and in writing.

8.   Each Party shall provide:

   (a)   a system for the electronic application, processing, registration, and maintenance of marks; and

---

[17-7] In determining whether a mark is well known, the reputation of the mark need not extend beyond the sector of the public that normally deals with the relevant goods or services.

(b)   a publicly available electronic database, including an on-line database, of applications for marks and registrations.

9.   Each Party shall provide that initial registration and each renewal of registration of a mark shall be for a term of no less than ten years.

10.   Neither Party may require recordal of licences for marks.

11.   Each Party shall endeavour to reduce differences in law and practice between the Parties' respective systems for the protection of marks, including differences that affect the cost to users. In addition, each Party shall endeavour to participate in international trademark harmonization efforts, including the WIPO fora dealing with reform and development of the international trademark system.

12.   (a)   Each Party shall provide a system that permits owners to assert rights in marks, and interested parties to challenge rights in marks, through administrative or judicial means, or both.

    (b)   Consistent with sub-paragraph (a), where a Party provides the means to apply for protection or petition for recognition of geographical indications, through a system for the protection of marks or otherwise, it shall accept such applications and petitions without the requirement for intercession by a Party on behalf of its nationals, and shall:

        (i)   process applications or petitions, as relevant, for geographical indications with a minimum of formalities;

        (ii)   make its regulations governing filing of such applications or petitions, as relevant, readily available to the public;

        (iii)   ensure that applications or petitions, as relevant, for geographical indications are published for opposition, and provide procedures for opposing geographical indications that are the subject of applications or petitions. Each Party shall also provide procedures to cancel any registration resulting from an application or a petition;

        (iv)   ensure that measures governing the filing of applications or petitions, as relevant, for geographical indications set out clearly the procedures for these actions. These procedures shall include contact information sufficient for applicants or petitioners, as relevant, to obtain specific procedural guidance regarding the processing of those applications or petitions; and

        (v)   provide that grounds for refusing an application for protection or recognition of a geographical indication include the following:

            (A)   the geographical indication is likely to cause confusion with a mark that is the subject of a good-faith pending application or registration; and

(B)   the geographical indication is likely to cause confusion with a preexisting mark, the rights to which have been acquired through use in good faith in the territory of the Party.

ARTICLE 17.3: DOMAIN NAMES ON THE INTERNET

1.   In order to address trademark cyber-piracy, each Party shall require that the management of its country-code top-level domain (ccTLD) provide an appropriate procedure for the settlement of disputes, based on the principles established in the Uniform Domain-Name Dispute-Resolution Policy.

2.   Each Party shall require that the management of its ccTLD provide online public access to a reliable and accurate database of contact information for domain-name registrants.

ARTICLE 17.4: COPYRIGHT

1.   Each Party shall provide[17-8] that the following have the right to authorise or prohibit[17-9] all reproductions, in any manner or form, permanent or temporary (including temporary storage in material form):

(a)   authors, in respect of their works;

(b)   performers, in respect of their performances;[17-10] and

(c)   producers of phonograms, in respect of their phonograms.[17-11]

2.   Each Party shall provide to authors, performers, and producers of phonograms the right to authorise or prohibit the making available to the public of the original and copies[17-12] of their works, performances, and phonograms through sale or other transfer of ownership.[17-13]

3.   In order to ensure that no hierarchy is established between rights of authors, on the one hand, and rights of performers and producers of phonograms, on the other hand, each Party shall provide that in cases where authorisation is needed from both the author of a work embodied in a phonogram and a performer or producer owning rights in the phonogram, the need for the authorisation of the author does not cease to exist because the authorisation of the performer orproducer is also required. Likewise, each Party shall provide that in cases where authorisation is needed from both the author of a work embodied in a phonogram and a performer or producer

---

[17-8] 8The Parties reaffirm that it is a matter for each Party's law to prescribe that works and phonograms shall not be protected by copyright unless they have been fixed in some material form.

[17-9] For the purposes of Articles 17.4, 17.5, and 17.6, a **right to authorise or prohibit** means an exclusive right.

[17-10] For the purposes of Articles 17.4, 17.5, and 17.6, a **performance** refers to a performance fixed in a phonogram unless otherwise specified.

[17-11] References in this Chapter to **authors, performers** and **producers of phonograms** include any successors in interest.

[17-12] The expressions **copies** and **original and copies** subject to the right of distribution in this paragraph refer exclusively to fixed copies that can be put into circulation as tangible objects.

[17-13] Nothing in this Agreement shall affect a Party's right to determine the conditions, if any, under which the exhaustion of this right applies after the first sale or other transfer of ownership of the original or a copy of their works, performances, or phonograms with the authorisation of the right holder.

owning rights in the phonogram, the need for the authorisation of the performer or producer does not cease to exist because the authorisation of the author is also required.

4.   Each Party shall provide that, where the term of protection of a work (including a photographic work), performance, or phonogram is to be calculated:

(a)   on the basis of the life of a natural person, the term shall be not less than the life of the author and 70 years after the author's death; and

(b)   on a basis other than the life of a natural person, the term shall be:

(i)   not less than 70 years from the end of the calendar year of the first authorised publication of the work, performance, or phonogram; or

(ii)   failing such authorised publication within 50 years from the creation of the work, performance, or phonogram, not less than 70 years from the end of the calendar year of the creation of the work, performance, or phonogram.

5.   Each Party shall apply Article 18 of the Berne Convention and Article 14.6 of the TRIPS Agreement, *mutatis mutandis*, to the subject matter, rights, and obligations in this Article and Articles 17.5 and 17.6.

6.   (a)   Each Party shall provide that for copyright, any person acquiring or holding any economic right in a work, performance, or phonogram:

(i)   may freely and separately transfer that right by contract; and

(ii)   by virtue of a contract, including contracts of employment underlying the creation of works, performances, and phonograms, shall be able to exercise that right in that person's own name and enjoy fully the benefits derived from that right.

(b)   Each Party may establish measures to give effect to the measures specified in Article 14*ter* of the Berne Convention.

7.   (a)   In order to provide adequate legal protection and effective legal remedies against the circumvention of effective technological measures that authors, performers, and producers of phonograms use in connection with the exercise of their rights and that restrict unauthorised acts in respect of their works, performances, and phonograms, each Party shall provide that any person who:

(i)   knowingly, or having reasonable grounds to know, circumvents without authority any effective technological measure that controls access to a protected work, performance, or phonogram, or other subject matter; or

(ii)   manufactures, imports, distributes, offers to the public, provides, or otherwise traffics in devices, products, or components, or offers to the public, or provides services that:

      (A)   are promoted, advertised, or marketed for the purpose of circumvention of any effective technological measure;

      (B)   have only a limited commercially significant purpose or use other than to circumvent any effective technological measure; or

      (C)   are primarily designed, produced, or performed for the purpose of enabling or facilitating the circumvention of any effective technological measure,

shall be liable and subject to the remedies specified in Article 17.11.13. Each Party shall provide for criminal procedures and penalties to be applied where any person is found to have engaged wilfully and for the purposes of commercial advantage or financial gain in any of the above activities. Each Party may provide that such criminal procedures and penalties do not apply to a non-profit library, archive, educational institution, or public non-commercial broadcasting entity.

(b)   **Effective technological measure** means any technology, device, or component that, in the normal course of its operation, controls access to a protected work, performance, phonogram, or other protected subject matter, or protects any copyright.

(c)   In implementing sub-paragraph (a), neither Party shall be obligated to require that the design of, or the design and selection of parts and components for, a consumer electronics, telecommunications, or computing product provide for a response to any particular technological measure, so long as the product does not otherwise violate any measures implementing sub-paragraph (a).

(d)   Each Party shall provide that a violation of a measure implementing this paragraph is a separate civil or criminal offence and independent of any infringement that might occur under the Party's copyright law.

(e)   Each Party shall confine exceptions to any measures implementing sub-paragraph (a) to the following activities, which shall be applied to relevant measures in accordance with sub-paragraph (f):

      (i)   non-infringing reverse engineering activities with regard to a lawfully obtained copy of a computer program, carried out in good faith with respect to particular elements of that computer program that have not been readily available to the person engaged in those activities, for the sole purpose of achieving interoperability of an independently created computer program with other programs;

      (ii)   non-infringing good faith activities, carried out by an appropriately qualified researcher who has lawfully obtained a copy, unfixed performance, or display of a work, performance, or phonogram and who has made a good faith effort to obtain authorisation for such activities, to the extent necessary for the sole purpose of identifying and analyzing flaws and vulnerabilities of technologies for scrambling and descrambling of information;

(iii)   the inclusion of a component or part for the sole purpose of preventing the access of minors to inappropriate online content in a technology, product, service, or device that itself is not prohibited under the measures implementing sub-paragraph (a)(ii);

(iv)   non-infringing good faith activities that are authorised by the owner of a computer, computer system, or computer network for the sole purpose of testing, investigating, or correcting the security of that computer, computer system, or computer network;

(v)   non-infringing activities for the sole purpose of identifying and disabling a capability to carry out undisclosed collection or dissemination of personally identifying information reflecting the online activities of a natural person in a way that has no other effect on the ability of any person to gain access to any work;

(vi)   lawfully authorised activities carried out by government employees, agents, or contractors for law enforcement, intelligence, essential security, or similar governmental purposes;

(vii)   access by a non-profit library, archive, or educational institution to a work, performance, or phonogram not otherwise available to it, for the sole purpose of making acquisition decisions; and

(viii)   non-infringing uses of a work, performance, or phonogram in a particular class of works, performances, or phonograms, when an actual or likely adverse impact on those non-infringing uses is credibly demonstrated in a legislative or administrative review or proceeding; provided that any such review or proceeding is conducted at least once every four years from the date of conclusion of such review or proceeding.

(f)   The exceptions to any measures implementing sub-paragraph (a) for the activities set forth in sub-paragraph (e) may only be applied as follows, and only to the extent that they do not impair the adequacy of legal protection or the effectiveness of legal remedies against the circumvention of effective technological measures:

(i)   any measures implementing sub-paragraph (a)(i) may be subject to exceptions with respect to each activity set forth in sub-paragraph (e);

(ii)   any measures implementing sub-paragraph (a)(ii), as they apply to effective technological measures that control access to a work, performance, or phonogram, may be subject to exceptions with respect to activities set forth in sub-paragraph (e)(i), (ii), (iii), (iv), and (vi); and

(iii)   any measures implementing sub-paragraph (a)(ii), as they apply to effective technological measures that protect any copyright, may be subject to exceptions with respect to the activities set forth in subparagraph (e)(i) and (vi).

8. In order to provide adequate and effective legal remedies to protect rights management information:

(a) each Party shall provide that any person who without authority, and knowing, or, with respect to civil remedies, having reasonable grounds to know, that it would induce, enable, facilitate, or conceal an infringement of any copyright:

(i) knowingly removes or alters any rights management information;

(ii) distributes or imports for distribution rights management information knowing that the rights management information has been removed or altered without authority; or

(iii) distributes to the public, imports for distribution, broadcasts, communicates, or makes available to the public copies of works, performances, or phonograms, knowing that rights management information has been removed or altered without authority, shall be liable and subject to the remedies specified in Article 17.11.13. Each Party shall provide for criminal procedures and penalties to be applied where any person is found to have engaged wilfully and for purposes of commercial advantage or financial gain in any of the above activities. Each Party may provide that these criminal procedures and penalties do not apply to a non-profit library, archive, educational institution, or public non-commercial broadcasting entity;

(b) each Party shall confine exceptions to measures implementing sub-paragraph (a)to lawfully authorised activities carried out by government employees, agents, or contractors for the purpose of law enforcement, intelligence, essential security, or similar government purposes;

(c) **rights management information** means:

(i) electronic information that identifies a work, performance, or phonogram; the author of the work; the performer of the performance; the producer of the phonogram; or the owner of any right in the work, performance, or phonogram; or

(ii) electronic information about the terms and conditions of the use of the work, performance, or phonogram; or

(iii) any electronic numbers or codes that represent such information, when any of these items is attached to a copy of the work, performance, or phonogram or appears in connection with the communication or making available of a work, performance, or phonogram to the public. Nothing in this paragraph shall obligate a Party to require the owner of any right in the work, performance, or phonogram to attach rights management information to copies of the work, performance, or phonogram, or to cause rights management information to appear in connection with a communication of the work, performance, or phonogram to the public.

9.   Each Party shall provide appropriate laws, orders, regulations, government issued guidelines, or administrative or executive decrees providing that its central government agencies not use infringing computer software and only use computer software as authorised in the relevant licence. These measures shall provide for the regulation of the acquisition and management of software for such government use and may take the form of procedures such as those under which an agency prepares and maintains inventories of software present on the agency's computers and inventories of software licenses.

10.   With respect to Articles 17.4, 17.5, and 17.6:

(a)   each Party shall confine limitations or exceptions to exclusive rights to certain special cases that do not conflict with a normal exploitation of the work, performance, or phonogram, and do not unreasonably prejudice the legitimate interests of the right holder;

(b)   notwithstanding sub-paragraph (a) and Article 17.6.3(b), neither Party may permit the retransmission of television signals (whether terrestrial, cable, or satellite) on the Internet without the authorisation of the right holder or right holders, if any, of the content of the signal and of the signal;

(c)   unless otherwise specifically provided in this Chapter, nothing in this Article shall be construed as reducing or extending the scope of applicability of the limitations and exceptions permitted under the agreements referred to in Articles 17.1.2 and 17.1.4 and the TRIPS Agreement.

ARTICLE 17.5: COPYRIGHT WORKS

Without prejudice to Articles 11(1)(ii), 11*bis*(1)(i) and (ii), 11*ter*(1)(ii), 14(1)(ii), and 14*bis*(1) of the Berne Convention, each Party shall provide to authors the exclusive right to authorise or prohibit the communication to the public of their works, by wire or wireless means, including the making available to the public of their works in such a way that members of the public may access these works from a place and at a time individually chosen by them.

ARTICLE 17.6: PERFORMERS AND PRODUCERS OF PHONOGRAMS

1.   Each Party shall accord the rights provided for in this Chapter with respect to performers and producers of phonograms to the performers and producers of phonograms who are nationals of the other Party and to performances first fixed or phonograms first fixed or first published in the territory of the other Party. A performance or phonogram shall be considered first published in the territory of a Party in which it is published within 30 days of its original publication.[17-14]

2.   Each Party shall provide to performers the right to authorise or prohibit:

(a)   the broadcasting and communication to the public of their unfixed performances, except where the performance is already a broadcast performance; and

(b)   the fixation of their unfixed performances.

[17-14]For the purposes of this Article, **fixation** includes the finalisation of the master tape or its equivalent.

3.   (a)   Each Party shall provide to performers and producers of phonograms the right to authorise or prohibit the broadcasting or any communication to the public of their performances or phonograms by wire or wireless means, including the making available to the public of those performances and phonograms in such a way that members of the public may access them from a place and at a time individually chosen by them.

      (b)   Notwithstanding sub-paragraph (a) and Article 17.4.10, the application of this right to traditional free over-the-air (*i.e.,* non-interactive) broadcasting, and exceptions or limitations to this right for such broadcasting activity, shall be a matter of each Party's law.

      (c)   Each Party may adopt limitations to this right in respect of other non-interactive transmissions in accordance with Article 17.4.10, provided that the limitations do not prejudice the right of the performer or producer of phonograms to obtain equitable remuneration.

4.   Neither Party may subject the enjoyment and exercise of the rights of performers and producers of phonograms provided for in this Chapter to any formality.

5.   For the purposes of this Article and Article 17.4, the following definitions apply with respect to performers and producers of phonograms:

      (a)   **broadcasting** means the transmission to the public by wireless means or satellite of sounds or sounds and images, or representations thereof, including wireless transmission of encrypted signals where the means for decrypting are provided to the public by the broadcasting organisation or with its consent; "broadcasting" does not include transmissions over computer networks or any transmissions where the time and place of reception may be individually chosen by members of the public;

      (b)   **communication to the public** of a performance or a phonogram means the transmission to the public by any medium, otherwise than by broadcasting, of sounds of a performance or the sounds or the representations of sounds fixed in a phonogram.

           For the purposes of paragraph 3, **communication to the public** includes making the sounds or representations of sounds fixed in a phonogram audible to the public;

      (c)   **fixation** means the embodiment of sounds, or of the representations thereof, from which they can be perceived, reproduced, or communicated through a device;

      (d)   **performers** means actors, singers, musicians, dancers, and other persons who act, sing, deliver, declaim, play in, interpret, or otherwise perform literary or artistic works or expressions of folklore;

      (e)   **phonogram** means the fixation of the sounds of a performance or of other sounds, or of a representation of sounds, other than in the form of a fixation incorporated in a cinematographic or other audiovisual work;

(f) **producer of a phonogram** means the person who, or the legal entity which, takes the initiative and has the responsibility for the first fixation of the sounds of a performance or other sounds, or the representations of sounds; and

(g) **publication** of a performance or a phonogram means the offering of copies of the performance or the phonogram to the public, with the consent of the right holder, and provided that copies are offered to the public in reasonable quantity.

ARTICLE 17.7: PROTECTION OF ENCRYPTED PROGRAMME-CARRYING SATELLITE SIGNALS

1.   Each Party shall make it a criminal offence:

(a)   to manufacture, assemble, modify, import, export, sell, lease, or otherwise distribute a tangible or intangible device or system, knowing or having reason to know that the device or system is primarily of assistance in decoding an encrypted programme-carrying satellite signal without the authorisation of the lawful distributor of such signal; and

(b)   wilfully to receive and make use of, or further distribute, a programme-carrying signal that originated as an encrypted programme-carrying satellite signal knowing that it has been decoded without the authorisation of the lawful distributor of the signal.

2.   Each Party shall provide for civil remedies, including compensatory damages, for any person injured by any activity described in paragraph 1, including any person that holds an interest in the encrypted program-carrying signal or its content.

ARTICLE 17.8: DESIGNS

1.   Each Party shall maintain protection for industrial designs that provides a right of presumptive validity and shall endeavour to simplify and streamline its administrative system for the benefit of users.

2.   Each Party shall endeavour to reduce differences in law and practice between the Parties' industrial design systems. In addition, each Party shall endeavour to participate in international activities concerning industrial designs, including those ongoing within WIPO.

ARTICLE 17.9: PATENTS

1.   Each Party shall make patents available for any invention, whether a product or process, in all fields of technology, provided that the invention is new, involves an inventive step, and is capable of industrial application. The Parties confirm that patents shall be available for any new uses or methods of using a known product. For the purposes of this Article, a Party may treat the terms "inventive step" and "capable of industrial application" as synonymous with the terms "non-obvious" and "useful", respectively.

2.   Each Party may only exclude from patentability:

(a)   inventions, the prevention within their territory of the commercial exploitation of which is necessary to protect *ordre public* or morality, including to protect human, animal, or plant life or health or to avoid serious prejudice to the environment, provided that such exclusion is not made merely because the exploitation is prohibited by law; and

(b)   diagnostic, therapeutic, and surgical methods for the treatment of humans and animals.

3.   A Party may provide limited exceptions to the exclusive rights conferred by a patent, provided that such exceptions do not unreasonably conflict with a normal exploitation of the patent and do not unreasonably prejudice the legitimate interests of the patent owner, taking account of the legitimate interests of third parties.

4.   Each Party shall provide that the exclusive right of the patent owner to prevent importation of a patented product, or a product that results from a patented process, without the consent of the patent owner shall not be limited by the sale or distribution of that product outside its territory, at least where the patentee has placed restrictions on importation by contract or other means.

5.   Each Party shall provide that a patent may only be revoked on grounds that would have justified a refusal to grant the patent, or on the basis of fraud, misrepresentation, or inequitable conduct.

6.   Consistent with paragraph 3, if a Party permits a third person to use the subject matter of a subsisting patent to generate information necessary to support an application for marketing approval of a pharmaceutical product, that Party shall provide that any product produced under such authority shall not be made, used, or sold in the territory of that Party other than for purposes related to generating information to meet requirements for marketing approval for the product, and if the Party permits exportation, the product shall only be exported outside the territory of that Party for purposes of meeting marketing approval requirements of that Party.

7.   A Party shall not permit the use[17-15] of the subject matter of a patent without the authorisation of the right holder except in the following circumstances:

(a)   to remedy a practice determined after judicial or administrative process to be anticompetitive under the Party's laws relating to prevention of anti-competitive practices;[17-16] or

(b)   in cases of public non-commercial use, or of national emergency, or other circumstances of extreme urgency, provided that:

(i)   the Party shall limit such use to use by the government or third persons authorised by the government;

(ii)   the Party shall ensure that the patent owner is provided with reasonable compensation for such use; and

---

[17-15] "Use" in this paragraph refers to use other than that allowed under paragraph 3 and Article 30 of the TRIPS Agreement.

[17-16] With respect to sub-paragraph (a), the Parties recognize that a patent does not necessarily confer market power.

(iii) the Party may not require the patent owner to provide undisclosed information or technical know-how related to a patented invention that has been authorised for use in accordance with this paragraph.

8. (a) If there are unreasonable delays in a Party's issuance of patents, that Party shall provide the means to, and at the request of a patent owner, shall, adjust the term of the patent to compensate for such delays. An unreasonable delay shall at least include a delay in the issuance of a patent of more than four years from the date of filing of the application in the Party, or two years after a request for examination of the application has been made, whichever is later. For the purposes of this paragraph, any delays that occur in the issuance of a patent due to periods attributable to actions of the patent applicant or any opposing third person need not be included in the determination of such delay.

(b) With respect to a pharmaceutical product[17-17] that is subject to a patent, each Party shall make available an adjustment of the patent term to compensate the patent owner for unreasonable curtailment of the effective patent term as a result of the marketing approval process.

9. Each Party shall disregard information contained in public disclosures used to determine if an invention is novel or has an inventive step if the public disclosure, (a) was made or authorised by, or derived from, the patent applicant and (b) occurs within 12 months prior to the date of filing of the application in the territory of the Party.

10. Each Party shall provide patent applicants with at least one opportunity to make amendments, corrections, and observations in connection with their applications.

11. Each Party shall provide that a disclosure of a claimed invention shall be considered to be sufficiently clear and complete if it provides information that allows the invention to be made and used by a person skilled in the art, without undue experimentation, as of the filing date.

12. Each Party shall provide that a claimed invention is sufficiently supported by its disclosure if the disclosure reasonably conveys to a person skilled in the art that the applicant was in possession of the claimed invention, as of the filing date.

13. Each Party shall provide that a claimed invention is useful if it has a specific, substantial, and credible utility.

14. Each Party shall endeavour to reduce differences in law and practice between their respective systems, including in respect of differences in determining the rights to an invention, the prior art effect of applications for patents, and the division of an application containing multiple inventions. In addition, each Party shall endeavour to participate in international patent harmonisation efforts, including the WIPO fora addressing reform and development of the international patent system.

[17-17] For Australia, the term pharmaceutical substance as used in Section 70 of the Patents Act 1990 on the date of entry into force of this Agreement may be treated as synonymous with the term **pharmaceutical product** as used in this sub-paragraph.

---

15.   Each Party shall endeavour to establish a cooperative framework between their respective patent offices as a basis for progress towards the mutual exploitation of search and examination work.

ARTICLE 17.10: MEASURES RELATED TO CERTAIN REGULATED PRODUCTS

1.   (a)   If a Party requires, as a condition of approving the marketing of a new pharmaceutical product, the submission of undisclosed test or other data concerning safety or efficacy of the product, the Party shall not permit third persons, without the consent of the person who provided the information, to market the same or a similar product on the basis of that information, or the marketing approval granted to the person who submitted such information, for at least five years from the date of marketing approval by the Party.

        (b)   If a Party requires, as a condition of approving the marketing of a new agricultural chemical product, including certain new uses of the same product, the submission of undisclosed test or other data concerning safety or efficacy of that product, the Party shall not permit third persons, without the consent of the person who provided the information, to market the same or a similar product on the basis of that information, or the marketing approval granted to the person who submitted such information, for ten years from the date of the marketing approval of the new agricultural chemical product by the Party.

        (c)   If a Party permits, as a condition of approving the marketing of a new pharmaceutical or agricultural chemical product, third persons to submit evidence concerning the safety or efficacy of a product that was previously approved in another territory, such as evidence of prior marketing approval, the Party shall not permit third persons, without the consent of the person who previously submitted information concerning safety or efficacy, to market the same or a similar product on the basis of evidence of prior marketing approval in another territory, or information concerning safety or efficacy that was previously submitted to obtain marketing approval in another territory, for at least five years, and ten years for agricultural chemical products, from the date of marketing approval by the Party, or the other territory, whichever is late.[17-18]

        (d)   For the purposes of this Article, a **new product** is one that does not contain a chemical entity that has been previously approved for marketing in the Party.

        (e)   If any undisclosed information concerning the safety or efficacy of a product submitted to a government entity, or entity acting on behalf of a government, for the purposes of obtaining marketing approval is disclosed by a government entity, or entity acting on behalf of a government, each Party is required to protect such information from unfair commercial use in the manner set forth in this Article.

[17-18] The Parties acknowledge that, at the time of entry into force of this Agreement, neither Party permits third persons, not having the consent of the person that previously submitted information concerning the safety and efficacy of a product in order to obtain marketing approval in another territory, to market a same or similar product in the territory of the Party on the basis of such information or evidence of prior marketing approval in another territory.

2.   With respect to pharmaceutical products, if a Party requires the submission of: (a) new clinical information (other than information related to bioequivalency) or (b) evidence of prior approval of the product in another territory that requires such new information, which is essential to the approval of a pharmaceutical product, the Party shall not permit third persons not having the consent of the person providing the information to market the same or a similar pharmaceutical product on the basis of the marketing approval granted to a person submitting the information for a period of at least three years from the date of the marketing approval by the Party or the other territory, whichever is later.[17-19]

3.   When a product is subject to a system of marketing approval in accordance with paragraph 1 or 2, as applicable, and is also subject to a patent in the territory of that Party, the Party shall not alter the term of protection that it provides pursuant to paragraph 1 or 2 in the event that the patent protection terminates on a date earlier than the end of the term of protection specified in paragraph 1 or 2, as applicable.

4.   Where a Party permits, as a condition of approving the marketing of a pharmaceutical product, persons, other than the person originally submitting the safety or efficacy information, to rely on evidence or information concerning the safety or efficacy of a product that was previously approved, such as evidence of prior marketing approval by the Party or in another territory:

   (a)   that Party shall provide measures in its marketing approval process to prevent those other persons from:

      (i)   marketing a product, where that product is claimed in a patent; or

      (ii)   marketing a product for an approved use, where that approved use is claimed in a patent, during the term of that patent, unless by consent or acquiescence of the patent owner; and

   (b)   if the Party permits a third person to request marketing approval to enter the market with:

      (i)   a product during the term of a patent identified as claiming the product; or

      (ii)   a product for an approved use, during the term of a patent identified as claiming that approved use, the Party shall provide for the patent owner to be notified of such request and the identity of any such other person.

ARTICLE 17.11: ENFORCEMENT OF INTELLECTUAL PROPERTY RIGHTS

General obligations

1.   For greater clarity, the obligations specified in this Article are limited to the enforcement of intellectual property rights, or, if mentioned, a particular intellectual property right.

[17-19] As an alternative to this paragraph, where a Party, on the date of entry into force of this Agreement, has in place a system for protecting information submitted in connection with the approval of a pharmaceutical product that utilizes a previously approved chemical component from unfair commercial use, the Party may retain that system, notwithstanding the obligations of this paragraph.

2.   Each Party shall provide that final judicial decisions or administrative rulings for the enforcement of intellectual property rights that under the Party's law are of general applicability shall be in writing and shall state any relevant findings of fact and the reasoning, or the legal basis on which the decisions or rulings are based. Each Party shall provide that such decisions or rulings shall be published[17-20] or, where such publication is not practicable, otherwise made available to the public, in a national language in such a manner as to enable governments and right holders to become acquainted with them.

3.   Each Party shall inform the public of its efforts to provide effective enforcement of intellectual property rights in its civil, administrative, and criminal system, including any statistical information that the Party may collect for such purpose.

4.   In civil, criminal, and if applicable, administrative procedures, involving copyright, each Party shall provide for a presumption that, in the absence of evidence to the contrary, the person whose name is indicated in the usual manner is the right holder in the work, performance, or phonogram as designated. Each Party shall also provide for a presumption, in the absence of evidence to the contrary, of all the factual elements necessary to establish under its law that copyright subsists in such subject matter.

Civil and Administrative Procedures and Remedies

5.   Each Party shall make available to right holders[17-21] civil judicial procedures concerning the enforcement of any intellectual property right.

6.   Each Party shall provide that:

   (a)   in civil judicial proceedings, its judicial authorities shall have the authority to order the infringer to pay the right holder:

      (i)   damages adequate to compensate for the injury the right holder has suffered as a result of the infringement; and

      (ii)   at least in the case of copyright infringement and trademark counterfeiting, the profits of the infringer that are attributable to the infringement and that are not taken into account in computing the amount of the damages referred to in clause (i).

   (b)   in determining damages for infringement of intellectual property rights, its judicial authorities shall consider, *inter alia*, any legitimate measure of the value of the infringed on good or service that the right holder submits, including the suggested retail price.

[17-20] A Party may satisfy the requirement for publication by making the measure available to the public on the Internet.

[17-21] For the purpose of this Article, the term **right holder** shall include exclusive licensees as well as federations and associations having the legal standing and authority to assert such rights; the term **exclusive licensee** shall include the exclusive licensee of any one or more of the exclusive intellectual property rights encompassed in a given intellectual property.

7.　　(a)　　In civil judicial proceedings, each Party shall, at least with respect to works, phonograms, and performances protected by copyright, and in cases of trademark counterfeiting, establish or maintain pre-established damages, which shall be available on the election of the right holder. Such pre-established damages shall be in an amount sufficient to constitute a deterrent to future infringements and to compensate fully the right holder for the harm caused by the infringement.

　　　　(b)　　As an alternative to the requirements in sub-paragraph (a) with respect to both copyright and to trademark counterfeiting, a Party may maintain a system of additional damages in civil judicial proceedings involving infringement of copyright in works, phonograms, and performances; provided that if such additional damages, while available, are not regularly awarded in proceedings involving deliberate acts of infringement where needed to deter infringement, that Party shall promptly ensure that such damages are regularly awarded or establish a system of pre-established damages as specified in sub-paragraph (a) with respect to copyright infringement.

8.　　Each Party shall provide that its judicial authorities shall have the authority to order, at the conclusion of civil judicial proceedings at least for copyright infringement and trademark counterfeiting, that the prevailing party be awarded payment of court costs or fees and reasonable attorney's fees by the losing party.[17-22] Further, each Party shall provide that its judicial authorities, at least in exceptional circumstances, shall have the authority to order, at the conclusion of civil judicial proceedings concerning patent infringement, that the prevailing party be awarded payment of reasonable attorney's fees by the losing party.

9.　　In civil judicial proceedings concerning copyright infringement and trademark counterfeiting, each Party shall provide that its judicial authorities shall have the authority to order the seizure of suspected infringing goods, any related materials and implements, and, at least for trademark counterfeiting, documentary evidence relevant to the infringement.

10.　　Each Party shall provide that:

　　　　(a)　　in civil judicial proceedings, at the right holder's request, goods that have been found to be pirated or counterfeit in breach of a copyright or trademark of the right holder shall be destroyed, except in exceptional circumstances;[17-23]

　　　　(b)　　its judicial authorities shall have the authority to order that materials and implements that have been used in the manufacture or the creation of such pirated or counterfeit goods be, without compensation of any sort, promptly destroyed or, in exceptional circumstances, without compensation of any sort, disposed of outside the channels of commerce in such a manner as to minimise the risks of further infringements; and

　　　　(c)　　in regard to counterfeit trademarked goods, the simple removal of the trademark unlawfully affixed shall not be sufficient to permit the release of goods into the channels of commerce.

[17-22] A Party may limit this authority in exceptional circumstances.

[17-23] A Party may give effect to paragraph 10(a) through, *inter alia*, the exercise of judicial discretion or pursuant to specific causes of action, as applicable.

11.   Each Party shall provide that in civil judicial proceedings concerning the enforcement of intellectual property rights, its judicial authorities shall have the authority to order the infringer to provide any information that the infringer possesses regarding any person involved in any aspect of the infringement and regarding the means of production or distribution channel of the infringing material, and to provide this information to the right holder's representative in the proceedings.[17-24]

12.   Each Party shall provide that in judicial proceedings concerning the enforcement of intellectual property rights, its judicial authorities shall have the authority to:

    (a)   fine or imprison, in appropriate cases, a party to litigation who fails to abide by valid orders issued by such authorities; and

    (b)   impose sanctions on parties to litigation, their counsel, experts, or other persons subject to the court's jurisdiction, for violation of judicial orders regarding the protection of confidential information produced or exchanged in a proceeding.

13.   (a)   In civil judicial proceedings concerning the acts described in Article 17.4.7 and 17.4.8, each Party shall provide that its judicial authorities shall have the authority to order or award at least:

        (i)   provisional measures, including the seizure of devices and products suspected of being involved in the proscribed activity;

        (ii)   damages of the type available for infringement of copyright;

        (iii)   payment to the prevailing party of court costs and fees and reasonable attorney's fees;[17-25] and

        (iv)   destruction of devices and products found to be involved in the proscribed activity.

    (b)   A Party may provide that damages shall not be available against a non-profit library, archive, education institution, or public non-commercial broadcasting entity that sustains the burden of proving that it was not aware or had no reason to believe that its acts constituted a proscribed activity.

14.   Each Party shall provide that its judicial authorities shall have the authority to enjoin a party to a civil judicial proceeding from the exportation of goods that are alleged to infringe an intellectual property right.

15.   If a Party's judicial or other authorities appoint technical or other experts in civil judicial proceedings concerning the enforcement of intellectual property rights, and require that the parties to litigation or other civil or criminal proceedings bear the costs of such experts, the Party should seek to ensure that these costs are reasonable and related appropriately to, *inter alia*, the

---

[17-24] For greater clarity, this provision does not apply to the extent that it would conflict with common law or statutory privileges, such as legal professional privilege.
[17-25] Reasonable attorney's fees may include those levied pursuant to relevant court fee schedules.

quantity and nature of work to be performed and do not unreasonably deter recourse to such litigation or proceeding.

Provisional measures

16.   Each Party's authorities shall act on requests for relief *inaudita altera parte* expeditiously in accordance with the Party's judicial rules.

17.   With respect to provisional measures, each Party shall provide that its judicial authorities shall have the authority to require the applicant to provide any reasonably available evidence in order to satisfy themselves with a sufficient degree of certainty that the applicant's right is being infringed or that such infringement is imminent, and to order the applicant to provide a reasonable security or equivalent assurance set at a level sufficient to protect the respondent and to prevent abuse, and so as not to unreasonably deter recourse to such procedures.

18.   In proceedings concerning the grant of provisional measures in relation to enforcement of a patent, each Party shall provide for a rebuttable presumption that the patent is valid.

Special requirements related to border measures

19.   Each Party shall provide that any right holder initiating procedures for that Party's customs authorities to suspend the release of suspected counterfeit[11-26] or confusingly similar trademark goods, or pirated copyright goods,[11-27] into free circulation is required to provide adequate evidence to satisfy the competent authorities, administrative or judicial that, under the laws of the territory of importation, there is *prima facie* an infringement of the right holder's intellectual property right and to supply sufficient information that may reasonably be expected to be within the right holder's knowledge to make the suspected goods reasonably recognizable by the Party's customs authorities. The requirement to provide sufficient information shall not unreasonably deter recourse to these procedures. Each Party shall provide that the application to suspend the release of goods shall remain in force for a period of not less than one year from the date of application or the period that the good is protected by copyright or the relevant trademark is registered, whichever is shorter.

20.   Each Party shall provide that its competent authorities shall have the authority to require a right holder initiating procedures to suspend the release of goods suspected of being counterfeit trademark or pirated copyright goods to provide a reasonable security or equivalent assurance sufficient to protect the defendant and the competent authorities and to prevent abuse. Each Party shall provide that such security or equivalent assurance shall not unreasonably deter recourse to these procedures. Each Party may provide that such security may be in the form of a documentary guarantee conditioned to hold the importer or owner of the imported merchandise harmless from any loss or damage resulting from any suspension of the release of goods in the event the competent authorities determine that the article is not an infringing good.

[11-26] For the purposes of paragraphs 19 through 24, **counterfeit trademark goods** means any goods, including packaging, bearing without authorisation a trademark that is identical to the trademark validly registered in respect of such goods, or that cannot be distinguished in its essential aspects from such a trademark, and that thereby infringes the rights of the owner of the trademark in question under the law of the country of importation.

[11-27] For the purposes of paragraphs 19 through 24, **pirated copyright goods** means any goods that are copies made without the consent of the right holder or person duly authorised by the right holder in the country of production and that are made directly or indirectly from an article where the making of that copy would have constituted an infringement of a copyright or a related right under the law of the country of importation.

21.   Where its competent authorities have made a determination that goods are counterfeit or pirated, a Party shall provide that its competent authorities have the authority to inform the right holder of the names and addresses of the consignor, the importer, and the consignee, and of the quantity of the goods in question.

22.   Each Party shall provide that its customs authorities may initiate border measures *ex officio* with respect to imported merchandise suspected of infringing being counterfeit trademark or pirated copyright goods, without the need for a specific formal complaint.

23.   Each Party shall provide that goods that have been suspended from release by its customs authorities, and that have been forfeited as pirated or counterfeit, shall be destroyed, except in exceptional cases. In regard to counterfeit trademark goods, the simple removal of the trademark unlawfully affixed shall not be sufficient to permit the release of the goods into the channels of commerce. In no event shall the competent authorities be authorised to permit the exportation of counterfeit or pirated goods that have been seized, nor shall they be authorised to permit such goods to be subject to movement under customs control, except in exceptional circumstances.

24.   Each Party shall provide that where an application fee or merchandise storage fee is assessed in connection with border measures to enforce a trademark or copyright, the fee shall not be set at an amount that unreasonably deters recourse to these measures.

25.   Each shall provide the other, on mutually agreed terms, with technical advice on the enforcement of border measures concerning intellectual property rights, and the Parties shall promote bilateral and regional cooperation on such matters.

Criminal procedures and remedies

26.   (a)   Each Party shall provide for criminal procedures and penalties to be applied at least in cases of wilful trademark counterfeiting or copyright piracy on a commercial scale. Wilful copyright piracy on a commercial scale includes:

           (i)   significant wilful infringements of copyright, that have no direct or indirect motivation of financial gain; and

           (ii)   wilful infringements for the purposes of commercial advantage or financial gain.

      (b)   Each Party shall treat wilful importation or exportation[17-28] of pirated copyright goods or of counterfeit trademark goods as unlawful activities subject to criminal penalties to at least the same extent as trafficking or distributing such goods in domestic commerce.

27.   In cases of wilful trademark counterfeiting or copyright piracy on a commercial scale, each Party shall provide:

      (a)   penalties that include imprisonment and monetary fines sufficiently high to provide a deterrent to infringement consistent with a policy of removing the

---

[17-28] A Party may comply with paragraph 26(b) in relation to exportation through its measures concerning distribution or trafficking.

monetary incentive of the infringer. Also, each Party shall encourage its judicial authorities to impose fines at levels sufficient to provide a deterrent to future infringements;

(b)   that its judicial authorities shall have the authority to order the seizure of suspected counterfeit or pirated goods, any related materials and implements that have been used in the commission of the offence, any assets traceable to the infringing activity, and any documentary evidence relevant to the offence;[17-29]

(c)   that its judicial authorities shall have the authority, among other measures, to order the forfeiture of any assets traceable to the infringing activity for at least indictable offences, and shall, except in exceptional circumstances, order the forfeiture and destruction of all goods found to be counterfeit or pirated, and, at least with respect to wilful copyright piracy, order the forfeiture and destruction of materials and implements that have been used in the creation of the infringing goods. Each Party shall further provide that such forfeiture and destruction shall occur without compensation to the defendant; and

(d)   that the appropriate authorities, as determined by each Party, shall have the authority to initiate criminal legal action *ex officio* with respect to the offences described in this Chapter without the need for a formal complaint by a private party or right holder.

28.   Each Party shall provide for criminal procedures and penalties for the knowing transport, transfer, or other disposition of, in the course of trade, or the making or obtaining control of, with intent to so transport, transfer, or otherwise dispose of, in the course of trade, to another for anything of value:

(a)   either false or counterfeit labels affixed or designed to be affixed to, at least the following:

(i)   a phonogram;

(ii)   a copy of a computer program or documentation;

(iii)   the packaging for a computer program; or

(iv)   a copy of a motion picture or other audiovisual work; or

(b)   counterfeit documentation or packaging for a computer program where the documentation or packaging has been made or obtained without the authorization of the right holder.

Limitations on liability for service providers

29.   Consistent with Article 41 of the TRIPS Agreement, for the purposes of providing enforcement procedures that permit effective action against any act of copyright infringement

---

[17-29] Each Party shall provide that items that are subject to seizure pursuant to any such judicial order need not be individually identified so long as they fall within general categories specified in the order.

covered under this Chapter, including expeditious remedies to prevent infringements and criminal and civil remedies, each Party shall provide, consistent with the framework specified in this Article:

(a) legal incentives for service providers to cooperate with copyright owners in deterring the unauthorised storage and transmission of copyrighted materials; and

(b) limitations in its law regarding the scope of remedies available against service providers for copyright infringements that they do not control, initiate, or direct, and that take place through systems or networks controlled or operated by them or on their behalf, as set forth in this sub-paragraph.[17-30]

    (i) These limitations shall preclude monetary relief and provide reasonable restrictions on court-ordered relief to compel or restrain certain actions for the following functions, and shall be confined to those functions:[17-31]

        (A) transmitting, routing, or providing connections for material without modification of its content, or the intermediate and transient storage of such material in the course thereof;

        (B) caching carried out through an automatic process;

        (C) storage at the direction of a user of material residing on a system or network controlled or operated by or for the service provider; and

        (D) referring or linking users to an online location by using information location tools, including hyperlinks and directories.

    (ii) These limitations shall apply only where the service provider does not initiate the chain of transmission of the material and does not select the material or its recipients (except to the extent that a function described in clause (i)(D) in itself entails some form of selection).

    (iii) Qualification by a service provider for the limitations as to each function in clause (i)(A) through (D) shall be considered separately from qualification for the limitations as to each other function, in accordance with the conditions for qualification set forth in clauses (iv) through (vii).

    (iv) With respect to function referred to in clause (i)(B), the limitations shall be conditioned on the service provider:

        (A) permitting access to cached material in significant part only to users of its system or network who have met conditions on user access to that material;

[17-30] Paragraph 29(b) is without prejudice to the availability of defences to copyright infringement that are of general applicability.

[17-31] Either Party may request consultations with the other Party to consider how to address under this paragraph functions of a similar nature to the functions identified in paragraphs (A) through (D) above that a Party identifies after the entry into force of this Agreement.

(B)   complying with rules concerning the refreshing, reloading, or other updating of the cached material when specified by the person making the material available online in accordance with a relevant industry standard data communications protocol for the system or network through which that person makes the material available that is generally accepted in the Party's territory;

(C)   not interfering with technology used at the originating site consistent with industry standards generally accepted in the Party's territory to obtain information about the use of the material, and not modifying its content in transmission to subsequent users; and

(D)   expeditiously removing or disabling access, on receipt of an effective notification of claimed infringement, to cached material that has been removed or access to which has been disabled at the originating site.

(v)   With respect to functions referred to in clause (i)(C) and (D), the limitations shall be conditioned on the service provider:

(A)   not receiving a financial benefit directly attributable to the infringing activity, in circumstances where it has the right and ability to control such activity;

(B)   expeditiously removing or disabling access to the material residing on its system or network on obtaining actual knowledge of the infringement or becoming aware of facts or circumstances from which the infringement was apparent, such as through effective notifications of claimed infringement in accordance with clause (ix);   and

(C)   publicly designating a representative to receive such notifications.

(vi)   Eligibility for the limitations in this sub-paragraph shall be conditioned on the service provider:

(A)   adopting and reasonably implementing a policy that provides for termination in appropriate circumstances of the accounts of repeat infringers; and

(B)   accommodating and not interfering with standard technical measures accepted in the Party's territory that protect and identify copyrighted material, that are developed through an open, voluntary process by a broad consensus of copyright owners and service providers, that are available on reasonable and nondiscriminatory terms, and that do not impose substantial costs on service providers or substantial burdens on their systems or networks.

(vii)   Eligibility for the limitations in this subparagraph may not be conditioned on the service provider monitoring its service, or affirmatively seeking facts indicating infringing activity, except to the extent consistent with such technical measures.

(viii)   If the service provider qualifies for the limitations with respect to the function referred to in clause (i)(A), court-ordered relief to compel or restrain certain actions shall be limited to terminating specified accounts, or to taking reasonable steps to block access to a specific, non-domestic online location. If the service provider qualifies for the limitations with respect to any other function in clause (i), court-ordered relief to compel or restrain certain actions shall be limited to removing or disabling access to the infringing material, terminating specified accounts, and other remedies that a court may find necessary provided that such other remedies are the least burdensome to the service provider among comparably effective forms of relief. Each Party shall provide that any such relief shall be issued with due regard for the relative burden to the service provider and harm to the copyright owner, the technical feasibility and effectiveness of the remedy, and whether less burdensome, comparably effective enforcement methods are available. Except for orders ensuring the preservation of evidence, or other orders having no material adverse effect on the operation of the service provider's communications network, each Party shall provide that such relief shall be available only where the service provider has received notice and an opportunity to appear before the judicial authority.

(ix)   For the purposes of the notice and take down process for the functions referred to in clause (i)(C) and (D), each Party shall establish appropriate procedures for effective notifications of claimed infringement, and effective counter-notifications by those whose material is the subject of a notice for removal or disabling, on the basis of a good faith belief that it was issued by mistake or misidentification in accordance with clause (v)(B). Each Party shall also provide for monetary remedies against any person who makes a knowing material misrepresentation in a notification or counter-notification that causes injury to any interested party as a result of a service provider relying on the misrepresentation.

(x)   If the service provider removes or disables access to material in good faith based on claimed or apparent infringement, each Party shall provide that the service provider shall be exempted from liability for any resulting claims, provided that, in the case of material residing on its system or network, it takes reasonable steps promptly to notify the person making the material available on its system or network that it has done so and, if such person makes an effective counter-notification and is subject to jurisdiction in an infringement suit, to restore the material online unless the person giving the original effective notification seeks judicial relief within a reasonable time.

(xi)   Each Party shall provide for an administrative or judicial procedure enabling copyright owners who have given effective notification of claimed infringement to obtain expeditiously from a service provider information in its possession identifying the alleged infringer.

(xii)   For the purposes of the function referred to in clause (i)(A), **service provider** means a provider of transmission, routing, or connections for digital online communications without modification of their content between or among points specified by the user of material of the user's choosing, and for the purposes of the functions referred to in clause (i)(B) through (D), **service provider** means a provider or operator of facilities for online services or network access.

ARTICLE 17.12: TRANSITIONAL PROVISIONS

Recognizing that Australian law currently restricts making and distributing devices or providing services to circumvent effective technological measures, Australia shall fully implement the obligations set forth in Article 17.4.7 within two years of the date of entry into force of this Agreement. In the interim, Australia may not adopt any new measure that is less consistent with Article 17.4.7 or apply any new or existing measure so as to reduce the level of protection provided on the date of entry into force of this Agreement.

[...]

*

AGREEMENT BETWEEN THE GOVERNMENT OF THE UNITED STATES OF AMERICA AND THE GOVERNMENT OF THE STATE OF KUWAIT CONCERNING THE DEVELOPMENT OF TRADE AND INVESTMENT RELATIONS *

> The Agreement Between the Government of the United States of America and the Government of the State of Kuwait Concerning the Development of Trade and Investment Relations was signed on 6 February 2004.

The Government of the United States of America and the Government of the State of Kuwait (individually a "Party" and collectively the "Parties"):

1.   Desiring to enhance the bonds of friendship and spirit of cooperation between the two countries, and to promote further both countries' international trade and economic interrelationship;

2.   Recognizing the importance of fostering an open and predictable environment for international trade, investment, and economic cooperation;

3.   Recognizing the benefits to each Party resulting from increased international trade and investment, and that trade-distorting investment measures and protectionist trade barriers would deprive the Parties of such benefits;

4.   Taking into account the membership of the two countries in the World Trade Organization (WTO) and noting that this Agreement is without prejudice to each Party's rights and obligations, where applicable, under the Marrakesh Agreement Establishing the WTO and the agreements, understandings, and other instruments relating thereto or concluded under the auspices of the WTO;

5.   Recognizing the essential role of private investment, both domestic and foreign, in furthering growth, creating jobs, expanding trade, improving technology, and enhancing economic development;

6.   Recognizing that foreign direct investment confers positive benefits on each Party;

7.   Recognizing the desirability of resolving trade and investment problems as expeditiously as possible;

8.   Desiring to encourage and facilitate private sector contacts between the two countries;

9.   Recognizing the increased importance of services in their economies and in their bilateral relations;

Source: The Government of the United States and the Government of the State of Kuwait (2004). "Agreement Between the Government of the United States of America and the Government of the State of Kuwait Concerning the Development of Trade and Investment Relations", available on the Internet (http://www.ustr.gov/assets/Trade_Agreements/Regional/MEFTA/asset_upload_file909_3528.pdf). [Note added by the editor.]

10.   Taking into account the need to eliminate non-tariff barriers in order to facilitate greater access to the markets of both countries and the mutual benefits thereof;

11.   Recognizing the importance of providing adequate and effective protection and enforcement of intellectual property rights and of membership in and adherence to intellectual property rights conventions;

12.   Reiterating the commitment reaffirmed in the Doha Declaration and recognizing the importance of providing adequate and effective protection and enforcement of worker rights in accordance with each nation's own labor laws and of improving the observance of internationally recognized core labor standards;

13.   Desiring to ensure that trade and environmental policies are mutually supportive in the furtherance of sustainable development;

14.   Desiring that this Framework Agreement reinforce the multilateral trading system by strengthening joint efforts to complete successfully the Doha Development Agenda; and

15.   Considering that it would be in their mutual interest to establish a bilateral mechanism between the Parties for encouraging the liberalization of trade and investment between them.

To this end, the Parties agree as follows;

ARTICLE ONE

The Parties affirm their desire to promote an attractive investment climate and expand trade in products and services consistent with the terms of this Agreement. They shall take appropriate meaures to encourage and facilitate the exchange of goods and services and to secure favorable conditions for long-term development and diversification of trade between the two countries.

ARTICLE TWO

The Parties shall establish a United States-Kuwait Council on Trade and Investment ("the Council"), which shall be composed of representatives of both Parties. The side of the State of Kuwait will be chaired by the Ministry of Commerce and Industry; and the U.S. side will be chaired by the Office of the U.S. Trade Representative ("USTR"). Both Parties may be assisted by officials of other government entities as circumstances require. The Council will meet at least once a year and at such times as agreed by the two Parties.

ARTICLE THREE

The objectives of the Council are as follows:

1.   To monitor trade and investment relations, to identify opportunities for expanding trade and investment, and to identify issues relevant to trade or investment, such as intellectual property, labor, or environmental issues that may be appropriate for negotiation in an appropriate forum.

2.   To hold consultations on specific trade and investment matters of interest to the parties.

3.   To identify and work toward the removal of impediments to trade and investment flows.

4.   To seek the advice of the private sector, where appropriate, in their respective countries on matters related to the work of the Council.

ARTICLE FOUR

Either Party may raise for consultation any trade or investment matter between the Parties. Requests for consultation shall be accompanied by a written explanation of the subject to be discussed and consultations shall be held within 30 days of the request, unless the requesting Party agrees to a later date. Each Party shall endeavour to provide for an opportunity for consultations before taking actions that could affect adversely the trade or investment interests of the other Party.

ARTICLE FIVE

This Agreement shall be without prejudice to the domestic law of either Party or the rights and obligations of either Party under any other agreement to which it is a party.

ARTICLE SIX

This Agreement shall become effective on the date that the Parties exchange notes stating that each has completed the required procedures under its domestic law.

ARTICLE SEVEN

This Agreement shall remain in force unless terminated by mutual consent of the Parties or by either Party upon six months written notice to the other Party.

In WITNESS WHEREOF, the undersigned, being duly authorized by their respective governments, have signed this Agreement.

Done at Washington this 6th day of February 2004, in the English and Arabic languages, with both texts being equally authentic.

*

AGREEMENT BETWEEN THE GOVERNMENT OF THE UNITED STATES OF AMERICA AND THE GOVERNMENT OF THE REPUBLIC OF YEMEN CONCERNING THE DEVELOPMENT OF TRADE AND INVESTMENT RELATIONS [*]

The Agreement Between the Government of the United States of America and the Government of the Republic of Yemen Concerning the Development of Trade and Investment Relations was signed on 6 February 2004. It entered into force on the date of signature.

The Government of the United States of America and the Government of the Republic of Yemen (individually a "Party" and collectively the "Parties"):

1.   Desiring to enhance the bonds of friendship and spirit of cooperation between the two countries;

2.   Desiring to promote further both countries' international trade and economic interrelationship;

3.   Recognizing the importance of fostering an open and predictable environment for international trade and investment;

4.   Recognizing the benefits to each Party resulting from increased international trade and investment, and that trade-distorting investment measures and protectionist trade barriers would deprive the Parties of such benefits;

5.   Recognizing the essential role of private investment, both domestic and foreign, in furthering growth, creating jobs, expanding trade, improving technology, and enhancing economic development;

6.   Recognizing that foreign direct investment confers positive benefits on each Party;

7.   Desiring to encourage and facilitate private sector contacts between the two countries;

8.   Recognizing the desirability of resolving trade and investment problems as expeditiously as possible;

9.   Acknowledging the Agreement Between the Government of the United States of America and Government of the Kingdom of the Yemen Concerning Friendship And Commerce, signed May 4, 1946;

10.   Noting that this agreement is without prejudice to the rights and obligations of the Parties under the agreement cited in the precedent paragraph 9;

---

[*] *Source*: The Government of the United States and the Government of the Republic of Yemen (2004). "Agreement Between the Government of the United States of America and the Government of the Republic of Yemen Concerning the Development of Trade and Investment Relations", available on the Internet (http://www.ustr.gov/assets/Trade_Agreements/Regional/MEFTA/asset_upload_file638_3529.pdf). [Note added by the editor.]

11.   Recognizing the increased importance of services in their economies and in their bilateral relations;

12.   Taking into account the need to eliminate non-tariff barriers in order to facilitate greater access to the markets of both countries and the mutual benefits thereof;

13.   Recognizing the importance of providing adequate and effective protection and enforcing intellectual property rights and of membership in and adherence to intellectual property rights conventions;

14.   Recognizing the importance of providing adequate and effective protection and of enforcing worker rights in accordance with each nation's own labor laws, and of improving the observance and promotion of internationally recognized core labor standards, as recognized in the 1998 ILO Declaration on Fundamental Principles and Rights at Work and reaffirmed in the Doha Declaration;

15.   Desiring to ensure that trade and environmental policies are mutually supportive in the furtherance of sustainable development;

16.   Desiring that this Framework Agreement reinforce the multilateral trading system; and

17.   Considering that it would be in their mutual interest to establish a bilateral mechanism between the Parties for encouraging the liberalization of trade and investment between them.

To this end, the Parties agree as fellows:

ARTICLE ONE

The Parties affirm their desire to promote an attractive investment climate and expand trade in products and services consistent with the terms of this Agreement. They shall take appropriate measures to encourage and facilitate the exchange of goods and services and to secure favorable conditions for long-term development and diversification of trade between the two countries.

ARTICLE TWO

The Parties shall establish a United States-Yemen Council on Trade and Investment ("the Council"), which shall be composed of representatives of both Parties. The side of the Republic of Yemen will be chaired by the Ministry of Planning and International Cooperation; and the U.S. side will be chaired by the Office of the U.S. Trade Representative ("USTR"). Both Parties may be assisted by officials of other government entities as circumstances require. The Council will meet at least once a year and at such times as agreed by the two Parties.

ARTICLE THREE

The objectives of the Council are as follows:

1.   To monitor trade and investment relations, to identify opportunities for expanding trade and investment, and to identify issues relevant to trade or investment, such as intellectual property, labor, or environmental issues that may be appropriate for negotiation in an appropriate forum.

2.   To hold consultations on specific trade and investment matters of interest to the Parties.

3.   To identify and work toward the removal of impediments to trade and investment flows.

4.   To seek the advice of the private sector, where appropriate, in their respective countries on matters related to the work of the Council.

ARTICLE FOUR

Either Party may raise for consultation any trade or investment matter between the Parties. Requests for consultation shall be accompanied by a written explanation of the subject to be discussed and consultations shall be held within 30 days of the request, unless the requesting Party agrees to a later date. Each Party shall endeavor to provide for an opportunity for consultations before taking actions that could affect adversely the trade or investment interests of the other Party.

ARTICLE FIVE

This Agreement shall be without prejudice to the domestic law of either Party or the rights and obligations of either Party under any other agreement to which it is a party.

ARTICLE SIX

This Agreement shall enter into force on the date of its signature by both Parties.

ARTICLE SEVEN

This Agreement shall remain in force unless terminated by mutual consent of the Parties or by either Party upon six months written notice to the other Party.

IN WITNESS WHEREOF, the undersigned, being duly authorized by their respective governments, have signed this Agreement.

DONE at Washington this 6th day of February 2004, in the English and Arabic languages, with both texts being equally authentic.

*

AGREEMENT BETWEEN THE GOVERNMENT OF THE UNITED STATES OF AMERICA AND THE GOVERNMENT OF THE UNITED ARAB EMIRATES CONCERNING THE DEVELOPMENT OF TRADE AND INVESTMENT RELATIONS*

> The Agreement Between the Government of the United States of America and the Government of the United Arab Emirates Concerning the Development of Trade and Investment Relations was signed on 15 March 2004.

The Government of the United States of America and the Government of the United Arab Emirates (individually a "Party" and collectively the "Parties"):

1.   Desiring to enhance the bonds of friendship and spirit of cooperation between the two countries',

2.   Desiring to promote further both countries' international trade and economic interrelationship;

3.   Recognizing the vast potential for economic cooperation and the importance of exploring business opportunities for enterprises in each country;

4.   Recognizing that both countries could deepen and broaden bilateral trade and investment based on the complementary characteristics of their economies;

5.   Recognizing the importance of fostering an open and predictable environment for international trade and investment;

6.   Recognizing the benefits to each Party resulting from increased international trade and investment, and that trade-distorting investment measures and protectionist trade barriers would deprive the Parties of such benefits;

7.   Taking into account the membership of the two countries in the World Trade Organization (WTO) and noting that this Agreement is without prejudice to each Party's rights and obligations, where applicable, under the Marrakesh Agreement Establishing the WTO and the agreements, understandings, and other instruments relating thereto or concluded under the auspices of the WTO;

8.   Acknowledging prior bilateral agreements signed by the Parties, including the Agreement Between the United States of America and the Government of the United Arab Emirates on Investment Guaranties signed September 29, 1991;

9.   Noting that this Agreement is without prejudice to the rights and obligations of the Parties under the agreements cited in the precedent paragraph 8;

Source: The Government of the United States and the Government of the United Arab Emirates (2004). "Agreement Between the Government of the United States of America and the Government of the United Arab Emirates Concerning the Development of Trade and Investment Relations", available on the Internet (http://www.ustr.gov/assets/Trade_Agreements/Regional/MEFTA/asset_upload_file305_3540.pdf). [Note added by the editor.]

10.   Recognizing the essential role of private investment, both domestic and foreign, in furthering growth, creating jobs, expanding trade, improying technology, and enhancing economic development;

11.   Recognizing that foreign direct investment confers positive benefits on each Party;

12.   Desiring to encourage and facilitate private sector contacts between the two countries;

13.   Recognizing the desirability of resolving trade and investment problems as expeditiously as possible;

14.   Recognizing the increased importance of services i~ their economies and in their bilateral relations;

15.   Taking into account the need to eliminate non-tariff barriers in order to facilitate greater access to the markets of both countries and the mutual benefits thereof;

16.   Recognizing the importance of providing adequate and effective protection and enforcement of intellectual property rights and of membership in and adherence to intellectual property rights conventions;

17.   Recognizing the importance of providing adequate and effective protection and enforcing workers rights in accordance with each nation's own labor laws, and of working toward the respect and promotion of internationally recognized core labor standards as reaffirmed in the

Doha Declaration;

18.   Desiring to ensure that trade and environmental policies are mutually supportive in the furtherance of sustainable development;

19.   Recognizing that this Framework Agreement shall reinforce the multilateral trading system by strengthening efforts to complete successfully the Doha Development Agenda; and

20.   Considering that it would be in their mutual interest to establish a bilateral mechanismbetween the Parties for encouraging the liberalization of trade and investment between them.

To this end, the Parties agree as follows:

ARTICLE ONE

The Parties affirm their desire to promote an attractive investment climate and expand trade in products and services consistent with the terms of this Agreement. They shall take appropriate measures to encourage and facilitate the exchange of goods and services and to secure favorable conditions for long-term development and diversification of trade between the two countries.

ARTICLE TWO

The Parties shall establish a United States-United Arab Emirates Council on Trade and Investment ("the Council"), which shall be composed of representatives of both Parties. The side of the United

Arab Emirates will be chaired by the Ministry of Finance and Industry; and the U.S. side will be chaired by the Office of the U.S. Trade Representative ("USTR"). Both Parties may be assisted by officials of other government entities as circumstances require. The Council will meet at least once a year and at such times as agreed by the two Parties.

ARTICLE THREE

The objectives of the Council are as follows:

1   To promote and enhance the economic cooperation between the Parties.

2.   To monitor trade and investment relations, to identify opportunities for expanding trade and investment, and to identify issues relevant to trade or investment that may be appropriate for negotiation in an appropriate forum.

3.   To hold consultations on specific trade and investment matters of interest to the Parties.

4.   To identify and work toward the removal of impediments to trade and investment flows.

5.   To seek the advice of the private sector, where appropriate, in their respective countries on matters related to the work of the Council.

ARTICLE FOUR

Either Party may raise for consultation any trade or investment matter between the Parties. Requests for consultation shall be accompanied by a written explanation of the subject to be discussed and consultations shall be held within 30 days of the request, unless the requesting Party agrees to a later date. Each Party shall endeavor to provide for an opportunity for consultations before taking actions that could affect adversely the trade or investment interests of the other Party.

ARTICLE FIVE

This Agreement shall be without prejudice to the domestic law of either Party or the rights and obligations of either Party under any other agreement to which it is a party.

ARTICLE SIX

This Agreement shall enter into force on the date that the Parties exchange notes stating that each has completed the required procedures under its domestic law.

ARTICLE SEVEN

This Agreement shall remain in force unless terminated by mutual consent of the Parties or by either Party upon six months written notice to the other Party.

IN WITNESS WHEREOF, the undersigned, being duly authorized by their respective governments, have signed this Agreement..

DONE at Washington this 15th day of March 2004, in the English and Arabic languages, with both texts being equally authentic.

AGREEMENT BETWEEN THE GOVERNMENT OF THE UNITED STATES OF AMERICA AND THE GOVERNMENT OF THE STATE OF QATAR CONCERNING THE DEVELOPMENT OF TRADE AND INVESTMENT RELATIONS[*]

The Agreement Between the Government of the United States of America and the Government of the State of Qatar Concerning the Development of Trade and Investment Relations was signed on 19 March 2004.

The Government of the United States of America and the Government of the State of Qatar (individually a "Party" and collectively the "Parties"):

1.   Desiring to enhance the bonds of friendship and spirit of cooperation between the two countries;

2.   Desiring to further develop the international trade and economic relationship between the two countries;

3.   Recognizing the importance of economic cooperation and of fostering an open and predictable environment for international trade and investment;

4.   Recognizing the benefits to each Party resulting from increased international trade and investment, and that trade-distorting investment measures and protectionism would deprive the Parties of such benefits;

5.   Taking into account the membership of the two countries in the World Trade Organization (WTO) and desiring that this Agreement reinforce the multilateral trading system by strengthening joint efforts to complete successfully the Doha Development Agenda, within the context of WTO rules and procedures;

6.   Noting that this Agreement is without prejudice to each Party's rights and obligations, where applicable, under the Marrakesh Agreement Establishing the WTO and the agreements, understandings, and other instruments relating thereto or concluded under the auspices of the WTO,

7.   Recognizing the essential role of private investment, both domestic and foreign, in furthering growth, creating jobs, expanding trade, improving technology, and enhancing economic development;

8.   Recognizing that foreign direct investment confers positive benefits on each Party;

9.   Desiring to encourage and facilitate private sector contacts between the two countries;

---

[*] *Source*: The Government of the United States (2004). "Agreement Between the Government of the United States of America and the Government of the State of Qatar Concerning the Development of Trade and Investment Relations", available on the Internet (http://www.ustr.gov/assets/Trade_Agreements/Regional/MEFTA/asset_upload_file318_3536.pdf). [Note added by the editor.]

10. Recognizing the desirability of resolving trade and investment problems as expeditiously as possible;

11. Recognizing the increased importance of services in their economies and in their bilateral relations;

12. Taking into account the need to eliminate non-tariff barriers in order to facilitate greater access to the markets of both countries and the mutual benefits thereof;

13. Recognizing the importance of providing adequate and effective protection and enforcement of intellectual property rights and of membership in and adherence to intellectual property rights conventions;

14. Recognizing the importance of providing adequate and effective protection and of enforcing worker rights in accordance with each nation's own labor laws and of improving the observance of internationally recognized core labor standards;

15. Desiring to ensure that trade and environmental policies are mutually supportive in the furtherance of sustainable development; and

16. Considering that it would be in their mutual interest to establish a bilateral mechanism between the Parties for encouraging the liberalization of trade and investment between them.

To this end, the Parties agree as follows:

ARTICLE ONE

The Parties affirm their desire to promote an attractive investment climate and expand trade in products and services consistent with the terms of this Agreement. They shall take appropriate measures to encourage and facilitate the exchange of goods and services and to secure favourable conditions for long-term development and diversification of trade between the two countries.

ARTICLE TWO

The Parties shall establish a United States-Qatar Council on Trade and Investment ("the Council"), which shall be composed of representatives of both Parties. The Qatari side will be chaired by the Ministry of Economy and Commerce; and the U.S. side will be chaired by the Office of the U.S. Trade Representative ("USTR"). Both Parties may be assisted by officials of other government entities as circumstances require. The Council will meet at least once a year and at such times as agreed by the two Parties.

ARTICLE THREE

The objectives of the Council are as follows:

1. To monitor trade and investment relations, to identify opportunities for expanding trade and investment, and to identify issues relevant to trade or investmenthat may be appropriate for negotiation in an appropriate forum.

2. To hold consultations on specific trade and investment matters of interest to the Parties.

3.   To identify and work toward the removal of impediments to trade and investment flows.

4.   To seek the advice of the private sector in their respective countries on matters related to the work of the Council where the Parties deem it appropriate. Private sector representatives may be asked to participate in Council meetings whenever both Parties agree it is appropriate.

ARTICLE FOUR

1.   Either Party may raise for consultation any trade or investment matter between the Parties.

Requests for consultation shall be accompanied by a written explanation of the subject to be discussed, and consultations shall be held within 30 days of the request, unless the requesting Party agrees to a later date.

2.   Each Party shall endeavor to provide for an opportunity for consultations before taking actions that could affect adversely the trade or investment interests of the other Party.

ARTICLE FIVE

This Agreement shall be without prejudice to the domestic law of either Party or the rights and obligations of either Party under any agreement to which it is a party.

ARTICLE SIX

This agreement shall be effective on the date that the Parties exchange notes stating that each has completed the required procedures under its domestic law.

ARTICLE SEVEN

This Agreement shall remain in effect unless terminated by mutual consent of the Parties or by either Party upon six months written notice to the other Party.

IN WITNESS WHEREOF, the undersigned, being duly authorized by their respective governments, have signed this Agreement.

DONE at Washington this 19th day of March 2004, in duplicate in the English and Arabic languages, with both texts being equally authentic.

*

PART THREE

PROTOTYPE INSTRUMENTS

GHANA MODEL 2003
AGREEMENT BETWEEN THE GOVERNMENT OF THE REPUBLIC OF GHANA AND THE GOVERNMENT OF THE REPUBLIC OF _____ FOR THE PROMOTION AND PROTECTION OF INVESTMENTS*

The Government of the Republic of Ghana and the Government of the Republic of _____ (hereinafter referred to as the "Contracting Parties").

Desiring to create favourable conditions for greater investment by nationals and companies of one state in the territory of the other.

Recognizing that the encouragement and reciprocal protection under international agreement of such investments will be conducive to the stimulation of individual business initiative and will increase prosperity in both States.

Have agreed as follows:

ARTICLE 1

Definitions

1.   For the purpose of this Agreement:

   (a)   "investments" means every kind of asset and in particular, though not exclusively, includes:

   (i)   movable and immovable property and any other property rights such as mortgages, liens or pledges;

   (ii)   shares in and stocks and debentures of a company and any other form of participation in a company;

   (iii)   claims to money or to any performance under contract having a financial value;

   (iv)   intellectual property rights, goodwill, technical processes and know-how;

   (v)   business concessions conferred by law or under contract, including concessions to search for, cultivate, extract, or exploit natural resources;

   A change in the form in which assets are invested does not affect their character as investments, provided such change is not contrary to the laws of the Contracting Party in whose territory the investment has been made. The term "investment" includes all investments, whether made before or after the date of entry into force of this Agreement.

---

* *Source*: The Government of Ghana, Ministry of Foreign Affairs (2003).

(b)   "returns" means the amount yielded by an investment and in particular, though not exclusively, includes profits, interest, capital gains, dividends, royalties and fees;

(c)   "national" means:

    (i)   in respect of the Republic of Ghana: natural persons deriving their status as Ghanaian nationals from the law in force in the Republic of Ghana

    (ii)   in respect of the Republic of ....: natural persons deriving their status as .... nationals from the law in force in the Republic of ....

(d)   "companies" means:

    (i)   in respect of the Republic of Ghana: any corporations, firms and associations incorporated or constituted under the law in force in the Republic of Ghana;

    (ii)   in respect of the ...., corporations, firms and associations incorporated or constituted under the law in force in any part of ....

(e)   "territory" means:

    (i)   in respect of Ghana: the present territory of the Republic of Ghana including the territorial sea and any maritime area situated beyond the territorial sea of Ghana which has been or might in the future be designated under the national law of Ghana in accordance with international law as an area within which Ghana may exercise rights with regard to the sea-bed and subsoil and the natural resources;

    (ii)   in respect of the Republic of ...., the present territory of the Republic of .... including the territorial sea and any maritime area situated beyond the territorial sea of .... which has been or might in the future be designated under the national law of .... in accordance with international law as an area within which .... may exercise rights with regard to the sea-bed and subsoil and the natural resources;

ARTICLE 2
Promotion of Investments

Each Contracting Party shall encourage and create favourable conditions for nationals and companies of the other Contracting Party to invest capital in its territory and, subject to its rights to exercise powers conferred by its laws, shall admit such investments.

ARTICLE 3
Protection of Investments

1.   Investments of nationals and companies of each Contracting Party shall at all times be accorded equitable treatment and shall enjoy full and adequate protection and security in the territory of the other Contracting Party.

2. .   Neither Contracting Party shall, in any way, impair by unreasonable or discriminatory measures, the management, maintenance, use, enjoyment or disposal of investments in its territory of nationals or companies of the other Contracting Party.

3.   Each Contracting Party shall observe any obligation it may have entered into with regard to investments of nationals or companies of the other Contracting Party.

ARTICLE 4
National Treatment and Most-Favoured-Nation Provisions

1.   Neither Contracting Party shall in its territory subject investments or returns of nationals or companies of the other Contracting Party to treatment less favourable than that which it accords to investments or returns of its own nationals or companies or to investments or returns of nationals or companies of any third state.

2.   Neither Contracting Party shall in its territory subject nationals or companies of the other Contracting Party, as regards their management, maintenance, use, enjoyment or disposal of their investments, to treatment less favourable than that which is accorded to its own nationals or companies or to nationals or companies of any third state.

ARTICLE 5
Compensation for Losses

Nationals or companies of one Contracting Party whose investments suffer losses in the territory of the other Contracting Party owing to war or other armed conflict, revolution, a state of national emergency, revolt, insurrection or riot in the territory of the latter Contracting Party, shall be accorded by the latter Contracting Party treatment, as regards restitution, indemnification, compensation or other settlement, no less favourable than that which the latter Contracting Party accords to nationals of companies of any third State. Resulting payments shall be freely transferable.

ARTICLE 6
Exceptions

The provisions of this Agreement relative to the grant of treatment not less favourable than that accorded to the nationals or companies of either Contracting Party on any third State shall not be construed so as to oblige one Contracting Party to extend to the nationals or companies of the other, the benefit of any treatment, preference or privilege resulting from:

   (a)   any existing or future customs union, common market, free trade area, or regional economic organization or measures leading to the formation of a customs union or free trade area of which either Contracting Party is or may become a member, or

(b)   any international agreement or arrangement relating wholly or mainly to taxation or any domestic legislation relating wholly or mainly to taxation.

(c)   any special policies or measures intended to address the specific internal needs of identified disadvantaged groups, person or regions in the territory of either Contracting Party.

ARTICLE 7
Expropriation

1.   Investments of nationals or companies of either Contracting Party shall not be nationalised, expropriated or subjected to measures having effect equivalent to nationalisation or expropriation (hereinafter referred to as "expropriation") in the territory of the other Contracting Party, except where for a public purpose related to its internal needs, a Contracting Party expropriates the investments of nationals or companies of the other Contracting Party, the following conditions shall be complied with:

(a)   the measures shall be accompanied by provision for the payment of compensation amounting to the full and genuine value of the investment expropriated immediately before the expropriation or before the impending expropriation became public knowledge whichever is the earlier.

(b)   the compensation shall be paid without undue delay. If the compensation is not paid within six months from the date of its determination, it shall after that date attract interest at the normal commercial rate until the date of payment.

2.   A national or company affected shall have a right, under the law of the Contracting Party making the expropriation, to prompt review, by a judicial or other independent authority of that Party, of his or its investment in accordance with the principles set out in paragraph (1) of this Article.

3.   Where a Contracting Party expropriates the assets of a company which is incorporated or constituted under the law in force in any part of its own territory, and in which nationals or companies of the other Contracting Party own shares, the provisions of paragraphs (1) and (2) of this Article shall apply.

ARTICLE 8
Repatriation of Investments and Returns

Each Contracting Party shall, in respect of investments, guarantee to nationals or companies of the other Contracting Party the unrestricted transfer to the country where they reside of their investments and returns. Transfers of currency shall be effected without undue delay in the convertible currency in which the capital was originally invested or in any other convertible currency agreed by the investor and the Contracting Party concerned, subject, however, to the right of the former Contracting Party to impose equitably and in good faith such measures as may be necessary to safeguard the integrity and independence of its currency, its external financial position and balance of payments. Unless otherwise agreed by the investor, transfers shall be made at the rate of exchange applicable on the date of transfer pursuant to the exchange regulations in force.

ARTICLE 9
Subrogation

1.   If one Contracting Party or its designated agency makes a payment under an indemnity given in respect of an investment in the territory of the other Contracting Party, the latter Contracting Party shall, recognise the assignment to the former Contracting Party or its designated agency by law or any legal transaction of all the rights and claims of the party indemnified and that former Contracting Party or its designated agency is entitled to exercise such rights and enforce such claims by virtue of its subrogation, to the same extent as the party indemnified.

2.   The former Contracting Party or its designated Agency shall be entitled in all circumstances to the same treatment in respect of the rights and claims acquired by it by virtue of the assignment and any payments received in pursuance of those rights and claims as the party indemnified was entitled to receive by virtue of this Agreement in respect of the investment concerned and its related returns.

3.   Any payments received by the former Contracting Party or its designated Agency in pursuance of the rights and claims acquired shall be freely available to the former Contracting Party for the purpose of meeting any expenditure incurred in the territory of the latter Contracting Party.

ARTICLE 10
Settlement of Investment Disputes between a Contracting Party
and an Investor of the Other Contracting Party

1.   Disputes between a national or company of one Contracting Party and the other Contracting Party concerning an obligation of the latter under this agreement in relation to an investment of the former which have not been amicably settled shall, after a period of six months from written notification of a claim, be submitted at the first instance to the competent court of the Contracting Party for decision, or to international arbitration if either party to the dispute so wishes.

2.   Where the dispute is referred to international arbitration, the investor and the Contracting Party concerned in the dispute may agree to refer the dispute either to:

(a)   the International Centre for the Settlement of Investment Disputes (having regard to the provisions, where applicable, of the Convention of the Settlement of Investment Disputes between states and nationals of other states, opened for signature at Washington DC on 18th march, 1965 and the Additional Facility for the Administration of conciliation, Arbitration and Fact-Finding proceedings); or

(b)   an international arbitrator or ad hoc arbitration tribunal to be appointed by a special agreement between the parties or established under the Arbitration Rules of the United Nations Commission on International Trade Law.

3.   If after a period of six months from written notification of the claim there is no agreement to one of the above alternative procedures, the parties to the dispute shall be bound to submit it to arbitration under the arbitration rules of the United Nations Commission on International Trade law as then in force. The parties to the dispute may agree in writing to modify these rules.

ARTICLE 11
Disputes Between the Contracting Parties

1.   Disputes between the Contracting Parties concerning the interpretation or application of this Agreement should, if possible, be settled through diplomatic channels.

2.   If a dispute between the Contracting Parties cannot thus be settled within six months, it shall upon the request of either Contracting Party be submitted to an arbitral tribunal.

3.   Such an arbitral tribunal shall be constituted for each individual case in the following way: Within two months of the receipt of the request for arbitration, each Contracting Party shall appoint one member of the tribunal. Those two members shall then select a national of a third State who on approval by the two Contracting Parties shall be appointed Chairman of the tribunal. The Chairman shall be appointed within two (2) months from the date of appointment of the other two members.

4.   If within the periods specified in paragraph 3 of this Article the necessary appointments have not been made, either Contracting Party may, in the absence of any other agreement, invite the President of the International Court of Justice to make the necessary appointments. If the President is a national of either Contracting Party or if he is otherwise prevented from discharging the said function, the Vice-President shall be invited to make the necessary appointments. If the Vice-President is a national of either Contracting Party or if he too is prevented from discharging the said function, the member of the International Court of Justice next in seniority who is not a national of either Contracting Party shall be invited to make the necessary appointments.

5.   The arbitral tribunal shall reach its decision by a majority of votes. Such decision shall be binding on both Contracting Parties. Each Contracting Party shall bear the cost of its own member of the tribunal and of its representation in the arbitral proceedings. The cost of the Chairman and the remaining costs shall be borne in equal parts by the Contracting Parties. The tribunal may, however, in its decision, direct that a higher proportion of costs shall be borne by one of the two Contracting Parties, and this award shall be binding on both Contracting Parties. The tribunal shall determine its own procedure.

ARTICLE 12
Amendments

At the time of entry into force of this Agreement or at any time thereafter, the provisions of this Agreement may be amended in such manner as may be agreed between the Contracting Parties. Each Contracting Party shall notify the other Contracting Party of the completion of the constitutional formalities in its territory for entry into force of the said amendments. Such amendments shall enter into force on the date of the latter of the two notifications.

ARTICLE 13
Application of other Rules

If the provision of the law of either Contracting Party or obligations under international law existing at present or established hereafter between the Contracting Parties in addition to the present Agreement contain rules, whether general or specific, entitling investments by investors of the other Contracting Party to a treatment more favourable than is provided for by the present

Agreement, such rules shall to the extent that they are more favourable prevail over the present Agreement.

ARTICLE 14
Scope of application

This Agreement shall be applicable to investments made before or after its entry into force by investors of either Contracting Party in the territory of the other Contracting Party. However, the provisions of this Agreement shall not apply to claims arising out of events which occurred or to claims which have been settled prior to its entry into force.

ARTICLE 15
Consultations

The Contracting Parties agree to consult each other at the request of either Party on any matters relating to investments between the two countries, or otherwise affecting implementation of this Agreement.

ARTICLE 16
Entry into Force, Duration and Termination

1.   Each Contracting Party shall notify the other Contracting Party of the completion of the constitutional formalities in its territory for the entry into force of this Agreement. This Agreement shall enter into force on the date of the latter of the two notifications.

2.   This Agreement shall remain in force for a period of ten (10) years. After the expiration of the initial period, it shall continue in force thereafter until the either Contracting Party notifies the other Contracting Party in writing of its decision to terminate this Agreement. The notice of termination shall become effective one year after the date of notification.

3.   In respect of investments made prior to the date of termination of this Agreement, the provisions of Articles 1 to 15 of this Agreement shall remain on force shall continue in effect for a period of five (5) years from the date of termination.

IN WITNESS WHEREOF, the undersigned, duly authorised thereto by their respective Governments, have signed this Agreement.

Done in duplicate at .... this .... day of............ in English Language.

*

AGREEMENT BETWEEN THE GOVERNMENT OF ROMANIA AND THE GOVERNMENT OF _____ ON THE PROMOTION AND RECIPROCAL PROTECTION OF INVESTMENTS*

Agreement Between the Government of Romania and the Government of _____ on the Promotion and Reciprocal Protection of Investments

The Government of Romania and the Government of the _____ herein referred to as the "Contracting Parties",

Desiring to intensify economic co-operation to the mutual benefit of both States,

Intending to create and maintain favourable conditions for investments by investors of the State of one Contracting Party in the State territory of the other Contracting Party,

Recognising the need to promote and protect foreign investments with the aim to foster the economic prosperity of both States,

Have agreed as follows:

ARTICLE 1
DEFINITIONS

For the purpose of this Agreement:

(1)   The term "investor" refers, with regard to either Contracting Party, to the following subjects who made investments in the State territory of the other Contracting Party:

- In respect of Romania:

a)   "natural person" means a citizen in accordance with the law of Romania;

b)   "legal person" means legal entities, including companies, corporations, business associations and other organizations which are constituted or otherwise duly organised in accordance with the law of Romania and have their seat, together with real economic activities, in the territory of Romania.

- In respect of the _____.

a)   "natural person" means a citizen or non-citizen in accordance with the law of the _____;

b)   "legal person" means any entity incorporated or constituted in accordance with the law of the _____.

(2)   The term "investments" shall mean every kind of assets invested by investors of one Contracting Party in the State territory of the other Contracting Party, in accordance with the laws and regulations of the State of the latter, and include particularly, but not exclusively:

---

* *Source*: The Government of Romania, Ministry of Foreign Affairs (2003).

a)   movable and immovable property as well as any other rights in rem, such as servitudes, mortgages, liens, pledges;

b)   shares, parts or any other kinds of participation in companies;

c)   claims to money or to any rights to any performance having an economic value;

d)   intellectual property rights, such as copyrights, patents, industrial designs or models, trade or service marks, trade names, know-how and goodwill, as well as other similar rights recognised by the national laws of the Contracting Parties;

e)   concessions under public law, including concessions to search, extract or exploit of natural resources as well as all other rights given by law, by contract or by decision of the authority in accordance with the law.

Any alteration of the form in which assets are invested or reinvested shall not affect their character as investment.

(3)   The term "returns" means amounts yielded by an investment and in particular, though not exclusively, includes profits, dividends, interests, capital gains, royalties, management and technical assistance or other fees, irrespective of the form in which the return is paid.

(4)   The term "territory means:

- In respect of Romania, the territory of Romania, including its territorial sea and the airspace above its territory and territorial sea over which Romania exercises its sovereignty, as well as the contiguous zone, continental shelf and exclusive economic zone over which Romania exercises its jurisdiction, respective sovereign rights, in accordance with its legislation and international law.

- In respect of the ...., the territory of the .... including the territorial sea, as well as any maritime area beyond which .... in conformity with international law, exercises sovereign rights with regard to the seabed and subsoil and the natural resources of such areas.

ARTICLE 2
PROMOTION, ADMISSION

(1)   Each Contracting Party shall, in its State territory, promote as far as possible, investments by investors of the other Contracting Party and admit such investments in accordance with its national laws and regulations.

(2)   When a Contracting Party shall have admitted an investment in its State territory, it shall, in accordance with its national laws and regulations, grant the necessary permits in connection with such an investment, including authorisations for engaging top managerial and technical personnel of their choice, regardless of citizenship, on a non-discriminatory basis.

ARTICLE 3
PROTECTION, TREATMENT

(1)   Each Contracting Party shall protect within its State territory investments made in accordance with its national laws and regulations by investors of the other Contracting Party and shall not impair by unreasonable or discriminatory measures the management, maintenance, use, enjoyment, extension, sale or liquidation of such investments. In particular, each Contracting Party or its competent authorities shall issue the necessary authorisations mentioned in Article 2, paragraph (2) of this Agreement.

(2)   Each Contracting Party shall ensure fair and equitable treatment within its State territory of the investments of the investors of the other Contracting Party. This treatment shall not be less favourable than that granted by each Contracting Party to investments made within its State territory by its own investors, or than that granted by each Contracting Party to the investments made within its State territory by investors of any third State, if this latter treatment is more favourable.

(3)   The most favoured nation treatment shall not be construed so as to oblige a Contracting Party to extend to the investors and investments of the other Contracting Party the advantages resulting from any existing or future customs or economic union, a free trade area or regional economic union, to which either of the Contracting Parties is or becomes a member. Nor shall such treatment relate to any advantage which either Contracting Party accords to investors of a third State by virtue of a double taxation agreement or other agreements on a reciprocal basis regarding tax matters.

ARTICLE 4
FREE TRANSFER

(1)   Each Contracting Party in whose State territory investments have been made by investors of the other Contracting Party shall grant those investors the free transfer of the payments relating to these investments, particularly of:

a)   returns according to Article 1, paragraph (3) of this Agreement;

b)   amounts relating to loans incurred, or other contractual obligations undertaken, for the investment;

c)   proceeds accruing from the total or partial sale, alienation or liquidation of an investment.

Transfers shall be effected without delay, in convertible currency.

(2)   Unless otherwise agreed with the investor, transfers shall be made pursuant to the national laws and regulations in force of the Contracting Party in whose State territory the investment was made, at the rate of exchange applicable on the date of transfer.

ARTICLE 5
DISPOSSESSION, COMPENSATION

(1)   Neither of the Contracting Parties shall take, either directly or indirectly, measures of expropriation, nationalisation or any other measures having the same nature or the same effect against investments of investors of the other Contracting Party, unless the measures are taken in the public interest as established by law, on a non-discriminatory basis and under due process of law, and provided that provisions be made for effective and adequate compensation. The amount of compensation, interest included, shall be settled in a convertible currency and paid without delay to the investor entitled thereto. Resulting payments shall be freely and promptly transferable.

(2)   The investors of one Contracting Party whose investments have suffered losses due to a war or any other armed conflict, revolution, state of emergency or rebellion, which took place on the State territory of the other Contracting Party shall benefit, from the part of this latter, of a treatment in accordance with Article 3, paragraph (2) of this Agreement. They shall, in all events, be entitled to compensation.

ARTICLE 6
PRE-AGREEMENT INVESTMENTS

The present Agreement shall apply to investments in the State territory of a Contracting Party made in accordance with its national laws and regulations by investors of the other Contracting Party whether prior to or after the entry into force of this Agreement. However, the Agreement shall not apply to disputes that have arisen before its entry into force.

ARTICLE 7
OTHER OBLIGATIONS

(1)   If the national legislation of either Contracting Party entitles investments by investors of the other Contracting Party to treatment more favourable than is provided for by this Agreement, such legislation shall, to the extent that it is more favourable, prevail over this Agreement.

(2)   Each Contracting Party shall observe any other obligation it has assumed with regard to investments in its State territory by investors of the other Contracting Party.

ARTICLE 8
PRINCIPLE OF SUBROGATION

If either Contracting Party or its designated agency makes payment to one of its investors under any financial guarantee against non-commercial risks it has granted in regard of an investment in the State territory of the other Contracting Party, the latter shall recognise, by virtue of the principle of subrogation, the assignment of any right or title of that investor to the first Contracting Party or its designated agency. The other Contracting Party shall be entitled to set off taxes and other public charges due and payable by the investor.

ARTICLE 9
SETTLEMENT OF DISPUTES BETWEEN A
CONTRACTING PARTY AND AN INVESTOR OF
THE OTHER CONTRACTING PARTY

(1)   For the purpose of solving disputes with respect to investments between a Contracting Party and an investor of the other Contracting Party, consultations will take place between the parties concerned with a view to solving the case, as far as possible, amicably.

(2)   If these consultations do not result in a solution within six months from the date of request for settlement, the investor may submit the dispute, at his choice, for settlement to:

    a)   the competent court of the Contracting Party in the State territory of which the investment has been made; or

    b)   the International Centre for Settlement of Investment Disputes (ICSID) provided for by the Convention on the Settlement of Investment Disputes between States and Nationals of the other States, opened for signature at Washington, on March 18, 1965; or

    c)   an ad hoc arbitral tribunal which, unless otherwise agreed upon by the parties to the dispute, shall be established under the arbitration rules of the United Nations Commission on International Trade Law (UNCITRAL).

(3)   Each Contracting Party hereby consents to the submission of an investment dispute to international conciliation or arbitration.

(4)   The Contracting Party which is a party to the dispute shall, at no time whatsoever during the procedures involving investment disputes, assert as a defence its immunity or the fact that the investor has received compensation under an insurance contract covering the whole or part of the incurred damage or loss.

ARTICLE 10
SETTLEMENT OF DISPUTES
BETWEEN CONTRACTING PARTIES

(1)   Disputes between Contracting Parties regarding the interpretation or application of the provisions of this Agreement shall be settled through diplomatic channels.

(2)   If both Contracting Parties cannot reach an agreement within twelve months after the beginning of the dispute between themselves, the latter shall, upon request of either Contracting Party, be submitted to an arbitral tribunal of three members. Each Contracting Party shall appoint one arbitrator, and these two arbitrators shall nominate a chairman who shall be a citizen of a third State.

(3)   If one of the Contracting Parties has not appointed its arbitrator and has not followed the invitation of the other Contracting Party to make that appointment within two months, the arbitrator shall be appointed, upon the request of that Contracting Party, by the President of the International Court of Justice.

(4)   If both arbitrators cannot reach an agreement about the choice of the chairman within two months after their appointment, the latter shall be appointed, upon the request of either Contracting Party, by the President of the International Court of Justice.

(5)   If, in the cases specified under paragraphs (3) and (4) of this Article, the President of the International Court of Justice is prevented from carrying out the said function or if he is a citizen of the State of either Contracting Party, the appointment shall be made by the Vice-President, and if the latter is prevented or if he is a citizen of the State of either Contracting Party, the appointment shall be made by the most senior Judge of the Court who is not citizen of the State of either Contracting Party.

(6)   Subject to other provisions made by the Contracting Parties, the tribunal shall determine its procedure.

(7)   Each Contracting Party shall bear the cost of the arbitrator it has appointed and of its representation in the arbitral proceedings. The cost of the chairman and the remaining costs shall be borne in equal parts by the Contracting Parties.

(8)   The decisions of the tribunal are final and binding for each Contracting Party.

ARTICLE 11
FINAL PROVISIONS

(1)   This Agreement shall enter into force thirty days after the date of the last notification which the Contracting Parties shall have communicated each other that their internal legal requirements for the entry into force of this Agreement have been fulfilled. It shall remain in force for an initial period of ten years. Unless official notice of denonciation is given six months before the expiration of this period, the Agreement shall be considered as renewed on the same terms for further periods of ten years.

(2)   In case of official notice as to the denonciation of the present Agreement, the provisions of the Article 1 to 10 shall continue to be effective for a further period of ten years for investments made before official notice was given.

IN WITNESS THEREOF the Undersigned, being duly authorised by their respective Governments, have signed this Agreement.

Signed at ...., on ...., in two originals, each in Romanian, ... and English languages, all texts being equally authentic. In case of difference of interpretation, the English text shall prevail.

*

LIST OF PUBLICATIONS ON FDI AND TNCS, 1973-2004
(For more information, please visit www.unctad.org/en/pub on the web.)

I. TRENDS IN FDI AND THE ACTIVITIES OF TNCs

A.   World Investment Report

UNCTAD, *World Investment Report 2004. The Shift Towards Services* (New York and Geneva, 2004). 470 pages. Sales No. E.04.II.D.33.

UNCTAD, *World Investment Report 2004. The Shift Towards Services. Overview*. 54 pages (A, C, E, F, R, S). Document symbol: UNCTAD/WIR/2004 (Overview). Available free of charge.

UNCTAD, *World Investment Report 2003. FDI Policies for Development: National and International Perspectives* (New York and Geneva, 2003). 303 pages. Sales No. E.03.II.D.8.

UNCTAD, *World Investment Report 2003. FDI Policies for Development: National and International Perspectives. Overview*. 42 pages (A, C, E, F, R, S). Document symbol: UNCTAD/WIR/2003 (Overview). Available free of charge.

UNCTAD, *World Investment Report 2002: Transnational Corporations and Export Competitiveness* (New York and Geneva, 2002). 350 pages. Sales No. E.02.II.D.4.

UNCTAD, *World Investment Report 2002: Transnational Corporations and Export Competitiveness. Overview*. 66 pages (A, C, E, F, R, S). Document symbol: UNCTAD/WIR/2002 (Overview). Available free of charge.

UNCTAD, *World Investment Report 2001: Promoting Linkages* (New York and Geneva, 2001). 354 pages. Sales No. E.01.II.D.12.

UNCTAD, *World Investment Report 2001: Promoting Linkages. Overview*. 63 pages (A, C, E, F, R, S). Document symbol: UNCTAD/WIR/2001 (Overview). Available free of charge.

UNCTAD, *World Investment Report 2000: Cross-border Mergers and Acquisitions and Development* (New York and Geneva, 2000). 337 pages. Sales No. E.00.II.D.20.

UNCTAD, *World Investment Report 2000: Cross-border Mergers and Acquisitions and Development. Overview*. 65 pages (A, C, E, F, R, S). Document symbol: UNCTAD/WIR/2000 (Overview). Available free of charge.

UNCTAD, *World Investment Report 1999: Foreign Direct Investment and the Challenge of Development* (New York and Geneva, 1999). 541 pages. Sales No. E.99.II.D.3.

UNCTAD, *World Investment Report 1999: Foreign Direct Investment and the Challenge of Development. Overview*. 75 pages (A, C, E, F, R, S). Document symbol: UNCTAD/WIR/1999 (Overview). Available free of charge.

UNCTAD, *World Investment Report 1998: Trends and Determinants* (New York and Geneva, 1998). 463 pages. Sales No. E.98.II.D.5.

UNCTAD, *World Investment Report 1998: Trends and Determinants. Overview*. 72 pages (A, C, E, F, R, S). Document symbol: UNCTAD/WIR/1998 (Overview). Available free of charge.

UNCTAD, *World Investment Report 1997: Transnational Corporations, Market Structure and Competition Policy* (New York and Geneva, 1997). 416 pages. Sales No. E.97.II.D. 10.

UNCTAD, *World Investment Report 1997: Transnational Corporations, Market Structure and Competition Policy. Overview*. 76 pages (A, C, E, F, R, S). Document symbol: UNCTAD/ITE/IIT/5 (Overview). Available free of charge.

UNCTAD, *World Investment Report 1996: Investment, Trade and International Policy Arrangements* (New York and Geneva, 1996). 364 pages. Sales No. E.96.11.A. 14.

UNCTAD, *World Investment Report 1996: Investment, Trade and International Policy Arrangements. Overview*. 22 pages (A, C, E, F, R, S). Document symbol: UNCTAD/DTCI/32 (Overview). Available free of charge.

UNCTAD, *World Investment Report 1995: Transnational Corporations and Competitiveness* (New York and Geneva, 1995). 491 pages. Sales No. E.95.II.A.9.

UNCTAD, *World Investment Report 1995: Transnational Corporations and Competitiveness. Overview*. 68 pages (A, C, E, F, R, S). Document symbol: UNCTAD/DTCI/26 (Overview). Available free of charge.

UNCTAD, *World Investment Report 1994: Transnational Corporations, Employment and the Workplace* (New York and Geneva, 1994). 482 pages. Sales No.E.94.11.A.14.

UNCTAD, *World Investment Report 1994: Transnational Corporations, Employment and the Workplace. An Executive Summary*. 34 pages (C, E, also available in Japanese). Document symbol: UNCTAD/DTCI/10 (Overview). Available free of charge.

UNCTAD, *World Investment Report 1993: Transnational Corporations and Integrated International Production* (New York and Geneva, 1993). 290 pages. Sales No. E.93.II.A.14.

UNCTAD, *World Investment Report 1993: Transnational Corporations and Integrated International Production. An Executive Summary*. 31 pages (C, E). Document symbol: ST/CTC/159 (Executive Summary). Available free of charge.

DESD/TCMD, *World Investment Report 1992: Transnational Corporations as Engines of Growth* (New York, 1992). 356 pages. Sales No. E.92.II.A.24.

DESD/TCMD, *World Investment Report 1992: Transnational Corporations as Engines of Growth: An Executive Summary*. 26 pages. Document symbol: ST/CTC/143 (Executive Summary). Available free of charge.

UNCTC, *World Investment Report 1991: The Triad in Foreign Direct Investment* (New York, 1991). 108 pages. Sales No. E.9 1.II.A. 12. $25.

B.   Other Studies

UNCTAD, *FDI in Landlocked Developing Countries at a Glance* (Geneva, 2003). Document symbol: UNCTAD/ITE/IIA/2003/5. Available free of charge.

UNCTAD, *Foreign Direct Investment in the World and Poland: Trends, Determinants and Economic Impact*. (Warsaw, 2002). ISBN 83-918182-0-9.

UNCTAD, *FDI in Least Developed Countries at a glance: 2002* (Geneva, 2002). Document symbol: UNCTAD/ITE/IIA/6. 150 pages. Available free of charge.

UNCTAD, *Tax incentives and FDI: A Global Survey* (Geneva, 2001). Sales No. E.01.II.D.5.

UNCTAD, *FDI in Least Developed Countries at a glance: 2001* (Geneva, 2001). Document symbol: UNCTAD/ITE/IIA/3. 150 pages. Available free of charge.

UNCTAD, Invest in France Mission, DATAR and Arthur Andersen, *International Investment: Towards the Year 2002* (Paris, 1998). 167 pages (E,F). Sales No. GV.E.98.0.15. $29.

UNCTAD, Invest in France Mission, DATAR and Arthur Andersen, *International Investment: Towards the Year 2001* (Paris, 1997). 81 pages. Sales No. GV.E.97.0.5. $35.

UNCTAD, *Sharing Asia's Dynamism: Asian Direct Investment in the European Union* (Geneva, 1997). 143 pages. Sales No. E.97.II.D. 1. $26.

UNCTAD and the European Commission, *Investing in Asia's Dynamism: European Union Direct Investment in Asia* (A joint publication with the Office for Official Publications of the European Communities, Luxembourg, 1996). 124 pages. ISBN 92-827-7675-1. ECU 14.

UNCTAD, *Foreign Direct Investment in Africa*. Current Studies, Series A, No. 28 (Geneva, 1996). 115 pages (E, F). Sales No. E.95.II.A.6. $20.

John H. Dunning and Khalil A. Hamdani (eds.), *The New Globalism and Developing Countries* (United Nations University Press, on behalf of UNCTAD, DITE, 1996). 336 pages (E). ISBN 92-808-0944-X. $25.

Karl P. Sauvant, Persephone Economou and Fiorina Mugione (eds.), *Companies without Borders: Transnational Corporations in the 1990s* (Published by International Thomson Business Press, for and on behalf of UNCTAD DITE, 1996). 224 pages. ISBN 0-415-12526-X. E47.50.

UNCTAD, *Transnational Corporations and World Development* (Published by International Thomson Business Press, for and on behalf of UNCTAD DITE, 1996). 656 pages. ISBN 0-415-08560-8 (hardback), 0-415-08561-6 (paperback). £65.00 (hardback), £20.99 (paperback).

UNCTC, *TNCs in South Africa: List of Companies with Investments and Disinvestments, 1990* (New York, 1991). 282 pages. Sales No. E.91.II.A.9. $22.

UNCTC, *Transnational Corporations in World Development: Trends and Prospects* (New York, 1988). 630 pages (A, C, E, F, R, S). Sales No. E.88.II.A.7. Out of print. Available on microfiche. Paper copy from microfiche: $650.

UNCTC, *Transnational Corporations in World Development: Trends and Prospects. Executive Summary* (New York, 1988). 63 pages. Sales No. E.88.II.A.15. Out of print. Available on microfiche.

UNCTC, *Foreign Direct Investment in Latin America: Recent Trends, Prospects and Policy Issues*. Current Studies, Series A, No. 3. (New York, 1986). 28 pages. Sales No. E.86.II.A. 14. Out of print. Available on microfiche. Paper copy from microfiche: $40.

UNCTC, *Trends and Issues in Foreign Direct Investment and Related Flows:* **A Technical Paper** (New York, 1985). 96 pages. Sales No. E.85.II.A.15. Out of print. Available on microfiche. Paper copy from microfiche: $110.

UNCTC, ***Transnational Corporations in World Development: Third Survey*** (New York, 1983). (Also published by Grahain and Trotman, London, 1985). 386 pages (A, C, E, F, R, S). Sales No. E.83.II.A. 14 and Corrigendum. Out of print. Available on microfiche. Paper copy from microfiche: $400.

UNCTC, ***Salient Features and Trends in Foreign Direct Investment*** (New York, 1983). 71 pages (A, C, E, F, R, S). Sales No. E.83.II.A.8. Out of print. Available on microfiche. Paper copy from microfiche: $82.

UNCTC, ***Transnational Corporations in World Development: A Re-examination*** (New York, 1978). 346 pages (E, F, S). Sales No. E.78.1I.A.5. Out of print. Available on microfiche. Paper copy from microfiche: $360.

United Nations Department of Economic and Social Affairs, ***Multinational Corporations in World Development*** (New York, 1973). (Also published by Praeger, New York, 1974, 200 pages). 196 pages (E, F, R, S). Sales No. E.73.II.A. 11. Out of print. Available on microfiche. Paper copy from microfiche: $204.

United Nations Department of Economic and Social Affairs, ***Summary of the Hearings Before the Group of Eminent Persons to Study the Impact of Multinational Corporations on Development and on International Relations*** (New York, 1974). 455 pages. Sales No. E.74.II.A.9. Out of print. Available on microfiche. Paper copy from microfiche: $450.

United Nations Department of Economic and Social Affairs, ***The Impact of Multinational Corporations on Development and on International Relations*** (New York, 1974). 162 pages (E, F, R, S). Sales No. E.74.II.A.5. Out of print. Available on microfiche. Paper copy from microfiche: $160.

The United Nations Library on Transnational Corporations. (The original, hardback version was published by Routledge, for and on behalf of UNCTAD, 1994). Twenty volumes, in five boxed sets of four volumes per set, ISBN 0-415-08559-4, £1,750 (£350 per set), can be ordered in the U.S.A. and Canada from Routledge, Inc., 29 West 35th Street, New York, NY 1000 1, U. S.A. (U.S.A. Tel.: ++ 1212 244 6412 and Fax: ++ 1212 268 9964; Canada Tel.: ++ 1 800 248 4724). In the U.K., by contacting: Routledge Customer Services Department, FREEPOST, ITPS, Cheriton House, North Way, Andover, Hants SP 10 5BR, U.K. (Tel.: ++44 1264 342811/342939; Fax: ++44 1264 364418).

Volume 1: Dunning, John H. (ed.). ***The Theory of Transnational Corporations.*** 464 pages. Also available in paperback version (published by International Thomson Business Press, for and on behalf of UNCTAD DITE). ISBN 0-415-14106-0. £20.99.

Volume 2: Jones, Geoffrey (ed.). ***Transnational Corporations: A Historical Perspective.*** 464 pages.

Volume 3: Lall, Sanjaya (ed.). ***Transnational Corporations and Economic Development.*** 448 pages. Also available in paperback version (published by International Thomson Business Press, for and on behalf of UNCTAD DITE). ISBN 0-415-14110-9. $29.95.

Volume 4: Lecraw, Donald J. and Allen J. Morrison (eds.). ***Transnational Corporations and Business Strategy.*** 416 pages. Also available in paperback version (published by International Thomson Business Press, for and on behalf of UNCTAD DITE). ISBN 0-415-14109-5. $29.95.

Volume 5: Stonehill, Arthur I. and Michael H. Moffet (eds.). ***International Financial Management.*** 400 pages. Also available in paperback version (published by International Thomson Business Press, for and on behalf of UNCTAD DITE). ISBN 0-415-14107-9.; £19.95.

Volume 6: Hedlund, Gunnar (ed.). ***Organization of Transnational Corporations***. 400 pages. Also available in paperback version (published by International Thomson Business Press, for and on behalf of UNCTAD DITE). ISBN 0-415-14108-7. $29.95.

Volume 7: Moran, Theodore H. (ed.). ***Governments and Transnational Corporations***. 352 pages.

Volume 8: Gray, H. Peter (ed.). ***Transnational Corporations and International Trade and Payments***. 320 pages.

Volume 9: Robson, Peter (ed.). ***Transnational Corporations and Regional Economic Integration***. 331 pages.

Volume 10: McKern, Bruce (ed.). ***Transnational Corporations and the Exploitation of Natural Resources***. 397 pages.

Volume 11: Chudnovsky, Daniel (ed.). ***Transnational Corporations and Industrialization***. 425 pages.

Volume 12: Sauvant, Karl P. and Padma Mallampally (eds.). ***Transnational Corporations in Services***. 437 pages.

Volume 13: Buckley, Peter J. (ed.). ***Cooperative Forms of Transnational Corporation Activity***. 419 pages.

Volume 14: Plasschaert, Sylvain (ed.). ***Transnational Corporations: Transfer Pricing and Taxation***. 330 pages.

Volume 15: Frischtak, Claudio and Richard Newfarmer (eds.). ***Transnational Corporations: Market Structure and Industrial Performanc***e. 383 pages.

Volume 16: Enderwick, Peter (ed.). ***Transnational Corporations and Human Resources***. 429 pages.

Volume 17: Cantwell, John (ed.). ***Transnational Corporations and Innovatory Activities***. 447 pages.

Volume 18: Chen, Edward (ed.). ***Transnational Corporations and Technology Transfer to Developing Countries***. 486 pages.

Volume 19: Rubin, Seymour and Don Wallace, Jr. (eds.). ***Transnational Corporations and National Law.*** 322 pages.

Volume 20: Fatouros, Arghyrios (ed.). ***Transnational Corporations. The International Legal Framework***. 545 pages.

II. DEVELOPMENT ISSUES AND FDI

Transnational Corporations. A refereed journal published three times a year. (Supersedes the *CTC Reporter* as of February 1992). Annual subscription (3 issues): $45. Single issue: $20.

UNCTAD, ***Investment and Technology Policies for Competitiveness: Review of Successful Country Experiences*** (Geneva, 2003). Document symbol: UNCTAD/ITE/ICP/2003/2.

UNCTAD, ***The Development Dimension of FDI: Policy and Rule-Making Perspectives*** (Geneva, 2003). Sales No. E.03.II.D.22. $35.

UNCTAD, *FDI and Performance Requirements: New Evidence from Selected Countries* (Geneva, 2003). Sales No. E.03.II.D.32. 318 pages. $ 35.

UNCTAD, *Measures of the Transnationalization of Economic Activity* (New York and Geneva, 2001). Document symbol: UNCTAD/ITE/IIA/1. Sales No. E.01.II.D.2.

UNCTAD, *FDI Determinants and TNC Strategies: The Case of Brazil* (Geneva, 2000). Sales No. E.00:II.D.2.

UNCTAD, *The Competitiveness Challenge: Transnational Corporations and Industrial Restructuring in Developing Countries* (Geneva, 2000). Sales No. E.00.II.D.35.

UNCTAD, *Foreign Direct Investment in Africa: Performance and Potential* (Geneva, 1999). Document symbol: UNCTAD/ITE/IIT/Misc.15. Available free of charge.

UNCTAD, *The Financial Crisis in Asia and Foreign Direct Investment An Assessment* (Geneva, 1998). 110 pages. Sales No. GV.E.98.0.29. $20.

UNCTAD, *Handbook on Foreign Direct Investment by Small and Medium-sized Enterprises: Lessons from Asia* (New York and Geneva, 1998). 202 pages. Sales No. E.98.II.D.4. $48.

UNCTAD, *Handbook on Foreign Direct Investment by Small and Medium-sized Enterprises: Lessons from Asia. Executive Summary and Report on the Kunming Conference.* 70 pages. Document symbol: UNCTAD/ITE/IIT/6 (Summary). Available free of charge.

UNCTAD, *Survey of Best Practices in Investment Promotion* (New York and Geneva, 1997). 81 pages. Sales No. E.97.II.D.11. $35.

UNCTAD, *Incentives and Foreign Direct Investment* (New York and Geneva, 1996). Current Studies, Series A, No. 30. 98 pages. Sales No. E.96.II.A.6. $25.

UNCTC, *Foreign Direct Investment in the People's Republic of China* (New York, 1988). 110 pages. Sales No. E.88.II.A.3. Out of print. Available on microfiche. Paper copy from microfiche: $122.

UNCTAD, *Foreign Direct Investment, Trade, Aid and Migration* Current Studies, Series A, No. 29. (A joint publication with the International Organization for Migration, Geneva, 1996). 90 pages. Sales No. E.96M.A.8. $25.

UNCTAD, *Explaining and Forecasting Regional Flows of Foreign Direct Investment* (New York, 1993). Current Studies, Series A, No. 26. 58 pages. Sales No. E.94.II.A.5. $25.

UNCTAD, *Small and Medium-sized Transnational Corporations: Role, Impact and Policy Implications* (New York and Geneva, 1993). 242 pages. Sales No. E.93.II.A. 15. $35.

UNCTAD, *Small and Medium-sized Transnational Corporations: Executive Summary and Report of the Osaka Conference* (Geneva, 1994). 60 pages. Available free of charge.

DESD/TCMD, *From the Common Market to EC 92: Regional Economic Integration in the European Community and Transnational Corporations* (New York, 1993). 134 pages. Sales No. E.93.11.A.2. $25.

DESD/TCMD, *Debt-Equity Swaps and Development* (New York, 1993). 150 pages. Sales No. E.93.11.A.7. $35.

DESD/TCMD, *Transnational Corporations from Developing Countries: Impact on Their Home Countries* (New York, 1993). 116 pages. Sales No. E.93.11.A.8. $15.

DESD/TCMD, *Foreign Investment and Trade Linkages in Developing Countries* (New York, 1993). 108 pages. Sales No. E.93.II.A. 12. Out of print.

UNCTC, *Foreign Direct Investment and Industrial Restructuring in Mexico*. Current Studies, Series A, No. 18. (New York, 1992). 114 pages. Sales No. E.92.11.A.9. $12.50.

UNCTC, *The Determinants of Foreign Direct Investment: A Survey of the Evidence* (New York, 1992). 84 pages. Sales No. E.92.11.A.2. $12.50.

UNCTC and UNCTAD, *The Impact of Trade-Related Investment Measures on Trade and Development* (Geneva and New York, 1991). 104 pages. Sales No. E.91 II.A. 19. $17.50.

UNCTC, *The Challenge of Free Economic Zones in Central and Eastern Europe: International Perspective* (New York, 1991). 442 pages. Sales No. E.90.11.A.27. $75.

UNCTC, *The Role of Free Economic Zones in the USSR and Eastern Europe*. Current Studies, Series A, No. 14. (New York, 1990). 84 pages. Sales No. E.90.11.A.5. $10.

UNCTC, *Foreign Direct Investment, Debt and Home Country Policies*. Current Studies, Series A, No. 20. (New York, 1990). 50 pages. Sales No. E.90.II.A. 16. $12.50.

UNCTC, *News Issues in the Uruguay Round of Multilateral Trade Negotiations*. Current Studies, Series A, No. 19. (New York, 1990). 52 pages. Sales No. E.90.II.A. 15. $12.50.

UNCTC, *Regional Economic Integration and Transnational Corporations in the 1990s: Europe 1992, North America, and Developing Countries*. Current Studies, Series A, No. 15. (New York, 1990). 52 pages. Sales No. E.90.II.A. 14. $12.50.

UNCTC, *Transnational Corporations and International Economic Relations: Recent Developments and Selected Issues*. Current Studies, Series A, No. 11. (New York, 1989). 50 pages. Sales No. E.89.11.A.15. Out of print. Available on microfiche. Paper copy from microfiche: $60.

UNCTC, *The Process of Transnationalization and Transnational Mergers*. Current Studies, Series A, No. 8. (New York, 1989). 91 pages. Sales No. E.89.11.A.4. Out of print. Available on microfiche. Paper copy from microfiche: $106.

UNCTC and ILO, *Economic and Social Effects of Multinational Enterprises in Export Processing Zones* (Geneva, International Labour Office, 1988). 169 pages. ISBN: 92-2106194-9. S1727.50.

UNCTC, *Measures Strengthening the Negotiating Capacity of Governments in Their Relations with Transnational Corporations: Regional Integration cum/versus Corporate Integration. A Technical Paper* (New York, 1982). 63 pages. Sales No. E..82.II.A.6. Out of print. Available on microfiche. Paper copy from microfiche: $71.

III. SECTORAL STUDIES

A.   TNCs in the Manufacturing and Extractive Sectors

UNCTC, *New Approaches to Best-Practice Manufacturing: The Role of Transnational Corporations and Implications for Developing Countries*. Current Studies, Series A, No. 12. (New York, 1990). 76 pages. Sales No. E.90.II.A. 13. $20.

Blomström, Magnus, *Transnational Corporations and Manufacturing Exports from Developing Countries* (New York, 1990). 124 pages. Sales No. E.90.II.A.21. $25.

UNCTC, *Transnational Corporations in the Plastics Industry* (New York, 1990). 167 pages. Sales No. 90.II.A. 1. $20.

Hoffman, Kurt and Raphael Kaplinsky, *Driving Force: The Global Restructuring of Technology, Labour and Investment in the Automobile and Components Industries.*. (Boulder: Westview and UNCTC, 1988). 385 pages. ISBN: 0-8133-7502-9. $32.50.

UNCTC, *Transnational Corporations in Biotechnology* (New York, 1988). 130 pages. Sales No. E.88.II.A.4. $17.

UNCTC, *Transnational Corporations and Non-fuel Primary Commodities in Developing Countries* (New York, 1987). 89 pages. Sales No. E.87.II.A. 17. Out of print. Available on microfiche. Paper copy from microfiche: $98.

UNCTC and ESCAP Joint Unit, *Transnational Corporations and the Electronics Industries ofASEAN Economies*. Current Studies, Series A, No. 5. (New York, 1987). 55 pages. Sales No. E.87.II.A. 13. $7.50.

UNCTC, *Transnational Corporations in the Man-made Fibre, Textile and Clothing Industries* (New York, 1987). 154 pages. Sales No. E.87.II.A. 11. $19.

UNCTC, *Transnational Corporations in the International Semiconductor Industry* (New York, 1986). 471 pages. Sales No. E.86.II.A. 1. $41.

UNCTC, *Transnational Corporations in the Pharmaceutical Industry of Developing Countries* (New York, 1984). 223 pages. Sales No. E. 84.II.A. 10. Out of print. Available on microfiche. Paper copy from microfiche: $238.

UNCTC, *Transnational Corporations in the International Auto Industry* (New York, 1983). 223 pages. Sales No. E.83.II.A.6. Out of print. Available on microfiche. Paper copy from microfiche: $242.

UNCTC, *Transnational Corporations in the Agricultural Machinery and Equipment Industry* (New York, 1983). 134 pages. Sales No. E.83.II.A.4. Out of print. Available on microfiche. Paper copy from microfiche: $148.

UNCTC, *Transnational Corporations in the Power Equipment Industry* (New York, 1982). 95 pages (E, F, S). Sales No.E.82.II.A.1 1. Out of print. Available on microfiche. Paper copy from microfiche: $108.

UNCTC, *Transnational Corporations in the Fertilizer Industry* (New York, 1982). 69 pages (E, F, S). Sales No. E.82.H.A.10. Out of print. Available on microfiche. Paper copy from microfiche: $80.

UNCTC, *Transnational Corporations in Food and Beverage Processing* (New York, 1981). 242 pages. Sales No. E.8 I.II.A. 12. Out of print. Available on microfiche. Paper copy from microfiche: $26 1.

UNCTC, *Transnational Corporations in the Bauxite and Aluminium Industry* (New York, 1981). 88 pages (E, F, S). Sales No. E.8 1.II.A.5. Out of print. Available on microfiche. Paper copy from microfiche: $104.

UNCTC, *Transnational Corporation Linkages in Developing Countries: The Case of Backward Linkages via Subcontracting* (New York, 1981). 75 pages. Sales No. E.8 1.II.A.4. Out of print. Available on microfiche. Paper copy from microfiche:

UNCTC, *Transnational Corporations in the Copper Industry* (New York, 1981). 80 pages (E, F, S). Sales No. E.81.II.A.3. Out of print. Available on microfiche. Paper copy from microfiche: $92.

UNCTC, *Transnational Corporations and the Pharmaceutical Industry* (New York, 1979). 163 pages. Sales No. E.79.II.A.3. Out of print. Available on microfiche. Paper copy from microfiche: $160.

B.   TNCs in the Services Sector and Transborder Data Flows

UNCTAD, *Tradability of Consulting Services and Its Implications for Developing Countries* (New York and Geneva, 2002).189 pages. UNCTAD/ITE/IPC/Misc.8.

UNCTAD and the World Bank, *Liberalizing International Transactions in Services: A Handbook* (New York and Geneva, 1994). 182 pages. Sales No. E.94.II.A. 11. $45.

UNCTAD, *Tradability of Banking Services: Impact and Implications*. Current Studies, Series A, No. 27. (Geneva, 1994). 242 pages. Sales No. E.94.II.A. 12. $50.

UNCTAD, *Management Consulting: A Survey of the Industry and Its Largest Firms* (New York, 1993). 100 pages. Sales No. E.93.II.A. 17. $25.

UNCTAD, *International Tradability in Insurance Services*. Current Studies, Series A, No. 25. (New York, 1993). 54 pages. Sales No. E.93.II.A. 11. $20.

UNCTAD, *The Transnationalization of Service Industries: An Empirical Analysis of the Determinants of Foreign Direct Investment by Transnational Service Corporations*. Current Studies, Series A, No. 23. (New York, 1993). 62 pages. Sales No. E.93.II.A.3. $15.

UNCTC, *Transnational Banks and the External Indebtedness of Developing Countries: Impact of Regulatory Changes*. Current Studies, Series A, No. 22. (New York, 1992). 48 pages. Sales No. E.92.1l.A.10. Out of print. Available on microfiche. Paper copy from microfiche: $60.

UNCTC, *Transnational Banks and the International Debt Crisis* (New York, 1991). 148 pages. Sales No. E.90.II.A. 19. $22.50.

UNCTC, *Transborder Data Flows and Mexico* (New York, 1991). 194 pages. Sales No. E.90.II.A.17. $27.50.

UNCTC and World Bank, *The Uruguay Round., Services in the World Economy* (Washington and New York, 1990). 220 pages. ISBN: 0-8213-1374-6.

UNCTC, *New Issues in the Uruguay Round of Multilateral Trade Negotiations*. Current Studies, Series A, No. 19. (New York, 1990). 52 pages. Sales No. E.90.II.A. 15. $12.50.

UNCTC, ***Transnational Corporations, Services and the Uruguay Round*** (New York, 1990). 252 pages. Sales No. E.90.II.A. 11. $28.50.

UNCTC, ***Services and Development: The Role of Foreign Direct Investment and Trade*** (New York, 1989). 187 pages. Sales No. E.89.II.A. 17. Out of print. Available on microfiche. Paper copy from microfiche: $200.

(Also published in Spanish as *Servicios y el Desarrollo: El Papel de la Inversion y el Commercio*, by Junta del Acuerdo de Cartagena (Lima, 1990). 206 pages.)

UNCTC, ***Transnational Service Corporations and Developing Countries: Impact and Policy Issues.*** Current Studies, Series A, No. 10. (New York, 1989). 50 pages. Sales No. E.89.II.A. 14. Out of print. Available on microfiche. Paper copy from microfiche: $60.

UNCTC, ***Transnational Corporations in the Construction and Design Engineering Industry*** (New York, 1989). 60 pages. Sales No. E.89.II.A.6. Out of print. Available on microfiche. Paper copy from microfiche: $74.

Dunning, John H., ***Transnational Corporations and the Growth of Services: Some Conceptual and Theoretical Issues***. Current Studies, Series A, No. 9. (New York, 1989). 80 pages. Sales No. E.89.II.A.5. Out of print. Available on microfiche. Paper copy from microfiche: $92.

UNCTC, ***Foreign Direct Investment and Transnational Corporations in Services*** (New York, 1989). 229 pages. Sales No. E.89.II.A. 1. Out of print. Available on microfiche. Paper copy from microfiche: $240.

UNCTC, ***Data Goods and Data Services in the Socialist Countries of Eastern Europe*** (New York, 1988). 103 pages. Sales No. E.88.II.A.20. Out of print. Available on microfiche. Paper copy from microfiche: $114.

UNCTC, ***Foreign Direct Investment, the Service Sector and International Banking***. Current Studies, Series A, No. 7. (New York, 1987). (Also published by Graham and Trotman, Londori, 1988). 71 pages. Sales No. E.87.II.A. 15. $9.

UNCTC, ***Transborder Data Flows: Transnational Corporations and Remote-Sensing Data*** (New York, 1984). 74 pages. Sales No. E.84.II.A.11 and Corrigendum. (book reads: E.84.II.A.8). Outofprint. Available on microfiche. Paper copy from microfiche: $82.

UNCTC, ***Transborder Data Flows and Poland. Polish Case Study. A Technical Paper*** (New York, 1984). (Also published by North-Holland, Amsterdam, 1984). 75 pages. Sales No. E.84.11.A.8. Out of print. Available on microfiche. Paper copy from microfiche: $86.

UNCTC, ***Transborder Data Flows and Brazil*** (New York, 1983). (Also published by NorthHolland, Amsterdam, 1984). 418 pages. Sales No. E.83.II.A.3. Out of print. Available on microfiche. Paper copy from microfiche: $400.

UNCTC, ***Transborder Data Flows: Access to the International On-line Data-base Market*** (New York, 1983). (Also published by North-Holland, Amsterdam, 1984.) 140 pages. Sales No. E.83.II.A. 1. Out of print. Available on microfiche. Paper copy from microfiche: S 154.

UNCTC, ***Transnational Corporations in International Tourism*** (New York, 1982). 113 pages. Sales No. E.82.II.A.9. Out of print. Available on microfiche. Paper copy from microfiche: $123.

UNCTC, *Transnational Corporations and Transborder Data Flows: A Technical Paper* (New York, 1982). 149 pages. Sales No. E.82.II.A.4. Out of print. Available on microfiche. Paper copy from microfiche: $159.

UNCTC, *Transnational Banks: Operations, Strategies and Their Effects in Developing Countries* (New York, 1981). 140 pages. Sales No. E.8 1.II.A.7. Out of print. Available on microfiche. Paper copy from microfiche: $15 1.

UNCTC, *Transnational Reinsurance Operations: A Technical Paper* (New York, 1980). 51 pages. Sales No. E.80.II.A.10. Out of print. Available on microfiche. Paper copy from microfiche: $59.

UNCTC, *Transnational Corporations in Advertising. A Technical Paper* (New York, 1979). 54 pages (E, F, S). Sales No. E.79.II.A.2. Out of print. Available on microfiche. Paper copy from microfiche: $62.

IV. TNCs, TECHNOLOGY TRANSFER AND INTELLECTUAL PROPERTY RIGHTS

UNCTAD, *Transfer of Technology for Successful Integration into the Global Economy* (New York and Geneva, 2003). Sales No. E.03.II.D.31. 206 pages.

UNCTAD, *Compendium of International Arrangements on Transfer of Technology* (Geneva, 2001). Sales No. E.01.II.D.28.

UNCTAD, *The TRIPS Agreement and Developing Countries* (Geneva, 1997). 64 pages. Sales No. E.96.II.13. 10. $22.

UNCTAD, *Fostering Technological Dynamism: Evolution of Thought and Technological Development Process and Competitiveness: A Literature Review* (Geneva, 1995). 183 pages. Sales No. E.95.II.D.21. $35.

UNCTAD, *Intellectual Property Rights and Foreign Direct Investment*. Current Studies, Series A, No. 24. (New York, 1993). 108 pages. Sales No. E.93.II.A. 10. $20.

UNCTC, *Foreign Direct Investment and Technology Transfer in India* (New York, 1992). 150 pages. Sales No. E.92.II.A.3. $20.

UNCTC, *Transnational Corporations and the Transfer of New and Emerging Technologies to Developing Countries* (New York, 1990). 141 pages. Sales No. E.90.II.A.20. $27.50.

UNCTC, *Transnational Corporations and the Transfer of New Management Practices to Developing Countries* (New York, 1993). ST/CTC/153.

UNCTC, *New Approaches to Best-Practice Manufacturing: The Role of Transnational Corporations and Implications for Developing Countries*. Current Studies, Series A, No. 12. (New York, 1990). 76 pages. Sales No. E.90.II.A. 13. $12.50.

UNCTC and ESCAP Joint Unit, *Technology Acquisition under Alternative Arrangements with Transnational Corporations: Selected Industrial Case Studies in Thailand*. Current Studies,

Series A, No. 6. (New York, 1987). 55 pages. Sales No. E. 87.II.A. 14. Out of print. Available on microfiche. Paper copy from microfiche: $64.

UNCTC, *Transnational Corporations and Technology Transfer: Effects and Policy Issues* (New York, 1987). 77 pages. Sales No. E.87.II.A.4. Out of print. Available on microfiche. Paper copy from microfiche: $90.

UNCTC, *Measures Strengthening the Negotiating Capacity of Governments in Their Relations with Transnational Corporations: Technology Transfer through Transnational Corporations. A Technical Paper* (New York, 1979). 37 pages. Sales No. E.79.II.A.6. Out of print. Available on microfiche. Paper copy from microfiche: $43.

United Nations Department of Economic and Social Affairs, *Acquisition of Technology from Multinational Corporations by Developing Countries* (New York, 1974). 50 pages. Sales No. E.74.II.A.7. Out of print. Available on microfiche. Paper copy from microfiche: $57.

V. POLITICAL, SOCIAL AND ENVIRONMENTAL IMPACTS OF TNCs

UNCTAD, *The Social Responsibility of Transnational Corporations*. Document symbol: UNCTAD/ITE/IIT/Misc.21. Available free of charge.

UNCTAD, *Self-regulation of Environmental Management: An Analysis of Guidelines Set by World Industry for Their Member Firms* (Geneva, 1996). 165 pages. Sales No. E.96.II.A.5. $35.

UNCTC, *Environmental Management in Transnational Corporations: Report on the Benchmark Corporate Environment Survey* (Geneva, 1993). 265 pages. Sales No. E.94.II.A.2.

UNCTAD, *Environmental Management in Transnational Corporations: Report on the Benchmark Corporate Environment Survey* (Geneva, 1994). 278 pages. Sales No. E.94.II.A.2. 529.95.

DESD/TCMD, *Climate Change and Transnational Corporations: Analysis and Trends* (New York, 1992). 110 pages. Sales No. E.92.II.A.7. $16.50.

UNCTC, *Transnational Corporations and Industrial Hazards Disclosure* (New York, 1991). 86 pages. Sales No. E.91.II.A.18. $17.50.

UNCTC and DIESA, *Consolidated, List of Products Whose Consumption and/or Sale Have Been Banned, Withdrawn, Severely Restricted or not Approved by Governments*, Fourth ed. (New York, 1991). 769 pages. Sales No. E.91.1V.4. Out of print. Available on microfiche. Paper copy ftom microfiche: $800.

UNCTC, *Transnational Corporations in South Africa: Second United Nations Public Hearings, 1989*:

Vol. I *Report of the Panel of Eminent Persons, Background Documentation* (New York, 1990). 162 pages. Sales No. E.90.II.A.6. $19.

Vol. II *Statements and Submissions* (New York, 1990). 210 pages. Document symbol: ST/CTC/102. Sales No.E.90.II.A.12. $21.

UNCTC and DESA, *Consolidated List of Products Whose Consumption and/or Sale Have Been Banned, Withdrawn, Severely Restricted or Not Approved by Government,* Second issue. Prepared jointly by the Food and Agriculture Organization of the United Nations, the World Health Organization, the International Labour Organization, the United Nations Centre on Transnational Corporations and other relevant intergovernmental organizations (New York, 1987). 655 pages. Sales No. E.87.1V. I. Out of print.

UNCTC, *Transnational Corporations in South Africa and Namibia*: United Nations Public Hearings, **1986**:

Vol. I **Reports of the Panel of Eminent Persons and of the Secretary-General** (New York, 1986). 242 pages. Document symbol: ST/CTC/68 (Vol. I). Sales No. E.86.II.A.6. Out of print. Available on microfiche. Paper copy from microfiche: $240.

Vol. II **Verbatim Records** (New York, 1986). 282 pages. Document symbol: ST/CTC/68 (Vol. II). Sales No. E.86.II.A.7. Out of print. Available on microfiche. Paper copy from microfiche: $300.

Vol. III **Statements and Submissions** (New York, 1987). 518 pages. Document symbol: ST/CTC/68 (Vol. III). Sales No. E.86.1I.A.8. Out of print. Available on microfiche. Paper copy from microfiche: $530.

Vol. IV **Policy Instruments and Statements** (New York, 1987). 444 pages. Document symbol: ST/CTC/68 (Vol. IV). Sales No. E.86.II.A.9. Out of print. Available on microfiche. Paper copy from microfiche: $474.

UNCTC, *Activities of Transnational Corporations in South Africa and Namibia and the Responsibilities of Home Countries with Respect to Their Operations in This Area* (New York, 1986). 59 pages (E, F, S). Sales No. E.85.II.A. 16. Out of print. Available on microfiche. Paper copy from microfiche: $66.

UNCTC, *Environmental Aspects of the Activities of Transnational Corporations: A Survey* (New York, 1985). 114 pages (E, F, S). Sales No. E.85.II.A. 11. Out of print. Available on microfiche. Paper copy from microfiche: $126.

UNCTC and ILO, *Women Workers in Multinational Enterprises in Developing Countries: A Contribution to the United Nations Decade for Women*. A joint publication by the United Nations Centre on Transnational Corporations and the International Labour Office (Geneva, International Labour Office, 1985). 119 pages (E, F, S). ISBN: 92-2-100532-1. SF15.

UNCTC and DIESA, *Listé récapitulative desproduits dont la consommation ou la vente ont été interdites ou rigoureusement réglementées, ou qui ont été retirées du marché ou n'ont pas été approuvés par les gouvernements. Première édition révisée* (New York, 1985). (E, F, S). Sales No. F.85.IV.8. Out of print. Available on microfiche. Paper copy from microfiche: $370.

UNCTC, *Policies and Practices of Transnational Corporations Regarding Their Activities in South Africa and Namibia* (New York, 1984). 55 pages (E, F, S). Sales No. E.84.1I.A.5.
Out of print. Available on microfiche. Paper copy from microfiche: $55.

UNCTC, *Transnational Corporations in Southern Africa: Update on Financial Activities and Employment Practices* (New York, 1982). 44 pages. Sales No. E.82.II.A. 12. Out of print. Available on microfiche. Paper copy from microfiche: $62.

UNCTC, *Activities of Transnational Corporations in Southern Africa: Impact on Financial and Social Structures* (New York, 1978). 80 pages. Sales No. E.78.II.A.6. Out of print. Available on microfiche. Paper copy from microfiche: $85.

VI. INTERNATIONAL ARRANGEMENTS AND AGREEMENTS

A.   Series on Issues in International Investment Agreements (IIAs)

UNCTAD, *Glossary of Key Concepts Used in IIAs*. UNCTAD Series on Issues in International Investment Agreements (New York and Geneva, 2003)

UNCTAD, *Incentives* UNCTAD Series on Issues in International Investment Agreements (New York and Geneva, 2003). Sales No. E.04.II.D.6. $15.

UNCTAD, *Transparency*. UNCTAD Series on Issues in International Investment Agreements (New York and Geneva, 2003). Sales No. E.03.II.D.7. $15.

UNCTAD, *Dispute Settlement: Investor-State*. UNCTAD Series on Issues in International Investment Agreements (New York and Geneva, 2003). 128 pages. Sales No. E.03.II.D.5. $15.

UNCTAD, *Dispute Settlement: State-State*. UNCTAD Series on Issues in International Investment Agreements (New York and Geneva, 2003). 109 pages. Sales No. E.03.II.D.6 $16.

UNCTAD, *Transfer of Technology*. UNCTAD Series on Issues on International Investment Agreements (New York and Geneva, 2001). 135 pages. Sales No. E.01.II.D.33. $16.

UNCTAD, *Illicit Payments*. UNCTAD Series on Issues on IInternational Investment Agreements (New York and Geneva, 2001). 112 pages. Sales No. E.01.II.D.20. $13.

UNCTAD, *Home Country Measures*. UNCTAD Series on Issues on International Investment Agreements (New York and Geneva, 2001). 95 pages. Sales No. E.01.II.D.19. $12.

UNCTAD, *Host Country Operational Measures*. UNCTAD Series on Issues on International Investment Agreements (New York and Geneva, 2001). 105 pages. Sales No. E.01.II.D.18. $18.

UNCTAD, *Social Responsibility*. UNCTAD Series on Issues on International Investment Agreements (New York and Geneva, 2001). 87 pages. Sales No. E.01.II.D.4.$15.

UNCTAD, *Environment*. UNCTAD Series on Issues on International Investment Agreements (New York and Geneva 2001). 106 pages. Sales No. E.01.II.D.3. $15.

UNCTAD, *Transfer of Funds*. UNCTAD Series on Issues on International Investment Agreements (New York and Geneva 2000). 79 pages. Sales No. E.00.II.D.38. $10.

UNCTAD, *Flexibility for Development*. UNCTAD Series on Issues on International Investment Agreements (New York and Geneva 2000). 185 pages. Sales No. E.00.II.D.6. $15.

UNCTAD, *Employment*. UNCTAD Series on Issues on International Investment Agreements (New York and Geneva, 2000). 64 pages. Sales No. E.00.II.D.15. $12.

UNCTAD, *Taxation*. UNCTAD Series on Issues on International Investment Agreements (New York and Geneva, 2000). 111 pages. Sales No. E.00.II.D.5. $15.

UNCTAD, *Taking of Property*. UNCTAD Series on Issues on International Investment Agreements (New York and Geneva, 2000). 78 pages. Sales No. E.00.II.D.4. $12.

UNCTAD, *Trends in International investment Agreements: An Overview.* UNCTAD Series on Issues on International Investment Agreements (New York and Geneva, 1999). 133 pages. Sales No. E.99.II.D.23. $12.

UNCTAD, *Lessons from the MAI.* UNCTAD Series on Issues on International Investment Agreements (New York and Geneva 1999). 52 pages. Sales No. E.99.II.D.26. $10.

UNCTAD, *National Treatment.* UNCTAD Series on Issues in International Investment Agreements (New York and Geneva, 1999). 88 pages. Sales No. E.99.II.D. 16. $12.

UNCTAD, *Fair and Equitable Treatment.* UNCTAD Series on Issues in International Investment Agreements (New York and Geneva, 1999). 80 pages. Sales No. E.99.II.D.15. $12.

UNCTAD, *Investment-Related Trade Measures.* UNCTAD Series on Issues in International Investment Agreements (New York and Geneva, 1999). 64 pages. Sales No. E.99.II.D.12.$12.

UNCTAD, *Most-Favoured-Nation Treatment.* UNCTAD Series on Issues in International Investment Agreements (New York and Geneva, 1999). 72 pages. Sales No. E.99.II.D.11. $12.

UNCTAD, *Admission and Establishment.* UNCTAD Series on Issues in International Investment Agreements (New York and Geneva, 1999). 72 pages. Sales No. E.99.II.D.10. $12.

UNCTAD, *Scope and Definition.* UNCTAD Series on Issues in International Investment Agreements (New York and Geneva, 1999). 96 pages. Sales No. E.99.II.D.9. $12.

UNCTAD, *Transfer Pricing.* UNCTAD Series on Issues in International Investment Agreements (New York and Geneva, 1999). 72 pages. Sales No. E.99.II.D.8. $12.

UNCTAD, *Foreign Direct Investment and Development.* UNCTAD Series on Issues in International Investment Agreements (New York and Geneva, 1999). 88 pages. Sales No. E.98.1I.D.15A12.

B.   Other studies

UNCTAD's Work Programme on International Investment Agreements: **From UNCTAD IX to UNCTAD X**. Document symbol: UNCTAD/ITE/IIT/Misc.26. Available free of charge.

UNCTAD, Progress Report. Work undertaken within UNCTAD's work programme on International Investment Agreements between the 10th Conference of UNCTAD 10th Conference of UNCTAD, Bangkok, February 2000, and July 2002 (New York and Geneva, 2002). UNCTAD/ITE/Misc.58. Available free of charge.

UNCTAD, *Bilateral Investment Treaties in the Mid-1990s* (New York and Geneva, 1998). 322 pages. Sales No. E.98.II.D.8. $46.

UNCTAD, *Bilateral Investment Treaties: 1959-1999* (Geneva and New York, 2000) Sales No. E.92.II.A.16. $22.

UNCTAD, *International Investment Instruments: A Compendium* (New York and Geneva, 1996 to 2003). 12 volumes. Vol. I: Sales No. E.96.A.II.A.9. Vol. II: Sales No. E.96.II.A.10. Vol. III: Sales No. E.96.II.A.11. Vol. IV: Sales No. E.00.II.D.13. Vol. V: Sales No. E.00.II.A.14. Vol. VI: Sales No. E.01.II.D.34. Vol. VII: Sales No. E.02.II.D.14. Vol. VIII: Sales No. E.02.II.D.15. Vol. IX: Sales No. E.02.II.D.16. Vol. X: Sales No. E.02.II.D.21. Vol. XI: Sales No. E.04.II.D.9. Vol. XII: Sales No. E.04.II.D.10. $60.

UNCTC and ICC, ***Bilateral Investment Treaties***. A joint publication by the United Nations Centre on Transnational Corporations and the International Chamber of Commerce (New York, 1992). 46 pages. Sales No. E.92.II.A. 16. $22.

UNCTC, ***The New Code Environment***. Current Studies, Series A, No. 16. (New York, 1990). 54 pages. Sales No. E.90.II.A.7. Out of print. Available on microfiche. Paper copy from microfiche: $68.

UNCTC, ***Key Concepts in International Investment Arrangements and Their Relevance to Negotiations on International Transactions in Services***. Current Studies, Series A, No. 13. (New York, 1990). 66 pages. Sales No. E.90.II.A.3. $9.

UNCTC, ***Bilateral Investment Treaties*** (New York, 1988). (Also published by Graham and Trotman, London/Dordrecht/Boston, 1988). 188 pages. Sales No. E.88.II.A. 1. $20.

UNCTC, ***The United Nations Code of Conduct on Transnational Corporations***. Current Studies, Series A, No. 4. (New York, 1986). 80 pages. Sales No. E.86.II.A. 15. Out of print. Available on microfiche. Paper copy from microfiche: $88.

Vagts, Detlev F., ***The Question of a Reference to International Obligations in the United Nations Code of Conduct on Transnational Corporations: A Different View***. Current Studies,

Series A, No. 2. (New York, 1986). 17 pages. Sales No. E.86.II.A.11. Out of print. Available on microfiche. Paper copy from microfiche: $24.

Robinson, Patrick, ***The Question of a Reference to International Law in the United Nations Code of Conduct on Transnational Corporations***. Current Studies, Series A, No.1. (New York, 1986). 22 pages. Sales No. E.86.II.A.5. $4.

UNCTC, ***Transnational Corporations: Material Relevant to the Formulation of a Code of Conduct*** (New York, 1977). 114 pages (E, F, S). UN Document Symbol: EX. 10/ 10 and Corr. 1. $7.

UNCTC, ***Transnational Corporations: Issues Involved in the Formulation of a Code of Conduct*** (New York, 1976). 41 pages (E, F, R, S). Sales No. E.77.II.A.5. Out of print. Available on microfiche. Paper copy from microfiche: $41.

VII. NATIONAL POLICIES, LAWS, REGULATIONS AND CONTRACTS RELATING TO TNCs

A. Investment Policy Reviews

UNCTAD, ***Investment Policy Review of Algeria*** (Geneva, 2004). 110 pages. UNCTAD/ITE/IPC/2003/9.

UNCTAD, ***Investment Policy Review of Sri Lanka*** (Geneva, 2003). 89 pages. UNCTAD/ITE/IPC/2003/8

UNCTAD, ***Investment Policy Review of Lesotho*** (Geneva, 2003). 105 pages. Sales No. E.03.II.D.18.

UNCTAD, ***Investment Policy Review of Nepal***. (Geneva, 2003). 89 pages. Sales No.E.03.II.D.17.

UNCTAD, ***Investment Policy Review of Ghana*** (Geneva, 2002). 103 pages. Sales No. E.02.II.D.20.

UNCTAD, ***Investment Policy Review of Botswana*** (Geneva, 2003). 107 pages. Sales No. E.03.II.D.1.

UNCTAD, *Investment Policy Review of Tanzania* (Geneva, 2002). 109 pages. Sales No. E.02.II.D.6. $ 20.

UNCTAD, *Investment and Innovation Policy Review of Ethiopia* (Geneva, 2001). 130 pages. Sales No. E.01.II.D.5.

UNCTAD, *Investment Policy Review of Ecuador.* (Geneva, 2001). 136 pages. Sales No. E.01.II.D.31. $25. Also available in Spanish.

UNCTAD, *Investment Policy Review of Mauritius* (Geneva, 2000). 92 pages. Sales No. E.00.II.D.11.

UNCTAD, *Investment Policy Review of Peru* (Geneva, 2000). 109 pages. Sales No. E.00.II.D.7.

UNCTAD, *Investment Policy Review of Uganda* (Geneva, 1999). 71 pages. Sales No. E.99.II.D.24.

UNCTAD, *Investment Policy Review of Uzbekistan* (Geneva, 1999). 65 pages. Document number: UNCTAD/ITE/IIP/Misc.13.

UNCTAD, *Investment Policy Review of Egypt* (Geneva, 1999). 119 pages. Sales No. E.99.II.D.20. $19.

B.   Investment Guides

UNCTAD and ICC, *An Investment Guide to Mauritania* (Geneva, 2004). Document symbol: UNCTAD/IIA/2004/4. Free of charge.

UNCTAD and ICC, *An Investment Guide to Cambodia* (Geneva, 2003). 89 pages. Document symbol: UNCTAD/IIA/2003/6. Free of charge.

UNCTAD and ICC, *An Investment Guide to Nepal* (Geneva, 2003). 97 pages. Document symbol: UNCTAD/IIA/2003/2. Free of charge.

UNCTAD and ICC, *An Investment Guide to Mozambique* (Geneva, 2002). 109 pages. Document symbol: UNCTAD/IIA/4. Free of charge.

UNCTAD and ICC, *An Investment Guide to Uganda* (Geneva, 2001). 76 pages. Document symbol: UNCTAD/ITE/IIT/Misc.30. Publication updated in 2004. New document symbol UNCTAD/ITE/IIA/2004/3. Free of charge.

UNCTAD and ICC, *An Investment Guide to Mali* (Geneva, 2001). 105 pages. Document symbol: UNCTAD/ITE/IIT/Misc.24. Publication updated in 2004. New document symbol UNCTAD/ITE/IIA/2004/1. Free of charge.

UNCTAD and ICC, *An Investment Guide to Ethiopia* (Geneva, 2000). 68 pages. Document symbol: UNCTAD/ITE/IIT/Misc.19. Publication updated in 2004. New document symbol UNCTAD/ITE/IIA/2004/2. Free of charge.

UNCTAD and ICC, *An Investment Guide to Bangladesh* (Geneva, 2000). 66 pages. Document symbol: UNCTAD/ITE/IIT/Misc.29. Free of charge.

C.   Contracts and Agreements

UNCTC and Moody's Investors Service, *Directory of the World's Largest Service Companies: Series I* (New York, 1991). 834 pages. ISSN 10 14-8507. $95.

(To order and other information, please write to: Moody's Investors Service, 99 Church St., New York, N.Y. 10003, USA.)

UNCTC, *International Hotel Chain Management Agreements: A Primer for Hotel Owners in Developing Countries.* Advisory Studies, Series B, No. 5. (New York, 1990). 60 pages. Sales No. E.90.II.A.8. $9.

UNCTC, *International Debt Restructuring: Substantive Issues and Techniques.* Advisory Studies, Series B, No. 4. (New York, 1989). 91 pages. Sales No. E.89.II.A.10. $ 10.

UNCTC, *Joint Ventures as a Form of International Economic Co-operation. Background documents of the High-Level Seminar organized by the United Nations Centre on Transnational Corporations in co-operation with the State Foreign Economic Commission, and the State Committee on Science and Technology of the Union of Soviet Socialist Republics, Moscow, 10 March 1988* (New York, 1988). (Also published by Taylor & Francis, New York, 1989). 205 pages (E, R). Sales No. E.88.II.A.12. Out of print. Available on microfiche. Paper copy from microfiche: $270.

UNCTC, *Licence Agreements in Developing Countries* (New York, 1987). 108 pages. Sales No. E.87.II.A.21. Out of print. Available on microfiche. Paper copy from microfiche: $118.

UNCTC/ESCAP Joint Unit, *Technology Acquisition under Alternative Arrangements with Transnational Corporations: Selected Industrial Case Studies in Thailand.* Current Studies, Series A, No. 6. (New York, 1987). 55 pages. Sales No. E.87.II.A. 14. Out of print. Available on microfiche. Paper copy from microfiche: $64.

UNCTC, *Financial and Fiscal Aspects of Petroleum Exploitation.* Advisory Studies, Series B, No. 3. (New York, 1987). 39 pages. Sales No. E.87.II.A.10. $6.

UNCTC, *Arrangements Between Joint Venture Partners in Developing Countries.* Advisory Studies, Series B, No. 2. (New York, 1987). 43 pages. Sales No. E.87.II.A.5. $6.

UNCTC, *Natural Gas Clauses in Petroleum Arrangements.* Advisory Studies, Series B, No. 1. (New York, 1987). 54 pages. Sales No. E.87.II.A.3. $8.

UNCTC, *Analysis of Engineering and Technical Assistance Consultancy Contracts* (New York, 1986). 517 pages. Sales No. E.86.II.A.4. Out of print. Available on microfiche. Paper copy from microfiche: $530.

UNCTC, *Analysis of Equipment Leasing Contracts* (New York, 1984). 138 pages. Sales No. E.84.II.A.4. Out of print. Available on microfiche. Paper copy from microfiche: $148.

UNCTC, *Measures Strengthening the Negotiating Capacity of Governments in Their Relations with Transnational Corporations. Joint Ventures Among Firms in Latin America: A Technical Paper* (New York, 1983). 97 pages. Sales No. E.83.II.A.19. Out of print. Available on microfiche. Paper copy from microfiche: $ 100.

UNCTC, *Issues in Negotiating International Loan Agreements with Transnational Banks* (New York, 1983). 103 pages. Sales No. E. 83.II.A. 18. Out of print. Available on microfiche. Paper copy from microfiche: $110. ~

UNCTC, *Transnational Corporations and Contractual Relations in the World Uranium Industry: A Technical Paper* (New York, 1983). 167 pages. Sales No. E.83.II.A. 17. Out of print. Available on microfiche. Paper copy from microfiche: $179.

UNCTC, *Features and Issues in Turnkey Contracts in Developing Countries: A Technical Paper* (New York, 1983). 156 pages. Sales No. E.83.II.A.13. Out of print. Available on microfiche. Paper copy from microfiche: $160.

UNCTC, *Main Features and Trends in Petroleum and Mining Agreements* (New York, 1983). 129 pages. Sales No. E.83.II.A.9. Out of print. Available on microfiche. Paper copy from microfiche: $140.

UNCTC, *Alternative Arrangements for Petroleum Development* (New York, 1982). 70 pages. Sales No. E.82.II.A.22. Out of print. Available on microfiche. Paper copy from microfiche: $82.

UNCTC, *Management Contracts in Developing Countries: An Analysis of Their Substantive Provisions* (New York, 1983). 139 pages (E, F, S). Sales No. E.82.II.A.21. Out of print. Available on microfiche. Paper copy from microfiche: $150.

D. Other Studies

UNCTAD, *Investment Regimes in the Arab World: Issues and Policies*. (Geneva, 2000). Sales No. E/F.00.II.D.32. $39.

UNCTC, *Debt Equity Conversions: A Guide for Decision-makers* (New York, 1991). 149 pages. Sales No. E.90.II.A.22. $27.50.

UNCTAD, *Comparative Analysis of Petroleum Exploration Contracts* (New York and Geneva, 1995). Advisory Studies, Series B, No. 21. 80 pages. Sales No. E. 96.1I.A.7. $35.

UNCTAD, *Administration of Fiscal Regimes for Petroleum Exploration and Development* (New York and Geneva, 1995). Advisory Studies, Series B, No. 20. Sales No. E.95.II.A.8. $28.

DESD/TCMD, *Formulation and Implementation of Foreign Investment Policies: Selected Key Issues*. Advisory Studies, Series B, No. 10. (New York, 1992). 84 pages. Sales No. E.92.II.A.21. $12.

UNCTC, *Government Policies and Foreign Direct Investment*. Current Studies, Series A, No. 17. (New York, 1991). 66 pages. Sales No. E.91.II.A.20. $12.50.

UNCTC, *National Legislation and Regulations Relating to Transnational Corporations*:

Vol. VIII	(Geneva, 1994), 263 pages. Sales No. E.94.1I.A. 18. $60.
Vol. VII	(New York, 1989). 320 pages. Sales No. E.89.II.A.9. Out of print. Available on microfiche. Paper copy from microfiche: $328.
Vol. VI	(New York, 1988). (Also published by Graham and Trotman, London/Dordrecht/Boston, 1988). 322 pages (E, F, S). Sales No. E.87.H.A.6. Out of print. Available on microfiche. Paper copy from microfiche: $330.
Vol. V	(New York, 1986). 246 pages (E, F, S). Sales No. E.86.II.A.3. Out of print. Available on microfiche. Paper copy from microfiche: $250.
Vol. IV	(New York, 1986). 241 pages (E, F, S). Sales No. E.85.II.A. 14. Out of print. Available on microfiche. Paper copy from microfiche: $250.

Vol. III	(New York, 1983). 345 pages (E, F, S). Sales No. E.83.II.A. 15. Out of print. Available on microfiche. Paper copy from microfiche: $360.
Vol. II	(New York, 1983). 338 pages (E, F, S). Sales No. E.83.II.A.7. Out of print. Available on microfiche. Paper copy from microfiche: $340.
Vol. I	(Part Two) (New York, 1980). 114 pages (E, F, S). Sales No. E.80.II.A.5 and corrigendum. Out of print. Available on microfiche. Paper copy from microfiche: $120.
Vol. I	(Part One) (New York, 1978). 302 pages (E, F, S). Sales No. E.78.II.A.3 and corrigendum. Out of print. Available on microfiche. Paper copy from microfiche: $300.

UNCTC, *International Income Taxation and Developing Countries* (New York, 1988). 103 pages. Sales No. E.88.II.A.6. Out of print. Available on microfiche. Paper copy from microfiche: $120.

UNCTC, *The Impact of Multinational Corporations on Development and on International Relations. Technical Paper*: **Taxation** (New York, 1974). 111 pages. Sales No. E.74.II.A.6. Out of print. Available on microfiche. Paper copy from microfiche: $110.

VIII. INTERNATIONAL STANDARDS OF ACCOUNTING AND REPORTING

UNCTAD, *International Accounting and Reporting Issue*s:

2003 Review (Geneva, 2003). UNCTAD/ITE/TEB/2003/4.

2002 Review (Geneva, 2002). UNCTAD/ITE/TEB/2003/9.

2001 Review (Geneva, 2001). 66 pages. Sales No. E.03.II.E.3

1999 Review (Geneva, 1999). 155 pages. Sales No. E.99.II.D.27.

1998 Review (Geneva, 1998). 463 pages. Sales No. E.98.II.D.5. $50.

1996 Review (Geneva, 1997). 175 pages. Sales No. E.97.II.D. 12. $50.

1995 Review (Geneva, 1995). 155 pages. Sales No. E.95.II.A. 11. $47.50.

1994 Review. (Geneva, 1995). 94 pages. Sales No. E.95.II.A.3. $27.50.

1993 Review. (Geneva, 1994). 245 pages. Sales No. E.94.II.A. 16. $25.

1992 Review (Geneva, 1993). 328 pages. Sales No. E.93.II.A.6. $25.

1991 Review (New York, 1992). 243 pages (E, F, S). Sales No. E.92.II.A.8. $25.

1990 Review (New York, 1991). 236 pages (E, F, S). Sales No. E.90.II.A.3. $9.

1989 Review (New York, 1990). 152 pages (E, F, S). Sales No. E.90.II.A.4. $17.

1988 Review (New York, 1989). 95 pages (E, F, S). Sales No. E.89.1I.A.3.

Out of print. Available on microfiche. Paper copy from microfiche: $165.

1987 Review (New York, 1988). (Also published by Graham and Trotman, London/Dordrecht/Boston, 1988). 135 pages. Sales No. E.88.II.A.8. Out of print. Available on microfiche. Paper copy from microfiche: $152.

1986 Review (New York, 1986). 158 pages. Sales No. E.86.II.A.16. Out of print. Available on microfiche. Paper copy from microfiche: $162.

1985 Review (New York, 1985). 141 pages (E, F, S). Sales No. E.85.II.A. 13. Out of print. Available on microfiche. Paper copy from microfiche: $152.

1984 Review (New York, 1985). 122 pages (E, F, S). Sales No. E.85.II.A.2. Out of print. Available on microfiche. Paper copy from microfiche: $138.

These annual publications report of sessions of the Intergovernmental Working Group of Experts on International Standards of Accounting and Reporting (ISAR).

UNCTAD, *A Manual for the Preparers and Users of ECO-efficiency Indicators* (New York and Geneva, 2004). Sales No. E.04.II.D.13

UNCTAD, *Selected Issues in Corporate Governance: Regional and Country Experiences* (New York and Geneva, 2003). Sales No. E.03.II.D.26

UNCTAD, *Accounting and Financial Reporting for Environmental Costs and Liabilities* (New York and Geneva, 1998).184 pages (A, C, E, F, R, S). Sales No. A/C/E/F/WS.98.II.D. 14. $19.

UNCTAD, *Financial Disclosure by Banks: Proceedings of an UNCTAD Forum* (New York and Geneva, 1998). 84 pages. Sales No. E.98.II.D. 13. $13.

UNCTAD, *Responsibilities and Liabilities of Accountants and Auditors: Proceedings of a Forum* (Geneva, 1995). Sales No. E.95.II.A. 10.

UNCTAD, *Accounting for Sustainable Forestry Management: A Case Study* (New York and Geneva, 1994). 46 pages. Sales No. E.94.II.A. 17. $22.

UNCTAD, *Conclusions on Accounting and Reporting by Transnational Corporations* (New York and Geneva, 1994). 47 pages. Sales No. E.94.II.A.9. $12.

UNCTAD, *Accounting, Valuation and Privatization* (New York and Geneva, 1994). 190 pages. Sales No. E.94.II.A.3. $25.

UNCTC, *Accounting for East-West Joint Ventures* (New York, 1992). 282 pages. Sales No. E.92.II.A. 13. $25.

DES13/TCMD, *Environmental Accounting: Current Issues, Abstracts and Bibliography*. Advisory Studies, Series B, No. 9. (New York, 1992). 86 pages. Sales No. E.92.II.A.23. $15.

UNCTC, *Accountancy Development in Africa: Challenge of the 1990s* (New York, 1991). 200 pages (E, F). Sales No. E.91.II.A.2. $25.

UNCTC, *Joint Venture Accounting in the USSR: Direction for Change*. Advisory Studies, Series B, No. 7. (New York, 1990). 46 pages. Sales No. E.90.II.A.26. $11.

UNCTC, *Curricula for Accounting Education for East- West Joint Ventures in Centrally Planned Economies.* Advisory Studies, Series B, No. 6. (New York, 1990). 86 pages. Sales No. E.90.II.A.2. $10.

UNCTC, *Objectives and Concepts Underlying Financial Statements* (New York, 1989). 32 pages (A, C, E, F, R, S). Sales No. E.89.II.A.18. $8.

UNCTC, *Conclusions on Accounting and Reporting by Transnational Corporations: The Intergovernmental Working Group of Experts on International Standards of Accounting and Reporting* (New York, 1988). 58 pages (A, C, E, F, R, S). Sales No. E.88.II.A.18. $7.50.

UNCTC, *International Standards of Accounting and Reporting: Report of the Ad Hoc Intergovernmental Working Group of Experts on International Standards of Accounting and Reporting* (New York, 1984). 55 pages (C, E, F, R, S). Sales No. E.84.II.A.2. Out of print. Available on microfiche. Paper copy from microfiche: $63.

UNCTC, *Towards International Standardization of Corporate Accounting and Reporting* (New York, 1982). 104 pages (E, F, R, S). Sales No. E.82.II.A.3. Out of print. Available on microfiche. Paper copy from microfiche: $25.

UNCTC, *International Standards of Accounting and Reporting for Transnational Corporations: Report of the Secretary- General, and Report of the Group of Experts on International Standards of Accounting and Reporting* (New York, 1977). 79 pages (E, F, R, S). Sales No. E.77.II.A.17. Out of print. Available on microfiche. Paper copy from microfiche: $80.

UNCTC, *International Standards of Accounting and Reporting for Transnational Corporations: Technical Papers* (New York, 1977). 96 pages (E, F, S). Sales No. E.77.II.A. 15. Out of print. Available on microfiche. Paper copy from microfiche: $ 100.

IX. DATA AND INFORMATION SOURCES

UNCTAD, *World Investment Directory.*

Volume VIII: Latin America and the Caribbean (New York and Geneva, 2004). Sales No. E.03.II.D.12. $25.

Volume VIII: Central and Eastern Europe (New York and Geneva, 2003). Sales No. E.03.II.D.12. $25.

Volume VII: Asia and the Pacific (New York and Geneva, 2000). 356 pages. Sales No. E.00.II.D.11. $80.

Volume VI: West Asia (New York and Geneva, 1997). 138 pages. Sales No. E.97.II.A.2. $35.

Volume V: Africa (New York and Geneva, 1997). 462 pages. Sales No. E.97.II.A.1. $75.

Volume IV: Latin America and the Caribbean (New York, 1994). 478 pages. Sales No. E.94.II.A.10. $65.

Volume III: Developed Countries (New York, 1993). 532 pages. Sales No. E.93.II.A.9. $75.

Volume II: Central and Eastern Europe (New York, 1992) 432 pages. Sales No. E.93.II.A.1. $65.

Volume I: Asia and the Pacific (New York, 1992). 3 56 pages. Sales No. E.92.II.A.11. Out of print. Available on microfiche. Paper copy from microfiche: $370.

The *World Investment Directory* contains time-series data on FDI, as well as corporate data on the largest foreign affiliates and legal information for the countries of each region. A number of volumes also contain analytical overviews and detailed technical introductions.

UNCTAD, *Investment Promotion Agencies: Directory of Members of the World Association of Investment Promotion Agencies 1999,* Fifth Edition (Geneva, 1999). An annual publication containing contact addresses of heads of investment promotion agencies and institutions worldwide. Available free of charge.

DESD/TCMD, *Transnational Corporations: A Selective Bibliography, 1991-1992* (New York, 1993). 736 pages (E, F). Sales No. E1F.93.II.A. 16. $75.

DESD)/TCMD, *The East- West Business Directory 1991-1992* (New York, 1992). 567 pages. Sales No. E.92.II.A.20. $65.

UNCTC, *Transnational Business Information: A Manual of Needs and Sources* (New York, 1991). 228 pages (E, F, S). Sales No. E.91.II.A. 13. $45.

The manual discusses the needs of developing countries for information in all phases of their relations with TNCs and identifies sources that can help to meet those needs.

UNCTC, *University Curriculum on Transnational Corporations*:

Vol. I	*Economic Development* (New York, 1991). 186 pages. Sales No. E.91.II.A.5. $20.	
Vol. II	*International Business* (New York, 1991).154 pages. Sales No. E.9 I.H.A.6. $20.	
Vol. III	*International Law* (New York, 1991). 180 pages. Sales No. E.91.II.A.7. $20.	

(The set: Document Symbol: ST/CTC/62. Sales No. E.91.II.A.8. $50.)

UNCTC, T*ransnational Corporations: A Selective Bibliography, 1988-1990 Les Sociétés Transnationales: Bibliographie Sélective, 1988-1990* (New York, 1991). 617 pages (E, F). Sales No. E/R9 1.II.A.10. $75.

UNCTC, *Workshop Papers of UNCM, Annotated Bibliography with Indexes, 1978-91* (New York, 1991). 153 pages. Free of charge.

UNCTC, *Documents of the Joint Units of UNCTC and the Regional Commissions, 1975-1991* (New York, 1991). 33 pages. Free of charge.

UNCTC, *Transnational Corporations in South Africa and Namibia: A Selective Bibliography* (New York, 1989). 98 pages. Sales No. E.89.II.A. 13. Out of print. Available on microfiche. Paper copy from microfiche: $ 100.

UNCTC, *Transnational Corporations: A Selective Bibliography, 1983-1987. Les Sociétés Transnationales: Bibliographie Sélective, 1983-1987*:

Main List by Category, Author Index, Title Index1Liste Principale par Catigorie, Index des Auteurs, Index des Titres. Volume I (New York, 1988). 442 pages. Sales No. E.88.H.A.9. Out of print. Available on microfiche. Paper copy from microfiche: $450.

Subject Index/Index des Matiéres. Volume II (New York, 1988). 458 pages (E, F). Sales No. E/F.88.II.A.10. Two-volume set. Out of print. Available on microfiche. Paper copy from microfiche: $170.

UNCTC, ***UNCTC Bibliography 1974-1987*** (New York, 1988). 83 pages. Sales No. E.87.H.A.23. Out of print. Available on microfiche. Paper copy from microfiche: $90.

UNCTC, ***Publication Reviews: 1975-1987*** (New York, 1988). 101 pages. Free of charge.

UNCTC, ***List of Company Directories and Summary of Their Contents/List d'Annuaires de Sociétés et Résumé de Leurs Données,*** *Second ed.* (New York, 1983). 160 pages (E, F). Sales No. E/E83.II.A. 10. Out of print. Available on microfiche. Paper copy from microfiche: $170.

UNCTC, ***Users Guide to the Info~tion System on Transnational Corporations: A Technical Paper*** (New York, 1980). 30 pages (E, F, R, S). Sales No. E.80.II.A.6. Out of print. Available on microfiche. Paper copy from microfiche: $35.

UNCTC, ***International Directory of Data Bases Relating to Companies*** (New York, 1979). 246 pages. Sales No. E.79.II.A. 1. Out of print. Available on microfiche. Paper copy from microfiche: $260.

UNCTC, ***Bibliography on Transnational Corporations*** (New York, 1979). 426 pages (E, F). Sales No. E/E78.II.A.4. Out of print. Available on microfiche. Paper copy from microfiche: $430.

UNCTC, ***Survey of Research on Transnational Corporations*** (New York, 1977). 534 pages. Sales No. E.77.II.A.16. Out of print. Available on microfiche. Paper copy from microfiche: $530.

UNCTC, ***List of Company Directories and Summary of Their Contents*** (New York, 1977). 60 pages. Sales No. E.77.11.A.8. Out of print. Available on microfiche. Paper copy from microfiche: $62.

UNCTC, ***Establishment of a Comprehensive Information System on Transnational Corporations: Government Replies*** (New York, 1977). 26 pages (E, F, S). Sales No. E.77.11.A.7. Out of print. Available on microfiche. Paper copy from microfiche: $30.

UNCTC, ***Curricula for Accounting Education for East-West Joint Ventures in Centrally Planned Economies.*** Advisory Studies, Series B, No. 6. (New York, 1990). 86 pages. Sales No. E.90.II.A.2. $10.

HOW TO OBTAIN THE PUBLICATIONS

The sales publications may be purchased from distributors of United Nations publications throughout the world. They may also be obtained by writing to:

United Nations Publications   or   United Nations Publications
Sales and Marketing Section, DC2-853   Sales and Marketing Section, Rm. C. 113-1
United Nations Secretariat   United Nations Office at Geneva
New York, N.Y. 100 17   Palais des Nations
U.S.A.   CH-1211 Geneva 10
Tel.: ++1 212 963 8302 or 1 800 253 9646   Switzerland
Fax: ++1 212 963 3489   Tel.: ++41 22 917 2612
E-mail: publications@un.org   Fax: ++4122 917 0027
                                              E-mail: unpubli@unog.ch

INTERNET: www.un.org/Pubs/sales.htm

For further information on the work on foreign direct investment and transnational corporations, please address inquiries to:

Karl Sauvant
Director
Division on Investment, Technology and Enterprise Development
United Nations Conference on Trade and Development
Palais des Nations, Room E-10052
CH-1211 Geneva 10 Switzerland
Telephone: ++41 22 907 5707
Fax: ++41 22 907 0498
E-mail: karl.sauvant@unctad.org

INTERNET: www.unctad.org/en/subsites/dite

QUESTIONNAIRE

International Investment Instruments: A Compendium

Volume XIII

In order to improve the quality and relevance of the work of the UNCTAD Division on Investment, Technology and Enterprise Development, it would be useful to receive the views of readers on this publication. It would therefore be greatly appreciated if you could complete the following questionnaire and return it to:

Readership Survey
UNCTAD Division on Investment, Technology and Enterprise Development
United Nations Office in Geneva
Palais des Nations
Room E-9123
CH-1211 Geneva 10
Switzerland
Fax: 41-22-907-0194

1. Name and address of respondent (optional):

_____

_____

2. Which of the following best describes your area of work?

Government	O	Public enterprise	O
Private enterprise	O	Academic or research institution	O
International organization	O	Media	O
Not-for-profit organization	O	Other (specify) _____	

3. In which country do you work? _____

4. What is your assessment of the contents of this publication?

Excellent	O	Adequate	O
Good	O	Poor	O

5. How useful is this publication to your work?

Very useful O   Of some use O   Irrelevant O

6. Please indicate the three things you liked best about this publication:

_____

_____

_____

7. Please indicate the three things you liked least about this publication:

_____

_____

_____

8. Are you a regular recipient of *Transnational Corporations* (formerly *The CTC Reporter*), UNCTAD-DITE's tri-annual refereed journal?

Yes   ○   No   ○

If not, please check here if you would like to receive
a sample copy sent to the name and address you have
given above   ○

*